# Quota Quickie

And more 'B' movies
to come!
Thanks for all
your help and
good work this
year Aidan.

Simon

# Quota Quickies

## The Birth of the British 'B' Film

Steve Chibnall

 Publishing

First published in 2007 by the
BRITISH FILM INSTITUTE
21 Stephen Street, London W1T 1LN

The British Film Institute's purpose is to champion moving image culture in all
its richness and diversity across the UK, for the benefit of as wide an audience as
possible, and to create and encourage debate.

Cover design: ketchup/SE14
Cover image: *Badger's Green* (Adrian Brunel, 1934)

Set by Fakenham Photosetting Limited, Fakenham, Norfolk
Printed in the UK by St Edmundsbury Press, Bury St Edmunds, Suffolk

British Library Cataloguing-in-Publication Data
A catalogue record for this book is available from the British Library

ISBN 1–84457–155–6 (pbk)
ISBN 1–84457–154–8 (hbk)

# Contents

# Acknowledgments

Many people and organisations have helped in the completion of this book. I must first thank the Arts and Humanities Research Council, whose study leave award financed a significant portion of this research, and De Montfort University and my Head of School, Tim O'Sullivan, for giving me generous time and support to work on what proved to be a thirty-month project. Brian McFarlane generously commented on drafts of this book when he had more than enough work of his own, while my colleagues Alan Burton and Robert Murphy supplied me with research materials that I might not otherwise have discovered. Lawrence Napper at the University of East Anglia and John Herron at the Canal + Archive at Pinewood also put themselves out to make material available for me.

I would also like to thank (in no particular order): Jeffrey Richards, Tom Ryall, Sue Harper, Steve Crook, Vincent Porter, Allen Eyles, Mark Glancy, Tony Hutchinson, Noel Pratt, Alan Kibble, Mike Taylor, David Williams, Ronald Grant, Don Schiac, Matthew Frost, Richard Dacre and the lads at Flashbacks, Janet Moat and the staff of the BFI Library, Sophia Contento and my editor Rebecca Barden, who gave full backing to this project at the earliest opportunity. Thanks are also due to the late Denis Gifford and John Huntley, part of whose collections of British cinema memorabilia are now in my safe-keeping. And, of course, *grazie* to 'La Principessa', without whom everything would be so much more difficult.

This book is dedicated to the man who put my home town, Bedford, on the film-making map, the Crown Prince of the Quota: Widgey Raphael Newman (1900–1944).

Widgey Newman

# Introduction: The Cuckoos in the Nest

Between 1933 and 1939, I directed no less than twenty-four pictures. And weren't they awful! With one or two exceptions. My punishment is that now, in my New York apartment, when I switch on my TV set, occasionally one of those dreadful abortions will float up out of its celluloid grave on to the screen.

Reginald Denham[1]

In autumn of 1935, a modest little British film, directed by the long-forgotten Leslie Hiscott, secured an extraordinary seven bookings in the provincial city of Leicester. The sixty-six-minute picture, made at Twickenham Studios and distributed by the American company Radio Pictures (RKO), was a conventional drama of mistaken identity set in a department store, and was not particularly distinguished or critically praised. The trade paper *Today's Cinema* summed it up as 'Moderate direction, adequate portrayal [. . .] for unexacting patrons.'[2] The cinemagoers of Leicester were apparently unexacting enough to tolerate its screening, in two venues, as a co-feature. The film was called *Bargain Basement*, and the title could have been a generic one for the hundreds of cheap and usually cheerful pictures that could be picked up by exhibitors to fill the bottom half of their double bills. They were not expensive and nobody expected a masterpiece, but they served a purpose and they passed the time. Of course, their own time is now passed, most are lost and almost all are forgotten. It would be easy – some might say kindest – to let them lie in those celluloid graves, but no cultural historian should be content to let the half-truths told about them go unchallenged.

Pictures like *Bargain Basement* came to be referred to as 'quota quickies' because they were speedily turned out to allow distributors and exhibitors to conform to the legal requirements of the 1927 Cinematograph Films Act. This protective legislation introduced a minimum quota of British films that distributors were obliged to offer and cinemas were expected to screen. The vast majority of these inexpensive productions were shown as supporting features, often with a Hollywood film as the main attraction, and were almost exclusively for domestic consumption rather than export. This pattern of production, distribution and exhibition was the unintended consequence of the so-called 'Quota' Act, which had ambitiously sought to stimulate the making of British pictures that might compete with Hollywood's best and promote imperial interests overseas. While the native film industry did succeed in producing many pictures of which the nation was proud, the quota quickies became a national disgrace, and their elimination a challenge for law reformers.

Cheap products: the title of Leslie Hiscott's quota quickie could not have been more appropriate. Trade advertisement for *Bargain Basement*. Author's collection

In his influential book on British cinema in the 1930s *The Age of the Dream Palace*, cultural historian Jeffrey Richards described the quota quickies unequivocally as 'a truly awful flood of cinematic rubbish'.[3] Veteran director and cinematographer, Ronald Neame, who worked on supporting features at Fox-British in the 1930s is equally dismissive: 'Quota quickies were bad films, and therefore bad for our industry.'[4] For the distinguished producer Michael Balcon, these cheap and tawdry pictures sullied the reputation of the entire national cinema: 'For many people "a British film" became the rubbishy second feature you had to sit through, or avoid, if you went to see a Hollywood picture.'[5] These commentators were doing little more than articulating a widespread opinion within the film trade and beyond. A contemporary Memorandum from the Cinematograph Exhibitors' Association (CEA) asserted that the British quota quickie was 'probably worse than the worst foreign film', and that its only competitors have been some Empire-made pictures 'which happen to qualify as British films'. It was in the 'public interest', said the CEA, that 'production of this type should be eliminated'.[6] Fifteen years later, the Political and Economic Planning (PEP) report, *The British Film Industry* described the quickies as 'a series of cheap films which had little or no entertainment value even for the meanest taste', adding that the 'disheartening effects on the actors and the technicians of producing such films can be imagined, and must largely have offset any satisfaction at being in employment at all'.[7]

The quota quickies were the shame of the nation, and apparently did lasting harm. The 1952 PEP report even feared that 'it is possible that even after many years of an infinitely higher standard of national film the opprobrium which the "quota quickie" earned may still affect the preferences of British audiences'.[8] It seems that, if ever there were a case of unpatriotic film-making, this was it. As World War II approached, the quota quickies must have appeared to be a cinematic fifth column, diligently engaged in the work of sabotaging the nation's pride in home-produced entertainments. However the blame for this could not be laid on Hitler. A much older enemy was at work: America. The PEP report puts the responsibility for these abominations squarely on the American distribution companies that cynically sponsored their production in order to fulfil legal obligations 'without impairing the competitive advantage of their own product'.[9] In this and many other accounts, an unmistakable strand of anti-Americanism bars the way to a proper understanding of the conditions that produced and sustained the quota quickie phenomenon. There is no hint here that British companies might have been involved in the production and distribution of quickies, or of the role played by these modest movies in servicing the needs of the popular two-feature cinema programme. There is certainly no suggestion that some might have received good reviews, many hundreds of bookings across the country and positive responses from audiences.

The blame attached to Hollywood companies for sponsoring a sub-industry of substandard film-making in Britain sits uneasily with the credit given to the same studios for making low-budget programmers in the USA. The differences in the treatment given to American 'B' movies and their British equivalents have been striking. The unfavourable comparison of British with American second features can be traced back to the contemporary judgment of the leftist *World Film News* in 1937:

> For some reason or other the English producer has decided that English audiences dislike any sort of realism, while the American producer concentrates on drawing his characterization, if not his situations, from life. The English second feature is practically always upper class. If it is a comedy, it is peopled with grotesque characters with whose facetious horseplay one is meant to maintain sympathy. Members of the aristocracy are presented with the intelligence of apes and a far lower moral standard. Their sense of humour finds an outlet in tiresome horseplay reminiscent of the dormitory rag. The mirthful *piece de resistance* is the spectacle of the hero dressing up as a woman. These characters do not live and are not meant to live.... The American second feature usually draws its characters from life. They are human beings, not pegs for 'funny dialogue'.[10]

In more recent years, the products of the 'B' units in Hollywood, the Poverty Row studios like Monogram and Republic, and independent merchants of exploitation cinema in the 1930s have generated waves of warm nostalgia, while a stream of fan magazines and scholarly works have analysed their texts, interviewed their makers, and celebrated their cultural value as expressions of vernacular taste and commercial inventiveness. In contrast, there is an almost uncanny silence around their British equivalents. Annette Kuhn's study of the popular memory of cinema in the 1930s gives no clue that the hundreds of indigenous second features of the era were ever part of the programme of entertainment.[11] It is as if they have been erased from history. The National Film Archive has preserved no posters and barely 5 per cent of the films themselves. There have been no fanzines dedicated to their memory and the only mentions in standard histories of British cinema have been pejorative.

Whereas historical work on American 'B' pictures dates back to the late 1960s and the prolific output of enthusiast Alan Barbour, the quota quickie barely surfaced in British film historiography until twenty years later. First, BFI employee Linda Wood decided to adopt low-budget British pictures of the 1930s as the subject of her M. Phil. thesis at the Polytechnic of Central London, and then, a few years later, Lawrence Napper picked a similar topic for his MA thesis at the University of East Anglia.[12] Napper's work can now be seen as part of a revisionist research project instigated at the same university in the mid-1980s, when Charles Barr commissioned articles for his edited collection *All Our Yesterdays*. The contribution from Robert Murphy had contained only a single page on the second features of the 1930s, but that was still a breakthrough at that time.[13] Paradoxically, the continuing neglected status of the quota quickies is evidenced by their prominence in Jeffrey Richards' indicatively titled collection *The Unknown 1930s*.[14] Napper has ascribed this neglect to a tradition of critical thought that has been 'unable to accommodate specifically British films in a meaningful way'.[15] However, I am more inclined to the idea that the hundreds of cheap 'knock-offs', which constituted half of the films made in Britain in the decade before World War II, have been difficult to reconcile with the prevailing definitions of a national cinema of quality enshrined in film culture after the end of those hostilities. Within this paradigm, the quota quickies must either be ignored as regrettable anomalies, or grudgingly acknowledged when they clearly constitute preparatory work by film-makers and actors who went on to produce quality work. When we view the examples of 1930s' low-budget production that have survived, there is usually little doubt that they are culturally 'specifically British' (usually specifically English), but they have always had one vital characteristic that has allowed them to be disowned by the guardians of a thoroughbred national cinema: most were made or commissioned and distributed by American companies. Thus, they can be denounced as – to use Anthony Asquith's phrase – 'cuckoo films', deposited illegitimately in the nest of British cinema.[16] The problem with such a dismissive nomenclature, however, is that it ignores the awkward fact that they were made overwhelmingly by Britons for domestic audiences.

If Asquith had been writing in a less genteel age, he might have conceptualised these pictures as 'bastard films', the progeny of an illicit liaison between American capital and English labour. The idea would have suited the moral climate of a time when children born out of wedlock were not talked about and only reluctantly acknowledged, but again it does not fit the facts. The quota quickie cannot be so easily disinherited and denied. It was the offspring of a shotgun marriage: the father of the bride was the British legislature, and no dowry was forthcoming. The offspring may have been under-socialised and may have exhibited symptoms of disability, but its legitimacy was without question. It must be treated as part of the lineage of British popular film.

It will, no doubt, be objected that the quickie was never popular, that it was merely tolerated until it could be eliminated. Perhaps, but this begs an empirical question. Any attempt to quantify the popularity of 'B' pictures is made difficult by the very status of these films as supporting features. Consequently, they have not been considered in surveys of cinema attendance, such as Julian Poole's work on the Majestic, Macclesfield.[17] In fact there is no indication in Poole's statistics that any supporting features were shown, although some must have been. Similarly, the otherwise meticulous measuring of audience preferences in the 1930s by John Sedgwick largely ignores the significance of the supporting feature, which might have been a factor for filmgoers when choosing among competing programmes.[18]

## Definitions

So far, the terms 'quota quickie', 'second feature' and 'supporting feature' have been used interchangeably. However, they are really overlapping categories, the first referring to a mode of production, the others to a mode of exhibition. 'Quota quickie' was a term used in the 1930s to describe a picture made in less than four weeks, at a cost of approximately £1 per foot of film, with the primary purpose of discharging the legal obligations (under the Quota Act) of American rental companies. The term might also be extended to films handled by British renters, but made under similar budgetary regimes. Less pejoratively, the term 'quota films' was also used to distinguish low-budget British production from indigenous films that might be expected to compete with Hollywood movies as major box-office attractions. Quota films served the needs of exhibitors with a clientele that was typically local, regular, female, older and more conscious of value-for-money than the patrons of the large circuit houses. While a few enjoyed screenings at pre-release and large circuit cinemas, these were films that generally only entered the cascade system of distribution described by John Sedgwick at its lower levels, with the second- and third-run cinemas.[19]

The 'second' or 'supporting' feature is a more slippery beast. The twin appellations 'second feature' or 'supporting feature' may be used synonymously to describe the subordinate positioning of a film within a two-feature cinema programme, a placing which, in spite of the manipulations of distributors, was ultimately subject to the judgment of individual exhibitors. Therefore, all but the most lavish productions of the 1930s might suffer the indignity of support billing at some stage in their distribution, at home or abroad. In practice, however, there usually existed a working consensus that allowed most films to be classified as either a first, second, or co-feature (i.e. a film that was to be given an equal billing with an equivalent attraction on the cinema bill). But such classifications were often provisional and subject to revision in the light of actual exhibition experience or predicted audience response in a given area.

Unlike the quota quickie, the second feature was not defined simply by budget or production schedule: George Formby's first film *Boots! Boots!* (1934) was made at Albany Studios, reputedly for only £3,000, but played as an eighty-minute feature attraction until it was edited for its second run as a supporting feature, first to seventy minutes and then to fifty-seven in 1936. The film is thought to have grossed £30,000, almost three times higher than the average box-office return.[20] BIP's smash hit musical revue *Elstree Calling* (1930) was filmed by Adrian Brunel in twelve days and, after additional scenes were added by Hitchcock, it was edited in a further eleven.[21] Nor was running time always a sure indication of a film's status. Even informed observers of the trade tended to assume that length was the primary indicator of a picture's status, but witnesses called to Lord Moyne's 1936 inquiry into the operation of the Cinematograph Films Act, repeatedly had to correct this misapprehension, insisting that the two films in a programme were often of similar length, and that second-feature status was a judgment of quality above all else.[22] British International Pictures' (BIP's) drama of sailors trapped in a sub-marine, *Men Like These* (directed by Walter Summers in 1931), clocked in at only three-quarters of an hour, but struck such a patriotic chord that it became a major attraction.[23] When the dashing, young bearded wonder Bernard Vorhaus directed his first film for United Artists in 1933, he thought he was making a supporting feature, but the appropriately titled *Money for Speed* (1933) was so dynamic that it frequently zipped into top billing – with no additional remuneration for its director.[24] BIP's crime thriller *The House Opposite* (1932) was thought by *Kinematograph Weekly* to be a 'fair, average supporting offering', but the popularity of its star, Henry Kendall, and its exciting climax in a blazing house, enabled it to play exclusively as a first feature in Leicester.[25] John Baxter's *Lest We Forget* (1934) was also made as a second feature, but was elevated to the top of the bill by many cinemas.[26]

The dividing line between first and second features was often thin. Films costing a little above the standard pound-a-foot but under £10,000 might fall either side of that line. Their status depended on the quality of the final cut, the trade reviews received and the prestige of the booking exhibitor. Sometimes these considerations could be contradictory: *Alibi*, Twickenham's 1931 adaptation of Agatha Christie's *The Murder of Roger Ackroyd*, was recommended in *The Bioscope* as a 'Good second feature offering', but was evidently intended by its distributors, W&F, as a 'super' production – which is how it was featured at London's Capitol Cinema and probably how most provincial bookers regarded it.[27] Conversely, there were a significant number of supporting features that once had loftier ambitions. One example was the disappointing *The House of the Spaniard* (1936). Made at Ealing with relatively high production values, reasonable notices and distributed by Associated British, it failed to inspire exhibitors and sank to second-feature status.[28] Sometimes the reaction of the Hollywood-hungry audiences in London's West End could sink the prospects of a British picture. For instance, when Twickenham made *Silver Blaze* (1937), they had reason to believe that a Sherlock Holmes story was a box-office banker, especially as Arthur Wontner in the role of Conan Doyle's sleuth had a good track record.[29] However, when Thomas Bentley's modern dress adaptation premiered at the Regal, Marble Arch, the youthful audience treated it as unsophisticated, old-fashioned melodrama, cheering the hero, hissing the villain and chuckling through the serious passages.[30] Film industry old-timers might have scratched their heads and agreed with Inspector Lastrade that 'there are things about this case that completely baffle me', but this well-publicised rejection of a proven formula was enough to condemn the film to supporting-feature status, even in less exalted halls than the Regal. Wontner never played Holmes again and the depiction of the great detective was left to Hollywood for the next twenty years. As the president of the CEA put it: 'the film that is made with the best of intentions and does not turn out right still has its uses, and its use is the second feature'.[31]

A failed first feature could expect little respect from provincial exhibitors, and their scissor-happy projectionists might mutilate it to fit their programmes' running times. The aggrieved Association of Cine-Technicians (ACT) cited one case in which a British programmer had been cut by eight minutes by an exhibitor keen to accommodate a short film into his programme. The effect was to eliminate the entire part played by an actress who subsequently found fame in Hollywood. At least she got her screen credit, but the crudeness of this re-editing was evidenced in another case in which the whole of the first reel, including the credit titles, was junked.[32] Presumably there was simply not time to wield the scissors. Some first features were re-cut by their distributors and reissued as supporting features. For example, New Era's stirring naval tale, *Q Ships*, directed by Geoffrey Barkas and Michael Barringer in 1928, was edited down to an accommodating seventy minutes, with sound added for its re-release as *Blockade* in 1932. Curiously, the new version was credited to Hugh Croise.[33] During the production shortage of 1938–9, the Stanley Lupino comedy *Honeymoon for Three* (1935) was cut by twenty minutes to make a sixty-eight-minute supporting feature for Victor Film Distributors.

Some attempt to map this jungle is made in this book's Filmography, by examining what was actually shown as supporting, co- and first features in one city, Leicester (according to the advertisements in the local paper), and then making a series of educated guesses about films that were apparently not exhibited in the city. Although the Filmography is provisional (and even speculative in places), it is at least empirically grounded, and, as the best data set available, has been used as a basis for quantitative projections and the estimation of production and exhibition rates. These, of course, should be treated with caution and regarded as merely indicative. With these explanations and warnings in mind, we can now begin the story of the British second feature by approaching its foundational event: the Quota Act.

## Notes

1. Reginald Denham, *Stars in My Hair* (London: T. Werner Laurie, 1958), p. 177.
2. *Today's Cinema*, 11 May 1935, p. 4.
3. Jeffrey Richards, *The Age of the Dream Palace: Cinema and Society in Britain, 1930–1939* (London: Routledge, 1984), p. 3.
4. Ronald Neame, *Straight from the Horse's Mouth* (Lanham, MD and Oxford: Scarecrow Press, 2003), p. 35.
5. Michael Balcon, *Michael Balcon Presents . . . A Lifetime of British Films* (London: Hutchinson, 1969), p. 28.
6. Cmd. 5320, *Cinematograph Films Act 1927: Report of a Committee Appointed by the Board of Trade*, Memorandum by the CEA, paragraphs 4 and 5.
7. PEP, *The British Film Industry* (London: Political and Economic Planning, 1952), pp. 50, 51.
8. Ibid., p. 51.
9. Ibid., p. 50.
10. *World Film News*, May 1937, p. 13.
11. Annette Kuhn, *An Everyday Magic: Cinema and Cultural Memory* (London: I. B. Tauris, 2002).
12. Linda Wood, 'Low-budget Film-making in 1930s Britain', unpublished M. Phil. thesis, Polytechnic of Central London, 1989. Lawrence Napper, 'British Scenes and British Humour: "Quota Quickies" in the 1930s', unpublished MA thesis, University of East Anglia, 1994. Articles based on both of these theses were published as (respectively) 'Low-budget Films in the 1930s', and 'A Despicable Tradition? Quota Quickies in the 1930s', in Robert Murphy (ed.), *The British Cinema Book* (London: BFI, 1997), pp. 48–57 and 37–47.
13. Robert Murphy, 'Under the Shadow of Hollywood', in Charles Barr (ed.), *All Our Yesterdays* (London: BFI, 1986), pp. 47–71.
14. Jeffrey Richards (ed.), *The Unknown 1930s: An Alternative History of British Cinema 1929–1939* (London: I. B. Tauris, 1998).

15. Napper, 'A Despicable Tradition?'.

16. *Kinematograph Weekly*, 20 April 1939, p. 5.

17. Julian Poole, 'British Cinema Attendance in Wartime: audience preference at the Majestic, Macclesfield, 1939–1946', *Historical Journal of Film, Radio and Television* vol.7 no.1, 1987, pp. 15–34.

18. John Sedgwick, *Popular Filmgoing in 1930s Britain* (Exeter: University of Exeter Press, 2000).

19. Ibid., pp. 56–61.

20. Rachael Low, *The History of the British Film, 1929–1939* (London: Allen and Unwin, 1985), p. 162.

21. Letter from Brunel to Michael Balcon, 30 July 1937, BFI Special Collections.

22. See, for example, the evidence of F. W. Baker and Captain R. Norton of the British Film Producers Group, Cmd. 5320: 370–1.

23. *Kinematograph Weekly* (12 November 1931, p. 39) accorded it almost unprecedented praise, stating that 'it is doubtful if any finer work of a realistic nature has been achieved' and finding it 'difficult to conjecture what sort of audience it would be that could not be thrilled and fascinated by this epic of courage'.

24. Bernard Vorhaus interview, BECTU Oral History Project, Interview 219, 23 October 1991.

25. *Kinematograph Weekly*, 24 March 1932, p. 27.

26. John Baxter, 'Stepping Stones', unpublished manuscript, BFI Special Collections, p. 18.

27. *The Bioscope*, 20 April 1931, p. 34.

28. It managed a single supporting-feature booking in Leicester, and this more than a year after its trade show.

29. Six years earlier, Wontner had played Holmes in *The Sleeping Cardinal* (1931), a film that was apparently acclaimed in the USA as 'the best British picture yet made'. *Picturegoer*, 1 August 1931, p. 5.

30. *Picturegoer*, 14 August 1937, p. 6.

31. Cmd. 5320: 887.

32. Cmd. 5320: 622.

33. *Q Ships* and *Blockade* press books.

# 1

# Protective Measures: The Quota Act

There appears to be a misguided opinion about this industry that there is a wish on the part of the producers to make greater and better films. We have not found that. What we have found is the wish to make money in this business.

T. H. Fligelstone, President of the CEA[1]

In the years that followed World War I, the once prominent British film industry was progressively displaced by foreign competition. By 1926, when English studios turned out just thirty-seven pictures, British films accounted for less than 5 per cent of screenings in UK cinemas. Stoll and Butcher's, the leading British distributors, could offer only seven indigenous pictures.[2] When a Joint Trade Committee for British Films, representing producers, distributors and exhibitors, failed to agree a plan to rescue the home industry, the government was obliged to introduce legislation. The resulting Cinematograph Films Act of 1927 is popularly known as the Quota Act because it required that a certain proportion of films distributed and exhibited in Britain had to be British in origin.

Thought of as a protectionist measure to create employment within a hard-pressed industry, the Act also addressed less tangible social and cultural concerns. At home, there were fears about the waywardness of youth and, particularly, the fate of young women (a prominent part of the cinema audience) exposed to the unadulterated influence of Hollywood decadence. Marek Kohn has documented the frequently overt racism and xenophobia among the press and politicians of the period, and the way in which foreign influences were regularly blamed for British social ills.[3] Xenophobic and anti-Semitic discourses were given legitimacy by an ultra-conservative Home Secretary, William Joynson-Hicks, who would readily accept the idea that the internationally dominant American film industry was controlled by a cabal of Jews. As far as the British Empire was concerned, fears were expressed at the 1926 Imperial Conference that the Hollywood film, with its attendant ideologies of independence, individualism and consumption, would not only make the colonies and dominions more difficult to govern, but would also undermine the lucrative trade relations with the 'Mother Country'. The imperial lobby, with its belief that 'trade follows the film', provided a vital impetus to the Quota Act.[4]

Thus, the 1927 Act should be seen as an attempt to protect and promote both British economic and cultural interests, at home and abroad. In symbolic terms, the Act opened the gates for the brave St George to venture out to slay the mighty dragon of Hollywood and restore British enlightenment. However, effective propaganda for the British way of life and British political interests depended on the national cinema attaining a quality of production that would reflect favourably on the country. Unfortunately, the Act failed to provide guarantees of quality, not least because the Board of Trade was loath to accept criteria that were not amenable to simple and unequivocal measurement techniques.

Like all legislation, the 1927 Act was a compromise between competing interest groups. The British producer/renters saw an opportunity to expand both their film-making and their access to desirable American films for distribution. Unsurprisingly, the cartel of American companies that dominated British film distribution was motivated by the desire to maintain its share of an overseas market that had become a vital source of profitability. To this end, they operated the advantageous practices of block and blind (advance) booking, which obliged exhibitors to hire inferior, or as yet unmade, films in order to obtain proven American successes. But, in spite of exploitative contracts, the thousands of British exhibitors who had founded profitable businesses on popular Hollywood product maintained an allegiance to the American companies. The exhibitors, most of whom managed a single picture house or small chain of cinemas, were ambivalent or hostile towards a growth of British films of unproven public appeal.[5] There were also sceptical voices among the primary group that the Act was designed to help: the established independent British film producers. T. A. Welsh of the Welsh Pearson Company pointed to the way in which quota legislation in Germany had led to the production of 'junk films in large quantities'.[6] Welsh certainly anticipated the advent of the cheap quota films that John Maxwell later claimed came as a complete surprise to distributors and 'quality' film-makers. Similarly, the film producer Herbert Wilcox described the Quota Bill as 'inept, fatuous, and suicidal', an opinion shared rather more diplomatically by the impartial journal *The Economist*.[7]

In the end, the Act was forced through by the Conservative government against the opposition of the Labour and Liberal parties and most sections of the film industry that it professed to assist. *The Bioscope* was the only one of the half dozen trade papers to give its unequivocal support. There was to be a quota of British films – films made by a British subject, or a company based in the British Empire, with all studio scenes shot within the Empire – for both exhibitors and distributors, the latter being a higher percentage than the former so that exhibitors would be guaranteed choice in their selection of films.[8] This quota was to rise incrementally over the next ten years from 5–20 per cent for exhibitors, and 7.5–20 per cent for distributors. The Act also sought to regulate the booking practices of distribution companies in the interests of protecting and promoting indigenous production.

The value of the Act has been a bone of contention in British film historiography. Those in the Rachael Low camp believed the Act was a failure because it led to the mass production of inferior films that exhibitors were forced to show; while revisionist historians have argued that the legislation produced films that competed successfully with American films in the domestic market, or that Low's 'inferior' films were not without merit or significance.[9] The Quota Act may not have succeeded in ensuring that the lofty goals of cultural dissemination across the globe were achieved, or even that British audiences were protected from the excesses of Americanisation. It may have failed to guarantee that the quality of indigenous pictures would be universally high. However, it did unlock American finance for the uncertain business of British film production and stimulate a mushroom growth of indigenous film companies. By 1936 it had helped to almost quadruple the number of stages in film studios, produce a sixfold increase in the number of pictures made, and establish the British cinema industry as the largest outside America.[10] It also gave birth to the British supporting feature.

## The fruits of protection

> When this Act was passed, we never dreamed of the quota quickie. The quota quickie was a complete surprise.
>
> John Maxwell, President of the Kinema Renters Society[11]

The Quota Act had been in force for only a few months when the trade press began to chatter about the poor quality of product the American renters were commissioning or acquiring in order to fulfil their quota obligations.[12] Worse still, there was a widespread belief (denied by the renters concerned) that the practice of block booking – the packaging of mediocre films with desirable new product – was still being used by US companies. As early as July 1928, the British renter George Smith of PDC predicted that the quota would prove 'unworkable'.[13] The first steps of British production into the brave, new, protected world created by the Act were faltering. Charles Oakley has noted that *Kinematograph Weekly* was scathing about the performance of the expanding British film industry in 1928:

> Thanks largely to mismanagement and to the appointment of unfit persons to boards of directors we have seen the failure of one company after another. They have been floated with high hopes, with much confidence in the spoon-feeding of the Quota Bill and with little executive competence. Few good British films were made.[14]

Edgar Wallace, the popular writer and prime mover behind the film producer and distributor, British Lion, put it more pithily: 'I think the average British picture is rotten.'[15] But then the national cinema was being redeveloped from a very low base. In 1927, it was suggested that there were only five or six directors and a similar number of cameramen of proven ability, while the number of art directors capable of designing major productions was even smaller.[16] Fly-by-night companies, which had grabbed finance in the early days of the quota, ground out the odd film before folding. One company, Carlton Films, run by an Italian entrepreneur, Giovani Glavany, collapsed when the picture it made for Warners failed to meet the requirements for quota registration. Even companies with previous experience of the film business, such as those set up by G. W. Pearson and George Banfield, often fared no better.[17]

The first three years of the Act coincided with the introduction of sound recording technology into studios and the gradual equipping of cinemas with sound-projection facilities. The sound revolution had not been anticipated by those who framed the Quota Act, and was dramatic in its speed. In November 1928 there were nineteen films in production at British studios. All were silent. A year later, the number of productions had almost halved, but all were talkies being produced at a faster rate.[18] Thus, the early producers of quota films had suddenly to make pictures more quickly, and for less money, while mastering a new technology that was more expensive and required a revolution in scenario construction.[19] Their efforts were never likely to scale the heights of artistic achievement. Nevertheless, in the early stages of the Quota Act's operation, there was considerable satisfaction within the industry, particularly among film producers and the burgeoning distribution circuits. For instance, John Maxwell, the head of British International Pictures (BIP), was quoted as saying that the Act had been responsible for the 'renaissance of the British picture'.[20] Certainly, the proportion of British films among all those registered under the Act rose steadily and far exceeded the legal minimum: from a little under 14 per cent in 1928 to 22 per cent in 1932.[21] It was a similar story for exhibition. In 1929, the exhibitors' quota was exceeded by 137 per cent, partly because of the growing vertical integration of the two main circuits.[22] When *Kinematograph Weekly* took stock of the progress made by British films during the first three years of the Quota Act's operation, it recorded with satisfaction that: 'The days are gone when an exhibitor used to paste . . . "Coming Shortly" over any publicity matter which indicated that a given picture was British.'[23] British production was now thought to be at least 'on the map', although a home-grown film was yet to figure in 'the best twelve of the year'. In the same issue, film-maker John Grierson also tempered satisfaction at progress with an awareness of its limitations:

> I would be sorry to minimise the great upstrides the English industry has made within the past year or two. It has made films comparable in technical quality to American films, and *it has begun to believe in itself*. But it has neither the money for so vast and luxurious a scheme of national publicity, nor, I think, has it achieved that box-office sense which makes for the widespread and almost ultimate popularity of American films. . . . We are, in spirit, too near the somewhat tired and somewhat shabby sophistication of Piccadilly, too close to the English stage and its traditions and personnel. . . . At present there is too much mental inbreeding in the studios, and a consequent loss of spontaneity and freshness in the work of our directors.[24]

The early days of quota production were volatile and confused. As City investors burned their fingers and looked for businesses with more secure prospects, the ground was largely cleared for the American distribution companies to finance British production on their own terms, or to set up their own satellite studios. At this time, according to film producer Edward Dryhurst:

> The major American companies considered their obligation to acquire quota footage as a form of taxation which they were well able to write off; and when appalling domestic films brought howls of anguish from British audiences, the Americans chortled with glee.[25]

Director Reginald Denham, who began his film career in 1931 as a dialogue director and production manager for Paramount British, recalled this as a time when 'a whole new bunch of incompetent people were churning out these pictures', and contracts were handed out by American renters 'like religious tracts on street corners'. He agreed with Dryhurst that, 'the worse they were the more delighted the Americans seemed. The one thing Hollywood didn't want was strong competition from the English film-makers.'[26] An indication of the lack of importance attached to quota production by one big American renter, MGM, was the awarding of the job of acquiring quota product to the head of prints and dispatch – an administrative rather than creative post. MGM reportedly bought Lawrence Huntington's seventy-minute silent film, *After Many Years* (1930), for around £1,000 (still more than double its cost) and a contract to direct a talkie, *Romance in Rhythm* (1934), featuring the popular Carroll Gibbons orchestra.[27]

Returning from a spell in Hollywood in the spring of 1930, the respected silent film director, George Pearson, cast an eye over the quota production in which he was soon to become involved. Not only had the 'talkie flood' swamped the silent film, but 'there were short-sighted film-makers' turning out 'catch-penny films made on shoe-string budgets'. Pearson feared that these 'ill-made Quickies' made 'the word "British" on a film a term of contempt'.[28] Pearson's view of the industry is typical of the social distinctions made at the time between gentlemen and players: respectable film-makers of 'integrity' and parvenu charlatans interested only in making a quick profit. Within it is the fear of competition, the threat to established orders and hierarchies. Gentlemen, it seemed, made their permanent homes in the studios of Islington and Shepherd's Bush, each a Mecca for Cambridge men, while the players moved peripatetically around the lesser floors.[29] Only a few directors – notably Major Sinclair Hill (OBE) – successfully negotiated the transitions between one production environment and the other. The distaste for what would come to be known as 'quota quickies' was almost inseparable from the dislike of the *nouveau riche*, the upwardly mobile: no breeding, no sense of responsibility. Pearson quotes with approval the words of his public school assistant Penrose Tennyson, a youth of 'fine fibre':

> The Public School type that is to-day, say twenty, finds himself up against the competition of the Secondary School product. The latter has no family tradition, no money, hence has only his brains; it is a very dangerous rival. Youth now realizes that prestige counts for little, ability only matters. The old worship of safety and security no longer exists; all around the world is in pieces.[30]

In a way, the quota quickies were some of the pieces the world was in: shoddy, tawdry things of little lasting substance – no tradition, no money. The class system was alive and well within British film production, and the distinction between 'quality' and 'quota' pictures has been further delineated over time; not least by Rachael Low, who views quota production as a cheap and vulgar flood which submerged the reputation of the industry.[31] The only quota films she is prepared to exonerate are some of Michael Powell's early efforts, the Old Mother Riley and Max Miller films (which were popular first features) and 'one that Douglas Fairbanks made for Warners' (*Man of the Moment*, 1935, another first feature). And there, with a sweep of the pen, go perhaps two-thirds of the decade's pictures, 'dead weight' as far as Low is concerned.[32]

Low is happy to validate a system of commodity differentiation in which the quota quickie occupied the bottom rung in the hierarchy of value. The common distinction between 'quality' and 'quota' was a major source of dissonance within the national film culture. As *Film Weekly*'s studio correspondent put it at the end of 1932: 'The word "quota" applied to a picture is, normally, not so much a description as a term of abuse . . . there are films and quota films.'[33] This differentiation connoted a set of binary oppositions:

| Quality | Quota |
|---|---|
| Slow | Fast |
| Careful | Careless |
| Crafted | Mass produced |
| Expensive | Cheap |
| Star value | Lack of star value |
| Innovative | Conventional |
| Metropolitan | Provincial |
| Prestigious | Debasing |
| Valuable | Worthless |
| Desired | Undesired |
| Enjoyed | Tolerated |
| Profit-making | Loss-making |
| Artful | Artless |
| Product | By-product |
| Superior | Inferior |
| Dominant | Subordinate |

This system of differentiation was rooted in the circumstances of film production, but it was the changes taking place in the organisation of exhibition that would ensure its cultivation.

## Two for the price of one: the double bill

> The double feature can be seen as an additional showman's attraction, part of the 'better business drive' that included cafés, ice-cream and cinema-organs, to bring the public back into the cinemas.[34]

While the Quota Act has taken the blame for a proliferation of low-budget British pictures of dubious quality, there were two other important factors in the development of an exhibition system which often relegated these films to secondary attractions on double bills:

1  The sudden and rapid adoption of the technology of synchronised sound.
2  The deepening economic depression of the early 1930s.

Although supporting attractions had long been a part of the silent film programme, they were mainly comedy and actuality shorts or live variety performances. The adoption of talkie technology by exhibitors in 1929 and 1930 created a surplus of silent films that the newly equipped cinemas were reluctant to show. The British silent productions, the first fruits of the quota legislation, were now chasing a rapidly shrinking market. Those picture houses that had not yet converted to sound could rent these films cheaply and add them to their programmes. Showing two features in a programme gave these cinemas something with which to compete with the talkie houses – they could point to a three-hour programme of features in opposition to a talking picture, which lasted not much more than one hour. To counter this, more affluent cinemas began to show a silent film with a talkie, or even two talkies, and the demand for sound second fea-

Last of the silents: Herbert Wilcox (centre) directs *The Bondman* (1929) in the presence of author Hall Caine (right)

tures was born.[35] Five years later, F. W. Baker of the British Film Producers Group attributed the two-feature programme to an excess of supply in the market and the desire of exhibitors 'to give the public as much as they could for their money'.[36]

The production industry was taken by surprise by the rapid conversion of cinemas to sound, and its distributors found they had a glut of silent features on their hands. Intended main features became programmers. This was the fate of Herbert Wilcox's picture *The Bondman* (1929), which the director later described as one of a series of unimportant but profitable films that he made in the last days of silent cinema.[37] That this particular picture was profitable is open to doubt. It took eighteen months to reach the provincial city of Leicester, where its three bookings were all as a supporting feature. Based on a Victorian novel of vendetta and self-sacrifice by Hall Caine, *The Bondman* is a thick and indigestible dollop of melodrama that requires an unreasonable effort in the suspension of disbelief. Burdened with conspicuous symbolism and unconvincing narrative development, it represented a style of storytelling that would be quickly displaced by the possibilities offered by the new technology of film-making. At the dawn of the 1930s it was already as outmoded as poorhouse gruel. The practice of distributors or exhibitors cutting films to fit the requirements of a double bill was condemned by the new Association of Cine-Technicians (ACT), but a little judicious editing of its bloated ninety-five minutes could only have benefited *The Bondman*.[38]

Soon, all cinema managers began to realise that, by making a proportion of their second features British, they could meet their quota obligations. This strategy would not have worked if audiences had proved indifferent or hostile to the double bill. But, on the contrary, they embraced the idea to such an extent that it became commercially risky for exhibitors to offer only one feature. As the economic slump deepened and disposable incomes began to dwindle, showmen had to market their programmes more vigorously and competitively. So, as the smaller, inner-city and suburban cinemas began to offer a double bill at half the price or less of the city-centre supers, the largely circuit-owned supers flexed their muscles and began to screen, as supporting features, those films which other picture houses might be happy to play as main attractions. Thus, lower-budget features became part of a system of distinction for exhibitors. At first the distribution of quota films destined for the bottom half of the bill was controlled by British renters, but their position would quickly be usurped by the rental arms of the five Hollywood majors. MGM provided a sign of things to come when, in September 1930, eight months after the original trade show by Alpha Films, it picked up the revue *Comets* and cut it down to convenient second-feature length. It was a move that *The Bioscope* praised as enhancing the film's entertainment value.[39] The excessive length of programmes was already causing concern to the CEA, who considered that the public was getting more than value for money, and that two-and-a-quarter hours should be sufficient time for a full programme.[40] However, the evidence from Leicester suggests that British second features did not become a regular part of provincial cinema programmes until the middle of 1931, when the American renters began to enter the field in earnest.

It is a moot point whether the double bill was adopted earlier and more readily in Britain than in the USA, where similar economic and technological conditions prevailed, but where there was no quota to provide an additional impetus to the two-feature programme. The CEA's President, T. H. Fligelstone, certainly believed that the two-feature programme originated in Britain as part of 'the natural evolution of the trade'.[41] Flynn and McCarthy date the first signs of double-bill programming in the USA to 1931, suggesting that by 1935, 85 per cent of cinemas had largely abandoned the single feature and specialist production houses had been established to satisfy audience demand for 'B' movies (indeed some had already folded).[42] John Izod also dates the adoption of the two-feature programme in the USA to 1931, and explains it as a way of marketing the cinema experience at a time of deepening economic depression: 'The three-hour programme gave the movie-goer the sense, important in a time of financial stringency, of getting good value for the ticket price, which stayed at the same level as for a single feature.'[43]

In Britain, as we have seen, the same marketing strategy was already supported by protectionist legislation and the backlog of indigenously produced silent films awaiting release. Thus, the early sound/silent double features suited the interests both of renters and exhibitors, as well as proving popular with audiences. But, with increasingly universal adoption, rather than being a way of securing an advantage over competitors, the double-feature programme ended up as an additional financial burden on exhibitors, who now had to rent two films instead of one.[44] Partly in recognition of this, distributors in both America and Britain developed a differential way of charging for first and second features. First features were typically rented for a percentage of audience revenue (usually 25–50 per cent), while supporting films were rented for a flat fee only. This meant that 'B' films came to represent a minor but steady and fairly predictable income stream for both renters and producers, and offset some of the financial risks of high-budget features of uncertain popularity. Most of the major Hollywood studios also quickly realised that the inauguration of a 'B' movie unit had a number of additional benefits:

1. The producer/renter could gain a competitive advantage by offering a complete programme package to the exhibitor.
2. The studios could use their 'B' movies as an elaborate screen test for prospective stars, with the additional benefit of audience feedback.
3. Contracted artists could be found work, rather than remaining idle until a suitable part appeared.
4. The 'B' units could be used to train and give experience to new technicians.
5. The short production schedule of the 'B' film meant that it could be slipped in between longer major productions, thus making full use of studio space and contracted technicians (often during unsociable hours and without overtime payments) while allowing another film a more leisurely development stage.

## Patriotic pictures

> Our biggest competitors, the Americans, are paying us the compliment of bringing their money over to this country to make films in British studios . . . The films they make will be branded as British, it is to be hoped that they will be worthy of the name.[45]

While some of the men who helped give impetus to the expansion of low-budget film-making in Britain have looked back on those days with jaundiced eyes, there is no doubt from contemporary accounts that the close of the 1920s was an exciting time to be making movies. *Picture Show*'s young studio correspondent Edith Nepean clearly experienced the first months after the Quota Act as a time of optimism and possibilities: 'One of the liveliest and most inspiring places to-day in this country is a British film studio', she wrote at the beginning of 1928, 'apparently things will be even more hectic if the rumour is true that the Americans are coming over here to make pictures.'[46] The Americans would arrive in due course, but some of the Brits were returning to an industry that was showing signs of revival. John Stafford, for example, came back to England to form his own production company after gaining experience in Hollywood. Others would soon join him, including a young man who had begun to learn the film-making trade in France: Michael Powell. Over the next few years, Nepean's dispatches from the production front would draw no significant distinction between first and supporting features – all were treated as films made in British studios, all indicative of an industry on the rise. This seems to have been a general policy at *Picture Show*, with the magazine reviewing films in alphabetical, rather than prestige, order and devoting a similar space to each.

The fan magazines became increasingly enthusiastic about British production, particularly the almost absurdly patriotic *The British Film-Studio Mirror*, which was launched at the end of 1931. Even *Film Weekly*, which had been so critical of the early quota films that there had been attempts to ban its reviewers from press screenings, proudly ran a special issue on British cinema in the spring of 1932, declaring: 'This British number – which is unique in film journalism –

represents the culmination of our campaign for better British pictures. It is both a record of progress and a promise of even greater things to come.'[47]

Certainly, the number of fan clubs for British stars springing up in the early 1930s and the patriotic support for British product evident in the letters columns of fan magazines attest to a substantial level of satisfaction among audiences. *Picture Show*, for instance, received the following letter from a woman in Hendon:

> It is really delightful to . . . find so many of our readers ready to support British films. Quite recently I organised a party of my girl friends to collect as many votes as possible for British and American films. The total amount was: British films 379 votes; American 152. Needless to say, I was delighted to find British films leading the way.[48]

Another reader from Hythe thought that: 'American films . . . lack the reality and homeliness that British pictures have. In my opinion, English talkies are by far the better, although they do not have such expensive frocks, nor such elaborate settings.'[49] Perhaps the most interesting thing about these opinions is that they were expressed in a magazine whose core readership was young and female, the constituency one might have assumed to be highly vulnerable to the seductions of Hollywood. When the fan weekly *Girl's Cinema* was re-launched as *The Film Star Weekly* in 1932, a reader calling herself 'Britisher' wrote in support of one of the early quota stars: 'I'm so glad John Stuart has not been lured to Hollywood, and hope British producers will keep him here. He's so refreshing after the American heroes with their ugly twang.'[50]

The advent of the talkies, with their ever-present differences of accent and language usage, seems to have sharpened the perception of the distinctiveness of British pictures. It is hard now to appreciate just how important 'correct' pronunciation was to many audience members in the early 1930s, and, with sudden exposure, how jarring and offensive many found 'slack' American speech. Vicky Lowe has drawn attention to the critical role played by the voice in influencing the reception of early sound films: 'In the 1930s, it is particularly clear that the sound of actors' voices on films was crucial in both reinforcing and challenging national, regional and gendered identities; the aural significance of what was considered to be "British" was being constantly negotiated.'[51]

Lowe goes on to argue that, for many audiences, the unconvincing and unacceptable sound of British actors' voices resulted in their performances being viewed as acts of 'cultural ventriloquism', disrupting the immersion in the reality of what was happening on screen. However, in the early days of sound, it appears that it was more often American speech that was experienced as jarring and disruptive of the easy suspension of disbelief. Exhibitors, writing in the trade press, frequently noted the alienating effect on their audiences of the 'nasal' American accent and 'crude American vernacular'.[52] *Picture Show's* redoubtable defender of the national culture, Edward Wood, cautioned against underestimating the corrosive effects of American slang:

> People in high places may argue that the slang of the people cannot affect the moral fibre or the financial stability of a nation, but this is a fallacy – and a very dangerous fallacy. A slang phrase, a music-hall joke, a popular song – all these have done more to mould public opinion than sermons and speeches.[53]

His readers were quick to support him. One wrote from north London recommending: 'For good acting and clear speech, go to any cinema showing a British film, and there you will get real entertainment.'[54] Even in the distant outposts of Empire like Madras, some gave thanks for the linguistic purity of English cinema in ways that would have gladdened the hearts of those who framed the Quota Act:

> The majesty of King's English is maintained in all its glory and dignity by those like Ralph Lynn, Tom Walls and Edna Best . . . . They are not only great stars but great teachers. Many a day have I gone home after the pictures pronouncing a word as an Englishman does.[55]

The problem for many of the readers and contributors to *Picture Show* was that the indigenous cinema struggled to gain the recognition and prestige it deserved. This was clearly evident in the magazine's first issue of 1932. The tone was set by the full-page advertisement by the Empire Marketing Board informing readers of 'Your Job for your country', which was 'to restore the nation's trade balance and to provide work for British men and women' by buying only home- and Empire-made goods 'produced at least as well there as in any foreign land'. That this injunction applied equally to films was emphasised in both the editorial and letter columns. Edward Wood predicted that 'instead of being used as fill-ups for programmes featuring American pictures', British films would become 'the programme feature, and deservedly so'.[56] This sort of rhetoric puts a different complexion on the maligned quota quickies, patriotically conferring on at least some of these modest productions the status of enforced subordination, victims of foreign domination. As it became clear that the quota legislation was failing fully to deliver cultural prowess (as opposed to economic success) to British pictures, Wood renewed his beating of the patriotic drum in support of bringing Old England to the screen:

> While American and foreign competitors are exploiting Vienna and other Continental cities let our British producers centre on Great Britain and the Empire. The castles and stately homes of England, its picturesque cottages and inns are still standing in sufficient quantities to provide natural backgrounds at small expense.[57]

His constant refrain: 'Show England, and every Englishman will be proud of his country' would again have been melodious to the ears of the authors of the Quota Act.[58] So too would patriotic and optimistic articles like *Film Pictorial*'s 'Showing Britain to the World: Ideas and Ideals on the Screen', which also indicated that the imperial intentions of the Act had not been forgotten:

> Now that British films are finding their place in the world, the natives of Timbuctoo and the Chinese of Shanghai will find out that all that has been best in the world is not represented by sky-scrapers and their inhabitants. They will learn that the Britain, of which they have heard, but unfortunately seen so little on the screen so far, is a pleasanter country than its mighty offspring.[59]

The key to cultural acceptance abroad was the same as that to pride at home: the romantic depiction of the British countryside, which was thought to have an irresistible effect on all viewers. Programmers like BIP's *Mr. Bill the Conqueror* (1932) and Butcher's *The Great Gay*

*Road* (1931) – showing the beauties of Sussex and Kent, respectively – certainly encapsulated the rural spell, but the latter's 'charming glimpses of Chiddington, Godstone, Forest Row, and Box Hill' probably struggled for bookings among the natives of Scotland and Tyneside, never mind Shanghai and Timbuctoo.

The detectable support for British product was certainly not confined to first features. In just one issue of *Picture Show* in 1934 there were three letters offering praise to British programmers. Ada Connell wrote to say that she had 'never seen such natural acting' as that in the MGM quickie *Commissionaire* (1933). Evelyn Speed suggested that American films could not match the 'sincerity' of Michael Powell's *Red Ensign* (1934); while Albert Race included John Baxter's *Doss House* (1933) and *Reunion* (1932) among his shortlist of memorable films free of 'love scenes'.[60] A few months earlier, *Film Pictorial* had published a letter comparing quota featurettes favourably with American short films:

> These little productions, some of them only forty or fifty minutes long, may well take the place of the miserable drivel from America purporting to be comedy which we have had to endure far too long. Surely the average English audience would prefer the robust but wholesome humour of [British quota films] . . . to the nonsensical antics of most American two-reel comedians.[61]

Reviews in the fan magazines could also often be favourable to low-budget British productions. For example, in its issue of 9 July 1932 *Film Pictorial* chose Paramount British's dockland drama *Ebb Tide* (1932) as its film of the week. It also enthused about PDC's 'unpretentious' but 'very good little effort', *Account Rendered* (1932), and ran a feature on its riches-to-rags star, Marilyn Mawn. It even managed to describe Universal's *Above Rubies* (1932), directed by one of the quota's less competent practitioners, Frank Richardson, as 'four thousand feet of pleasing enough entertainment'. It did admit that BIP's *The Strangler* (1932) was 'not a film which is likely to add lots of laurels to Britain's talkie crown', but could still advise that there was a thrill to be had 'if you like haunted rooms and storms, and badly lighted old houses'. In the early years of sound, there was less of a divide between low- and high-budget productions. At BIP, one of the national cinema's most significant studios, for example, the average expenditure on a film was only £10,000 – less than double that of the standard quickie.[62]

While there was widespread patriotic support for the idea of a British cinema, there were substantial doubts about the effect that the exhibition trend towards double-feature programmes might have on its development. At the 1931 CEA Summer Conference in Brighton, the double bill was an urgent topic of debate. An editorial in *The Bioscope* expressed the concerns of many in the film business about the growing acceptance of two-feature programming, and invited resistance:

> Single Feature Bills . . . would mean a more critical study by the exhibitor of the feature films he was buying, and also a more critical study of the short supporting subjects. The effect of this could not fail quickly to raise the standard of quality in both cases. . . . There are many films still being produced for Quota requirements which are only securing – and, indeed, deserving – a second place on the programme. With a reduced demand for feature-length subjects, every British film made would have to be produced with an eye to its suitability for 'topping the bill'. There would

be a reduced market for mere long-length Quota subjects and increased concentration on first class subjects capable of holding a premier position.[63]

But it was to be *The Bioscope* that disappeared in the following year while the position of the double bill strengthened. In London, by 1932, leading general-release cinemas like the Stoll Picture Theatre, Kingsway and the Trocadero in the Elephant and Castle, were engaged in cut-throat competition to show the biggest double-feature programme. These giant cinemas gave their patrons two (and even three) films that would each top the bill at lesser venues. *Film Weekly* thought that these super programmes 'must make provincial filmgoers green with envy', as smaller cinemas had to rely on purpose-made supporting features or more expensive flops to complete their bills.[64] However, the rise of these British supporting features is evident from the table below. The films identified are those listed in the Filmography, and the classification is based on the knowledge or strong supposition that these pictures played mainly as supporting features on their first release.

There are a number of observations to be made from this data:

1. Supporting features constitute almost half the films made in Britain between the first two Quota Acts. In 1932, 1933, 1934 and 1937 they were in a majority.

**Table 1.1** British film production 1928–37

| Year | 1928 | 1929 | 1930 | 1931 | 1932 | 1933 | 1934 | 1935 | 1936 | 1937 | Total |
|---|---|---|---|---|---|---|---|---|---|---|---|
| **British films produced** | 108 | 65 | 114 | 144 | 152 | 177 | 195 | 187 | 230 | 191 | 1563 |
| **British films registered** | 91 | 83 | 132 | 145 | 156 | 189 | 190 | 198 | 222 | 225 | 1631 |
| **Supporting features** | | | | | | | | | | | |
| **33–9 minutes** | 2 | 2 | 14 | 10 | 8 | 4 | 3 | 2 | 5 | 4 | 54 |
| **40–70 minutes** | 12 | 12 | 30 | 45 | 50 | 84 | 81 | 67 | 71 | 75 | 527 |
| **>70 minutes** | 15 | 6 | 6 | 10 | 20 | 20 | 24 | 23 | 34 | 32 | 190 |
| **Total** | 29 | 20 | 50 | 65 | 78 | 108 | 108 | 92 | 110 | 111 | 771 |
| **% films made in Britain** | 26.8 | 30.8 | 43.9 | 45.1 | 51.3 | 61.0 | 55.3 | 49.2 | 47.8 | 58.1 | 49.1 |
| **Exhibitors' quota %** | 5 | 7.5 | 10 | 10 | 12.5 | 15 | 17.5 | 17.5 | 20 | 20 | |

2. The number of British supporting features produced increased by almost 550 per cent between 1929 and 1933, and then remained fairly constant until the second Quota Act.

3. Second features are often identified by their briefer running time, but almost a quarter ran over seventy minutes. In the last days of silent film, these longer films were the majority. We can regard many of them as 'sunken' first features or films that failed. Their accommodation on double bills usually meant a lengthening of the programme.

4. The average length of supporting features increased as the second Quota Act approached. In 1933, films over seventy minutes constituted only 18.5 per cent of the total, but in 1937 they were 28.1 per cent. At the same time, short supporting featurettes under forty minutes were squeezed out: there were fourteen in 1930, but only four in 1937.

5. The number of British supporting features produced each year was not related simply to quota requirements: in 1933, when the exhibitors' quota was 15 per cent, 108 were produced (61 per cent), in 1935 when the quota was 17.5 per cent, only ninety were made (48 per cent). We might attribute this to the Korda effect: the success of *The Private Life of Henry VIII* (1933) meant that finance was more readily available for bigger-budget films.

Now that we have some idea of the population size of British supporting features and have identified some of their salient characteristics, it is time to see how they were made.

## Notes

1. Cmd. 5320: 702.

2. PEP, *The British Film Industry* (London: Political and Economic Planning, 1952), p. 42. On the dominance of Hollywood over the British film industry see Kenton Bamford, *Distorted Images: British National Identity and Film in the 1920s* (London: I. B. Tauris, 1999).

3. Marek Kohn, *Dope Girls: The Birth of the British Drug Underground* (London: Lawrence and Wishart, 1992), especially Chapter 8.

4. Linda Wood, 'Low-budget British Films in the 1930s', in Robert Murphy (ed.), *The British Cinema Book* (London: BFI, 2001), p. 53. See also Margaret Dickinson and Sarah Street, *Cinema and State: The Film Industry and the British Government 1927–84* (London: BFI, 1985), pp. 15–16, 29–30. See also Tom Ryall, *Alfred Hitchcock and the British Cinema* (London: Croom Helm, 1986), Chapter 3, which remains one of the best introductions to the act and its effect on British production.

5. Fears were expressed by exhibitors' representatives on the Joint Committee about 'whether British films of a suitable quality for exhibition would be forthcoming in sufficient numbers and at a suitable price'. *The Times*, 4 August 1926, p. 10.

6. 'Why Has the Quota Been Introduced?', *Daily Film Renter,* 22 March 1927.

7. *Daily Film Renter,* 22 March 1927; *The Economist,* 20 March 1927.

8. There were further stipulations in the definition of a British film, concerning the nationality of the scenarist and the percentage of labour costs paid to British subjects. See Dickinson and Street, *Cinema and State,* pp. 5–33; Rachael Low, *The History of the British Film 1918–29* (London: Allen and Unwin, 1971).

9. Revisionist work includes: Napper, 'A Despicable Tradition? Quota Quickies in the 1930s', in Murphy (ed.), *The British Cinema Book,* pp. 45–52; Wood, 'Low-budget British Films'; Matthew Sweet, *Shepperton Babylon* (London: Faber and Faber, 2005); H. Mark Glancy, 'Hollywood and

Britain: MGM and the British "Quota"', in Jeffrey Richards (ed.), *The Unknown 1930s: An Alternative History of British Cinema 1929–1939* (London: I. B. Tauris, 1998), pp. 57–72; John Sedgwick, 'Cinema-going Preferences in Britain in the 1930s', in Richards (ed.), *The Unknown 1930s*, pp. 1–35.

10. Cmd. 5320: Memorandum of the Film Producers' Group.

11. 'Final Evidence on Quota Act Revision', *Kinematograph Weekly*, 15 October 1936, p. 11.

12. For example, *Kinematograph Weekly*, 21 June 1928.

13. *The Cinema*, 4 July 1928, p. 3.

14. Quoted in Charles Oakley, *Where We Came In* (London: Allen and Unwin, 1964), pp. 101–2.

15. Quoted in P. L. Mannock, 'Will British Films Improve?', *Kinematograph Weekly*, 2 January 1930, p. 67.

16. R. G. Martin, 'Prospects of the Film Industry', *Financial Review of Reviews*, July 1927, p. 41.

17. British Screen Productions, British Filmcraft Productions and Audible Filmcraft.

18. *Kinematograph Weekly*, 21 November 1929, p. 47.

19. Sound virtually doubled the average cost of film production. Dickinson and Street, *Cinema and State*, p. 42.

20. *The Bioscope*, 6 June 1930.

21. *The Cinema*, 3 January 1934.

22. Dickinson and Street, *Cinema and State*, p. 41.

23. *Kinematograph Weekly*, 8 January 1931, p. 73.

24. Ibid., p. 87.

25. Edward Dryhurst, *Gilt Off the Gingerbread* (London: Bachman & Turner, 1987), p. 172.

26. Reginald Denham, *Stars in My Hair* (London: T. Werner Laurie, 1958), p. 175. Denham regarded the time devoted to his film career as time lost to his real love: the theatre. Twenty years after making them, he had forgotten the titles of all the twenty-four quota pictures he made for Paramount, Fox, George Smith and others. Only a handful of the larger-budget films gave him any pleasure and he remained ashamed of the others.

27. Profile of Huntington supplied by Rank's publicity department in the 1940s.

28. George Pearson, *Flashback* (London: Allen and Unwin, 1957), p. 187.

29. On the significance of Cambridge University in Gaumont-British recruitment see BECTU Oral History Project, Interview 108 with Hugh Stewart, 23 November 1989.

30. Pearson, *Flashback*, pp. 190, 192.

31. 'Unfortunately British production was swamped by the boring, badly made and routine work of the quota producers.' Rachael Low, *The History of the British Film, 1929–1939* (London: Allen and Unwin, 1985), p. 115.

32. Ibid., p. 116.

33. Stephen Watts, 'High-Speed Film Making', *Film Weekly*, 16 December 1932, p. 12.

34. PEP, *The British Film Industry*, p. 54.

35. The 1930 *Kinematograph Year Book* (p. 12) could report that it was 'generally recognized that an entertainment should consist of a talkie, a silent, and either a comedy or a variety turn'. Cameraman, Leonard Harris recalled that his small local cinema in north London began to show silent films as second features when it first converted to sound. BECTU Oral History Project, Interview 189, 18 March 1991. In Berlin, double bills of talkies were being shown as early as the summer of 1930,

although renters and other exhibitors had already combined to try to prevent this practice. *The Bioscope*, 10 September 1930, p. 25.

36. Cmd. 5320: 366.

37. Herbert Wilcox, *Twenty-Five Thousand Sunsets* (New York: A. S. Barnes, 1967), p. 83.

38. An Aberdeen cinemagoer also complained about this practice to *Picture Show*, 29 September 1929, p. 4.

39. *The Bioscope*, 24 September 1930, p. 43.

40. Ibid., p. 49.

41. Cmd. 5320: 872–4.

42. Charles Flynn and Todd McCarthy, 'The Economic Imperative: Why Was the B Movie Necessary?', in Todd McCarthy and Charles Flynn (eds), *Kings of the Bs: Working within the Hollywood System* (New York: E. P. Dutton, 1975), p. 15.

43. John Izod, *Hollywood and the Box Office 1895–1986* (New York: Columbia University Press, 1988), p. 99.

44. Industry analyst, Simon Rowson, estimated that the two-feature programme had been adopted by more than 50 per cent of cinemas in both Britain and the USA by 1936. Cmd. 5320: 1276. In Leicester, adoption was near universal.

45. *The British Film-Studio Mirror* no. 3, February–March 1932, p. 3.

46. *Picture Show*, 21 January 1928, p. 9.

47. *Film Weekly*, 29 April 1932, p. 7.

48. Letter from Q. L. T. of Hendon, *Picture Show*, 15 August 1931, p. 5.

49. Letter from V. H. of Hythe, *Picture Show*, 31 October 1931, p. 4. Correspondents from 'The Empire' expressed similar sentiments. A reader in Bombay, India, conceded that American films had 'more originality, more scenery and better material', but insisted that British films were 'of more solid worth, with clear dialogue, and clever, good stories'. *Picture Show*, 31 October 1931, p. 4.

50. Letter from 'Britisher', *The Film Star Weekly*, 26 November 1932, p. 37.

51. Vicky Lowe, 'The Best Speaking Voices in the World: Robert Donat, Stardom and the Voice in British Cinema', *Journal of British Cinema and Television* vol. 1 no. 2, 2005, p. 182. Conscious of the appeal to audiences of ordinary English speech, BIP adopted the slogan 'Talkies that talk as you talk!' See the press book for Thomas Bentley's 'symphony of everyday life', *After Office Hours* (1932).

52. *Kinematograph Weekly,* 8 January 1931, p. 101.

53. *Picture Show*, 23 July 1932, p. 18.

54. Letter from 'Hussar', *Picture Show*, 2 July 1932, p. 27.

55. Letter from B. B. A., *Picture Show*, 27 August 1932, p. 4.

56. *Picture Show*, 2 January 1932.

57. 'More Costume Plays Wanted', *Picture Show*, 23 January 1932, p. 21.

58. 'Show England', *Picture Show*, 23 July 1932, pp. 18–19. See also C. B. Cochran, 'Let Us Have Really British Films', *Cinematograph Times*, 3 January 1931, p. 62.

59. *Film Pictorial*, 17 September 1932, p. 20.

60. Letters from Ada Connell of Wandsworth, Evelyn Speed of Enfield and Albert Race of Sheffield, *Picture Show*, 18 August 1934, p. 28.

61. Letter to *Film Pictorial*, 30 December 1933, p. 30. Rather than supporting Stephen Shafer's contention that British productions were enjoyed by the 'poor and unemployed', the letter's middle-

class language and syntax bolster George Perry's argument that that national cinema catered predominantly to bourgeois taste in a year when almost 30 per cent of films were based on stage plays. Stephen Shafer, *British Popular Films 1929–1939: The Cinema of Reassurance* (London: Routledge, 1997), p. 20. George Perry, *The Great British Picture Show* (London: Hart-Davis, MacGibbon, 1974).

62. *Kinematograph Weekly*, 23 October 1930, p. 19.

63. *The Bioscope*, 1 July 1931, p. 1.

64. *Film Weekly*, 22 April 1932, p. 5.

# 2

# The Pound-a-foot Merchants

'What's the budget?' I asked. He gulped, 'A pound a foot.'

Michael Powell[1]

The Quota Act provided a vital impetus for the mushroom growth of small and medium-sized production companies, turning out pictures on frugal budgets, under conditions that would make most union officials apoplectic. An astonishing 233 new production companies were registered in the first five years of the Act, although few survived to see the next five years.[2] New independents were not saddled with obsolete equipment or reluctant personnel, and could often negotiate the change to sound production more easily than established firms. Their greater flexibility and lower operating costs gave them the opportunity to accept the penny-pinching contracts offered by the American renters.

The explosion of British production companies was aided by, and in turn stimulated, a rapid growth in film studio facilities. The number of stages in British studios increased from nineteen to seventy between 1928 and 1938.[3] In the last days of silent film production, the mushroom companies used the facilities at the Nettlefold Studios at Walton-on-Thames, the cavernous Stoll Studios at Cricklewood, the minuscule Bushey Studios and the converted aircraft hangar at Southall. G&S Productions even made a couple of comedy featurettes – including the provocatively titled *Nick's Knickers* (1929) – at the old Preston Studios in Brighton. However, the most frequently used studio was Worton Hall in Isleworth, a manor that had been converted into a film studio by G. B. Samuelson in 1914. The studio hosted at least a dozen quota pictures in the late 1920s. Pioneer producer/director Harry B. Parkinson made half of them, before the arrival of the talkies persuaded him to hang up his megaphone. Titles like *Human Cargo*, *The Streets of London* and *A Broken Romance* (all 1929) suggest that the urge to exploit issues of morality, which he had given full expression in the earlier *Cocaine* (1922), remained with him until the end. His last supporting feature was *Scrags*, chronicling the adventures of a stray dog, and directed by Norman Lee in March 1930.

The other Isleworth films were largely the work of British Screen Productions and Edward Whiting. Edward Dryhurst worked as a scenario editor for British Screen Productions, a company headed by G. W. Pearson, which had bought Worton Hall from G. B. Samuelson in 1928. In his remarkably frank autobiography Dryhurst recalls returning from a working visit to the USA in 1928, hearing about the 'bucket shop' companies that had been floated on the quota wave, and being introduced to the swaggering G. W. Pearson:

Pearson exuded the confidence of one whose precarious existence had been made secure by a wind-fall of easy money. His suit was new and expensive, his cigar enormous, his manner inclined to be patronizing. . . . Talking pictures were a nine days' wonder, he averred, and would soon fizzle out.[4]

Dryhurst's first assignment, *Houp-la!* (1928), was already going into production, and he judi-ciously withheld his opinion that: 'The story was bilge, the characterizations absurd, the writing amateurish.' When the film was eventually trade shown, however, the notices were predictably 'scathing', but the reaction of the director, Frank Miller, was that the critics were 'cretins' and the exhibitors 'oafs'.[5] The script for the next production, George Cooper's *Master and Man* (1928) was only a marginal improvement on the first, and the film's reception was equally frosty.[6]

Deserting the sinking ship, Dryhurst decided to try his luck as an independent producer in partnership with a London exhibitor. They approached distributor George Smith of PDC who offered them a contract for their first picture, a comedy melodrama titled *The Dizzy Limit*, filmed at Isleworth in the autumn of 1929. The dizzy limit for Smith was a miserly £2,000, con-firming Rachael Low's assertion that Smith's pictures were 'the cheapest of the cheap', and making Adrian Brunel's recollection that Smith 'paid better than most' all the more puzzling.[7] Incredibly, the eighty-minute silent film, shot by leading cameraman D. P. Cooper, was actually made for £1,200. Smith then added a musical soundtrack. PDC went on to make a series of musical featurettes at Isleworth during 1930 – including *The New Waiter* and *The Musical Beauty Shop* – but the directorial duties passed to Monty Banks, the diminutive Italian comic.[8] In Jan-uary 1930, Dryhurst's partner, Edward Whiting, secured a contract from MGM to deliver a silent film to be trade shown before the end of the quota year on 31 March. Dryhurst quickly paid George Cooper £20 for one of his scripts and got cracking at Worton Hall, with his partner's exotic girlfriend, Julie Suedo, starring as *The Woman from China*. By this time it was the end of February and the unit had to begin work with the shooting script only half-finished. Filming took place from morn 'til midnight, using a steam engine to generate power when the inability of the Hall's owners to pay their bill led to the electricity being cut. The final scenes were shot five days before the scheduled trade show, and director Dryhurst was obliged to double as editor with the help of one young assistant. The two worked ninety hours without sleep to meet the deadline, although the first of the two shows was lacking the final reel.[9]

Soon after Dryhurst's ordeal, in the summer of 1930, Pat Heale set up production at Worton Hall, producing three lacklustre features by the end of the year. All exploited the musical possi-bilities of the new sound medium. Heale's partner was Alfred Woodley, a builder with cinema interests in Surrey, and Isleworth veteran Fred Paul was in charge of production. Paramount was among the renters handling their product and, in the quota euphoria of the early 1930s, there were ambitious plans to construct new studios at Hayes, Middlesex. Worton Hall was also used by Reginald Fogwell Productions from September 1930.[10] Fogwell had been Fox's London publicity manager in the 1920s, and had written and directed a number of silent films before setting up his own production unit. The trade reviews of both Heale's and Fogwell's films were frequently scornful. For example, *Kinematograph Weekly* dismissed the Fogwell featurette *The Tem-perance Fete* (1932) without ceremony: 'The conception, treatment and presentation bear the stamp of the amateur, and at no period does the picture rise above the low level of mediocrity.'[11] This was both disappointing and surprising, as the film starred the popular music-hall performer

George Robey and was directed by Graham Cutts, a mentor of Alfred Hitchcock with a reputation as a visual stylist. Cutts was one of a number of successful directors of silent films who
found themselves in straitened circumstances with the arrival of the talkies. Albert Bramble,
Manning Hayes, Frank Richardson and the innovative and adventurous Guy Newall all found
themselves reduced to making cheap programmers.

A few production houses continued to turn out silent pictures during 1930 and even 1931,
notably the company run by John F. Argyle, a precocious teenager who, after camera training at
Gainsborough Studios, wrote, produced and directed his early films. He also took the lead role
in the mining drama *Flames of Fear* (1930) and the horse-racing films *Thoroughbred* and *The
Game of Chance* (both 1932). Argyle liked to depict working-class heroism and prided himself
on his promotion of traditional English virtues. He described *The Game of Chance*, made at the
obscure Reel Arms Studio in Argyle's home town of Tamworth, as 'a picture that is British in
every foot' set amid 'the rural beauty of England' with 'a theme near to every Englishman's
heart'.[12] The response of the critics, however, made it clear that he should move with the
times.[13] Eventually he did, making his first talkie, *Smilin' Along*, in February 1932.

Argyle was not the only young entrepreneur to capitalise on the growing demand for
second features. Bedford-born Widgey R. Newman began his film career with Gaumont and
continued with de Forest Photofilms, before organising the introduction of sound for Astra. He
registered his first film company in 1929, aged twenty-six. A 'gloriously eccentric and erratic
character', he operated as writer, producer and director of shorts and featurettes.[14] By the begin-

King of the quota: George King

ning of 1932, he had set up Delta Pictures with the producer Geoffrey Clarke and studio supervisor and cameraman John Miller to make films at Bushey. Towards the end of 1935 he completed the first second features for Butcher's Film Service, the novelty featurettes *What the Parrot
Saw* (to support *Lieut. Daring R.N.*) and *What the Puppy Said* (to support the revue *Stars on
Parade*, 1936).

Perhaps the most prolific of all the independent producer/directors working in second features was George King. Starting as an assistant in the machinery department of an equipment
company, he later gained some experience of film exhibition before joining the London staff of
a Hollywood producer. He began his own production at the age of thirty in summer 1930,
completing three talkies for Fox before the end of the year.[15] He made more than fifty quota
films at a variety of studios hired for the purpose. They earned him enough to buy an
eighteenth-century mansion on the Thames near Shepperton, and helped four of the actors
working in his early films – Heather Angel, Benita Hume, Sari Maritza and Laurence Olivier –
to secure Hollywood contracts. King maintained a long association with Fox, producing mainly
at Walton and Twickenham (see below), but he switched to MGM for his most lucrative collab-
oration with the monarch of melodrama, Tod Slaughter. Beginning with *Maria Marten* in 1935,
these barnstorming productions, with their dastardly villains, endangered maidens and thick
slices of ham acting, constitute the last flowerings of the Victorian theatrical tradition. By 1937,
with a network of distribution deals with British and American renters, King's productions were
becoming more ambitious, and he imported the Hollywood star Zasu Pitts to star in *Wanted* and

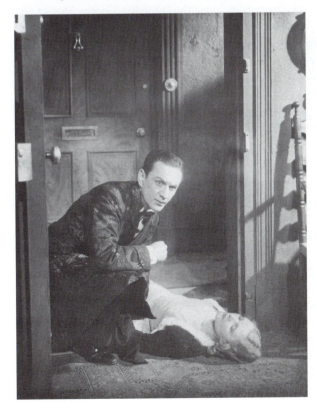

Spies in the night: John Stuart and
Eve Gray in George King's thriller
*Midnight* (1931)

*Merry Comes to Town*. King's wife, Odette, was his production supervisor and financial director and, together with Widgey Newman's wife, was one of the few women involved in the organisation of quota production. King met Odette when, soon after leaving school, she was screen tested by Warners. *Picturegoer's* studio correspondent, E. G. Cousins, was clearly smitten, describing her as 'that tiny, beautifully tailored, black-haired, dusky-complexioned little wisp of a thing with dark Oriental eyes and a vivid smile', and commenting, 'you'd hardly imagine her capable of budgeting for the Sunday joint'.[16]

King's production company was part of the continuing growth of independents in the early 1930s that included Clifton Hurst Productions, Anglo-Cosmopolitan, Grafton Films, Vogue Films, Progress Pictures, Triumph Films, Apex Pictures, Thames International Pictures. At the time, director Vernon Sewell was one of the bright young men trying their luck in the film business and he recalled that most of these companies had very little background in cinema: 'George King, he had no experience of anything but he became a quota film director. They were really entrepreneurs.'[17] Many offered work to new directors eager to make their way in the film business. Tribune Films, for example, was set up by a young enthusiast named Peter Saunders, and established a production base at the tiny Marylebone Studios in the heart of London, making *Eight Cylinder Love* in the summer of 1934. But the company that was to become the most famous of British 'B' film producers began with a modest fanfare at the end of that year. A full-page advertisement and a couple of column inches in *Kinematograph Weekly* heralded the arrival of Hammer Productions.[18] The company was set up by theatrical agent and performer William Hinds (aka Hammer), and the company directors included the comedian George Mozart and the director James Elder Wills, among whose credits was the Anna May Wong film *Tiger Bay* (1933). Their first picture, financed by a jewellery business, was entrusted to Bernerd Mainwaring, and was made for MGM at the ATP Studios, Ealing.[19] The title, *The Public Life of Henry the Ninth* (1934), traded on the success of Korda's transatlantic hit, but the Hammer film was aimed squarely at the domestic market, and featured the popular radio personality, Leonard Henry, as a devotee of the bar room. Its sound recordist, John Mitchell recalled:

> The whole film was shot in two weeks, and the Hammer logo with Bombardier Billy Wells (later the famous Rank man with the gong) was filmed one lunch hour. . . . The background music for the film was recorded on a Saturday with the film being dubbed and re-recorded on the Sunday, taking twenty-four hours of non-stop work. Total production time to delivery was three weeks in spite of which it was a very successful box office draw with cinema patrons.[20]

Judging it as 'quite a useful supporting proposition for popular and industrial halls', *Kinematograph Weekly* commented that the film made 'no attempt to compete seriously with slick American entertainment of the same calibre, but it does in its modest way fill an hour quite pleasingly'.[21] However, when Hammer joined forces with the owner of the Blue Hall cinema and theatre circuit, Enrique Carreras, the company's ambition became a good deal broader, with plans for a costume film set in the Louis XV period.[22] The project was still-born, but in anticipation of its later fame as a horror studio, Hammer instead brought over Bela 'Dracula' Lugosi to star in *The Mystery of the Marie Celeste* (1935). His star name was enough to win the film distribution in the USA (as *The Phantom Ship*).

British Lion's Beaconsfield Studios were another venue hired by producers of supporting features. Producer/director John Harvel (Amalgamated Films Association) booked the studios for six films at the end of 1931. The first was the Ruritanian operetta, *The Beggar Student*, which was turned out in thirteen days.[23] Beaconsfield also hosted Maurice Elvey's ATP production *The Water Gipsies* (1932).[24] British Lion liked to think of itself as making first features, although early sound productions such as *Should a Doctor Tell?* (1930) and *To Oblige a Lady* (1931), both directed by Manning Hayes, were equally suitable for the lower half of the bill. Late in 1932, studio manager Sam Smith offered Fox the opportunity to use his facilities to make slightly superior programmers, using the designers, technicians and elements of sets from the studio's more ambitious in-house productions. Resident director Leslie Hiscott was soon employed on a series of quickies for Fox and MGM at a rate of almost one per month. Hiscott developed a reputation for 'speed without haste', rehearsing with care and re-shooting when necessary.[25] When Hiscott departed for pastures new, production continued, with Herbert Smith taking over most of the directorial assignments. After the studios ran into the financial difficulties that led to temporary closure in 1937, Herbert Wilcox produced the low-budget hit *Blondes for Danger* (1937), directed by Jack Raymond.[26] Ideal-Gainsborough showed their appreciation of the emerging market for the British comedy programmer at the end of 1930 with a series of 'musical burlesques' at their Islington studios – *Aroma of the South Seas*, *My Old China*, *Bull Rushes* (all 1931) and *Who Killed Doc Robin?* (1930) etc. – satirising popular fiction. However, they quickly abandoned this type of production in favour of more prestigious projects.

Islington was one of those studios that had first been equipped to make silent pictures; but independent production of quota films was also facilitated by a studio-building boom. The new facilities at Wembley, north London, were used in 1933 by a motley collection of producers – including Pat Heale, Steven Edwards, George Smith, Arthur Maude and Edward Whiting – to make quickies for almost all the American renters, before being taken over by Fox the following year. Henry Edwards' re-built studios at Teddington were quickly snapped up by Warners as the base for their British production operation. Sound City Studios at Shepperton opened in the late spring of 1932 and booked in eleven independent productions before the end of the year. In addition, they produced two films of their own, including the well-received John Baxter/Ivar Campbell programmer *Reunion*, which, like most Sound City product, was handled by MGM. The studios' founders were mostly enthusiastic amateurs, many from wealthy families with good connections in the city and the services.[27] The studios' owner was a young Scot, Norman Loudon, who had made a fortune from publishing novelty 'flicker' books. Loudon's stated intention was to make 'vigorous, dramatic' films about the 'everyday life' of ordinary British people, and to counter the 'flirtatious farce' and 'cocktail effervescence' that passed for screen entertainment among British film-makers.[28] The watchwords of Loudon's productions were to be sincerity and optimism with attention given to the reality of characterisations. He was only occasionally susceptible to the lure of international markets – the over-blown loss-making *Colonel Blood* (1934), for instance – and generally ran his studios on financial lines as 'sound' as their name. If the budget for Baxter's 1935 film *A Real Bloke* (billed as 'A Story of the British Working Man') is anything to go by, Sound City operated on MGM payments that were a little more generous than usual. The film was budgeted at £8,000, or £1.20 per foot, for a fifteen-day shooting schedule.[29] The studios provided a training ground for some stalwarts of

British film-making, including John Paddy Carstairs, Anthony Kimmins, Raymond Stross, Ralph Thomas, Guy Green and the costume designer Elizabeth Haffenden.

The most important independent production base for British second features was Twickenham Studios in west London, established in 1929 by Julius Hagen, an actor and film renter. In association with the aforementioned Leslie Hiscott, who had worked in a number of production jobs during the 1920s, Hagen made films for Radio, Fox and Universal. Although Hiscott moved to Beaconsfield in 1933, Hagen was successful in retaining a team of capable and reliable directors, including many seasoned veterans, as well as new talents like John Baxter and Bernard Vorhaus. Like most of the American majors, Hagen quickly realised the benefit of a mixed economy of first and second features, the latter providing a steady income to compensate for the financial vicissitudes of the former. He charged a flat fee per foot, but ensured the possibility of extra revenue if a film attracted above average bookings.[30]

Until 1934, the production facility could boast only a single sound stage, but it was operated on American studio lines, with artists often placed under contract rather than hired on a one-off basis. This system, combined with the standardising effect of the studios' resident scriptwriter, H. Fowler Mear, and the recycling of sets, gave Twickenham films a kind of house style and continuity of treatment – particularly among the murder mysteries, which accounted for 50 per cent of the studio's output. In many respects, the studios at Twickenham became an extension of the West End stage, which was the major source of their scenarios, actors and *mise en scène*. One of Hagen's most reliable directors was George Pearson, who was obliged to explore the employment possibilities offered by quota quickie production as 'the only field open to the few pioneers remaining from the silent film days'. He slotted into Twickenham's roster of directors, which included George Cooper and Henry Edwards, 'all, like myself, victims of circumstance'. His description of the 'Spartan economy' and 'slave-driving effort' under which he toiled, makes Twickenham Studios sound more like a Soviet labour camp than a privileged environment for the production of entertainment in the leafy Home Counties:

> Though the studio was more or less a film factory, there was a keen spirit amongst the staff to raise the quality of its product. . . . Remuneration was small, but just enough for existence. All vaulting ideas of film as an art had to be abandoned; only as a capable and speedy craftsman could one survive in that feverish and restless environment.[31]

So successfully did Pearson adapt, that he completed his night-shoot on *That's My Uncle* ahead of schedule in March 1935.[32] Bernard Vorhaus recalled that two weeks constituted a long shooting schedule, and that if any director fell a day behind, Hagen would rip six pages out of the script. If the schedule was maintained, however, Hagen allowed his directors considerable autonomy. As Maurice Elvey put it: 'He let one make strange films – on condition you made them cheaply enough.'[33] Vorhaus realised the value of this relatively light touch when he was headhunted by the largest American 'B' movie studio. Although it had been 'terribly difficult' shooting films on tight budgets and schedules at Twickenham, Republic was 'very, very restrictive' by comparison.[34] In its twenty-five year history, Republic turned out an astonishing 386 Westerns – more than one each month – together with a host of mysteries, serials and other action pictures.[35] Neither Twickenham, nor any other British studio could approach this kind of volume

production. Nor were British producers ever quite able to emulate – at least until the 1950s –
the long-running series in which Monogram, Republic's chief competitor, specialised.[36]

Rather than Westerns, Twickenham specialised in what Lawrence Napper has termed
'middle-class quota-quickies'. These were often thrillers, whodunits and society melodramas
adapted from novels and stage plays.[37] Twickenham persisted in the fallacy that the Englishman's
home is a castle, and that only the murder of the wealthy is worthy of investigation.[38] The studios varied the formula and treatment little between different grades of feature and, consequently, the up-grades of quality often proved too subtle for exhibitors. For example, take two
films produced in the first half of 1934.

*Tangled Evidence*, directed by George A. Cooper, was a classic body-in-the-library whodunit
in which everyone is suspected of stabbing a studious old colonel, including his pretty nieces,
randy chauffeur and Oxford-accented librarian. No one in this unsavoury ménage is a sympathetic character. The Victorian Gothic country house is a perfect setting for a screaming maid
and the solemn declaration that 'Yesterday this was a peaceful house and now . . . .It's horrible!'
Clues are laid out for the camera with meticulous precision, and action is largely sacrificed to
either expository dialogue or the comedy of life below stairs.[39] Appropriately enough, the villain turns out to be a writer who has plagiarised the colonel's manuscript – just as the writer
of the film has appropriated and recycled any number of previous scenarios of this type. As if to

The body in the study: Edgar Norfolk and Sam Livesey amid the typical Twickenham *mise en scène*
in *Tangled Evidence* (1934)

underline this self-referentiality, the murderer even discusses the film rights for his story with his publisher. Three months later, there was another corpse on the library floor when the same studio made *Lord Edgware Dies* (1934), directed by Henry Edwards. The script was again by H. Fowler Mear, but this time it was adapted from an Agatha Christie novel, probably a more expensive purchase than *Tangled Evidence*, which had been penned by the rather less well-known Mrs Champion De Crespigny. Hercule Poirot was played by Austin Trevor, who had already starred as the Belgian detective in Twickenham's *Alibi* and *Black Coffee* (1931), a film that had been a main attraction (at least in Leicester). There is also evidence of a larger budget for *Lord Edgware Dies* in the use of extras for crowd scenes and bought-in footage of a horse-race meeting. Another indication that this film had pretensions to co-feature or first-feature status is the running time of eighty-two minutes, twenty-five minutes longer than *Tangled Evidence*. Beyond these differences, however, the two films are depressingly similar in their narratives, *mise en scène*, characterisations and treatment. Cinematically, Edwards is a little fonder than Cooper of static tableaux, but a similar faux baronial hall provides the dominant setting, there are the same dress suits and dressing gowns, the same passages of wordy exposition, and Michael Shepley, *Tangled Evidence*'s irritating librarian, returns as the equally irritating Captain Marsh. Even the colonel's desk is brought out of storage to serve the Duke of Merton. It is little wonder that many exhibitors had difficulty in identifying *Lord Edgware Dies* as qualitatively different from the earlier *Tangled Evidence* – both were Real Art productions – and booked it as a supporting feature.[40]

Hagen developed a successful partnership with American renter, Radio, for whom one supporting feature per month was produced under the 'Real Art' banner during 1934.[41] As his confidence grew during the 1930s, Hagen would steadily increase his production of more expensive films, made with one eye on international markets. These 'super' productions were mostly costume films inspired by the success of *The Private Life of Henry VIII*, and they would ultimately bankrupt the studio and the company Hagen set up to distribute them, when they continued to flop in the United States. Towards the end of a career that blazed briefly but brilliantly, Hagen bought the new Riverside Studios at Hammersmith, which had been opened in January 1934 to supply PDC with product. Both Hammersmith and Twickenham would become part of the chain of Alliance Film Studios after World War II.[42] Mixed economies like Hagen's meant that the British film industry was never simply bifurcated into quality or quickie producers.

The two leading production houses, BIP and Gaumont-British, spent more on their films than most of the independents, and promoted their product vigorously, but the pictures found their own level, at least outside the company circuits. Although studio head, John Maxwell maintained that BIP pictures were intended as first features, he conceded that 'the luck of the game' meant that as many as 50 per cent might not fully achieve that status.[43] In truth, the company always kept one eye on the second-feature market, using the small Welwyn Studio to make inexpensive programmers like *The Price of Folly* (1937) and *What Happened Then?* (1934), both directed by Walter Summers and based on stage plays.[44] The latter film is a particularly fanciful murder mystery with dialogue that verges on the parodic, and a ludicrously overwrought performance from Richard Bird as a psychopathic killer.[45] His guilt is blindingly obvious from the start, but like Cagney in *White Heat* (1949), he retains the love of his mother until the end. After 1934, BIP decided to dedicate their Elstree Studios to first features, on the rationale that:

Women in charge: Betty Amann rises above the crowd in *Strictly Business* (1932), the only quota quickie directed by women

> Programme pictures, which held the public for so many years, interest them no longer. . . . The success of British films during the past year and the insistent demand from the public and the kinema owners for more have given our producers fresh confidence. They are no longer content to play second fiddle, they are determined that the British picture will be the feature of the programme.[46]

The Welwyn programmers at least offered a hard-won opportunity for women film-makers to dip their toes in male-dominated feature production. The society comedy-drama, *Strictly Business* (1932), judged a 'pleasant diversion of second feature calibre', was not only written by actress Jacqueline Logan, but directed by Logan and Mary Field.[47] In fact, *The Bioscope* picked out the film's direction as its strongest element.[48] However, Welwyn stuck mostly to thrillers, and they were mostly undistinguished. One of the last before World War II was Harold French's *Dead Men Are Dangerous* (1939), which drew on the Hitchcockian formula of an innocent man on the run from both villains and the police. Unfortunately, it failed to better its title. The plot strained credulity, the characterisation was weak and the treatment lacked Hitchcock's dark humour.

By the mid-1930s, British low-budget features were pouring off the assembly line faster than model T Fords. In one issue in March 1935, *Kinematograph Weekly* reviewed no less than eight, including Pearson's *That's My Uncle* and two from John Baxter (*A Real Bloke* and *The Small*

*Man*).[49] Film production, in general, was also swelling to unsustainable levels. Fuelled by money from city speculators and insurance companies impressed by Korda's breakthrough into the American market, British studios were able to produce, at the rate of four every week, nearly half as many films as Hollywood. At one time in 1936 there were no fewer than forty in production. The bubble burst at the end of the year. Julius Hagen was the most high-profile casualty, but Hammer Productions also went into liquidation. *The Private Life of Henry VIII* had proved to be the exception rather than the rule, as far as the American box office was concerned.

In the context of the costly collapse of larger enterprises, the cottage industry of quota quickie production began to look lean and efficient rather than cheap and vulgar – at least to the Manager of Nettlefold Studios, Desmond S. Tew:

> It *is* possible to make an excellent second feature film for £1 per foot, and many examples of these can be found which have earned over 1,000 bookings. . . . More interest on capital has been made out of quota quickies by all concerned with them than with any other phase of British production. It is because there are so few really competent producers and directors in this country that everybody is convinced that at least twelve thousand pounds must be spent on a film for it even to gross its costs, let alone make a profit.
>
> Mushroom companies with little or no film producing experience are still springing up every day, and the City is gaily financing productions costing anything up to £80,000, and placing such incredible sums of money at the disposal of concerns with no conscience and still less ability. If the City made it a condition that every new company should produce a 'Quota Quickie' for £1 per foot before being allowed to make a feature picture, film finance would be a commercial undertaking instead of the appalling gamble it is today. There is no better training ground for competence in film production than having to provide genuine entertainment at £1 per foot. For every 'Quota Quickie' that has failed to provide any entertainment at all there is to be found one feature film, irrespective of cost, which means just as little at the box office.[50]

If the renter financing the film receives an unsaleable product, argued Tew, then it should have taken more care in its approval of producer, director, cast, scenario and budget.

## Pictures for peanuts

> Cost is, of course, not the only or even the best criterion of quality, but it is probably true that a good film cannot be produced for the amount of money these [American] renters are prepared to pay.
>
> R. D. Fennelly of the Board of Trade[51]

During the 1930s, the basic rules of low-budget 'B' film-making were laid down, and all were designed to minimise expenditure. Scenarios were to be adapted by staff writers from modest stage, novel, magazine or radio sources. Casts were to be kept small and extras used sparingly. Whenever possible, films were to be made in series featuring the same main character(s) and places. Sets were to be reused whenever practical. Elaborate new sets were to be avoided and location filming should either utilise the studio grounds or be confined to a single day, thus saving accommodation costs. Like sets, plots might be redressed and reused. Contemporary settings were to be used to minimise costume and design budgets. Ideally actors were to wear their own clothes. The number of retakes and the extent of 'coverage' of a scene were to be tightly controlled, and set-ups kept to a minimum, or a quota per day specified. If actors with extensive stage experience were used, takes could be longer. Stock footage or scenes from cheaply acquired foreign films were to substitute for overseas location shooting or the staging of large crowd scenes. Footage from previous films might be reused in montage sequences. Special effects ought not to be required unless they were key to the film's exploitation. Process shots (back-projected backgrounds) could be reused again and again. Some care ought to be taken to create the illusion that the production values were higher than they were in reality.[52]

Of course it was possible, even under so austere a regime, to make the occasional low-budget film of quality. The example most often referred to at the time was Paramount's whimsical story of endangered village life, *Badger's Green* (1934), directed by Adrian Brunel, a film-maker who had built a high reputation during the silent period, but had fallen on harder times. According to *Picturegoer's* E. G. Cousins, *Badger's Green* 'showed just what could be done by a judicious mix-ture of a great deal of brains with very little time and money'.[53] Valerie Hobson, the future British star whose career was launched by the film, declared that, in making it, Brunel 'estab-lished what many of our producers have since forgotten – that screen entertainment does not depend entirely, or even mainly, on money spent'.[54] Brunel, himself, felt that, in low-budget picture-making 'the odds are usually so heavily stacked against you that a good film is more a matter of luck than of design . . . It is not every day a *Badger's Green* falls from Heaven'. He was one of the few directors to explain exactly why 'it is possible to make quite a good pound-a-foot film in twelve days, but the chances of you doing so are remote':

> Amongst an otherwise competent cast there may be one artist who is just passable in most of his scenes, but who is definitely bad in one or two of them; being a cheap production, a better artist could not have been employed, neither was there time to remedy the situation with extra rehearsals, extra takes, extra close-ups, changes of angle and the score of devices that exist for correcting such a state of affairs. Or, perhaps a sequence dragged, because the editor had to deliver the cutting copy to the laboratories before he could get the last ounce out of the material to hand, or because the director was unable to provide the close-ups necessary for achieving speed in cutting, or because the director was afraid to risk confusing artists by trimming dialogue on the floor when he had to finish shooting before eight o'clock, or because the producer was afraid he might not have enough footage . . . Such things happen in even the best quickies.[55]

While quickies, could often hold their own with more expensive productions in camerawork, art direction and sound recording, Brunel believed, they struggled in those areas where the prob-lem of time shortage was most acute: direction, acting, cutting and, above all, scripting. In fact, there was widespread agreement among critics and film-makers that scripting was the prime weakness of British cinema. John Maxwell believed that 'to get people who can write scenarios' was 'our biggest difficulty in this country'.[56] The writer/director John Paddy Carstairs, who occasionally scripted for Paramount-British, singled out the same problem in his contemporary survey of the film business, complaining that, even at the top studios: 'It is heart-breaking to see some of the so-called script jobs that are filmed in England to-day'.[57] If this was true of more

A heaven-sent hit: Valerie Hobson (centre) is given an early opportunity in *Badger's Green* (1934). Bruce Lester is on the left

prestigious productions, it was certainly the case with second features. As George Pearson recalled, the production of scripts for the quickies followed 'a rigid formula':

> first an agreement on some inexpensive subject, some story selected from the scores of such submitted by would-be authors, since the cost of the film-rights of a published novel would swamp the budget, followed by a fortnight's team work by the film-director and a dialogue writer usually attached to the studio staff.[58]

The dialogue writer would work with a stopwatch, concerned as much with the time the words would take to say as with their quality. If the running time appeared too short, it could always be padded out with discussions of the weather or one character asking another to repeat a line, 'I didn't catch what you said'. This approach to scripting was often frustrating for writers with loftier ambitions, and it was anathema to Pearson, a film-maker who believed that 'the secret of every fine film is enshrined in the script, which should never go to the floor till every second of time entailed in its screening has been proved necessary and rightfully used'.[59]

The British approach to dialogue dismayed visiting American film-makers. Otto Ludwig, one of Radio's Hollywood editors, sent over to work at Basil Dean's Ealing Studios in 1931, found that there was 'too much dead footage' in English films:

The good meat is hopelessly hidden by a lot of useless dialogue and action which is not helping the story at all. . . . Directors have a habit of allowing a character to mention something – say the rain – and then they go and show a photograph of it as well.[60]

Five years later, when Warners sent William 'Buster' Collier Jr, one of the producers working on their Hollywood 'B' picture unit, over to their Teddington Studios he found that the British emphasis on dialogue was still in stark contrast to the American supporting feature's stress on action:

We don't have important stars in [Hollywood 'B'] pictures. They have to rely simply on their speed. They just have to possess plenty of action. And that is where your British 'programme pictures' fail. Because of the Quota Act, you pad them instead of cut them. Apart from your 'A' films, I reckon I could cut a thousand feet at least out of practically every British picture I have seen.[61]

For many film-makers working on Hollywood's Poverty Row, 'action' was actually the defining characteristic of the 'B' film. Phil Karlson, who served his time on the treadmills at Monogram, and in the second-feature units at Universal and Columbia, maintained that 'a B movie was an action movie, and an A movie was a characterization of people'.[62] The British supporting feature never shared this approach to product differentiation. Instead of emphasising physicality and pace, British 'Bs' generally attempted to emulate the discursive attributes of the first feature, but with significantly lower production values.[63]

The results of verbal padding, coupled with artificial storylines, were frequently disastrous. Paramount's *The Price of Wisdom* (1935) provoked *Kinematograph Weekly*'s reviewer to opine: 'Here is a typical English quota comedy drama, it is all tone and talk, most of which is superfluous, and no story, at least not one to carry the slightest conviction.'[64] Radio's *Anything Might Happen* (1934) was guilty of the same sin: 'This crime drama is never lost for a word: it is talk, talk, talk from beginning to end.'[65] While the aforementioned *Lord Edgware Dies* was not only guilty of 'too much verbiage', but of being 'a literal translation' rather than a screen adaptation of Agatha Christie's novel.[66] One of the worst culprits was journalist-turned-director Donovan Pedelty, whose garrulous Irish films were regularly condemned by reviewers for offences against verbal continence.[67] At one point, Paramount handed Pedelty *Behind Your Back* (1937), the most self-referential West End play it could find, set entirely in the 'Loyalty Theatre' (mostly in the dress circle bar while a play is in progress). The film's publicity suggested that this 'Brilliant comedy-drama of theatre life', showed 'how happenings in "front-of-house" may be more entertaining than the play itself'.[68] It was a view that many critics would have endorsed. However, by the time Pedelty made this picture, the techniques of adaptation had become more sophisticated than they had been in the early days of sound. As he remarked:

Filming a play is scarcely a matter of 'photographing' it just as it stands . . . A play is naturally hemmed in by the limits of the stage, and the theatre audiences have been trained to accept the necessary restrictions on action. But your film audience demands action – and plenty of it – therefore, the original script has to be transposed – often cut down – into nicely trimmed, and even fluctuating camera shots; the canvas of the plot has to be broadened by the introduction of fresh action, and frequently the dialogue has to be altered to suit the microphone.[69]

Textual fidelity: Vera Lennox and Robert Harris in the Shaw adaptation *How He Lied to Her Husband* (1931)

The most literal translation of a stage play for the screen had been George Bernard Shaw's *How He Lied to Her Husband* (1931). Shaw agreed to the filming only on the condition that it precisely replicated the 1904 stage production. Not a word was to be changed, and no concessions were to be made to ideas of the cinematic. The playwright supervised the filming, and in his programme notes for a screening at the Malvern Festival, he explicitly rejected the notion that plays needed to be adapted for the cinema. He also valorised the dialogue saturation and location restrictions for which quota quickies (and British cinema more generally) were to become notorious:

> The points for connoisseurs are (a) that the dialogue is continuous from end to end, except when Mr Gwenn purposely makes a silence more dramatic than words could be, and (b) that the entire action takes place in the same room, the usual changes from New York to the Rocky Mountains, from Marseilles to the Sahara, from Mayfair to Monte Carlo, are replaced by changes from the piano to the sideboard, from the window to the door, from the hearth rug to the carpet.[70]

The film's director, Cecil Lewis, later described *How He Lied to Her Husband* as 'about as unmovielike as anything could be', and it failed to recoup its cost of £5,000.[71]

Shaw's film was made at BIP, a studio that maintained a scripting department. Studio head Walter Mycroft would recruit talented young playwrights and place them under contract. Surprisingly little was then expected as the novices learned various aspects of film production. It could be a frustrating experience for a writer with any artistic pretensions, as Rodney Ackland discovered when he went to work at Elstree in the early 1930s. Any signs of an intellectual approach to the cinema were quickly suppressed and, like a number of his fellow scenarists, he came to regard his period of apprenticeship as his 'Borstal days'. The studio's second features were regarded as a suitable reformatory: 'They gave me *The Black Hand Gang* (1930) to write. It was to be a comedy thriller, about a bunch of "Dead End" kids, starring Wee Georgie Wood and directed by Monty Banks. The Ibsen in me winced, the Checkov in me shuddered.'[72] Worse still, when his script was nearly finished, he discovered that the film was already in production, scripted by another hand: Victor Kendall.

As scenario writing was relatively poorly paid, quickie producers like George King could afford the luxury of employing writers previously associated with more prestigious material. For example, two of King's 1931 films, *Midnight* and *Number Please*, were scripted by Charles Bennett, the writer of Hitchcock's *Blackmail* (1929). 'In those days I was rather good at writing something in about two weeks', recalled Bennett, 'a complete script, including the story, in about two weeks, for which I'd be paid three or four hundred pounds – which was a lot of money in those days. I wrote about ten of them, and I can't remember what any of 'em are about now.'[73] The up-and-coming Sidney Gilliat, moonlighting from Gaumont, helped out Bennett on another King production (*Two Way Street*, 1931), while, astonishingly, the Paramount programmer *The Belles of St. Clement's* (1936) was scripted by none other than Terence Rattigan (from an original girls' school story by director Ivar Campbell and his wife Sheila). At Warner's Teddington operation, studio head Irving Asher would make regular scavenging visits to the parent company in Hollywood. On his return, he would toss the scripts, many of them already used for filming at Burbank, over to his own scenario department for modification and recycling.[74] Perhaps the most expensive script of any British supporting feature in the 1930s was the one for *Murder on the Second Floor* (1931). Intending it for American production, Warners apparently bought the rights to the play for £6,000.[75] This would have swallowed the entire budget of most quota quickies, which were more likely to pay £60 for a scenario than £6,000. However, serviceable dialogue could sometimes be obtained for the sort of sums that a producer like George Smith was prepared to stump up. Basil Mason's dialogue for Smith's *Paid in Error* (1938), with George Carney and Googie Withers, was considered 'as good as we have heard in a British film in some time'.[76]

## Cheap shots

> Now, take the director of a quickie. He is almost inevitably an Englishman – we never insult foreigners with the task of making films without adequate material or remuneration.
>
> Adrian Brunel[77]

When the screenplay had been knocked into some sort of shape, principal photography could begin. Speed was of the essence. George King's *Too Many Crooks* (1930), the one-set featurette that gave an early starring role to Laurence Olivier, took just three weeks of production and post-production.[78] Sidney Cole recalled that the schedule for shooting second features often depended on back-to-back filming: 'Quota quickies were shot continuously, two weeks each,

Knight shoot: the future Sir
Laurence Olivier is challenged (by
A. Bromley Davenport) in his first
film role, *Too Many Crooks* (1930)

and one was finished on Saturday night at midnight and the next started Monday morning at
eight.'[79] Even this punishing schedule was too pedestrian for Julius Hagen, and Twickenham
Studios were often kept busy day and night, with two simultaneous productions. For example,
Henry Edwards helmed *Lord Edgware Dies* on Twickenham's day shift in May 1934, while
George Cooper directed *Anything Might Happen* on the night shift:

> The studio floor was never idle for a moment. Only by its constant use could the studio make any
> profit, and this meant both day and night filming. As one film unit working by day left the floor,
> another unit took over for night work on another subject, complete with its director, artists and
> technicians, only to reappear with the morrow's dawn. This night unit's midnight entry to the studio
> was sportively known as 'Going down the Mine'.[80]

In just over a year in 1933–4, George Pearson made seven films for Hagen, three of them at
night.[81] A few months before Pearson arrived at Twickenham, John Mills had worked the day
shift on Bernard Vorhaus's *The Ghost Camera* (1933):

> The atmosphere when I walked on the set at eight o'clock the first morning was almost inde-
> scribable: the night shift staggered out at 7.30 a.m., leaving in their wake an aroma – a delicate
> blend of cigarette butts, orange-peel, stale beer, make-up and several unmentionable gases. The
> schedule for a picture was eight days; they never went over.[82]

All-night filming was accommodated by scripts that staged their action exclusively during the hours of darkness. In fact, the titles of pictures filmed on Twickenham's night shift frequently indexed the conditions of their production: *When London Sleeps* (1932) and *Night Work* (1933, released as *A Safe Proposition*), for example. Contrarily, *Open All Night* (1934) was apparently filmed on the day shift.[83] The night shift had fewer disturbances from the trains that regularly passed by the studio, creating constant problems for sound recordists already overburdened by the weight of dialogue in most productions. Unforeseen problems could arise, however, as they did on one of Twickenham's earliest experiments with night production in 1930. George King's *Too Many Crooks* was a night shoot in which Laurence Olivier was obliged to open a safe. But the door refused to budge and the manufacturers could not be contacted out of office hours.[84] Tilly Day, who joined Kings's team as a continuity girl in autumn 1930, remembered spending one week working on both the day and night shift, with barely time for a wash and brush-up between.[85]

In spite of the demands made upon him, one of Twickenham's leading actors, Henry Kendall, had quite fond memories of working for Julius Hagen:

> Although 'Uncle Julius' worked us until we were dropping, the place had a wonderfully happy atmosphere and no one complained. We thought nothing of working round the clock [to finish a picture]. I remember one day beginning at the usual nine o'clock and working through till two the next morning. . . . The film was aptly called *Death on the Set* . . . Next morning I was on set again at eight o'clock, after four hours sleep, being made up for a starring role in the next picture.[86]

Hagen drove himself just as hard, overseeing the production of fifteen films in the first six months of 1934. One of them was *Tangled Evidence*, and when Anne Wilmot (Joan Marion) made the impassioned plea in that film – 'If there's one thing in the world I'd like to do, it's to get away from this house!' – she was probably speaking for all the toilers at Twickenham. Occasionally, directors of sufficient standing, such as Maurice Elvey, might successfully intervene to improve conditions, which obliged technicians who lived at some distance from St Margaret's to sleep on the studio premises after public transport had finished running for the night:'I thought it was all wrong. . . . So I said,"Look, I am not going to let these people work these ridiculous hours, unless they get a square meal in their bellies".' Hagen, his wife and his cook would then cook a large joint at their home next to the studios. 'And then 'round about seven o'clock everybody was given an enormous free meal with Julius and myself carving away like mad.'[87] The growing strength of the unions would soon put a stop to unsociable hours, but while they lasted, they contributed to the feeling of teamwork and camaraderie that often characterised quota production.

Conditions were not so different at other studios, although the family atmosphere might not have been as strong as it was under Uncle Julius. When not engaged by Hagen, George Pearson worked on Paramount quickies at B&D Studios:

> The first one I made, Tom White was in charge, and he came to me on the third day and said, 'You'll never make it, old chap. You've got so many minutes in today on the screen and you've got to finish within the week, . . . but finish that film I did. Instead of thinking, 'How good is this shot?' It was, 'Have I got this one in the bag? Yes. Good. How long was it? Two minutes. Right. Print it'. You

dare not think about quality, about having another take, you still had another three or four minutes to get in the bag for that day.[88]

Cinematographer Desmond Dickinson has described the regime at Cricklewood, as he and his crew were put to work by a succession of tenant production companies, as 'true slavery':

> We worked any hours. I had one year when I only had three days off, that was three Sundays. And we used to work normally one all-nighter each week . . . On one of those pictures I worked all day, all night, all day the next day till two a.m. the next morning, without going off the set except to go to the lavatory.

Eventually, the studio manager was made to realise that Stolls was losing rental money by tolerating these excessive hours, and extra fees were charged after 9 pm. But, in practice, it had little effect on the 'diabolical hours'.[89]

Speed of production, of course, did not necessarily lead to narrative economy. Ronald Neame has recalled an incident at Fox's Wembley Studios that nicely illustrates the contradiction between the methods of remuneration for the independent producer and the requirements of good storytelling:

> There was a permanent street set on the lot behind Wembley studios, which was used on practically every film. One sequence I shot called for a man to come out of a house, cross the road, and go into a phone booth. The next day, after he had seen the rushes, the producer stormed onto the set in a great rage asking me why I hadn't put the phone booth at the far end of the street. He yelled, 'You idiot, it would have taken the actor ten more seconds to walk there. That's fifteen feet and that's fifteen extra pounds for me.' He did have a point.[90]

When set against the leisurely pace of post-war British first feature production it might seem that the quota quickies were made at almost impossible speed, but by contemporary international standards their conditions of production were really nothing out of the ordinary. In fact, in comparison to the schedules in operation at some American 'B' movie units, the British rhythm of production appears positively leisurely. Many American supporting features were shot in five or six days. The prolific director, Joseph Kane, recalled that the early Republic films he made with crooning cowboys Roy Rogers and Gene Autry were produced in the mid-1930s under exactly those conditions, and often in the desert in sweltering heat.[91] Of course, working in bright and constant natural light could increase the number of daily set-ups considerably, but impressive films could also be made in the studio on similar schedules. Edgar G. Ulmer's seminal 'B' thriller *Detour* (1946) was made in six days.[92]

Among the fastest directors working in British quickie production was Adrian Brunel, whose effort in breaking the studio production record with *A Taxi to Paradise* (1933) was rewarded by Fox with a contract to have his next ready for trade showing in one month; and this without a completed script. Remarkably, the result, *I'm an Explosive* (1933), was a considerable hit.[93] Brunel, himself, pursued a picture's completion like a guided missile. While making Paramount's *Love at Sea* (1936) at Elstree's B&D Studios, fire gutted three sound stages, including the sets for

Billy's whiz-bang: an early role for William Hartnell (centre) in Adrian Brunel's hit, *I'm an Explosive* (1933)

the decks of a luxury liner. Brunel immediately hired another studio and finished the film on schedule.[94] However, Brunel was as capable of producing a quota dud as almost every other director. One effort for Fox was described by *Kinematograph Weekly* as a 'nebulous' entertainment that did little but 'eat up celluloid for quota purposes'.[95] The title of this 'slight, transparent comedy drama', *The Laughter of Fools* (1933), might have been selected to describe the reaction of its audience. But Brunel took the rough with the smooth: 'Instead of being ashamed, I was rather pleased with myself, for I believed that we were evolving a technique that showed what could be done when facing fearful odds.'[96] And it does indeed seem that the hard slog of quota production was not without romance. In order to complete *Mayfair Girl* (1933) in two weeks, George King's unit worked until 4 am on the final day, but then relaxed by bathing in the Thames and breakfasting in the Teddington Studio grounds as dawn broke.[97]

The relentless production schedules for quota pictures could be equally demanding for crews and casts. On *Mayfair Girl*, forty set-construction workers were expected to build a replica of an Old Bailey courtroom overnight, commencing at 8 pm when the actors finished filming on the previous set and working for a solid twelve hours to have the new set finished for the next day's filming. The film's stars John Stuart and Sally Blane may have got a night's sleep, but their noses were as close to the grindstone as any craftsman's. Stuart, a stalwart of quota production, had at one time in the previous year worked on three films simultaneously; and, although *Mayfair Girl* was Sally Blane's first British film, she had already completed over thirty American pictures by the age of twenty-three.[98] Some directors, like Fox's Al Parker, were reluctant to be bound by the tight shooting schedules imposed on quota productions, making frequent alterations to the scenario, as one of his actors, James Mason, recalled:

> None of us ever knew precisely how long one of Al Parker's films would take to shoot. . . . In those days budgets and schedules were sacred, especially if you were in the quota film game. So Al's habit of shooting off the cuff did not go down very well with the production staff.[99]

The solution of the studio head was to inform the director that at the end of the following day the sets would be struck to make way for the next production. Parker would then be obliged to work flat out, as he did on the last two days of *Late Extra* (1935). 'We were at it for thirty-six hours with no more than a short tea break from time to time,' Mason remembered.[100]

For *Late Extra*, Mason's first picture, Parker was able to assemble an 'A' grade cast including Alastair Sim, Cyril Cusack, Michael Wilding, Donald Wolfit and Virginia Cherrill. It is hardly surprising, then, that Bernard Vorhaus identified acting as the greatest strength of the quota film: 'What was marvellous to me was that you could get such wonderful acting talent here, even on very cheap pictures. Because top West End actors really commanded very small salaries at that time.'[101] For George Pearson, it was the skill and stamina of the actors that ultimately made quota production possible.[102] In the early days of sound films, the low-budget features gave silent and stage actors an opportunity to develop the techniques required by the new medium, and most seem to have enjoyed the experience. Their work was often the saving grace of quota productions for reviewers. For instance, the performance of Raymond Massey (fresh from his one outing as Sherlock Holmes) was said to be the highlight of the otherwise turgid Leslie Hiscott melodrama *The Face at the Window* (1932).[103] *Kinematograph Weekly*'s reviewer was far more impressed by the acting of Felix Aylmer and the promising Sally Gray in Pearson's Paramount crime drama *Checkmate* (1935) than with the 'poor' direction: 'Good acting alone rescues the entertainment from complete mediocrity.'[104] This was a little unfair on Pearson and his lighting cameraman, who bravely battled against dire dialogue, prosaic plot and cardboard characters to craft some atmospheric cinematography. Pearson's experience of silent film-making meant that he knew how to point a camera, but it took him some time to come to terms with the subtleties of directing dialogue. Thus, in an early effort like the Twickenham shocker *A Shot in the Dark* (1933) he elicits only the most stilted and histrionic of performances from his players. In this case, the acting only exacerbates the artificiality of the script and the preposterousness of the plot.

The stalwarts of the West End stage could usually be relied upon to deliver the King's English as it should be spoken, and this, in itself, was enough to evoke the sympathy of many critics. Their elocution might be thought to give a degree of sophistication to British attempts to emulate American genres, as in this review of Alex Bryce's juvenile *Sexton Blake and the Mademoiselle* (1935): 'Adults may find satisfaction in the uniformly good English voices of the actors, who contribute a gentlemanly note to the . . . gangster drama.'[105] Standard elocution, however, was not always appropriate, especially when the characters being portrayed were ordinary labouring men and women or denizens of the underworld. The well-brought-up young ladies who sought fame on stage and screen after World War I often found it difficult to impersonate someone from a less exalted station. The problem was evident in Paramount's docklands melodrama *Ebb Tide*:

> With few exceptions, the cast seems to be composed of refined young ladies and gentlemen with little knowledge or observation of the diction and manners of the submerged tenth, with the result that the whole atmosphere is artificial and unreal. Dorothy Bouchier plays Cassie with considerable dramatic feeling, though she quite fails to convey the sordidness of the character.[106]

Among the refined young ladies playing bit parts was the future screen goddess Merle Oberon, who had been promised a starring role by director Art Rossen after he had seen her Paramount screen test. Directors, as we know, have a habit of not keeping those kinds of promises.[107]

British actresses had, in the words of Jane Austen in *Mansfield Park*, 'all the disadvantages of decorum and education to struggle through'. The ladylike Ann Todd found it difficult to play a bargee with anything resembling conviction in *The Water Gipsies*. *The Bioscope* thought she failed to 'suggest in the slightest the kind of girl that would fill [her] position in life'.[108] When something more exotic than the sort of convent-educated Surrey girls who populated the West End stage really *was* required, the choice was fairly limited. Anna May Wong's brand of dangerous Orientalism might be brought in, if the budget allowed, or the glamorous Russian exile, Tamara Desni might be cast. Fox paired Desni with Harold French for Anthony Kimmins' romantic musical *How's Chances?* (1934), probably in an attempt to improve the film's chances of playing as a first

The 'disadvantages of decorum': Ann Todd struggles to shed her airs and graces with Richard Bird in *The Water Gipsies* (1932)

Talent spotted: Errol Flynn (far right) in Warners' *Murder at Monte Carlo* (1935)

feature. The film's publicity described it as 'one of the most lavish and scintillating entertainments which have yet been produced in this country', and the trade press reviews were enthusiastic, but in Leicester *How's Chances?* achieved only one booking and that as a supporting feature.[109]

Many celebrated actors made their screen debuts in quota quickies. The young Errol Flynn was whisked across the Atlantic after impressing Warners' Teddington Studio head, Irving Asher in Ralph Ince's programmer *Murder at Monte Carlo* (1935), even before the film was shown to the trade. Asher's judgment was vindicated when the reviewer for *The Cinema* declared Flynn 'a real find among British juvenile leads'.[110] The modest 1936 Herbert Mason crime comedy *First Offence* could boast a cast featuring John Mills and Lilli Palmer, in her first picture (happily, she did not offend the critics). Near the bottom of the cast list of the George King romantic comedy *Get Your Man* (1934) was the soon-to-be-illustrious name of Rex Harrison, while Michael Powell's disastrous *His Lordship* (1932) had Valerie Hobson and Anna Lee in bit parts. Hobson would follow Flynn to Hollywood after her success in *Badger's Green*, briefly becoming a 'scream queen' in films like *The Bride of Frankenstein* (1935) before returning home. Evelyn Ankers played in four Fox British quickies before being shipped to the States to spend the war screaming her way through innumerable 'B'-grade horrors and minor noirs. Future star Kathleen Harrison could be seen in the minor role of a kitchen maid in Bernerd Mainwaring's *Line Engaged* (1936). The last second feature to go into production before the outbreak of World War II, Warners' Irish drama *Dr. O'Dowd* (1940), could boast the rising talents of fourteen-year-old Peggy Cummins

– who would go on to star in perhaps the most revered of American 'B' movies, *Gun Crazy* (1949) – and future Gainsborough leading lady, Patricia Roc.

The fan magazines occasionally drew attention to the value of British supporting features for the talent-spotter. 'Keep your eyes on the "quickies",' advised E. G. Cousins in *Picturegoer*, 'you may be watching history in the making.' He pointed to Paramount-British's track record in grooming future stars such as Vivien Leigh, Sally Gray, Anna Lee and Gyles Isham (who went on to play in 1935's *Anna Karenina* with Garbo).[111] The parsimonious quota department at Herbert Wilcox's British and Dominion Studios turned out a quickie a month for Paramount. Vivien Leigh made her first film, *The Village Squire*, there in 1935, thanks to John Payne's casting agency Bramlyn's, which recruited for quota quickies on a typical casting budget of £750.[112] George Pearson then cast her as an unemployed typist living in an East End doss house in *Gentleman's Agreement* (1935). Both performances passed largely unnoticed by the critics of the trade press, who were not always helpful to rising stars.[113] When Fox made *All at Sea* (1935), an Anthony Kimmins romantic comedy, it cast the now-forgotten Tyrrell Davis with future stars Rex Harrison and Googie Withers. It was Davis who won the critic's plaudits: 'Tyrrell Davis is quite good as the hesitant, self-conscious Joe, but Googie Withers is very colourless as Daphne, and Rex Harrison overacts as Aubrey.'[114] Alastair Sim was thought to '"mug" overmuch' and exaggerate his character in Fox's *The Big Noise* (1936), his first starring role.[115] Renee Houston was also slated in her first leading role in MGM's *Come into my Parlour* (1932).[116] The debonair George

Critical failures: Googie Withers (left) and Rex Harrison (right) were apparently *All at Sea* in this 1935 rom-com

Sanders received some dreadful notices for his early roles in Paramount's *Strange Cargo* and Fox's *Find the Lady* (both 1936), and still made it to Hollywood.[117]

The departure of a quota star for California evoked mixed feelings, but the dominant response was generally optimism that the actor would at last be free from the restrictions imposed by budget and inferior scriptwriting. When *Film Pictorial* reviewed Florence Desmond's last quota picture before making what turned out to be her only American film, it had this to say about Warners' *Long Live the King* (1933):

> Wonder what Florence Desmond thinks of film-making now she's in Hollywood? Probably get a few different ideas. She's certainly not had many breaks in British productions . . . Here's another one of those stupid affairs, showing the efforts of a cockney girl and a Prime Minister to save a baby Crown Prince during a revolutionary attack on a palace. Oh, dear![118]

In the same issue of *Film Pictorial*, the review of Warners' *Out of the Past* (1933) lamented the predicament of another quota labourer who would shortly leave for a more successful Hollywood career than Desmond's:

> Rather sad seeing Lester Matthews in an affair such as this. Admittedly it doesn't set out to be a super-super, and maybe it will please somebody, somewhere. But it is all rather pathetic. It is a blackmail story stretching the long arm of coincidence to its uttermost length.

Calculating the footage: Henry Kendall gets out the tape measure in *The Shadow* (1933). John Turnbull is on the left

In the elevator shafts of quota production, the rising stars could pass others on the way down. In 1934, Buster Keaton, the celebrated American comedian, was directed by one of the most respected of British silent film directors, Adrian Brunel, in MGM's *The Invader*. *Kinematograph Weekly* described the result as 'just a slipshod symposium of theatrical knockabout gags resurrected from the silent two-reeler'. Buster Keaton, wrote the reviewer, 'finds it impossible to raise a laugh, so feeble is the story and the gags'.[119] The film had been shelved for two years before being sheepishly exposed to trade ridicule. Quota star Henry Kendall had held a contract with BIP and boasted a considerable fan following when, in 1933, he decided to maintain his glamorous lifestyle by grabbing the regular work that studios like Twickenham offered and, as he put it, 'fell into the snare of the "quota quickie"'. He made one film a month for the next two years, rating most of them as 'pretty bad', with the exceptions of *The Ghost Camera*, *Death on the Set* (1935) and *The Shadow* (1933).[120] Britain's 'It Girl', Chili Bouchier, had also been groomed for stardom, playing a succession of wanton vamps in silent films before being given a sophisticated make-over by Herbert Wilcox. However, Wilcox only really succeeded in consigning this spirited actress to the salt mines of quota production, where she laid claim to the title of Queen of the Quickies. Her performance with a pneumatic drill in Paramount's *The Mad Hatters* (1935) was not easily forgotten by the fortunate few who witnessed it.[121] Virginia Cherrill was another actor who had tasted success in first features – this time in Hollywood – who had to lower her sights. Edward Dryhurst, assistant director on the aptly named *Troubled Waters* (1936), recalled having to let the haughty Miss Cherrill know where she stood: 'I told her in effect that while she may have been Chaplin's leading lady in *City Lights*, she was now in England playing in B pictures and that she had better be content with her lot and pipe down.'[122]

Strapped for cash, the quickies could not afford the luxury of lengthy casting sessions. Sometimes the easiest and cheapest solution was to grab what was near at hand and hope for the best. When Fox's Al Parker needed a young man to play Horace Hodges' grandson in *After Dark* (1932), he looked no further than one of the company's office boys, fourteen-year-old George Padbury. One minute the startled Padbury was licking stamps, the next he was on set at Walton, marvelling at the size of the studios and scenes that ran to as many as four takes. A week or so later, he was back licking stamps. The film's leading lady, twenty-year-old Gertha Hansen, leapt 'to stardom in one bound', when Parker decided she had 'spark', or 'that compelling personality that makes people turn round to look at her in whatever company she may be'.[123] But by the time they turned, she had disappeared. However, the *ad hoc* casting policies of the quickies did sometimes bear fruit. When Milton Rosmer needed a girl to play an innkeeper's daughter in *The Secret of the Loch* (1934), he perversely chose a nineteen-year-old with no experience of acting or public houses, on the basis of a friend's introduction. Happily, she was Rosamund John, who enjoyed a successful career on screen over the next twenty years. Patricia Roc's recruitment into 'B' films was equally casual when the young Felicia Riese (as she was christened) was offered a screen test at a cocktail party in France.

While for some, quota quickies were a runway and for others a landing strip, for a third group they were simply a field in which they worked. Wally Patch and George Carney, for instance, consistently received enthusiastic notices for their numerous character roles but remained too down-to-earth to be stars. Wally Patch acted in dozens of second features, at one time forming a successful cockney comedy duo with Gus McNaughton in Radio's *Not So Dusty* and *Busman's Holiday* (both 1936), produced by George Smith and directed by Maclean Rogers.

Between licks: George Padbury (second from left) gets relief from stamp duty in *After Dark* (1932)

Patch struck up another screen partnership with the comic actor Julian Vedey in Paramount's *Night Ride* and *Missing, Believed Married* (both 1937). The epitome of the cockney character, Patch had started out as a music-hall athletic act, also working as a bookmaker, nightclub manager, commercial traveller and boxing promoter. His wide experience of life contributed greatly to the authenticity of his performances, which began with villainous parts, but soon became predominantly comic. Usually to be seen sporting a bowler hat at a jaunty angle, his proud boast was that he had played in more talking pictures than any other English actor. The director Robert Stevenson once insisted on including Patch in his cast because 'No British film would be complete without him'.[124] His fan base was said to be exclusively male, with a particular following among servicemen and sportsmen. George Carney, who tended to play, in supporting features, the sort of cockney parts which Gordon Harker took in higher-budget productions, was meticulous in his preparations for a role. Carney told *Picturegoer* he would 'make a point of spending as much of my time as possible with the type of man I am to play' and would 'quietly study them first hand'.[125] One or two of those refined young actresses would have benefited from studying his technique.

Typically, quota quickies were confined to a small number of studio sets. Paramount's slow, garrulous comedy *Show Flat* (1936), for example, did precisely what the title indicated, its action largely taking place within four walls. Director Bernerd Mainwaring readily accepted the challenge, commenting:

The point to remember is not to make a scene too long. By varying the tempo, cutting, and by changing the camera angle, the audience receives an impression of variety, even when the action is confined to a comparatively small space.[126]

It was a doctrine G. B. Shaw would have applauded and other quickie directors would have done well to remember; but ultimately it failed to address the problem of the film's 'abundance of talk over action'.[127] Limited funds for production design, meant an art director like J. Elder Wills could find himself working on four or five productions simultaneously. Where possible, sets were dragged from the scene dock and redressed. Even at some of the better-equipped studios, such as those leased by Paramount at Elstree, strict financial control and shortage of time for set design resulted in inadequate space for cameras and actors. Thus *Film Weekly* could note of the 'would-be rollicking melodrama' *Strange Cargo*: 'So cramped are the aboard-ship settings that the players have the utmost difficulty in not tripping over one another.' As a consequence, 'Most of the dramatic sequences in this film are just funny, while the humorous sequences are unconsciously tragic.'[128] One might have expected the success of Fox's *The Riverside Murder* (1935) to be due in some part to atmospheric location work, but despite the film's title, director Al Parker included not a single shot of a river, or any other exterior. Always conscious of costs, he used the facilities immediately available, having his police investigator (Basil Sidney) visit Wembley Studios, where, in a frenzy of self-referentiality, an American director is filming a thriller (constantly issuing orders to 'hurry up' and reluctant to allow his crew a tea break). Presumably, he reasoned that his audience had all seen a river, but few had been inside a film studio.[129] If so, it was the sort of reasoning that frustrated an imaginative director like Bernard Vorhaus, who had experience of American film-making and deplored the fact that quota pictures were mostly confined to the studio 'with as much dialogue and as little movement as possible'. Vorhaus was 'always keen to get out on location and was much more interested in cinema than theatre'.[130]

Not all productions were studio-bound. Three units went down to Devon and Cornwall in the summer of 1930 to film Paramount's *Contraband Love* and *The Road to Fortune* and the Edward Whiting production *Dangerous Seas*. While appreciating the scenery, most critics wished the film-makers had stayed at home.[131] Undeterred, Paramount later allowed Adrian Brunel to take a unit to Cornwall to shoot *Cross Currents* (1935) 'a drama of action, excitement, romance and thrills played out against beautiful natural scenic backgrounds'; while Henry Edwards spent a week in the same county filming *The Rocks of Valpre* (1935).[132] Leslie Hiscott's British Lion unit also went down to Land's End, and Beachy Head, to film 'angry seas dashing all their weight against the slim lighthouse' for Fox's *Marooned* (1933). Unfortunately, their visit coincided with a rare heat wave, and much of the dramatic storm that isolates the lighthouse and its escaped prisoner had to be faked back in the grounds of Beaconsfield Studios. Apparently enough authentic footage remained for the trade press to comment enthusiastically on the way in which location filming had contributed to the drama.[133] Anthony Gilkison's *Breakers Ahead* (1935), another supporting feature set in Cornwall, also received praise for the 'polish and sensibility' of its cinematography (although its characterisations were less than realistic).[134] However, although producers were keen to give their pictures the cinematic quality granted by filming in genuine locations, they remained wary of allowing them to evoke too precise a sense of place. *Marooned's*

Cornish corn: the glamorous Julie Suedo stays on the sands in *Dangerous Seas* (1930)

press book, for example, reassured exhibitors that 'care has been taken not to identify *Marooned* too closely with any particular county. Broad West of England dialects have been avoided so that the picture will be equally acceptable in all parts of the country.' Conversely, the publicity for *Old Roses* (1935) made much of its Devon locale, its 'remarkable shots of the glorious countryside' and director Bernerd Mainwaring's ambition to depict life in the place of his birth.

Almost as popular as the West Country for location filming was Scotland. The historical romance *Flame in the Heather* (1935), much of which was filmed at Fort William, boasted 'picturesque Highland scenery', with 'interesting glimpses of Highland customs, sports and pastimes at the time of the Jacobite rebellion'.[135] But location work could be a hazardous business:

A camera tripod came tumbling down from a transport van and struck Rani Waller, one of the feminine leads, a disabling blow over her eye; then, during one of the cavalry sequences, Ben Williams, second leading man, was thrown from his horse, his injuries stealing time from the production schedule. The assistant cameraman was yet another victim. A lightning heart attack, and he had to be rushed to the nearest hospital, which was 16 miles away . . . The sun went in whenever shooting commenced: rain was a frequent visitor: two horses cast their shoes at a most inopportune moment, and the cameras, not to be outdone, jammed continuously.[136]

Director Donovan Pedelty must have thought the Gods of the Highlands were extracting their revenge for Culloden, but he pressed on and miraculously seems to have completed the film on schedule – but possibly not on budget, which must have been unusually large for the thrifty Paramount. He might just as well not have bothered, because the reviews were scathing, and the picture failed to make much of a stir south of the border.[137]

Sometimes film units actually took to the water. In the case of George King's *To Be a Lady* (1934) – the adventures of a country girl in London – this was no more than a punt on the river near Shepperton. Similarly, it was a punt near Teddington Weir that fished the body out of the river in Warners' *A Voice Said Goodnight* (1932). Peter Godfrey filmed motor boat chases on the Thames for *Down River* (1930), the docklands thick-ear melodrama that starred Charles Laughton as a sinister Oriental. John Baxter took his *Flood Tide* (1934) unit down the Thames from Westminster Bridge to the mouth of the estuary for a few days before being condemned to the Twickenham night shift.[138] A handful of productions even made it to the ocean. *The Woman from China* was an early example, with a day's filming aboard the P&O liner *Viceroy of India* on Plymouth Sound.[139] BIP's *Verdict of the Sea* (1931) was filmed aboard a cargo boat, the *Capri*.[140] Lawrence Huntington chartered a steamer from Goole to Copenhagen to film his own screenplay *Full Speed Ahead* (1936) for Fox. Paramount's *The Fear Ship* (1933), an adaptation of R. F. W. Ree's story *The Second Mate*, also put to sea. The tag line was 'Love on a windjammer . . . with "fire down below"!', a reference to the blaze that brave director James Edwards was obliged to light on the hired clipper, *Ivy*.[141] Chartering a windjammer was a relatively inexpensive way of enhancing production values in some of the generously budgeted co- and second features. Sometimes these were adventure films with greater pretensions, which failed to justify the expectations of their producers or distributors. Wardour's *McGlusky the Sea Rover* (1935), directed by the erratic Walter Summers, is a good example of a prestige project that was scaled down to more modest proportions when things failed to gel. *Kinematograph Weekly* remarked on the gaps in its continuity created by drastic editing.[142] The Leslie Fuller vehicle *The Stoker* (1935), released at the same time as *McGlusky* is another example of money being committed to location filming on land and sea without results good enough to justify top billing for the finished film.

Unable to profit from the pictorial joys of open water Ivar Campbell's unit did the next best thing and hauled twenty tons of lighting equipment to the new swimming baths at Watford for two days' filming on *The Belles of St. Clement's*.[143] More adventurously, the intrepid Mr A. Cyran led his unit underground to shoot the climax of Paramount's *The Love Wager* (1933): a chase and fight filmed overnight at Holloway Road tube station, with additional scenes shot on a facsimile built at the studio under the supervision of London Transport engineers.[144] London Transport had already helped Warners by allowing scenes for *Murder on the Second Floor* to be shot from the top of a tramcar.[145] Usually, however, the Warners' units did not venture much beyond Teddington, where the final scenes of the film were shot outside an ironmongers in the High Street. Henry Edwards filmed interiors for Paramount's shoplifting drama *Purse Strings* (1933) in several London department stores. A number of Michael Powell's early quota quickies were praised for their London exteriors; while American director Rowland Lee, making *That Night in London* (an early starring role for Robert Donat) in 1932, took his cameras to a number of locations in the city, including an all-night shoot at Waterloo station. MGM's bizarrely titled

*Chin Chin Chinaman* (1931) was praised for photography that included 'Piccadilly by night'.[146] Similarly, much of the appeal of George Pearson's Paramount thriller *Midnight at Madame Tussaud's* (1936) lay in its use of the actual waxworks' Chamber of Horrors for the setting of its (rather tame) finale.

In spite of the popularity of books like Priestley's *English Journey* and Orwell's *The Road to Wigan Pier*, few units attempted to film in cities other than London. This did not escape the notice of critics like P. L. Mannock, who complained: 'London is only one great city in a country of cities, each teeming with a peculiarly individual atmosphere. Can it be that we are afraid to label a British film as a story about Manchester, Glasgow, Birmingham or Leeds?'[147] Reginald Denham's use of Liverpool locations in *The House of the Spaniard* was one exception to the London rule, although it was never labelled as a story of Merseyside. The film had its shortcomings, but at least evoked a sense of place. This was one of only a handful of productions – made almost exclusively for British renters – which also ran to the expense of foreign location work. The ill-conceived *Tea Leaves in the Wind* (1937) – a comparatively elaborate production featuring a large-scale attack on a plantation – involved shipping the cast and crew to Ceylon where they were almost washed away by floods.[148] A few films ventured as far as France – Gainsborough's *First Offence*, for example – but most productions confined their location work to the British countryside.

On location: Lilli Palmer, John Mills and director Herbert Mason (left) filming *First Offence* (1936)

*The Price of Wisdom* crew enjoyed a day in the country filming a pheasant shoot comfortably close to Elstree at Whitwell in Hertfordshire. But the favoured country location was the race meeting. Horse-racing was a national obsession before World War II, and a string of films recorded its thrills and spills. Britain's first Technicolor feature *Wings of the Morning* (1937) was the story of a Derby winner and included actual footage of the race, but more modest films also used the proven lure of the turf, as well as actuality filming, to attract bookings. One of the first quota films made by British and Dominions was 'a rousing drama of the Turf', *Warned Off* (1928), directed by Walter West and featuring 'the English Clara Bow', Chili Bouchier, in a supporting part. West had already directed a number of silent features with a horse-racing theme, and a series of shorts with leading jockey Steve Donoghue. His assistant on *Warned Off* was ex-jockey Billy Asher and ex-bookie Wally Patch also had a part as a turf accountant. The film prided itself on the authenticity of its milieu:

> All the multiform intricacies of racing life, all the details from the preliminary try-outs at the training quarters to the thrilling moment when the racing thoroughbreds thunder neck and neck down the course to the winning post are shown in entrancing fashion in this exciting drama. We see the training of the race-horse in all its details, we follow the jockeys into the weighing-in-room, meet 'bookies' without financial loss, see entrancing glimpses of actual racing at Sandown Park, Aintree, Newmarket and Epsom.[149]

The *Sunday Pictorial*'s critic was apparently particularly impressed, describing *Warned Off* as 'a tonic to those who have recently spent their film life in court-rooms and cabarets'.[150] Later, George Smith signed up the popular racing writer John Hunter to pen a couple of horsey dramas for RKO release: Randall Faye's *Luck of the Turf* (filmed in 1936 under the rather more intriguing title *Gay Reality*), and Maclean Rogers' crowd-pleasing comedy *Racing Romance* (1937), the latter including 'Actual scenes from the course where the Oaks is run' (Epsom).[151]

In the second half of the 1930s location filming became more common, but this did not always mean that the films became more fluid and expansive. Paramount's *Night Ride* is a case in point. Starring Jimmy Hanley and the story's author, Julian Vedey, the production was the first in a distinguished line of truck operas that includes the much better-known *They Drive by Night* (1939) and *Hell Drivers* (1957). The press book celebrated the 'varied backgrounds' in the film and announced that John Paddy Carstairs, had taken his cameras on the Great North Road. Commer, apparently, had lent a fleet of twenty lorries for the production and Hanley was given special lessons in how to drive (and crash) them.[152] One expects a film of movement and pace set on the open road. In fact, no more than two of the fleet of trucks are ever in the same shot, and the open road is glimpsed only in a short montage sequence and is otherwise hidden in a fog that conveniently disguises the studio environs. As Carstairs admitted: 'We couldn't afford to get as many exterior scenes of the English countryside as we had wanted. So we rather ingeniously and artfully played our action chase sequence at the end of the film – in a fog!'[153] The thick mist ensures that the lorries cannot be driven faster than a brisk walking pace. Much of the action, in fact, takes place on a small studio set of a transport café and office. *Hell Drivers* it ain't. Carstairs was faced with similar problems when trying to make the action-adventure *Incident in Shanghai* (1938) in eleven days on a budget of £7,000:

Truck opera: Julian Vedey (left) and Jimmy Hanley (right) take refuge from the fog in *Night Ride* (1937)

Nothing would have given me greater pleasure than a spectacular air fight or a running gun battle in the Chinese streets, but, for the money, we just could not do it. . . . The 'crowd' scenes were all filmed in *one day*. To use another crowd the next day would have been a very heavy item on our budget, so we had to be systematic. To work through set after set getting my long shots was excellent experience, and, of course, helped to teach me economy. But, oh, for just a few thousand pounds more to avoid having to shoot long, static dialogue scenes because we hadn't the money to build more sets for those action scenes! Oh for another week on the schedule to re-take certain scenes which wanted polishing.[154]

Rather than the extravagance of taking a unit on location, the standard tactic to give low-budget pictures the illusion of high production value was to insert footage shot by other crews for other purposes. Challis Sanderson's seafaring yarn *King of Whales* (1934) used this technique, but critics were not fooled: 'Authentic shots of the Durban whaling station, a whaler at sea, and the harpooning operations have been cut in, not so brilliantly . . . a fog scene alternates alarmingly between South Africa's brilliant sunshine and synthetic studio mist.'[155] The whole thing might have been more satisfactory as a documentary, but it would not have counted as quota for MGM.

Special effects could seriously inflate budgets, so were largely dispensed with by the quickies. There were exceptions, however. Paramount agreed to Donovan Pedelty's staging of the *Landslide* that engulfs a Welsh theatre and provides the title of a Wembley Studios' production of

1936. Tons of concrete and rubble were used to create what the film's press book hailed as 'spectacular effects'. However, the landslide was really only a sideshow to a murder mystery and a portrait of 'young love faced at the outset with dire calamity'. Not that the leading players, Jimmy Hanley and Dinah Sheridan were daunted: they married a few years later. For George Cooper's London dockland thriller *The World, the Flesh and the Devil* (1932), the Twickenham Studios setbuilders constructed a replica Wapping wharf with ale house on the back lot, before flooding it with a 50,000-gallon tank of water for the climax of the film. This time the effects played a more symbolic role in the narrative as the film's publicity indicated: 'The swirling waters of the flooded Thames take a hand on the side of justice.'[156]

'Process' shots were cheaper, but usually required a second unit, and were little used in supporting-feature production in England before 1935. Twickenham's first use of back projection was in that year on Bernard Vorhaus's *The Last Journey*.[157] Model shots were also sometimes employed: in Milton Rosmer's creature feature *The Secret of the Loch*, and Vernon Sewell's creepy directorial debut *The Medium* (1934). The latter, which also experimented with foreground mattes, was shot in Sewell's tiny Knightsbridge Studio, and scripted by his friend Michael Powell.[158] Powell preferred making quickies at Teddington, partly because Warners could supply the talents of Poppa Day 'the greatest trick photographer and double-exposure merchant that the movies have ever seen'.[159] Poppa's mastery of glass mattes would eventually be spectacularly showcased in Powell's *Black Narcissus* (1947).

Although the quota quickies were not renowned for the opulence of their sets or the ingenuity of their camerawork, their publicity was quite capable of singing the praises of production designer and cinematographer when the occasion arose. The press book for Paramount's murder mystery *The Girl in the Flat* (1934), for example, rather desperately drew attention to the film's 'tricky camera work' and 'modern settings':

> For Vera Boggetti's bedroom, which is one of the principal scenes of the picture, [art director] Mr Pusey chose a very fine sycamore suite consisting of bed, dressing table, wardrobe cabinet and telephone desk. Hidden lighting and attractive colour schemes of red, black and yellow complete the cosy setting.

It makes one rather sorry that the film was in black and white, a sentiment evidently shared by Paramount's publicist, who went on to a detailed description of the cut and colour of Miss Boggetti's cossack pyjamas and fellow actress Belle Chrystall's 'pale pink crepe-de-chine nightdress'.[160] Paramount's publicity maestros could make a virtue out of the most modest production values, as they did with the Edgar Wallace story *The Jewel* (1933), the first picture made by Reginald Denham and Hugh Percival's Venture Films:

> Although not an expensive picture, several weeks were spent on preparation, in order to obtain 100 per cent results. *The Jewel* was filmed in twelve days, including two days' exteriors, and the use of twenty sets. This efficiency was possible owing to the close co-operation of the unit.[161]

Had they possessed the gift of clairvoyance, the publicists might have made rather more of the contribution of the young actor playing the villain: Jack Hawkins. As it was, the future star barely rated a mention except for the attachment of the wildly misleading label of 'England's James Cagney'. In the same year, he had delivered one of the worst performances in the ensemble acting disaster that was *A Shot in the Dark*, and, five years later, he recalled: 'Many of my films have been "quickies" over which I'd like to draw a veil. We finished them in ten days, and hadn't the faintest idea what it was all about. We were given our lines just before we were to speak them.'[162]

By and large, the producers of second features preferred to make their films behind closed doors. In this way, the corners cut on the studio floor could be concealed and the impression might be created that the films were grander efforts than their makers knew them to be. This became increasingly important as British production values rose and criticism of cheap quota films grew. While Warners and Julius Hagen were usually happy to receive visiting journalists, other companies were more circumspect. In November 1936, for instance, *Picturegoer*'s studio correspondent grumbled about Paramount and Fox's reluctance to grant him access to their productions: 'Maybe it's modesty that keeps these Quota companies so secretive,' he remarked, 'but I for one should feel more confident in their activities if they would take me a little more into their confidence.[163] He was immediately invited onto the set of Paramount's *The Scarab Murder Case* (1936), and Fox began releasing publicity stills of their current production, *Strange Experiment* (1937). But, while they were sometimes shy, the quickie production houses employed quick-witted publicists like Billie Bristow and Victor Taylor, who set up his own press agency in 1931 after working for British Filmcraft and Pat Heale and as a film journalist on *The Cinema* and *Empire News*. Bristow, a widely respected woman working in an overwhelmingly male business, also turned her talents to scriptwriting and doctoring. Her first scenarios were for the early

A Bennett–Bristow thriller: a poster image for *Warn London* (1934). Author's collection

George King's featurettes *Too Many Crooks* and *Leave It to Me* (1930) – the latter penned with trade journalist P. L. Mannock – and she formed a regular writing partnership with the more celebrated Charles Bennett on films like *Warn London* (1934) and *The Secret of the Loch*.[164]

## Thrown together

> The picture wears that hurried look; it appears to have been thrown together for one purpose only – quota.
>
>                                                 Review of Paramount's *Ticket of Leave* (1935)[165]

If actors, directors, and the production crew had it hard on quota quickies, the films' editors were often faced with even more arduous schedules. Before he became an internationally famous director, David Lean was a cutter at Shepherd's Bush, Elstree and Ealing studios. One of his early editing jobs was a Bernard Vorhaus motorbike drama called *Money for Speed*, a title which summed up the expectations of a film editor working on low-budget pictures. He was just twenty-two years old when he cut his first quota picture, *The Night Porter* (1930), a comedy of mistaken identity directed by an American, Sewell Collins, for Gaumont.[166] Other quickies followed: Vorhaus's *The Ghost Camera*; the controversial docklands thriller *Tiger Bay*; John Baxter's *Song of the Plough* (1933); *The Secret of the Loch*; and, finally, the John Stafford production *The Wife of General Ling* (1937). Sidney Cole had also worked on a couple of Stafford films – *The Avenging Hand* and *Beloved Imposter* – made back to back at Welwyn early in 1936. They were cut simultaneously on sixteen-hour shifts by Cole and his assistant, Julian Wintle, to squeeze in their press shows before the close of the renters' quota year (31 March): 'It got so that we would stagger into the studio as the boys were leaving and I never really knew what day it was.'[167]

The results were less than satisfactory. The musical, *Beloved Imposter*, ended up running over eighty-five minutes – too long for a second feature – and required further pruning. *The Avenging Hand*, directed by Frank Richardson, an American director of such incompetence that some believed he was an Englishman faking the accent, needed considerable rescuing:

> [It] was supposed to be a mystery story, but it really wasn't any good. I thought I had better try and jazz it up a bit, and I asked for inserts to enable me to cut scenes around, and so on. . . . I still have a notice somewhere which says, 'The storyline of this picture presumably was rather obscure to begin with, but the editor has made it totally incomprehensible'.[168]

Cole's anecdote suggests that editors were given considerable freedom and were invited to do their best to cure the ills of hasty production. Certainly, he came to relish the challenge of working 'on a film which isn't very good' because 'there are so many things to be put right'.[169]

However, the editor's attempts to bring pace and continuity to lumbering and incoherent assemblages of footage could be frustrated by the nature of a producer's contract. Adrian Brunel recalled of *Prison Breaker* (1936), the film he made with James Mason for Columbia:

> The so-called finished film was full of those blemishes which a patient editor can whittle out, if he has the time. In our case our editor was additionally handicapped by our contract, as for every foot

A paragon of virtue: Frank Vosper in David Lean's first feature as a film editor, *The Night Porter* (1930)

cut out that brought the total footage below the guaranteed total of 6,000 feet, one pound was charged against us. To have cut from the film, say five minutes, might have made it an acceptable little film of 64 minutes running time, instead of a rather terrible film lasting 69 minutes – but such a cut would have eliminated most of the producer's profits.[170]

The film was released without the cuts and dissolves that Brunel had suggested to his editor, and remained for the director 'the perfect example of the bad type of ultra-quickie . . . a shocker'.[171] As we have seen, films were sometimes further edited by distributors, and some, particularly revues, were distributed in more than one version, the shorter version being available for use as a second feature.[172]

Hard though the work was in the quota factories, in the hungry 1930s it was the only work around, especially for the more skilled technicians who were being increasingly displaced in the larger studios by European émigrés. Most technicians were grateful for it. Electrician B. A. Tobin made this clear in a letter to a fan magazine:

Although we do all of us fully admit that a quota is undoubtedly 'tripe' when in production, it is these films which keep us in fairly regular employment when the British companies have a break in their production schedules. So although we dislike this type of film from a filmgoer's viewpoint . . . we are only too pleased to work on them.[173]

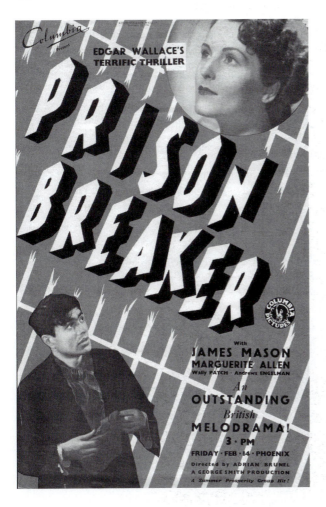

'A shocker': James Mason features
in this trade advertisement for
*Prison Breaker* (1936). Author's
collection

However, as his letter indicates, there were many who wanted to see the back of this particular
sector of the film business.

## Notes

1.  Michael Powell, *A Life in Movies* (London: Methuen, 1987), p. 114.
2.  Margaret Dickinson and Sarah Street, *Cinema and State: The Film Industry and the British
    Government 1927–84* (London: BFI, 1985), p. 39.
3.  PEP, *The British Film Industry* (London: Political and Economic Planning, 1952), p. 67.
4.  Edward Dryhurst, *Gilt Off the Gingerbread*, (London: Bachman & Turner, 1987), pp. 157–8. G. W.
    Pearson should not be confused with the aforementioned George Pearson, the distinguished
    director who had been with Samuelson when Worton Hall was founded. Unfortunately Patricia
    Warren makes this mistake in her useful *British Film Studios: An Illustrated History* (London:
    Batsford, 2001) (2nd edn), p. 99.
5.  Dryhurst, *Gilt Off the Gingerbread*, p. 165.

6.   George A. Cooper began his career as a film editor before becoming a director in 1922.

7.   Rachael Low, *The History of the British Film, 1929–1939* (London: Allen and Unwin, 1985), p. 185; Adrian Brunel, *Nice Work: Thirty Years in British Films* (London: Forbes Robertson, 1949), p. 169. Brunel liked working with George Smith because he 'gave his directors a free hand within the limitations he had to set'. Smith made his first films in Africa before World War I, coming to England via America as Goldwyn's head of operations in Britain. He was involved with fifty productions between 1927 and 1933.

8.   Monty Banks (Mario Bianchi) was born in Italy, the son of a composer. He left for the USA at the age of seventeen and eventually established himself in Hollywood as a comedy performer. He joined BIP in 1928, directing and producing a string of comedies in which he also sometimes acted.

9.   Dryhurst, *Gilt Off the Gingerbread*, pp. 174–80. Remarkably, the results of their red-eyed delirium survive in the National Film Archive.

10.  The Isleworth studios were refitted and extended in the spring of 1934, and began to host rather more prestigious productions like René Clair's *The Ghost Goes West* (1935).

11.  *Kinematograph Weekly*, 28 January 1932, p. 29.

12.  *The Bioscope*, 6 May 1931, p. 33.

13.  *Kinematograph Weekly*, 3 March 1932, thought *The Game of Chance's* points of appeal 'difficult to find', while *The Bioscope*, 9 March 1932, p. 15, recommended *Thoroughbred* 'for audiences lacking critical sense'.

14.  Peter Cotes, *Thinking Aloud* (London: Peter Owen, 1993), p. 42.

15.  King's brief biography in the *Kinematograph Year Book 1938* noted that he was an 'exploitation expert', while Edward Dryhurst (*Gilt Off the Gingerbread*, p. 213) described him as 'tall, good-looking and something of a ladies' man'. His production manager in the mid-1930s, E. M. Smedley-Aston, had warm memories of King as 'a delightful person to work with'. BECTU Oral History Project, Interview 407, 30 April 1997.

16.  *Picturegoer*, 16 January 1937, p. 9.

17.  Vernon Sewell interview, BECTU Oral History Project, Interview 329, 7 July 1994.

18.  *Kinematograph Weekly*, 10 January 1935, pp. 132, 135.

19.  Bernerd Mainwaring had an extraordinarily varied career as an acrobat, athlete, sailor and dance-band leader. After flying in the RAF during World War I, he entered the film business as an extra, and eventually won opportunities to act, and then direct. He was put under contract by British Lion at the end of 1935 after impressing with *Line Engaged*.

20.  John Mitchell, *Flickering Shadows – A Lifetime in Films* (Malvern Wells: Harold Martin & Redman, 1997), p. 24. The story of the early Hammer productions is told in Wayne Kinsey, *Hammer Films: The Bray Studio Years* (Richmond: Reynolds & Hearn, 2002), pp. 8–10; Howard Maxford, *Hammer, House of Horror* (London: Batsford, 1996), pp. 10–13; Marcus Hearn and Alan Barnes, *The Hammer Story* (London: Titan Books, 1997), pp. 8–9.

21.  *Kinematograph Weekly*, 7 February 1935.

22.  Carreras' cinemas had in fact been sold to the expanding Associated British circuit in 1932.

23.  *The Bioscope*, 11 November 1931, p. 15.

24.  *The Water Gipsies* was a troubled production that Elvey preferred to forget. He fell out with producer Basil Dean: 'I'm sorry to say that I thought he knew nothing about filmmaking, and he

thought I knew nothing about acting. We were both wrong, of course. And I walked out of that film halfway through and said, "well you'd better do it yourself!"' BECTU Oral History Project, Interview 110, 10 January 1963.

25.   Stephen Watts, 'High-Speed Film Making', *Film Weekly*, 16 December 1932, p. 12.

26.   The film received a record ten bookings in Leicester, four as a first feature.

27.   Low, *The History of the British Film, 1929–1939*, pp. 179–80; Derek Threadgall, *Shepperton Studios: An independent view* (London: BFI, 1994), pp. 4–16.

28.   'Put Britain on the Map', *Picturegoer*, 6 May 1933, p. 13.

29.   Geoff Brown and Tony Aldgate, *The Common Touch: The Films of John Baxter* (London: BFI, 1989), p. 125.

30.   Low, *The History of the British Film, 1929–1939*, p. 175.

31.   George Pearson, *Flashback* (London: Allen and Unwin, 1957), p. 192–3. Pearson would have made an ideal protagonist for a John Baxter film: a man of noble character, fallen on hard times, struggling to survive in a changing world.

32.   *Kinematograph Weekly*, 14 March 1935, p. 55.

33.   Interview with Maurice Elvey, BECTU Oral History Project.

34.   Bernard Vorhaus interview, BECTU Oral History Project, Interview 219, 23 October 1991.

35.   Richard Maurice Hurst, *Republic Studios* (London: Scarecrow Press, 1979).

36.   The nearest equivalents to Monogram's Mr Wong, Bomba, the Cisco Kid and the East Side Kids were, perhaps, the Sexton Blake films and the Tod Slaughter melodramas.

37.   They were the sort of films one of *Picturegoer's* readers had in mind when complaining that the 'mystery melodrama, in which the lights are mysteriously extinguished, doors slam, and so many screams and shots in the dark are heard . . . is becoming tedious'. Letter from A. A. Bates, *Picturegoer*, 20 January 1933.

38.   The phrase 'an Englishman's home is a castle' is borrowed from *Kinematograph Weekly's* review of Twickenham's *Lazybones*, 24 January 1935, p. 36.

39.   An adenoidal maid with a ready flow of malapropisms ('He's making insinuendoes at me') is the chief comic relief, but Cook holds her own when she responds to the police inspector's enquiry as to whether she is a heavy sleeper with, 'Well I turn the scales at 14 stone, but that's my business!'

40.   *Lord Edgware Dies* did receive three bookings, compared to *Tangled Evidence's* single playdate, in Leicester.

41.   *Picturegoer's* droll E. G. Cousins was probably not alone in spotting the irony of Hagen's choice of name for quota productions: 'I am grateful to Twickenham for one thing,' he wrote, 'they have handed me the best smile I have had for some time by describing this film [*Tangled Evidence*] as a Real Art production.' *Picturegoer*, 17 March 1934.

42.   For assessments of Hagen as a producer see Kenton Bamford, *Distorted Images: British National Identity and Film in the 1920s* (London: I. B. Tauris, 1999), pp. 170–1, and Linda Wood, 'Julius Hagen and Twickenham Film Studios', in Jeffrey Richards (ed.), *The Unknown 1930s: An Alternative History of British Cinema 1929–1939* (London: I. B. Tauris, 1998), pp. 37–55.

43.   Cmd. 5320: 1020 and 1023.

44.   Walter Summers was born in Barnstaple and entered the entertainment business at ten years old. He worked as a stage director before taking charge of his first film in 1913. During World War I, Summers rose to the rank of captain in the Royal Flying Corps and was decorated for bravery. He

went on to specialise in films about the war as well as churning out thrillers for BIP. He seems to have been exiled to Welwyn after a notorious court case exposed his penchant for asking actresses to audition in the nude. Rather unwisely, he had previously praised the silent film, *Damaged Goods*, as a potent warning of the 'terrible penalties of sexual promiscuity'. Walter Summers, 'Pictures with a Purpose', *Film Weekly*, 16 January 1932, p. 7. Summers was presumably the bully and sexual predator at Welwyn whom Muriel Box declined to name in her autobiography, *Odd Woman Out* (London: Leslie Frewin, 1974), p. 113.

45.  Perversely, *Picturegoer*'s Lionel Collier judged that Bird gave a 'clever character study' and that his final confession was 'an exceedingly good piece of acting' (16 February 1935, p. 24). One can only be struck by how radically tastes in acting styles have changed.

46.  Arthur Dent, 'British and Proud of It', *Picturegoer*, 24 January 1935, p. 34.

47.  *Kinematograph Weekly*, 7 January 1932. According to the first woman producer of a British talking picture, editing and continuity were the only avenues of opportunity that might allow women to advance to director and producer roles. M. Haworth-Booth, 'The Place for Women in the Film Studios', *Picturegoer*, 16 November 1935, p. 15. Unfortunately, Mrs Haworth-Booth's only production – a remake of a risqué French farce entitled *Runaway Ladies*, made partly at Elstree – was not a runaway success, taking three years to gain release (1938).

48.  *The Bioscope*, 30 December 1931, p. 11. *Film Weekly*'s John Gammie, on the other hand, thought that Logan and Field failed to 'interpret the feminine viewpoint on the screen', and that their work was unlikely to make male directors 'tremble for the security of their jobs'. *Film Weekly*, 2 January 1932, pp. 21-2.

49.  *Kinematograph Weekly*, 28 March 1935.

50.  *Kinematograph Weekly*, 23 April 1936, p. 4.

51.  Cmd. 5320: 78.

52.  The application of these rules in American 'B' film-making of the 1940s is discussed in Nick Grinde's 'Pictures for Peanuts', reprinted in R. K. Neilson-Baxter, Roger Manvell and H. H. Wollenberg (eds), *The Penguin Film Review*, no. 1 (London: Penguin, 1946).

53.  *Picturegoer*, 6 July 1935, p. 28.

54.  Quoted in Max Breen, 'There's Value in Valerie', *Picturegoer*, 16 April 1938, p. 9.

55.  Adrian Brunel, 'The Danger of Quickies to British Technicians', *The Journal of the Association of Cine-Technicians*, May 1936, pp. 6–8.

56.  Cmd. 5320: 1002.

57.  John Paddy Carstairs, *Movie Merry-Go-Round* (London: Newnes, 1937), pp. 54–5.

58.  Pearson, *Flashback*, p. 193.

59.  Ibid.

60.  *Kinematograph Weekly*, 8 October 1931, p. 48.

61.  *Film Weekly*, 20 February 1937, p. 5.

62.  Todd McCarthy and Charles Flynn (eds), *Kings of the Bs: Working within the Hollywood System* (New York: E. P. Dutton, 1975), p. 344.

63.  Some attempts at improvement were made, however. For example, when the ex-Fleet Street journalist, Reginald Pound, was appointed head of the scenario department at Fox's Wembley Studios, his call for film treatments indicated that they should be full of action and limited in dialogue. *Picturegoer*, 5 October 1935, p. 40.

64.   *Kinematograph Weekly*, 14 February 1935.

65.   *Kinematograph Weekly,* 20 August 1934.

66.   *Kinematograph Weekly,* 9 August 1934.

67.   See, for example, *Picturegoer*, 1 January 1938. Donovan Pedelty began his career as a publicist, before spending time in Hollywood as the representative of a film magazine, and absorbing everything he could learn about directing. Returning to England, he joined Paramount as a talent scout, and was given the arduous task of making the screen tests for the company's 'Search for Beauty' initiative, before finally landing a series of quota quickie directorial assignments. He returned to journalism in the 1950s – ironically as editor of *Picturegoer*.

68.   *Behind Your Back* press book.

69.   Ibid.

70.   Quoted in Donald P. Costello, *The Serpent's Eye: Shaw and the Cinema* (Notre Dame, IN: University of Notre Dame, 1965), p. 37.

71.   Ibid., p. x.

72.   Rodney Ackland and Elspeth Grant, *The Celluloid Mistress* (London: Allan Wingate, 1954), p. 26.

73.   Charles Bennett interview, BECTU Oral History Project, Interview 250, 3 March 1992. With a growing surplus of scripts £100-150 became a more usual fee.

74.   Michael Powell, *A Life in Movies*, p. 238.

75.   *The Bioscope*, 1 April 1931, p. 17.

76.   *Kinematograph Weekly,* 3 February 1938.

77.   Brunel, 'The Danger of Quickies'.

78.   *The Bioscope*, 2 July 1930, p. 23. The brevity of the production schedule did not prevent the paper's review heaping praise on the picture's 'excellent characterisation', 'first-rate direction', 'witty dialogue' and 'profound sense of mystery'. Exhibitors were told that they need not 'have any qualms in booking it'. 6 August 1930, p. 27.

79.   Sidney Cole interview, BECTU Oral History Project.

80.   Pearson, *Flashback*, p. 194.

81.   Pearson believed he made eight but seven is all I can trace.

82.   John Mills, *Up in the Clouds, Gentlemen Please* (Harmondsworth: Penguin, 1981), p. 177. The eight-day shooting schedules should perhaps be taken with a pinch of salt. At Twickenham, two, or even three, weeks was a standard shooting schedule for a supporting feature, but for more ambitious films like *Bella Donna* (1934) an eight-week allocation was made. For an account of a similar practice at Fox's Wembley Studios see Ronald Neame, *Straight from the Horse's Mouth* (Lanham, MD and Oxford: Scarecrow Press, 2003), p. 36. Mills was again on the Twickekenham day shift, shooting *The Lash*, while poor Pearson toiled at night to complete *Whispering Tongues*.

83.   *Picturegoer,* 4 August 1934.

84.   *Too Many Crooks* press book. *Number Please,* a story of a London telephone exchange, was another George King production which was beset with problems. On one disastrous day, the studio carpenter's dog rushed on set and savaged a leading actor (Warwick Ward), another actor (Richard Bird) fell through a glass screen and his assistant damaged his knee falling down a flight of steps. *The Bioscope*, 22 April 1931, p. 36.

85.   Tilly Day interview, BECTU Oral History Project, Interview 30, 15 January 1988.

86.    Henry Kendall, *I Remember Romano's* (London: MacDonald, 1960), p. 133. Vernon Sewell recalled that it was quite common on quota films for shooting to finish as late as 1 am, and begin the following morning at 8 am. BECTU Oral History Project, Interview 329, 7 July 1994.

87.    Maurice Elvey, BECTU Oral History Project.

88.    Belfarge, *All Is Grist*, p. 108.

89.    Desmond Dickinson interview, BECTU Oral History Project, Interview 111, 5 July 1963.

90.    Neame, *Straight from the Horse's Mouth*, p. 36. The film was almost certainly Garrick's *Café Colette*, the only independent production that Neame shot at Wembley.

91.    Kane made forty-three films with Rogers and seventeen with Autry. McCarthy and Flynn, *Kings of the Bs*, p. 320.

92.    Ibid., p. 403.

93.    *Kinematograph Weekly*, 16 February 1933, p. 35. The film scored eight-and-a-half marks from the *CEA Film Report* and garnered excellent reviews from all of the trade journals.

94.    *Love at Sea* press book.

95.    *Kinematograph Weekly*, 26 October 1933. Brunel commented that 'It would be fairer to say that the promoters of this type of picture show a lack of imagination. Without money you cannot buy imagination, without time imagination cannot flourish.' Brunel, 'The Danger of Quickies.'

96.    Adrian Brunel, *Nice Work: Thirty Years in British Films* (London: Forbes Robinson, 1949), p. 171.

97.    *Kinematograph Weekly*, 15 June 1933, p. 27.

98.    *Mayfair Girl* press book.

99.    James Mason, *Before I Forget* (London: Sphere, 1982), p. 121.

100.    Ibid. John Mitchell, whose first job as a sound recordist was on Parker's *The Third Clue* (filmed at Ealing in the summer of 1934), recalled that he was 'a man of fiery temperament' who could become thoroughly exasperated with the performances of his actors. His reaction terrified the inexperienced Anna Lee; 'she sobbed her heart out, so much so that shooting had to be stopped for the day'. Mitchell, *Flickering Shadows*, p. 23.

101.    Bernard Vorhaus interview, BECTU Oral History Project.

102.    Pearson could not recall any of the actors with whom he had worked on these productions ever speaking 'with scorn of that association, but only of happy memories of those early, though somewhat rough adventures'. Pearson, *Flashback*, pp. 194–5.

103.    *Kinematograph Weekly*, 20 October 1932, p. 43. This should not be confused with the later Tod Slaughter film with the same title.

104.    *Kinematograph Weekly*, 3 October 1935, p. 31. But not all actors who received critical praise went on to become stars. Reviews of Paramount's *The Girl in the Flat* (1934) clearly indicated that Belle Chrystall, who had first attracted attention in *Hindle Wakes* (1931) was indeed the girl and the rest was flat; (*Kinematograph Weekly*, 28 July 1934, p. 21; *Picturegoer*, 1 December 1934). But if the fragile Chrystall is now remembered, it is only as the hardy island maiden in Michael Powell's *The Edge of the World* (1937).

105.    *Kinematograph Weekly*, 24 October 1935.

106.    *The Bioscope*, 17 March 1932, p. 18.

107.    Merle Oberon, 'The Debts I Owe', *Picturegoer*, 5 October 1935, p. 15.

108.    *The Bioscope*, 23 March 1932, p. 19.

109. A. Ronald Thornton of the *Daily Express* thought that Tamara Desni 'will be Dietrich before you can say Garbo'. *How's Chances?* press book. Her entry into quota pictures is described in Stephen Watts, 'A Studio Falls for a Star', *Film Weekly*, 9 February 1934, p. 25.

110. *The Cinema*, 23 January 1935, p. 9. Flynn's 'discovery' by Asher is described in Errol Flynn, 'Give Me the Life of Adventure', *Picturegoer*, 2 January 1937, p. 32.

111. *Picturegoer*, 4 January 1936, p. 13.

112. For four day's work the future star of *Gone With the Wind* (1939) had received the princely fee of twenty guineas. Alexander Walker, *Vivien: The Life of Vivien Leigh* (London: Mandarin, 1990), pp. 75–6. Leigh had previously been an extra in the 1935 Gainsborough film *Things Are Looking Up*.

113. For example, there were no comments on Leigh's performances in *Today's Cinema*'s reviews of the films on 17 April 1935, p. 12, and 27 April 1935, p. 4. See also E. G. Cousins, 'A New Star Is Born', *Picturegoer*, 6 July 1935, p. 28.

114. *Kinematograph Weekly*, 31 October 1935, p. 29. Born in Surrey, Tyrrell Davis had developed his acting career in Hollywood before returning to England for a part in Fox's Ernie Lotinga comedy *Smith's Wives*.

115. *Kinematograph Weekly*, 26 March 1936, p. 35.

116. *The Bioscope*, 30 March 1932, p. 17.

117. Of course, some later luminaries got better reviews. Margaret Lockwood's leading role in Ralph Ince's *Jury's Evidence* (1936), for example, was praised by *Kinematograph Weekly* (9 January 1936, p. 30) for its 'sincerity and feeling'. This was one of American actor/director Ralph Ince's last films before he was killed in a car accident near the Albert Hall in April 1936. He was first brought to Britain by Warner Bros. to star in and direct *No Escape* in 1934.

118. *Film Pictorial*, 12 August 1933, p. 19.

119. *Kinematograph Weekly*, 16 January 1936, p. 26.

120. Henry Kendall, *I Remember Romano's* p. 133.

121. Her career is remembered in Chili Bouchier, *Shooting Star: The Last of the Silent Film Stars* (London: Atlantis, 1995).

122. Dryhurst, *Gilt Off the Gingerbread*, p. 196. Virginia Cherrill's 'discovery' was directly attributable to meeting Chaplin at a society party when she was only seventeen. She was emblematic of the well-to-do young actresses who were drafted into British films thanks to the right social connections. Born into a monied family, Cherrill (favourite pastime: yachting) was offered a leading part without even having a screen test and was later put under contract by Irving Thalberg. *Film Pictorial*, 17 September 1932, p. 6.

123. *After Dark* press book. Some of the film's advertising even put Padbury's name above the title.

124. Lionel Clynton, 'One Hundred Per Cent Cockney', *Film Weekly*, 8 October 1938, p. 27. It was estimated that Patch had appeared in over a hundred films in the first ten years of the talkies.

125. 'When Observation Spells Success', *Picturegoer*, 11 April 1936, pp. 12–13.

126. *Show Flat* press book.

127. *Kinematograph Weekly*, 15 October 1936.

128. *Film Weekly*, 18 June 1936, p. 37.

129.  Surprisingly, *Kinematograph Weekly* (7 March 1935, p. 21) thought 'the technical work comparable with the best' and the characterisation 'competent'.

130.  Bernard Vorhaus interview, BECTU Oral History Project.

131.  See, for example, *CEA Film Report*, 21 March 1931. One exception was Lionel Collier, who 'thoroughly recommended' *Contraband Love* as very well directed and 'redolent of Cornish atmosphere'. *Picturegoer*, 26 September 1931, p. 19. *The Bioscope* (18 March 1931) clearly detected that *Dangerous Seas* had been conceived as a silent film: 'The dialogue [by Edward Dryhurst] is trite and appears to have been written by one whose appreciation of present day dramatic values is infinitesimal. The general tone of the dialogue is too old-fashioned to promote any feeling other than a desire to laugh in derision.'

132.  *Cross Currents* press book.

133.  *Marooned* press book. One of *Film Weekly*'s readers agreed, commenting that the film's rocky settings provided 'a good example of well-used scenery'. Letter from E. I. Ward of Woodbridge, Suffolk,

      4 May 1934, p. 68.

134.  *Today's Cinema*, 12 January 1935.

135.  *Flame in the Heather* press book.

136.  Ibid.

137.  *Kinematograph Weekly* (26 September 1935, p. 31) found the Scottish scenery and accuracy of period detail the only praiseworthy elements in a 'vague and artless' picture suffering from 'complete narratal confusion'.

138.  *Kinematograph Weekly*, 14 June 1934, p. 52.

139.  Edward Dryhurst, *Gilt Off the Gingerbread*, p. 178.

140.  *The Bioscope*, 9 September 1931, p. 29.

141.  *The Fear Ship* press book. For the Redd Davis comedy *Seeing Is Believing*, however, Paramount preferred to build an elaborate set of an ocean liner at Elstree's Imperial Studios. *The Windjammer* itself (Grace Hawar) was the eponymous star of John Orton's docu-drama for Pro Patria (1930).

142.  *Kinematograph Weekly*, 11 July 1935. *Picturegoer* (11 January 1936, p. 25) remarked that the production was 'theatrical and badly pieced together'.

143.  *The Belles of St. Clements'* press book.

144.  *The Love Wager* press book.

145.  *The Bioscope*, 21 October 1931, p. 15.

146.  *CEA Film Report*, 5 September 1931.

147.  *Kinematograph Weekly*, 10 January 1935.

148.  *Picturegoer*, 21 August 1937, p. 8.

149.  *Warned Off* press book.

150.  Ibid.

151.  *Racing Romance* press book.

152.  The film was given a special Sunday screening, attended by director and cast members, to 2,800 company employees in Luton. *Kinematograph Weekly*, 24 June 1937, p. 34.

153.  John Paddy Carstairs, 'Thanks for the Remittance', *Film Pictorial*, 31 December 1938, p. 17.

154.  Ibid.

155.  *Kinematograph Weekly*, 7 June 1934, p. 31.

156. *The World, the Flesh and the Devil* press book.

157. Bernard Vorhaus interview BECTU Oral History Project.

158. Vernon Sewell interview BECTU Oral History Project.

159. Powell, *A Life in Movies*, p. 239.

160. The 'tricky camera work' consisted of an 'intricate tracking shot, combining trolley movement and pan' and was accomplished by Percy Strong after several rehearsals with his three assistants. *The Girl in the Flat* press book.

161. *The Jewel* press book.

162. David Welsh, 'Jack Hawkins Awaits', *Film Weekly*, 26 November 1938, p. 23.

163. *Picturegoer*, 7 November 1936, p. 17. However, Paramount's stills cameramen regularly took over a hundred pictures of each production for press distribution.

164. Bristow worked mainly with George King, Bray Wyndham and British Lion. Other female publicists included Margaret Marshall, the young Press Manager at Gaumont-British Distributors.

165. *Kinematograph Weekly*, 9 January 1936, p. 30.

166. Stephen M. Silverman, *David Lean* (New York: Abrams, 1992), p. 27.

167. Belfarge, *All Is Grist*, p. 107. Editor Reginald Beck had a similar experience on Michael Powell's *Born Lucky*, made at Wembley in 1932, working ninety-six hours without sleep. Ibid, p. 121.

168. Ibid., p. 107.

169. Sidney Cole interview, BECTU Oral History Project.

170. Brunel, *Nice Work*, p. 169.

171. Ibid.

172. See the editorial 'Those Cut-Down Features', *Kinematograph Weekly*, 26 March 1936, p. 4.

173. Letter from B. A. Tobin of Edgware, *Picturegoer*, 25 October 1935.

# 3

# Mere Footage?: Criticising the Quickie

Many a good film has been made on a modest budget. And many a bad picture has resulted from reckless expenditure. But – ever since the Act came into force – some renters have been content to provide – *mere footage* – for quota purposes. Some have offered preposterous films that were quite useless for any screen in this country.

Editorial in *The Cinema*[1]

## The villains of the piece: the American renters

Quota Quickies weren't in any way serious. The American companies regarded them as a Tax as it were, on their right to import their real pictures into this country.

Sidney Cole[2]

If an American renter had been a character in a quota quickie, the role would surely have been taken by the mustachioed Tod Slaughter because, in the writing on 1930s' British cinema, it is invariably the cunning and self-interested foreign distributor who is the villain of the piece. John Grierson, writing in 1937, certainly subscribed to this casting policy. Describing the Hollywood companies as 'imperial traders' who were 'mobilized in packs', he complained that they had 'squeezed every penny' out of the British market and 'given as little in return as the law allowed'. They had obliged English producers to make films for them for 'starveling' sums, which meant 'the deliberate and cynical exploitation of British technicians' and 'grinding the faces of young English directors in the dust of cheap and nasty production conditions'. He concluded that 'their activities during the past ten years will take some forgetting. They have brought contempt on the British film, and viciously.' Their quota quickies were nothing more than 'a sinister example of American commercial manoeuvre'.[3]

Grierson was certainly not alone in accusing the American firms of cynical or underhand business practices. Their attitudes towards British film production provoked irritation and resentment in many quarters, not least among film technicians. Always ready to bite one of the hands that fed them, the ACT accused their American paymasters of not simply exploiting their labour, but of using its product to undermine the British industry and bring it into disrepute.[4] When she came to write her history of the period, Rachael Low drew on opinions like these, emphasising the ways in which the American renters would buy up cheap footage of any quality to satisfy the quota regulations, and force their wares on powerless exhibitors through block book-ing.[5] Was this reputation deserved?

By the early 1930s the financial and technological mists were beginning to clear, and it became possible to discern developing patterns of quota production. For the most part, the American renters had decided on a strategy of commissioning supporting pictures from British production companies, thus minimising the competition for their costly Hollywood features. Emblematic of this policy to commission second features rather than form partnerships with British producers to make first features were Basil Dean's attempts to persuade Radio Pictures to enter into the joint production at Ealing of quality pictures for international distribution. Dean's efforts eventually foundered on the American company's unwillingness to make suffi-cient finance available.[6] Instead, British films were to be bought outright as close as possible to the minimum cost for quota registration allowed in the Act – £1 per foot of film. This would mean that the average cost of their British films would be approximately 10 per cent of the Hol-lywood movie it would normally support. The American firms maintained that this strategy was forced upon them as a means of accommodating a Quota Act, on which they had not been con-sulted. Making larger-budget pictures was never a viable option for two reasons. First, each firm had only sufficient capital available to make a handful of decently budgeted films in England. Once the quota rose above 10 per cent, the number of films required to meet it militated against adequate financing for each picture. Second, when the quota was lower than 10 per cent, the infrastructure and production personnel available in England were woefully inadequate for making pictures of a Hollywood standard. When the quota rose to 20 per cent, they pointed to the fact that the leading British producers Gaumont-British and BIP were, by their own admis-sion, over-stretched in trying to make twenty pictures per year. Korda's London Films main-tained quality by making only two or three per year. If this was the limit for indigenous producers with their own studio facilities, it was unreasonable to expect foreign companies, whose core business was distribution rather than production, to each make fifteen to eighteen films of good quality per annum.

These arguments were hard to fault. The shortage and paucity of technical personnel and creative talent in the early years of the Quota Act were widely acknowledged, even by the fiercest critics of the American firms. Moreover, much of the best talent was monopolised by the largest British studios, which, with the exception of London Films, had their own distribution companies and showed no desire to transfer their business to foreign concerns. Once United Artists had secured Korda's output, there was precious little of any real quality remaining on the market. Therefore, it was hardly the fault of the other American renters that they had been obliged to meet their legal obligations by procuring (by their own admission) 'a large number of cheap, poor pictures' that were no advertisement for British film-making.[7] With the excep-tion of United Artists, each firm acquired just enough British footage each year to stay within the law. The implications for the indigenous industry were clearly profound when one consid-ers that the US renters were responsible for the distribution of roughly two-thirds of all sup-porting features made in Britain during the life of the first Quota Act. However, this overall figure conceals a massive shift in distribution from British firms to their American cousins after 1931. From this date, American renters distributed nearly three out of every four British sup-porting features. The figures in the table below are based on the films listed in the Filmography.

**Table 3.1** Distributors of British supporting features 1928–37

| Years | British renters (per cent) | Total | US renters (per cent) | Total |
|---|---|---|---|---|
| 1928–31 | 64.5 | 107 | 35.5 | 59 |
| 1932–37 | 26.4 | 160 | 73.6 | 445 |
| 1928–37 | 34.6 | 267 | 65.4 | 504 |

Perhaps the most villainous US renter was one of the smallest: Universal Pictures were the chief exponents of the quota dodge that involved buying up cheap footage from Empire producers in Australia, Canada and India. The review of Universal's Australian crime picture *The Cheaters* (1934) in *The Cinema* will give some idea of the trade's adverse reaction to unusable films of this type:

> A completely primitive level in both material and technique deters this elementary Australian melo-drama from rising above the level of less than mediocre. The cutting is frankly tantalising, the photography crude, and both dialogue and portayal of that hyper-melodramatic type favoured by penny gaffs and school prize givings. . . . Quota fare for uncritical only.[8]

Columbia was also adept at fulfilling its small quota obligations from 'terribly bad' Empire productions, favouring Canada more than Australia.[9] When a shortfall needed to be made up from British studio production, almost anything would do, as this anecdote from Roy Boulting illustrates. The Boulting brothers began their career at the end of 1937, making short films. They were shooting their third when:

> A very debonair looking and highly sinister man arrived at the studios. This chap said he had read in the trade papers that we were making this film and was wondering whether we'd thought about distribution. So John told him we hadn't, that we wanted to see what the film was going to be like. He seemed convinced that the film was going to be fine, even though he hadn't read the script. He had contacts in Wardour Street, with Columbia Pictures, who were in need of British product. He said he could get us a pound a foot. Well, the film budget was only £1,600. A pound a foot gave us almost 100 per cent profit, and what a marvellous thing to be able to tell our shareholders who'd advanced the money for the company. Unfortunately, the film must be 3,100 feet to conform to the Quota Act. I argued that it was only a short story – how could we extend it to twice the length? Anyhow, . . . we accepted the arrangement, and I had the job of trying to stretch the story out. It was called *The Landlady* [1938]. The whole thing was set in a boarding house. . . . I knew, having cut the damn thing, that it was a disaster. John said, 'The big problem, Roy, is how do we prevent this film being shown to anybody else.' We learned from that the important thing is never listen to anybody who has a life rooted in Wardour Street.[10]

On the other hand, the lone hero among the renter villains is often said to be United Artists, which embraced the spirit of the Act by distributing the work of 'quality' British producers such as Alexander Korda and Herbert Wilcox. Low even asserts that the company 'did not make, sponsor or acquire quota quickies', which is a little economical with the truth.[11] In fact, the few British supporting features released by United Artists do not appear to have been of better quality than those of any other American renter. Those made by Michael Powell were thought to be among his poorest, and the fantastical whodunit *The Call-Box Mystery* (1932) was considered 'amateurish' and badly directed.[12]

## Other birds' nests

> I have discovered that the companies that are willing to make films for us, and that spend £20,000 to £25,000 to make them, can make no better films than other companies who spend £7,000 to £10,000. They lack the ability even though they have the money.
>
> MGM's Sam Eckman[13]

Most of the other US renters soon established production facilities in Britain to make their notorious 'cuckoo films'. Asquith's phrase conveys not only the resentment of many indigenous producers towards them, but also the idea of inauthenticity. By the end of 1931, Paramount and Warners were renting their own production facilities at B&D, Elstree and Teddington, respectively. Paramount, which already had studios in Paris, devoted a page of its *Finsbury Park Astorian* magazine to announcing its new British films, proclaiming that they would be 'Equal to Hollywood Productions'.[14] Said to feature 'the cream of British stage and screen talent', the early films were a mixture of first and second features. Special attention was drawn to the relatively lavish *Stamboul* (1931), made in British and Spanish versions, but the company also ensured that more modest productions had exploitation value: Manning Hayes' *The Officers' Mess* (1931) was set to put the West-End original 'in the shade', thanks to its 'brilliant cast of stage favourites'; while Sidney Morgan's *Contraband Love* starred C. Aubrey Smith, a successful émigré to Hollywood.

Initially, the trade papers and fan magazines seemed to take Paramount's publicists at their word.[15] *Picture Show*'s Edith Nepean reported enthusiastically on Paramount's new initiative at Elstree:

> New buildings are being shot up, vast resources for exteriors are being gathered together, and production is in full swing. . . . Paramount Company have taken to picture making as seriously in this country as they have done in Hollywood and France, and . . . are out to make the best possible pictures.[16]

Reviewers were less easily convinced, and soon cast doubt on the sincerity of Paramount's intentions. The *CEA Film Report* did not mince words in slating *Contraband Love*:

> This film ranks for quota, which is, perhaps, its principal value to the firm exploiting it. As entertainment it is nebulous, is wretchedly produced, with a story possessing little original material, and with a cast worthy of better stuff. . . . Recording very bad, and dialogue poor in material and delivery. Patchy photography, and settings cramped and tawdry.[17]

Paramount's claims might have been exposed as propaganda, but the new operation did have genuine successes, notably Alexander Korda's first British film, *Service for Ladies* (1932). However, the company soon realised that it could not sustain the level of investment – and subsequent loss – incurred on its first eight pictures. Once it had been demonstrated that most of these films could not attract international sales, because their themes and writers were too Anglocentric, expenditure was cut back, and no attempt was made to market the films abroad.[18] Paramount's quota films, each of which was expected to lose money, were produced by a semi-autonomous unit under Richard Norton and Anthony Havelock-Allan of B&D at Elstree until the studios burned down in 1936, and later at Pinewood.[19] At Elstree, the standard roster of jobbing directors was used, including Adrian Brunel, George Pearson, George Cooper, Henry Edwards and Sidney Morgan. At Pinewood, more scope was given to young directors like David Macdonald, John Paddy Carstairs and Donovan Pedelty, whose independent production company, Crusade Films, also made some Paramount pictures in Ireland. Paramount's managing director, J. C. Graham was said by Low to be 'notorious for his intransigence towards British exhibitors', and, although no evidence to substantiate this was produced, it may to some extent account for the apparent lack of bookings for the company's supporting features.[20] Graham admitted that most of his quota pictures 'lay in the offices largely unsold and unused'.[21]

Warners announced in August 1931 that, it would spend £200,000 on its first ten to twelve films, suggesting that it would double the standard expenditure on supporting features.[22] This

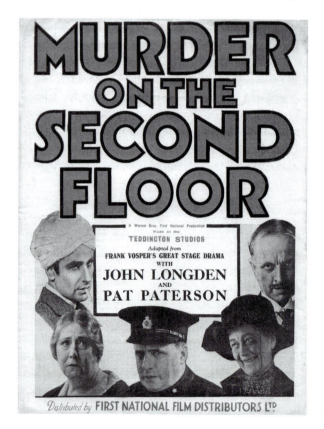

'Simply not trying': Warners'
publicity brochure for the first
Teddington production *Murder on
the Second Floor* (1931). Author's
collection

has to be taken with a pinch of salt – £7,000–10,000 per picture might be nearer the mark. Six years later, the studio claimed to have spent over £2.5 million on its first 116 films, but one assumes this was the total cost of running Teddington, with its staff and contract players.[23] Although most of Teddington's films were, by all accounts, undistinguished, Warners did give aspiring British writers and technicians the opportunity to work alongside Hollywood veterans like studio manager Doc Salomon and directors William McGann and Ralph Ince. Despite its notoriety as an anti-trades union studio, by 1938, Teddington had trained a substantial workforce of technicians and creative personnel that would prove to be of enormous value to the British film industry. Brock Williams was one of the writers who benefited from the experience, going on to head the scenario department and become one of the most prolific writers of British crime programmers.[24]

*Kinematograph Weekly* judged the initial Teddington production, *Murder on the Second Floor* (1931), 'a praiseworthy first effort', but *The Bioscope* was disappointed.[25] *Film* Weekly's editor was less inhibited in his criticisms:

> After seeing the 'British' talkies so far made with American backing, I have gathered the impression, not without due cause, that the people responsible for them are simply not trying . . . Neither critics nor public will suffer feeble entertainment gladly because Hollywood must keep within the letter of the quota law.[26]

However, bolstered by a favourable report from an American preview audience, the film was actually released in the USA. It was the first time that a picture made in Britain had been accepted for American release before being trade shown in its country of origin.[27] There was a generally more appreciative reception for the 'clever and well-presented' George Cooper featurette *A Voice Said Goodnight* (1932).[28] There is every indication that Warners and their distribution arm, First National, were keen to promote and market their new British product. First National bused its sales force to Teddington to see the work of the studios. Chief executive Irving Asher told them that it was not his intention 'to make pictures at Teddington merely for quota purposes', and that he intended to turn out films that would 'compare favourably with any from Hollywood and which would give the salesman something which he would be proud to handle'.[29] This may have been hot air, but a small selection of Hollywood actresses, notably Sally Blane and Asher's wife Laura La Plante, did come to Britain for Teddington productions. Warners also fostered British talent like comic Max Miller, who made a series of popular features at Teddington, and director Arthur Woods, whose short career included one of the first genuine British film noirs, *They Drive by Night*. Extensive advertising space was taken in the trade press, occasionally employing striking copy, like the tag line for *The Office Wife* (1934), a story in which a businessman (the homely Cecil Parker) is 'vamped' by his secretary (Dorothy Bouchier) on a visit to Amsterdam: 'Press the Button and She'll Take Down Whatever You Want!'[30] Warners' press books also indicate that the company was prepared to give every help to the showman in promoting its pictures. Even for a forty-nine-minute quickie like *As Good as New* (1933), Warners offered a litho six-sheet and hand-painted twelve and forty-eight-sheet posters, 24x30in 'framed photographic oils' in sets of four or six 'especially suited to front of cinema display', colour slides, large litho and hand-painted panels and cut-outs, as well as black-and-white stills in sizes up to 20x30in. They referred to this advertising as 'Patron pulling posters'. It indicated that the company was not content to let their British films rest on warehouse shelves.

The genuine achievements of the Hollywood distributor-producers in meeting their British quota obligations were acknowledged in a *Kinematograph Weekly* editorial:

> In the present effort of our important American houses to provide adequate quota pictures for their schedules one can see something more than a mere attitude of self-defence, of complying with an irksome Act of Parliament. Although the work already done might never have been put in motion except as a result of a legal obligation, experience has proved that there is real money in British pictures. Recent results of our own production units have emphasized the lesson. Quota pictures are good business – that is the lesson of today.[31]

Fox was rather slower to grasp the nettle of British production, continuing to commission films from some of the more prolific quota suppliers well beyond the autumn of 1932, when Fox-British leased the studios at Wembley.[32] Rachael Low may have been correct when she asserted that Fox's films were 'only made to comply with the law'; but without Fox's legal obligations, Laurence Olivier might not have made his screen debut, and Michael Powell might have been left scratching around for work instead of turning out his first five films.[33] Certainly, Edward Dryhurst thought Fox and Warners were unusually conscientious in their approach to the Quota Act.[34] The Wembley Studio was efficiently run by a Lancastrian accountant called Ernie Gartside. The documentarist Kay Mander, who joined the Fox publicity department in 1935, remembered the set-up at Wembley as 'very well organised – they worked six months a year, and they worked with two crews, and I think they had – if I remember rightly – three-week schedules'.[35] According to James Mason, Fox-British was keen to make pictures that 'were to be the very best they could turn out for the strictly limited budgets'.[36] The budgets, however, were a little more generous than those of the British independent producers who had to build their own profit margins into the price they charged American renters for their product. Fox were prepared to provide appropriate resources for promising young directors such as Bernard Vorhaus, for whose *Dark World* (1935) they probably had first-feature ambitions. The company brought over a number of directors from America, notably Albert Parker, who had been responsible for 'discovering' Rudolph Valentino and William Powell. Mason has insisted that Parker 'wanted to make a little masterpiece of each of his pictures' and had no desire to return to 'the Hollywood jungle'. Fox also nurtured British talent, including the celebrated production designer Carmen Dillon, who was assistant art director to Ralph Brinton.[37] Fox could not quite match Warners' publicity materials, but usually offered exhibitors a six-sheet poster, to go with its linen banners, coloured slides, sepia lobby cards and black-and-white stills.[38]

But in spite of the toil and ambition, Simon Rowson estimated that the American renters, as a group, lost £500,000 a year on their quota productions. Paramount, alone, claimed to lose £100,000 a year by complying with the Act.[39] However, these figures should be treated with caution. They are more a function of accounting procedures than the level of bookings for quota pictures. If a supporting feature was not booked at a flat rate, profit and loss depended on the percentage of the booking fee assigned to the second feature. This could be crucial to a British producer like Twickenham whose contacts with the renter entitled them to a share of the film's receipts. The creative accounting practices of the American firms could lead them to assigning only 2 or 3 per cent of gross on a double bill to the British picture that had been supplied as a booking inducement for the exhibitor (rather than the usual 10–20 per cent).[40] As Edward Dryhurst later complained:

> The fact is the distributors were only interested in getting their money back on the film, when they got the money back they stopped selling it. So . . . if you were relying on the sales to make you a profit, you were out of luck. They had no consideration at all for anybody except themselves.[41]

## Quota critics

> We want to find a way out of selling rotten apples.
>
> Leeds exhibitor, Arthur Cunningham[42]

Lawrence Napper has suggested that concerns about the quality of low-budget features only really surfaced in 1934, after the American market had been prised ajar by the success of a couple of more prestigious British offerings.[43] But, while it is true that the debate about quota quickies entered its most urgent phase in the mid-1930s as the exhibitor's quota reached 15 per cent and above, there is ample evidence of anxiety well before that time.[44] For example, as early as 19 February 1930, *The Times* reported:

> In recent months much criticism has been directed against the poor quality of British quota films. Steps are now being taken, by the exhibitor representatives on the Cinematograph Films Advisory Committee to draw up a workable scheme, under which quality will be a condition of eligibility for registration.

The first attempts to amend the Quota Act by introducing a quality test were made by a joint deputation to the Board of Trade by the CEA and the Federation of British Industries in 1929. The following July, the Liberal MP Geoffrey Mander (brother of actor-director Miles) attempted to amend the Act by introducing a minimum production cost of £12,000 for British productions. He argued that the distribution of British films was largely in the hands of American companies, which had a deliberate policy of facilitating the production of low-quality pictures that would undermine the reputation of the indigenous industry. The solution was the sort of strategy adopted in France and Germany – drastically to raise the quota to 50 per cent over four years in order to force the American companies to invest in making good films in Britain or risk a massive drop in profits.[45] Later in the same year, *The Bioscope* offered a critical judgment on the 118 British films trade shown during the year ending 30 September. Only 19 per cent were considered 'good', while 50 per cent were 'poor' or 'definitely bad'.[46] At the beginning of 1931, leading exhibitor, Oscar Deutsch, suggested that the general tendency of British films to be studio-bound and dialogue-heavy was particularly marked among the cheaper productions:

The Quota pictures made by small independent producers for American houses up to the present, do not seem to have, so far, been very well received. This is probably due to the very restricted prices offered in many cases by the American houses.[47]

The American renters were again the subject of criticism at the 1931 CEA Conference when the delegate from Leeds raised issues about their commitment to the production of quality British films.

The role of the American renters in commissioning and distributing substandard British product was again emphasised by the *The Bioscope*'s editor, W. H. Mooring, in his 1932 New Year address to readers, but he also indicated that the problem had largely being solved: 'The trashy quota film "invented" by certain American distributors is all but dead, and British exhibitors will do the rest.'[48] But three months later, concern was still being expressed by *Kinematograph Weekly*'s studio correspondent about the 'menace' of 'mediocre' British pictures from muddled and amateurish producers.[49] This issue was taken up in the *Daily Mail* the following day, and by Arthur Elton, a director of films for the Empire Marketing Board, who told the National Union of Students that 90 per cent of British films were 'bad' and were made solely to meet the quota.[50] The Federation of British Industries and the Trades Union Congress General Council presented a joint memorandum to the President of the Board of Trade suggesting practical ways (via an increased cost per foot of film for quota registration) to ensure 'the elimination of worthless films made especially in this country for quota purposes'.[51] At meetings of the CEA General Council, there was a motion condemning 'the methods adopted by certain foreign distributors as calculated and intentional evasions of the British Quota Act', and concern was again expressed about the marks given to unscreenable American-financed quota films in the organisation's own *Film Reports*. This time, however, the problem seemed to be that the marking was over-generous.[52]

The ratings given by the *CEA Film Report* became the prime 'impartial' indicators of quality in the debate about quota quickies, and some explanation of them is necessary. Rather confusingly, they used only a restricted range of the marking scale, and mixed judgments of cinematic worth with assessments of the suitability of films for the two positions on the double bill. Film producers interpreted their meaning as follows:

Under 7       a bad film
7.0–7.25    a second feature for small country cinemas
7.5–7.75    a first feature for small cinemas, and a possible second feature elsewhere
8–8.5         a first feature for most cinemas
8.75 +        films of the 'super' type.[53]

Condensed, formulaic and subjective, the ratings were a highly imperfect guide to quality. Even the cheapest and shoddiest of films seemed to score seven points out of twelve or better. George Smith and Maclean Rogers would later be proud to announce to the trade that the eleven films they made for Columbia and Radio in 1937 had averaged 7.5 marks from the *Report*.[54] BIP's featurette *Bill and Coo* (1931) somehow managed to clock up the same score despite the following assessment: 'This is a crude amateurish affair. The plot is negligible, the continuity non-existent, the dialogue very poor, the direction hopeless, the photography moderate, the humour doubtful.'[55] Moreover, even a score of 8.5 was no guarantee of bookability: BIP's film tran-

scription of George Bernard Shaw's *How He Lied to Her Husband* (1930) achieved this rating, but
was not thought to have much appeal beyond 'devotees of G.B.S.', and even they were 'not likely
to enthuse over it'.[56] When Shaw's film crossed the Atlantic, one New York newspaper described
it as 'the world's biggest flop'.[57] Nevertheless, the CEA ratings were given considerable credence
by all sections of the industry and went largely unchallenged in the deliberations on the future
of the Quota Act. Most importantly, they revealed 'a considerable difference in estimated value'
between quota films distributed by British companies (average score: 8) and those distributed by
the Americans (average score: 7).[58] This is not so surprising when one considers that the American firms were largely handling second features while the British renters were dealing predominantly in main attractions. The breakdown of scores for each American renter in the
calendar years 1934 and 1935 is given in Table 3.2 below.

**Table 3.2** *CEA Film Report* scores for quota films distributed by American renters in 1934 and
1935[59]

| US renter | Under 7 | 7–7.25 | 7.5–7.75 | 8+ |
|---|---|---|---|---|
| Columbia | 11 | 5 | 1 | — |
| Fox | 5 | 7 | 9 | 2 |
| MGM | 15 | 11 | 4 | — |
| Paramount | 8 | 13 | 8 | 1 |
| Radio | 7 | 13 | 8 | 2 |
| United Artists | — | — | 2 | 14 |
| Universal | 9 | 6 | 10 | 4 |
| WB–First National | 11 | 6 | 7 | 7 |

MGM and Columbia do predictably badly, while United Artists does predictably well. The more
surprising results are the relatively high numbers of reasonable films produced by Warner Bros.-
First National and Fox and commissioned or acquired by Radio and Universal. It should also
be noted that, in the same period the British renters Pathe and Equity were also responsible for
distributing some thoroughly bad films. In spite of its public assurance that all its productions
would be of 'high quality' and would reflect creditably on all concerned, Pathe handled four
quota films that scored less than seven points, while neither of Equity's two British pictures
could manage that mark.[60]

The *CEA Film Report* scores also suggested that the general standard of the quota pictures
handled by the American firms was declining. In the renter's quota year ending in March 1933,
only one-third of these films had scored less than 7.5, while 46 per cent had managed a
respectable 8 or over. Two years later, the proportion of those rated at less than 7.5 had increased
to two-thirds, and the percentage achieving the top marks had plummeted to 16.[61]

Exhibitors appeared to have quite different expectations of a supporting feature from newspaper critics and those involved at the more prestigious end of British production. Provincial

exhibitors' needs were satisfied by supporting features that would furnish a moderately entertaining introduction to the main feature, without attempting to upstage the costly star attraction. Films, in short, which knew their station. This was the tradition of supporting acts at the
music hall, and it was all most audiences really expected. 'B' films were there to provide a warm-
up to the main event. For example, *Kinematograph Weekly*, recommending Graham Cutts' adaptation of *Three Men in a Boat* (1933) as a 'useful supporting proposition', suggested that 'Within
its limitations, the film makes pleasant, innocuous entertainment and can be safely exploited on
the average two-feature programme'.[62] While a naturally adventurous director like Cutts may
have been frustrated, 'pleasant, innocuous entertainment' was really as much as the trade
demanded from a programmer. When something more than this was attempted, as, for instance
with John Baxter's *Doss House* (1933) or Brian Desmond Hurst's *The Tell Tale Heart* (1934), trade
reviewers were nervous of public reaction and offered more qualified endorsements than those
offered in the broadsheet press. So, in the case of *Doss House*, it was thought that, 'in spite of its
shortcomings, lifelike types, born of sound characterisation, are productive of sufficient interest
and entertainment to enable the film's novelty angles to get it over on the average two-feature
programme'.[63] The studio correspondents of the fan magazines were less conservative in their
recommendations. *Film Pictorial's* 'Nomad', for instance, encouraged readers to see *Doss House*
as a refreshing change from 'all the "bedroom" dramas and "society" pictures which the British
studios have pelted at us so persistently'.[64]

A refreshing change; John Baxter's *Doss House* (1933)

The internal enquiry conducted by the Board of Trade in 1933, in response to the well-orchestrated criticisms of the quality of low-budget British films, found that, in the previous year, less than 10 per cent of American-commissioned British films had cost more than one pound and five shillings (£1.25) per foot. Sixty of the eighty-three (77 per cent) had been produced for 15 shillings (75p) or less per foot. On the other hand, only fifteen out of seventy-three (21 per cent) British films not sponsored by American renters had cost this little to make. However, the relationship between production cost and 'quality' was by no means unproblematic. Overall, the Board of Trade rated a little under half of the American renters' quota films as 'good programme pictures', but they also concluded that some renters had higher standards than others. MGM failed to emerge smelling of roses, but even they looked good against Universal, who were condemned for acquiring only 'rubbish' to meet their quota obligations. More favourable comments were made on the efforts of United Artists and Paramount to distribute half-decent British product, while Fox, Radio and Warner Bros. were seen to occupy the middle ground. But here, too, there were differences: Warner Bros. spent more money on their films, but Fox's were thought to beat them for quality. Overall, the Board felt that there was no cause for alarm and that British films were making satisfactory progress.[65]

The Board's corporate view was not shared by all its advisors, as its most recent recruit, C. T. Cramp (General Secretary of the NUR), demonstrated in an inflammatory article in *Kinematograph Weekly*.[66] What is particularly interesting about Cramp's complaint about the quality of quota production is that 'quality' is not assessed on economic or cinematic criteria, but on moral ones:

> Our producers seem to have overlooked the fact that consciously or subconsciously every picture plays upon the minds of the patrons either for good or evil. Unfortunately, the greater number of feature films shown in the past have been definitely bad from the social, educational and cultural standpoints.

One does not need to scratch too far below the surface of arguments like this to find a vein of anti-Americanism. Cramp accuses British producers of 'slavishly following the American type of picture, chiefly based on stories of demoralised characters such as gangsters, etc'. Such 'depravity', he regrets, has worsened since the arrival of sound 'owing to the addition of suggestive words and slang in disagreeable twang peculiarly American'. Unsurprisingly, it is the American renters who take most of the blame for depressing the moral tone of British pictures and the morale of the industry:

> I am informed that certain renting houses fill their British quota by making or purchasing rubbishy or mediocre films . . . It may pay such renters to obtain pictures to put on the shelf, but indirectly the *morale* of the industry suffers from such action. Therefore it should be stopped – by law, if necessary.'[67]

*Kinematograph Weekly* quickly canvassed British producer, Basil Dean, for his view. After his unhappy experience with Radio Pictures, his response was predictable: 'The compulsory needs of American distributing firms in London have resulted in the making of scores of cheap indifferent quota offerings, which, under other circumstances, would not have been made at all.' Dean was quick to deny that he was 'anti-American', but felt it 'unreasonable to expect Americans to sell the British showman British films in preference to American ones'. The consequence of this folly had been that 'No British film, apparently, is too bad for quota purposes'. The prestige of the national cinema, he argued, was being lowered by 'the shoddy rubbish which is made for quota purposes on lines which actually put a premium on slapdash inefficiency'. The only reason such films got bookings and risked 'the active derision of audiences', he felt was 'the difficulty in getting better ones'.[68] There was a certain hypocrisy about these criticisms, coming as they did, from a man who was quite prepared to hire his facilities to an American renter like Fox, or to British independents to make 'shoddy rubbish' like *The Secret of the Loch*. But support for Dean's criticism was evident in the same issue of *Kinematograph Weekly*, with a showman from the East Midlands complaining about 'cheaply produced' and 'crude' quota films 'acquired by American concerns solely for the purpose of defeating the Quota Act and degrading British pictures'.

Because so few of the cheap quota films survive, it is difficult to assess the validity of the blanket criticism thrown at the quickies. However, if we examine a sample of trade reviews at the time of Dean's remarks, we find considerable support for the Board of Trade's view that British supporting features displayed the same 'curate's egg' properties as any other area of film production. Some pictures, like Warners' comedy-drama *Going Straight* (1933), clearly exasperated reviewers, who were weary of sitting through the accumulating hours of quota screentime. *Kinematograph Weekly*'s comments on John Rawlins' fifty-minute disaster are worth reproducing

'Fifty-minute disaster': Moira Lynd and a couple of old lags in *Going Straight* (1933)

in full, because they capture the depressing effect of the worst type of threadbare production, and convey the unmistakable impression of the ends of tethers being reached:

> Thin crook comedy-drama, entirely lacking in pep and originality. The flimsy story leaves the players to their own resources and their painful lack of experience lets the entertainment heavily down. Eligibility for quota purposes is the picture's only booking angle.
>
> **Story.** Peggy, attractive secretary to Lady Peckham, a nouveau riche Society woman, finds jobs for two ex-crooks, Hawkins and Macklin, as butler and chauffer, out of gratitude because they had saved her father from a criminal charge. Their misguided efforts to protect her from the attentions of John, son of the house, however, leads to their arrest on a charge of robbery, but their alibi paves the way to romance.
>
> **Acting.** Moira Lynd shows a little promise as Peggy, but Helen Farrers, Hal Waters, Gilbert Davis and Tracy Holmes, the supporting players are weak.
>
> **Production.** Comedy, drama and romance are mixed with little skill, and the entertainment, such as it is, is flat and stodgy. The technique suggests the amateur.
>
> **Settings and Photography.** The settings, mainly restricted to interiors, are cramped, and the lighting and photography are very ordinary.
>
> **Points of Appeal.** Quota.[69]

Clearly, the quality control at Warners left something to be desired. Normally, the trade press found something to recommend in a film, as *Kinematograph Weekly* did with the other five quota quickies reviewed in the same issue. Two of them, *Double Wedding* and *Too Many Wives* (both 1933), were also Warner offerings, and just scraped into 'the possible second-feature category', the former in 'halls that cater for the not too exacting patron'. Particular praise was given to Paramount's second or co-feature *Counsel's Opinion* (1933), which was described as offering 'diverting light entertainment of quality' and making 'a special appeal to good-class patrons'. One might have expected an avalanche of dismissive judgments over the four weeks that followed, because they were the last of the quota year, when the most perfunctory of the quickies were whisked into their trade shows. But on the contrary, positive reviews exceeded negative ones by eight to five:

## Negative

*Side Streets* (MGM), 'modest quota supporting entertainment for the unsophisticated'.[70]
*A Moorland Tragedy* (Equity), 'Only the most tolerant patron will accept this effort.'[71]
*Double Bluff* (Universal), 'has little to recommend it outside of its convenient length and eligibility for quota purposes'.[72]
*The Golden Cage* (MGM), 'Quota booking for uncritical audiences'.[73]
*Till the Bells Ring* (Bayley), 'Artless comedy sketch, restricted in scope and movement, and dated in technique'.[74]

## Positive

*Hiking with Mademoiselle* (International Productions), 'Good light supporting offering.'[75]
*The Crime at Blossoms* (Paramount), 'Useful two-feature programme proposition, particularly for good-class halls.'[76]

*I'm an Explosive* (Fox), 'The film provides forty-five minutes of good fun and represents capital supporting entertainment.'[77]
*That's My Wife* (British Lion), 'Capital comedy booking.'[78]
*Excess Baggage* (Radio), 'good team work'.[79]
*As Good as New* (Warners), 'The picture has feminine appeal, and this, together with its convenient length, makes it a quota supporting offering of possibilities.'[80]
*The Thirteenth Candle* (Warners), 'Useful quota offering.'[81]
*Matinee Idol* (United Artists), 'Safe, dramatic fare for the masses.'[82]

Trade reviews, while assessing the quality of a supporting picture, ultimately concentrated on its suitability for identifiable audiences. Occasionally, as was the case with Paramount's 'elaborated music-hall sketch' *Veteran of Waterloo* (1933), the best will in the world could not identify a viable market for a piece originally written by Conan Doyle for Henry Irving. Taste had moved on: 'The character of the entertainment is old-fashioned and the slender story not only lacks point, but is of little interest to the modern generation. . . . it is difficult to suggest an outlet as it stands.'[83] Conversely, some supporting films were able to overcome deficiencies of acting and treatment by making a clear appeal to a significant audience segment. For example, the theme of another Paramount programmer of 1933 *Purse Strings*, concerning a wife denied an allowance by a wealthy husband, was thought to be of sufficient interest to 'the weaker sex', and 'especially married women', to assure the film 'some measure of success as a second feature'.[84]

By May 1933 there was speculation that the government was about to respond to representations from the trade by inserting a quality clause into the quota legislation. One MP reportedly again evoked fears of damage being done to the nation's image overseas: 'It is not only that these films are of poor entertainment quality and thus entail anxiety to the exhibiter at home; but British films as a whole are being prejudiced abroad by being offered on the world's markets as representative of British film achievement.'[85] It must have been news to many a quickie merchant that his goods were being offered anywhere overseas. *Kinematograph Weekly*, a champion of the Quota Act, was sceptical about the effectiveness of any attempt to ensure quality entertainment by specifying a minimum cost for quota films: 'Whether the expenditure of a given sum of money on production means a box-office attraction is very much open to question. . . . Quality, in fact, cannot be estimated in advance, nor can it be guaranteed by the spending of money.'[86] As the periodical later made clear, what it called for was not legislative change, but the voluntary exercise of responsibility: 'What we really want is a change of heart, and a genuine attempt to fulfil obligations honourably and honestly.'[87]

## Life is cheap in Chelsea

The criticisms in the article were directed to quota quickies generally and we wish to make it quite clear that we had no intention of casting any reflection either on Mr Sidney Morgan or the film *Chelsea Life*.

A *Picturegoer* apology[88]

Making a picture with the minimum of coverage: Louis Hayward shows how it's done in *Chelsea Life* (1933)

*Picturegoer's* studio correspondent, E. G. Cousins, took the debate further by reporting, in some detail, on the making of a Paramount quickie, *Chelsea Life* (1933), at the British and Dominions Studio. The report, titled 'The Crime of the Quota Quickies', was prefaced by one of Cousins' typically sardonic descriptions of this genre of pictures:

> Films made in a hurry and much too cheaply, for an American distributing company to offer for sale, in order to comply with the law of the land. These are made by 'independent' companies – so called, presumably, because they can't afford to be independent. Once the distributing company has bought them, its responsibility – to the public as well as to the law, apparently – is at an end. It doesn't care whether they're seen or not.[89]

These were brave, and possibly injudicious, words for a journalist dependent on studio access, but Cousins pressed fearlessly on to describe the making of Sidney Morgan's film, noting that it was unlikely to be seen in the West End of London, but might go to 'a few small provincial theatres':

> Hurry is the operative word. A six-reel picture, it will have to be made in eight days. This means that dozens of shots a day must be taken. Needless to say, Morgan has to have everything cut and

dried before he goes on to the floor. There is no time for reconsideration, for hesitation, for retakes. In fact, he has earned the title of 'One-shot Morgan'. He is no slave-driver, but his tremendous enthusiasm carries everybody with him. . . . All the same, it isn't fair – to director, cameraman, players, audiences, or to the reputation of British films. . . . no one can make the best British films under those conditions. However, it certainly won't be for want of trying.[90]

Before enthusing about the comeliness of some of the bit players, Cousins offered praise to the leading actors, Louis Hayward and Molly Johnson, and the cinematographer, Henry Harris, hoping possibly to escape recriminations from the studio. He hoped in vain. His editor was obliged to run a clarification of the article's intentions, doubtless in response to strong protestations from studio and film-maker:

> It was not intended to convey the impression that the film *Chelsea Life* directed by Mr Sidney Morgan, was made by an independent company or that it had to be made cheaply. *Chelsea Life* was, of course, made for British and Dominions. Twenty thousand feet of negative were used for this 6,000-ft film and many scenes were shot four or five times. We understand that speedier production was obtained by Mr Morgan's system of giving all artists their script many days in advance and by rehearsing all the principals in their parts before bringing them to the studio.[91]

The film never played the West End, and they probably never saw it in Chelsea.
   Undaunted, Cousins was on the case of the 'quota scandal' again six months later:

> In the last few weeks we have had at trade and press shows a minor deluge of new English-made talkies and the standard of a great many of them makes one wonder if the authorities should not seriously consider if the time has arrived for the revision of the Quota Act in the direction of a Quality Clause.[92]

In August, Cousins again informed *Picturegoer's* readership that the quota quickie had 'served its purpose' and 'must go'.[93] However, he took a discriminating approach to the new breed of low-budget directors, singling out Bernard Vorhaus and John Baxter as 'the most important directorial finds of the past year'.[94] Both film-makers exemplified Cousins' preference for an authorial approach to production for which Poverty Row production offered the opportunity.
   Disquiet about the quality of quota films also surfaced in other fan magazines. In June 1934, the usually patriotic *Film Weekly* decided it was time for 'plain speaking' about 'inferior British pictures which have been produced, not to stand on their own merits as entertainment, but to enable some American film company to fulfil its legal obligations'. The British film business should no longer have to bear 'with great fortitude' the burden of these films, and it was time for filmgoers to voice their disapproval and force reform.[95] The outburst may finally have been provoked by the news carried in the same issue that one of the acting luminaries of low-budget production, Henry Kendall, was 'fed up to his aristocratic back teeth with some of the films in which he has appeared during the past two years' and had decided 'to eschew quota quickies from now on'.[96]

*Film Weekly* would also have been aware of the annual report of the CEA, which had revealed that complaints about the effect of the quota on film quality had 'passed unheeded' by the Board of Trade but would be renewed. The report concluded that unless something was done about quota quickies, 'the subject is bound to be one of major importance to the industry within a comparatively short time'.[97] One must presume that the crisis was likely to be provoked by the incremental rise in the quota percentage. Perhaps the most revealing thing about the *CEA Report* is the exclusiveness of the blame placed on the US renters. No criticism is made directly of the British production units for churning out substandard wares or of the restrictive distribution practices of the major British film companies. The CEA General Council took the cudgel to quota quickies again at its annual conference, where strong demands were made for a nationwide survey of exhibitor opinion on the issue.[98] It managed to get a question asked in Parliament about the quality of quota productions, and followed it up with yet another deputation to the Board of Trade to seek reform of the Quota Act.[99] The delegation was cordially received by the Board, but tangible results were hard to spot.[100] Undeterred, the CEA continued to lobby Tory MPs and, by the close of the year, had succeeded in gaining the support of the Films Advisory Committee, which joined in pressing for the amendment of the Quota Act to discourage the low-quality film.[101]

Unfortunately, the clamour of the small exhibitors for better, and therefore more expensive, pictures took little account of the economics of film production and renting. By and large, the making of British films was a loss-making activity. While the American firms could absorb their losses from quota pictures, thanks to the income generated by their core business, the British companies did not have the same luxury. John Maxwell, whose BIP production company was almost the only one to make a modest profit, could state that; 'The margin of receipts over cost at present got by the purely British producing companies is narrow, very narrow indeed. Indeed, I am safe in saying that very few of these companies' pictures show any profit.'[102] By 1936, something close to £4 million was being invested in indigenous production, although the domestic market for British films was really worth no more than £2.5–3 million per annum. There were around 200 films competing for a slice. The lion's share went to the hundred-or-so pictures distributed by British renters, but at an average cost of £20,000, their prospects of profitability were decidedly shaky. The proliferation of cinemas and the common practice of changing double-feature programmes twice per week meant that too many pictures were chasing too little box-office revenue.[103] Expensive productions chasing the pot of gold of £100,000 made by four or five British films annually were always likely to lose money, even with additional income from overseas sales. Paradoxically, then, the cheap 'quickies', so associated with the American renters, perhaps should have been important to British renting houses as low-risk investments to offset higher-risk ventures. The American renters, after all, were offering Hollywood pictures that had often already gone into profit in their home market. This remains one of many curious anomalies in the unstable and precarious film economy of the 1930s. At the same time that cheap quota pictures were receiving vilification out of all proportion to their deleterious effects on the cinema trade, more expensive productions were being over-praised and 'hyped' to an extent that would prove ruinous to the production sector by 1937.

At New Year 1935, however, the bubble was yet to burst. *The Cinema* was typically upbeat. Its studio correspondent welcomed the 'overwhelming improvement in British pictures' and asserted that there was 'scarcely an exhibitor of consequence now who does not readily exceed his quota by as many as ten or fifteen features a year'. The euphoria even extended to the better productions of the quickie studios and the director of the surprise hit, *Badger's Green*: 'Men like Adrian Brunel, working frequently under difficulties not met in the major companies, have generally succeeded in delivering a surprisingly high standard of product.'[104]

However, beneath the sunny rhetoric, support for the Quota Act among the film press was rapidly beginning to haemorrhage. Only ten days later, the same trade paper lost patience and printed an open letter to 'Quota Quickie Purveyors', advising them that, unless they reformed their practices, legislative change was inevitable:

> The quota quickie, always bad film art, has now become short-sighted commercial policy. There is no point blaming the Quota Act which, in our opinion, is an extraordinarily clever piece of legislation considering the complexity of the problem with which it was called upon to deal. The Board of Trade was probably wise in not including a 'quality clause', . . . but if the spate of quickies continues, the Board will have a certain excuse for refusing to maintain the status quo. Yet the only alteration that it can conceivably make in order to see that the good name of British production shall not be 'let down' by inferior product is a clause specifying minimum expenditure.
>
> It will be no use complaining that this will not necessarily result in good films, for the obvious retort is that its absence has resulted in a good many bad ones. Would it not be commercially wiser for the film industry to make a good job of setting its own house in order by sweeping out the quota quickies once and for all, instead of allowing the law to make a bad job of it?[105]

The law, however, remained intransigent, and the Board of Trade finally issued a statement in March 1935 to the effect that it had no intention of amending the Quota Act before its expiry in 1938.[106] The response of the independent exhibitors was predictable. In May, a front-page headline in *Today's Cinema* declared: 'War on Quota Quickies: CEA Organises Militant Action'.[107] The *Daily Mail*, ever the friend of the small businessman, reported that 'Thousands of cinema owners are in revolt'.[108]

Among the fan magazines, *Film Weekly* was already calling for repeal of the Quota Act, but *Picturegoer* maintained its support for legislation which had 'very materially helped to build up the British industry to its present healthier state', and warned that 'The invalid who throws away his crutches too soon is asking for trouble.'[109] The magazine's attitude towards low-budget pictures was to treat them strictly on their merits, and it cited examples of inexpensive films that had achieved a 'very high level of quality', including *Badger's Green* and Michael Powell's *Something Always Happens* (1934):

> *Picturegoer* has certainly never attempted to conceal its dislike of 'Quota Quickies' – the rubbishy films turned out merely to fulfil American distributing companies' obligations under the Act. But the fact remains that these quickies are not by any means invariably the worst British films to be seen . . . It is the 'mammoth super-productions' on which, not for lack of money but for lack of kinematic sense, we most frequently fall down.[110]

But within weeks, the magazine seemed to be having second thoughts about dispensing with crutches. A reader from Salford had written in complaining that the quota legislation was forc-

ing viewers to substitute patriotism for enjoyment in tolerating inferior British supporting features. In an editorial unequivocally titled 'Quota Quickies Must Go', *Picturegoer* was moved to
declare this an intolerable situation, even though it felt that the film in question was 'not as bad
as all that'. Recanting its support for the 'useless' Quota Act, it called for the legislation to be
'tightened up and generally revised' because the only beneficiaries now appeared to be the
American renters 'who are thus allowed to create a falsely low standard of British production'.[111]

## A change of heart

> More and more American producing companies are realising that 'quota quickies' are not enhanc-
> ing their reputation with British audiences, and are making plans to produce British films worthy
> of their sponsors.[112]

The American renters were already beginning to appreciate the damage that their British product was doing to them, and developing a more serious attitude towards their quota obligations.
As early as the spring of 1934, Warners' British boss, Irving Asher, returned from a visit to his
Hollywood head office with new instructions. More money was to be spent on Teddington's
productions, and by the time John Maxwell was making his comments about unwanted British

Upgrading quality: Ian Hunter (right) and John Singer in *Something Always Happens* (1934)

Gothic ghastliness: Molly Lamont in the clutches of Basil Sidney in *The Third Clue* (1934)

films, Asher had already instigated the new policy on *No Escape*, *The Office Wife* and *Something Always Happens* (all 1934). They were to have bigger casts with prominent actors in the leading roles, more location work and generally higher production values.[113] After another visit to head office in the spring of 1935, Asher declared the quota quickie dead as far as Teddington was concerned – by which he probably meant that his studio would continue to make supporting features, but would spend more on them.[114] His current production *Crime Unlimited* (1935) was a case in point, with sixty speaking parts and fifty sets, it was said to be 'comparable with the best production quality of Hollywood in entertainment values'.[115] Starring Lilli Palmer as a Russian girl and Esmond Knight as a Scotland Yard detective, it was enthusiastically received on its release as a 'vigorous melodrama on a spectacular scale' with 'the utmost in romance and thrills'.[116] But it was not unusual for Teddington's big strides forward to be followed by long slides back. Within a year of E. G. Cousins announcing that Warner Bros. had 'done with quickies', was also complaining about their 'habit of yelling about making super-films at Teddington, and then not doing it'.[117] But at least Warners had invested heavily in improving their studio facilities.

Fox, too, were letting it be known that they were increasing their production values. Albert Parker's *The Third Clue* (1934) was announced as 'a production on a big scale'. The standard two-week shooting schedule for the quickie had been doubled, and seventeen sets had been constructed. The picture, originally titled *The Shakespeare Murders*, was clearly meant to be a really

British film, with location filming near the Houses of Parliament.[118] Indeed, John Barrow, Fox's Production Manager, would later confirm a 'definite policy of giving a thoroughly British flavour to our work'.[119] This entailed appealing not only to London, but to provincial audiences as well. Fox had tried to make *Old Roses*, their latest production, 'essentially English in spirit, and yet of a wider interest by virtue of its human appeal'.[120] The film did not reach the box-office heights expected, but Fox's *The Riverside Murder* (1935) was a considerable hit with well over 1,000 bookings.[121] In October 1934, Fox had moved into the refurbished studios at Wembley, which would become the home of their quota productions. The company's MD, Walter Hutchinson, was conscious that if standards were raised, a market in the USA might be opened up and Australia was also identified as an important potential contributor to profits.[122] A year later, Fox productions like *Late Extra* and *Twice Branded* (both featuring a young James Mason) were being very well received by the trade press.[123] *Picturegoer* could report that, although Fox-British were yet to 'set the Thames on fire', they were 'certainly putting a little more money and care into their product than was the case with British branches of American companies a few years ago'.[124]

With Warners and Fox showing the way, even the most recalcitrant of American renters were coming to heel by 1935. With the quota percentage rising, they could no longer afford simply to write off their British films as a loss. Under the heading 'Good News', E. G. Cousins reported that MGM 'intend to pay a little more attention to their British-made films'. He went on to comment,

> This is a New Year resolution that will please everybody (almost) because the kind of films that M–G–M have been in the habit of buying from anywhere and anyone and flogging on the screen to satisfy the letter of the Quota Act was doing very little good to the name of M–G–M or the reputation of British films in general.[125]

The previous July, the company's vice-president, Louis Mayer had given a press conference at London's Savoy Hotel in which he condemned every quota quickie as another nail hammered into the coffin of the trade; and assured his listeners that MGM was ready to send over a production unit to work in England, possibly at Elstree.[126] When MGM finally announced, a year later, that it was to produce quality first features in Britain, *Film Weekly* popped a Champagne cork in its editorial and looked forward to 'the final doom of the "quota" picture, that wretched, bastard production', which had succeeded only in bringing 'unimaginable boredom' to filmgoers: 'One by one, the big American film companies are going off the quota standard, and making arrangements for the production in England of important pictures, worthy of their reputations.'[127] Universal set up its own studios at Sound City (Shepperton), declaring that its pictures were to be 'of such a box-office quality that they will be released throughout the world'.[128] Radio was rather slower to change, having had considerable success with the pictures that it commissioned from Twickenham. When Hagen went upmarket, Radio relied mainly on the quota factory at Walton-on-Thames, where George Smith and Randall Faye kept up a steady supply to the renter. But by the summer of 1936, Radio, too, was spending a little more and getting films from John Stafford like the treasure-seeking adventure *Wings over Africa* and the Gene Gerrard musical *Wake Up Famous*. Both enjoyed a high percentage of bookings as first features.

However, Columbia remained relatively cautious in its commissioning of quota pictures. Edgar Wallace adaptations were usually a sure bet, and the company had its greatest British success with *The Feathered Serpent* in 1934.[129] Thereafter, it reverted to a reliance on quota films made in the dominions.

There were four principal reasons for the policy shift of the US distributors:

1. As the number of films required by the quota rose, more money had to be invested, and British production became a more significant percentage of the American companies' business, and a larger factor in their profitability. It became more of a problem to leave the films on the shelf.
2. The possibility of making better films presented itself as British production houses became more experienced, and the increasing number of competent technicians and directors in British studios was boosted by skilled European migrants.
3. Films made by major British producers such as Balcon and Korda proved that there was a substantial home market and an export potential for the right kind of indigenous product.
4. As the major circuits expanded and the independent cinemas began to be squeezed, the American companies realised that they would have to sharpen up their act and supply quota films that the British circuits were prepared to handle.

It is now time to see just what all the fuss was about by examining the quota quickie itself in more detail.

## Notes

1.  *The Cinema*, 3 April 1935, p. 5.
2.  Quoted in Belfrage, *All Is Grist*, p. 107.
3.  John Grierson, 'The Film Situation', *London Mercury*, September 1937, pp. 459–63.
4.  Cmd. 5320: Memorandum of the Association of Cine-Technicians.
5.  Rachael Low, *The History of the British Film, 1929–1939* (London: Allen and Unwin, 1985), pp. 34–5.
6.  Ibid., pp. 150–4. Radio distributed one of Dean's most critically praised supporting features, *The Impassive Footman* (1932).
7.  Cmd. 5320: Memorandum of the Kinematograph Renters Society, and by Mr J. Maxwell on behalf of the KRS. MGM's Sam Eckman maintained that he had repeatedly tried to persuade some of the top British producers to allow his company to distribute their pictures. Ibid., p. 957.
8.  *The Cinema*, 7 March 1934, p. 10. Empire-made films have not been included in the Filmography of this book.
9.  Cmd. 5320: 91, evidence from R. D. Fennelly.
10.  Roy Boulting, interview with Alan Burton, 1998.
11.  Low, *The History of the British Film, 1929–1939*, p. 194.
12.  *Kinematograph Weekly*, 31 March 1932, p. 41.
13.  Cmd. 5320: 1084.
14.  *Finsbury Park Astorian* vol. 2 no. 3, 6 July 1931.
15.  For example, *The Bioscope* appeared fully to endorse Paramount's press release. 'Kane Outlines Paramount British Plans', 18 August 1931, p. 17. Even Michael Balcon conceded that Paramount

did make a genuine effort to 'comply with the Act in the proper spirit'. *Michael Balcon Presents. . . A Lifetime of British Films* (London: Hutchinson, 1969), p. 93.

16.  *Picture Show*, 15 August 1931.

17.  *CEA Film Report*, 21 March 1931. So much for the press book's claim that the picture was 'filmed almost exclusively in the open air, with lovely Cornish scenery'. Star C. Aubrey Smith was apparently given 'not much to do'.

18.  Cmd. 5320: 966–8, 1031,1065.

19.  Richard Norton was an aristocratic ex-Guards officer who had previously arranged quota films for United Artists at Walton and Isleworth. United Artists distributed the Korda films made at the B&D Studios after Norton joined the board in 1933.

20.  Low, *The History of the British Film, 1929–1939*, p. 188.

21.  Cmd. 5320: 1057.

22.  'Warners' £200,000 for British Production', *The Bioscope*, 2 September 1931, p. 16. The key studio personnel at Teddington were Irving Asher (chief executive), Harry Lorraine (studio manager), George Groves (in charge of recording), Willard Vananger (chief cameraman), George Ayre (publicity director), William McGann and John Daumery (directors).

23.  'Teddington Makes for World', *Kinematograph Weekly*, 13 January 1938, p. 155. The estimated total spend given in evidence to the Moyne Committee in 1936 was almost £1 million. Cmd. 5320: 1087.

24.  Other British writers employed by Warners included Roland Pertwee, John Hastings Turner, Frank Launder, Sidney Gilliat and Reginald Purdell.

25.  'There are so many twists, thrills and surprises that the interest is always held, and there is no time to dwell upon the improbabilities.' *Kinematograph Weekly*, 7 January 1932, p. 73. *The Bioscope*, 6 January 1932, p. 79.

26.  *Film Weekly*, 16 January 1932, p. 4.

27.  *Kinematograph Weekly*, 14 January 1932.

28.  For example, *Kinematograph Weekly*, 31 March 1932, p. 37. The film played as support to *The Expert* at London's New Gallery cinema and was booked by three cinemas in Leicester.

29.  *Kinematograph Weekly*, 3 December 1931, p. 20. Asher's first job with Warners in Hollywood was as a property boy. He rose to unit production manager before leaving to gain experience with Universal and Paramount and then British Lion, where he worked alongside Edgar Wallace. When the talkies arrived he returned to Warners in Hollywood to learn all he could about the new medium, and was subsequently entrusted with setting up Warners' British operation. He supervised an astonishing twenty-six pictures in the first year of operation on just two sound stages. Oliver Baldwin 'These People Make British Pictures: Irving Asher', *Picturegoer*, 12 August 1939, pp. 12, 13, 32.

30.  *Kinematograph Weekly*, 9 August 1934.

31.  *Kinematograph Weekly*, 1 October 1931.

32.  George Smith continued to make films for Fox at Nettlefold Studios. Other units produced for Fox at Sound City and Cricklewood.

33.  Low, *The History of the British Film, 1929–1939*, p. 187. She estimates that Fox were spending around £130,000 per year on British production.

34.  Edward Dryhurst, *Gilt Off the Gingerbread*, (London: Bachman & Turner, 1987) p. 191.

35.   Interview with Kay Mander, BECTU Oral History Project, Interview 57, 28 September 1998.

36.   James Mason, *Before I Forget* (London: Sphere, 1982), p. 118.

37.   The conservative Ernie Gartside was displeased that she wore trousers on the set. Kay Mander interview.

38.   MGM could supply twelve- and six-sheet posters, linen banner, advertising slide and set of stills to promote its popular Tod Slaughter films. Paramount's press books were slightly more modest, but offered six- and twelve-sheet posters, 36x14in 'artistic insert cards', coloured and black-and-white lobby cards as standard issue. But the most elaborate campaigns were usually supplied by Radio, including a full range of posters up to forty-eight-sheet, large cut-outs, banners, colour lobby cards and black-and-white stills.

39.   Low, *The History of the British Film, 1929–1939*, p. 39.

40.   Cmd. 5320: 624.

41.   Edward Dryhurst interview, BECTU Oral History Project, Interview 36, 26 April 1988.

42.   *Kinematograph Weekly*, 23 April 1936, p. 10.

43.   Lawrence Napper, 'British Scenes and British Humour: "Quota Quickies" in the 1930s', unpublished MA thesis, University of East Anglia, 1994, p. 52

44.   Although it should be noted that there was no criticism of quota quickies in the 1931 CEA Report, only thanks for British producers supplying bookable product at a time of shortfall in Hollywood supply. *The Bioscope*, 4 March 1931, p. 31.

45.   Details of the Parliamentary campaign are supplied in Low, *The History of the British Film, 1929–1939*, p. 36.

46.   *The Bioscope*, 5 November 1930. However, the same paper had earlier repudiated suggestions that American renters continued to finance bad British pictures as a deliberate policy. Editorial, 6 August 1930, p. 15.

47.   *Kinematograph Weekly*, 8 January 1931, p. 102.

48.   *The Bioscope*, 6 January 1932, p. 36.

49.   *Kinematograph Weekly*, 31 March 1932, p. 48.

50.   *Kinematograph Weekly*, 7 April 1932, p. 25.

51.   *Kinematograph Weekly*, 28 April 1932, p. 21.

52.   *Kinematograph Weekly*, 10 November 1932, p. 36, and 20 October 1932, p. 47.

53.   Cmd. 5320: 51

54.   *Kinematograph Weekly*, 13 January 1938, p. 146. Peter Maclean Rogers was one of the most prolific and longest-serving directors working in British second-feature production. During the silent film period, he worked in a variety of departments, including publicity and editing. As a scriptwriter in the early days of sound, he adapted the Whitehall farces *Rookery Nook* and *Tons of Money*, before directing a series of Sidney Howard comedies. Rogers formed a commercially successful partnership with producer George Smith, and although many of their pictures plumbed the depths of quota production, some were considerable hits.

55.   *CEA Film Report*, 1 August 1931.

56.   *CEA Film Report*, 17 January 1931.

57.   Donald P. Costello, *The Serpent's Eye: Shaw and the Cinema* (Notre Dame, IN: University of Notre Dame, 1965), p. 39. The trade advertisements, on the other hand, had hailed the film as the 'Biggest Scoop in the History of the Screen', claiming that this 'Bernard Shaw talkie will not only

bring thousands to your cinemas, but will help to make them regular patrons through their being able to experience a new joy in talking pictures'. *Kinematograph Weekly*, 4 December 1930.

58. Cmd. 5320: 51.

59. Adapted from data supplied in Cmd. 5320: Appendix VI to first day of evidence.

60. Ibid., 'Good quality British productions', insisted Pathe's managing director, W. J. Gell, 'besides earning dividends, add prestige and make for good will between renter and exhibitor.' *Kinematograph Weekly*, 24 May 1934, p. 25.

61. Radio and Fox had each registered seven well-liked films in 1932–3, while Universal had been responsible for the majority of films falling well below the threshold of acceptability. Cmd.5320: Appendix VI.

62. *Kinematograph Weekly*, 1 June 1933.

63. *Kinematograph Weekly*, 29 June 1933.

64. *Film Pictorial*, 12 August 1933, p. 15.

65. Public Records Office, BT64/97.

66. 'Film Quality under the Quota', *Kinematograph Weekly*, 9 March 1933, p. 4.

67. For a fuller discussion of anti-American sentiments in the cinema debates of the period see Peter Stead, 'Hollywood's Message for the World: The British Response in the Nineteen Thirties', *Historical Journal of Film, Radio & Television* vol. 1 no. 1, 1981, pp. 19–32.

68. 'More British Films – but Good Ones', *Kinematograph Weekly*, 30 March 1933, p. 4. Dean's solution was to call for a larger supply of quality British films, but this rather elided the crucial issue of the restrictive distribution practices of the major British producers with their own cinema chains. As Dean implicitly acknowledged, Gaumont-British and BIP productions were simply not available as first-run attractions to the vast majority of exhibitors.

69. *Kinematograph Weekly*, 9 March 1933.

70. *Kinematograph Weekly*, 16 March 1933.

71. Ibid.

72. *Kinematograph Weekly*, 30 March 1933.

73. *Kinematograph Weekly*, 6 April 1933.

74. Ibid.

75. *Kinematograph Weekly*, 16 March 1933.

76. Ibid.

77. *Kinematograph Weekly*, 23 March 1933.

78. *Kinematograph Weekly*, 30 March 1933.

79. Ibid.

80. Ibid.

81. Ibid.

82. *Kinematograph Weekly*, 6 April 1933.

83. *Kinematograph Weekly*, 13 July 1933.

84. *Kinematograph Weekly*, 20 July 1933.

85. *Kinematograph Weekly*, 4 May 1933.

86. *Kinematograph Weekly*, 20 July 1933, p. 4. See also the editorial 'Don't Meddle with the Quota', *Kinematograph Weekly*, 8 February 1934, p. 4.

87. *Kinematograph Weekly*, 28 June 1934, p. 4.

88.  *Picturegoer*, 21 October 1933, p. 5.

89.  *Picturegoer*, 9 September 1933.

90.  Ibid. Ironically, Sidney Morgan had been one of the first advocates of a British film quota. A Londoner, he began his career as a playwright in 1911 and entered the film industry just before World War I, directing a string of silent pictures. With the arrival of sound and the quota, he applied himself to making supporting features for Paramount. He applied himself so well that he became the Hon. Sec. of the British Association of Film Directors.

91.  *Picturegoer*, 21 October 1933, p. 5.

92.  *Picturegoer*, 14 April 1934.

93.  'Quota Quickies Must Go', *Picturegoer*, 4 August 1934.

94.  *Picturegoer*, 14 April 1934.

95.  *Film Weekly*, 29 June 1934, p. 3.

96.  Ibid., p. 11.

97.  *Kinematograph Weekly*, 15 March 1934, p. 11.

98.  *Kinematograph Weekly*, 14 June 1934.

99.  *Kinematograph Weekly*, 5 July 1934, p. 1, and 19 July 1934, p. 7.

100.  *Kinematograph Weekly*, 4 October 1934.

101.  *Kinematograph Weekly*, 27 December 1934, p. 3.

102.  Cmd. 5320: Memorandum on behalf of the KRS. The vertically integrated Gaumont-British relied on income from film exhibition to cover its production losses when its pictures struggled to gain American distribution.

103.  See *Kinematograph Weekly*, 5 September 1935, p. 19, and Rowson's discussion of the domestic market in Cmd. 5320: 1313.

104.  *The Cinema*, 2 January 1935, p. 143.

105.  *Today's Cinema*, 12 January 1935, p. 3.

106.  *Kinematograph Weekly*, 21 March 1935, p. 3.

107.  *Today's Cinema*, 11 May 1935, p. 1. The article detailed complaints from London and Home Counties exhibitors about the falling standard of quota quickies, singling out colonial product for particular criticism. Ten days later, another front-page headline announced: 'Quota: Exhibitors': Leeds Press for Abolition of Exhibition Clauses: Rising Protest against "Quickies".'

108.  *Daily Mail*, 12 June 1935.

109.  *Picturegoer*, 29 June 1935, p. 5.

110.  Ibid.

111.  *Picturegoer*, 17 August 1935, p. 5.

112.  *Picturegoer*, 9 November 1935, p. 5.

113.  *Kinematograph Weekly*, 14 June 1934. Among the casts were Cecil Parker, Chili Bouchier and Ian Hunter, who was quickly offered a Hollywood contract.

114.  *Kinematograph Weekly*, 18 April 1935, p. 43.

115.  *Kinematograph Weekly*, 8 May 1935, p. 12.

116.  *Picturegoer*, 25 January 1936, p. 25. Not surprisingly, it was one of the most heavily booked supporting features in Leicester.

117.  *Picturegoer*, 25 January 1936, p. 10, and 17 October 1936, p. 21.

118.  'Fox British Production Progress', *Kinematograph Weekly*, 23 August 1934, p. 40.

119.  *Kinematograph Weekly*, 25 April 1935, p. 33.

120.  Ibid.

121.  *Kinematograph Weekly*, 15 August 1935, p. 13.

122.  'Quality from Fox British', W. J. Hutchinson, *Kinematograph Weekly*, 10 January 1935, p. 72.

123.  See, for example, *Kinematograph Weekly*, 9 January 1936, p. 30.

124.  *Picturegoer*, 7 March 1936, p. 13.

125.  *Picturegoer*, 2 February 1935, p. 29.

126.  'MGM Plans British Production', *Kinematograph Weekly*, 2 August 1934, p. 3.

127.  *Film Weekly*, 30 November 1935, p. 3.

128.  *Kinematograph Weekly*, 9 January 1936, p. 114.

129.  *Kinematograph Weekly*, 23 January 1935, p. 41.

# 4

# Quota Entertainments

The kind of film that earned 'Quota' its quotes.

Review of MGM's The Temperance Fete (1932)[1]

The conventional wisdom in the cinema trade, that the surest way to box-office success was cheerful entertainment, was certainly older than the Quota Act. Edward Wood was articulating the importance of the happy ending in *Picture Show* before the Act was drafted:

> There is not the slightest doubt that the vast majority of picture-goers visit the cinema to be entertained. They would rather be amused than instructed, and they will not stand being preached at. Their chief motive in going to the cinema is to get away from the worries and troubles of everyday life. . . . In selecting a programme the wise exhibitor will avoid booking those stark tragedies that are merely harrowing. Such a picture may be a masterpiece from an artistic standpoint, but I am convinced the general public do not want it. Such pictures may well be left to the highbrows to whom nothing is art except that which portrays the negation of human happiness.[2]

This populist view was largely unaffected by the operation of the quota legislation. Arthur Dent of BIP (Associated British) put it even more starkly ten years later when he argued that films must appeal to 'tired brains': 'The masses do not change: they still go to the kinema for relaxation. A picture which demands too much mental exertion does not give them the relaxation they demand, and is therefore a failure.'[3] Dent agreed with Howard S. Cullman of New York's Roxy Cinema that 'thinking was the direct antithesis of entertainment'; and that mass entertainment should 'cause emotional excitation of some sort, but this emotional content must be set forth in the clearest kind of black and white'.[4]

When these ideas were put into practice – as they were in the formulaic 'low' comedies of BIP, starring Leslie Fuller or Ernie Lotinga – the easy distinction between quality and 'quota' begins to break down. Although made by one of the 'quality' studios, usually as first features, they were generically and in their address to audiences little different from 'quota comedies'. Differences of genre, discourse, treatment and modes of address were more likely to be used to target stratified classes of audience than to identify an appropriate position in the cinema programme. What then was it that distinguished those British films that were consigned to the bottom of the bill from those destined for the top? It was certainly not that quality films aspired to art, while 'quota' pictures settled for entertainment. Rather, it was a matter of star appeal and production values. Apart from a small minority of films that aspired to significant American distribution, British cinema in the 1930s was an indigenous cinema, made for a local audience and indexing its social divisions. This does not mean that quota quickies were designed exclusively for those in the lower strata of the nation's class hierarchy, or the upper reaches of its age pyramid. Nor were quota quickies some inferior race of films that could be easily distinguished, by their appearance, from superior brethren. As a production category, the quota quickie was highly permeable at its margins; and viewed today, its films may be difficult for the untrained eye to distinguish from more illustrious products. Quota quickies were simply standard British films made more cheaply and featuring less attractive stars, or stars of unproven box-office appeal.

The vast majority of supporting features over 3,000 feet in length were fiction films. Actuality film-making was largely confined to 'shorts', and did not (automatically) count towards the renter's or exhibitor's quota – although a short travelogue could sometimes be turned into a quota featurette by grafting on an unconvincing storyline. Exclusive's *Smuggler's Harvest* is an appropriately titled example. D. F. Cantley and John R. Phipps smuggled a criminal plot into their 1938 documentary of Cornish life and reaped a quota harvest. The proudly British production company, Pro Patria, specialised in what would now be termed 'docu-dramas', illustrating some valued aspect of national character or culture. Its silent featurette *The Woodpigeon Patrol* (1930), for instance, was an animated recruiting poster for the Boy Scouts filmed on location in Kent and featuring the illustrious Baden-Powell. From the contemporary description, the film hardly qualifies as entertainment by modern standards, but its lengthy depictions of everyday Scouting activities won indulgent praise from *The Bioscope's* critic, 'though the story is slight, and the adventures free from excitement'.[5] *The Woodpigeon Patrol*, was 'worthy' enough to be given an easy ride, but critics were generally suspicious of mixing drama and documentary. Ward Wing's melodrama *Tea Leaves in the Wind* (1937), filmed uncomfortably on a plantation in Ceylon, was attacked for being 'neither fiction nor travelogue', but a 'mixture of both, without the merits of either'.[6] Actuality footage was occasionally included in fiction films, as it was in *Wings over Africa*, Roy Tuckett's account of an air journey from Croydon to Cape Town and subsequent jungle adventures.[7] More representative, however, was *Paris Plane* (1933), a crime drama set on a flight from Croydon to France, which was praised for its 'authentic Imperial Airways detail', but derided for 'the weakness of the scenario, the feebleness of the humour, the thinness of the dialogue and the crudeness of most of the characterisation'.[8]

Realism, or naturalism in the treatment of action and dialogue, were not qualities particularly sought by most makers of quota films, although verisimilitude did occasionally raise its ugly head. Director Redd Davis once let two cockney cabbies (employed for a car accident scene) ad-lib their parts in Paramount's *Ask Beccles* (1933). Unfortunately their language would never have got past the censor, and the sound engineer hurriedly switched off. 'Even Elstree was shocked', the press book reported. By the late 1930s, however, British studios had begun to respond to pressure from critics to increase the level of realism in drama. Somewhat ahead of its time, William Cameron Menzies' race gang thriller *Four Dark Hours* was written by Graham Greene, and filmed convincingly against the atmospheric backgrounds of Paddington station, Covent Garden and Soho. Distributors, however, were in no hurry to expose their audiences to anything resembling the reality of the criminal underworld and the film was shelved for three dark years. When it was eventually given a release by 20th Century-Fox as *The Green Cockatoo*

(1940), its publicity stressed its adherence to an established taste for verisimilitude: 'Since the public's demand for stricter realism in films, it is no longer possible for lovely stars who play humble roles to dress in expensive "Bond Street" models and look as though they can afford a hair set every day of the week.' Consequently, its leading lady, Rene Ray 'goes through the picture dressed in a cheap mackintosh, a dark blue suit and inexpensive-looking felt hat, all of which are in keeping with the role she plays'. Clearly the trend towards greater realism was a godsend to the hard-pressed wardrobe budgets of the quota quickies. Paramount had already saved a make-up budget on its slice of East End life, *Down Our Street* (1932), which it claimed was 'probably the first picture to be made in this country with the cast dispensing entirely with grease paint'. The only form of 'facial adornment' allowed had been 'the slight embellishments which the fair sex permit themselves in everyday life'.[9] The press book was also pleased to report that most of the clothes worn in the picture had been bought 'for a few shillings in a London rag market'. No wonder the film was granted the indulgence of running to eighty-three minutes.

## Genre

John Baxter summed up the period's conventional approach to scriptwriting when he wrote: 'At that time there was a general recognition that "laughter and tears" were safe box-office ingredients and that the motto "touch their hearts and you touch their pockets!" had a ring of truth about it.'[10] As the table below demonstrates, laughter and tears – roughly translated into the generic categories of comedy and crime – were the staple of quota production, together accounting for almost two-thirds of all films made.[11]

**Table 4.1** British supporting features 1928–37 by genre

| Genre | 1928 | 1929 | 1930 | 1931 | 1932 | 1933 | 1934 | 1935 | 1936 | 1937 | Total |
|---|---|---|---|---|---|---|---|---|---|---|---|
| Comedy | 9 | 7 | 21 | 24 | 33 | 50 | 41 | 31 | 41 | 30 | 287 |
| % | 31.3 | 35.0 | 42.0 | 36.9 | 42.3 | 46.3 | 38.0 | 33.7 | 37.6 | 26.8 | 37.2 |
| Crime | 3 | 4 | 8 | 21 | 24 | 28 | 31 | 31 | 23 | 33 | 205 |
| % | 10.3 | 20.0 | 16.0 | 32.3 | 30.8 | 25.9 | 28.7 | 33.7 | 21.1 | 29.5 | 26.7 |
| Drama | 6 | 1 | 8 | 7 | 8 | 15 | 13 | 12 | 11 | 15 | 96 |
| % | 20.7 | 5.0 | 16.0 | 10.8 | 10.3 | 13.9 | 12.0 | 13.0 | 10.3 | 13.4 | 12.5 |
| Musical/ | 0 | 1 | 7 | 5 | 5 | 2 | 4 | 11 | 22 | 19 | 76 |
| Revue % | 0.0 | 5.0 | 14.0 | 7.7 | 6.4 | 1.9 | 3.7 | 12.0 | 20.2 | 17.0 | 9.9 |
| Romance | 2 | 2 | 3 | 7 | 5 | 6 | 9 | 5 | 6 | 7 | 52 |
| % | 6.9 | 10.0 | 6.0 | 10.8 | 6.4 | 5.6 | 8.3 | 5.4 | 5.5 | 6.3 | 6.7 |
| Other | 9 | 5 | 3 | 1 | 3 | 7 | 10 | 2 | 6 | 8 | 54 |
| % | 31.3 | 25.0 | 6.0 | 1.5 | 3.8 | 6.5 | 9.3 | 2.2 | 5.5 | 7.1 | 7.0 |
| **Total** | 29 | 20 | 50 | 65 | 78 | 108 | 108 | 92 | 109 | 112 | 771 |

## Hen-pecked hubbies and men in frocks

Critic Andrew Sarris once wrote that 'nothing is more depressing about a bad movie' than 'bad jokes' and 'unimaginative slapstick'.[12] This is, perhaps, one of the reasons why so few quota quickies are remembered: so many were comedies. According to the classifications assigned by Denis Gifford, comedies made up about one-third of British production in the 1930s, peaking at 45 per cent of all British films released in 1933.[13] Comedy, much of it unsophisticated and personality centred, was the backbone of a nascent national cinema and a bulwark against American cultural domination. As David Sutton has argued:

> It was the one area in which British films could offer audiences something strongly differentiated from the otherwise more popular products of Hollywood, a genre possessing both 'essentially British' qualities and an inbuilt appeal to tastes formed by a wider popular culture beyond specifically cinematic ideas of entertainment.[14]

It is a pity, then, that Sutton's study of the genre largely neglects the torrent of pictures designed to put smiles on faces before the main feature, although it does dissect the principal subgenres employed. Between 1928 and World War II, there were over 300 comedies released as second features, some 37 per cent of all films of this status. Comedies were considered safe bets by renters and exhibitors, were relatively cheap to make, and were more likely to be chosen for a supporting feature than a main attraction. But, if comedies were the mainstay of low-budget quota production, they were also frequently a source of embarrassment. Sutton even lays the blame for the low esteem in which the quota quickie was held at the door of a certain type of light comedy:

> A surprisingly large number of bland comedies, in which handsome young men–about–town pursue young women with cut-glass accents, were churned out by quota studios; the sheer unpopularity of so many British films, and the terrible reputation of the 'quota quickie', is probably explicable largely in terms of comedies of this sort, which were cheaply made, utterly predictable and lacking in any sort of comic energy or invention.[15]

One case in point was MGM's *A Little Bit of Bluff* (1935), directed by the prolific Maclean Rogers. It was such a light confection that one trade reviewer misread its title as *A Little Bit of Fluff*:

> Nothing but a network of aimless inanities, this farcical comedy has little to recommend it outside of its title, which admirably sums up its nebulous qualities in a phrase. . . . Here is a farce without an original idea; the mixture has been dished up on the stage and screen with such frequency that it no longer tickles the palate or sense of humour. In fact it is boring and irritating.[16]

Some titles invited adverse criticism. Paramount's *Simply Terrific* (1938) was another example, provoking a predictable response from *Picturegoer's* Lionel Collier: 'Pedestrian in development and laboured in humour, this Claude Hulbert comedy is not even moderately entertaining.'[17]

Andy Medhurst has rightly concluded that 'any history of British cinema that realises the need to situate the cinematic institution within its shifting webs of social relationships needs to pay great attention to the legacies of music hall'.[18] John Grierson certainly realised this in the 1930s when he referred approvingly to this 'vulgar tradition', and noted that 'the native vitality of this music hall contribution has been strong enough to survive bad production, bad scripts and bad direction alike'.[19] There were plenty of examples among the quota comedies. When they were not employing the dubious talents of graduates of the Henry Kendall school of silly asses, they often drew on the talents of music-hall performers who usually went through their 'business' with few cinematic refinements. One of the more accomplished was the rubber-faced Lancashire comic Herbert Mundin. He starred in a string of successful Fox featurettes in the early 1930s, including *The Wrong Mr Perkins* and *Immediate Possession* (both 1931) before enjoying a brief career in Hollywood films with character roles in *David Copperfield*, *Mutiny on the Bounty* (both 1935), *Under Two Flags* (1936), and others, before his death in 1939. Although most of the major renters distributed the films of variety stars at one time or another, one renter/producer, Butcher's, absorbed music hall into its corporate image of British working-class traditionalism. When, in 1935, the company made *Variety* (tag line: 'The Romance of the Music Hall') its trade ads for its current batch of releases were designed as an old-fashioned play bill, listing the 'All Star British Screen Casts' in rectangles of varying sizes.[20] As the palaces of variety closed their doors, the alternative bolthole for their performers was radio, and quota comedies also drew on this new medium for their stars. *The Scat Burglars* made for PDC at Riverside Studios in 1936 was one example, but few now remember the stars:

Music-hall star: Rubber-faced Herbert Mundin in *The Wrong Mr Perkins* (1931)

Haver and Lee. At the time, however, they were the only act under longterm contract to the BBC as guest comedians.

One of the most robust traditions of music-hall burlesque, cross-dressing, had its origins in pagan rites. The cinema gladly accepted the trope as a staple of comic performance. Indeed, a skilled performer like Arthur Lucan could lift a low-budget comedy to star attraction status as the combative Old Mother Riley. In supporting features, masquerade of this type tended to be used more sparingly as an adjunct to the narrative rather than its *raison d'être*. Drag would be a temporary disguise, as in the bedroom farce, rather than a permanent persona, as in pantomime.[21] Twickenham's featurette, *The Other Mrs. Phipps* (1931), is a good example, with an impoverished peer (Richard Cooper) donning the disguise of an old woman to escape creditors and becoming entangled in romantic misunderstandings. Gender masquerade often went hand-in-hand with class masquerade, in the tradition of the carnivalesque. The trope became so over-used in quota films that it must have become difficult to distinguish *Girls Will Be Boys* (1934) from *Boys Will Be Girls* (1937). There were probably plenty of filmgoers who agreed with one of the characters in *Everything Is Rhythm* (1936) when she remarked: 'I don't know if I approve of people posing as something they're not.'

Like Leslie Fuller's popular character, Old Bill, the protagonist of the comedy featurette was frequently a hen-pecked husband struggling to find fleeting pleasure in his oppressive situation. His antagonist was usually his wife or that traditional butt of vaudeville comedy, his mother-in-law. The plot of PDC's *The Spare Room* (1932), a poorly photographed featurette indifferently directed by Redd David, is fairly representative of the low-comedy version of domestic strife:

> Jimmy (Jimmy James) takes his wife (Ruth Taylor) to a second-rate dance club, where he spends his time decrying his wife during the intervals when she is not accusing him of flirting with blondes. She takes him home early, but he slips out after she has gone to bed, goes to a friend's flat and returns home very drunk in the early hours of the morning. The rest of the film is practically a monologue of advanced intoxication.[22]

In fact, the male-centred comedy of domestic suffering knew no class barriers. We might expect to find Leslie Fuller or Jimmy James in the BIP farce *His Wife's Mother* (1932), but it turns out instead to be another of those lightweight stories of young men in silk dressing-gowns who alternate between smart West End apartments and country retreats. The film's middle-brow pre-occupation with mad masquerades in baronial surroundings betrays its theatrical origins in a play by Will Scott, but its description of a mother-in-law as 'worse than the gypsy's warning' and its disparaging reference to 'do-*mess*-ticity,' would have been at home in one of Ernie Lotinga's low-brow *Josser* films. Lotinga's vulgarities were regular recipients of critical opprobrium in the early 1930s. But, while Lotinga certainly had his imitators among the lower ranks of comedians, his pictures were popular enough to play as main features until his star began to descend with 1934's *Josser on the Farm*.[23]

An alternative to the domestic comedy was provided by depositing the music-hall comedian in a Ruritanian setting. *Hot Heir* (1931) was a case in point, with cockney comic Charles Austin clowning around in pyjamas and a crown as a ballet-obsessed king. *The Bioscope's* reviewer was certainly impressed: 'The rich music hall vein of Austin's comedy is sure to make big popular appeal.'[24] Not content with burlesquing imaginary foreigners, W. P. Kellino took the rise out of real ones in a series of musical featurettes for Ideal. The Spanish got the treatment in *Bull Rushes*, while the Americans were lampooned in *Who Killed Doc Robin?*, which – sad to report – ended with a custard-pie fight. The comedy in some second features, however, was rather more refined. Bert Coote's performance in Gaumont's *Bracelets* (1931), for instance, was thought especially suitable for 'first-class halls'.[25]

## Jewel thieves and bodies in the library

Gifford suggests that between one in four and one in five quota films released in the 1930s dealt with crime in a more or less serious way.[26] Apart from a dip in 1933 and a rise in 1939, the proportion of crime films stayed remarkably constant at between 20 and 30 per cent. Like comedies, crime pictures were slightly more likely to be supporting features: approximately 27 per cent of British second features between 1928 and 1937. Although crime was a prominent genre, the films were not generally gangster melodramas of the type that enjoyed a vogue in Hollywood at the beginning of the 1930s. The influential *CEA Film Report* recommended that 'British stories of this class should aim at originality both in material and treatment.'[27] Most, like Radio's *The Shadow of Mike Emerald* (1935), were found wanting: 'So amateurish is this roughhouse melodrama compared with the polished American product of similar type that its chances of success on the average programme are far from promising.'[28] Roland Gillett's *Under Proof* (1936) got similarly short shrift:

> The presumption of attempting an American gangster comedy in this country gets the reward it deserves. Little else but feeble dialogue written in pseudo-wisecracking vein, the picture runs its leisurely course without as much as inviting a laugh or manufacturing a thrill.[29]

Budget-conscious film-makers found it particularly difficult to mix drama and comedy into a picture with the sureness of touch of the Hollywood studios. Even when MGM commissioned a quota picture – *Money Mad* (1934) – from an American director, success could not be guaranteed: step forward the unfortunate Frank Richardson:

> Here is a typical quota picture. . . . The Americans are adept at this type of entertainment, entertainment which requires pep and punch, but we have a lot to learn before we can hope to enter the field. The story certainly has possibilities, but they are neglected by the producer, the result being a hotch-potch of romance, comedy, melodrama and slap-stick, no more exciting than Monday's hash.[30]

Even at the end of the decade, after years of modest endeavour, it seemed that the British gangster film remained a *non sequitur*, as the reaction to ABPC's *Murder in Soho* (1938) demonstrated: 'In this country we cannot hope to make a gangster film that weighs up with the American product, and this one with a Soho background leaves one very unimpressed.'[31]

   The British version of the crime film was expected to be an altogether more genteel affair, partly because of the tighter control exercised by the British censor over domestic productions, but also because of the need to appeal to an audience which was predominantly female.[32]

Women might not have favoured gangster stories, but they were known to be fond of a good mystery, especially if it was lightened by a little comedy and romance, and set in affluent surroundings. Therefore, the strapline of Fox's comedy-drama *After Dark* – 'Thrills, love and laughter in an old country house' – became a mantra for quota pictures in search of bookings. Almost inevitably, the plot of *After Dark* revolved around an attempt to steal jewels, because murder and jewel robbery (usually from the wall safe which every country house and luxury flat seemed to accommodate) became the stock crimes for supporting features that depended for their bookings primarily on small and medium-sized local cinemas. In fact so many criminals had designs on so many gems that it became hard to tell Radio's *The Vandergilt Diamond Mystery* (1935) from Fox's *The Villiers Diamond* (1938).

In BIP's comedy drama of hidden gems and secret identities, *Someone at the Door* (1936), a solicitor remarks that 'it's not easy to find tenants for these old country houses'. But in fact, the Gothic pile imagined by the makers of quota pictures was never unoccupied for long, because the plush country retreat rather than the mean streets of the city was the preferred venue for the mystery thriller. Twickenham Studios may have specialised in the genre, but there were plenty of competitors, including BIP, whose *The Man at Six* (1931), was set entirely in a 'lonely country mansion' and its grounds.[33] The story by Jack de Leon and Jack Celestin Donohue was popular enough for it to be re-made at Welwyn for MGM in 1938 as *The Gables Mystery*. Its press book cheerfully celebrated the absurdities of the plot:

> Seldom has any film contained so many characters at cross purposes with each other and all appearing to be what they are not . . . The leading character, played by Francis L. Sullivan, is ostensibly a private detective, but is, in reality, a master criminal who has also adopted the disguise of an elderly woman. The heroine, Antoinette Cellier, poses as the mysterious old lady's secretary but is, in reality, the accredited representative of a company which seeks to discover the brain behind a series of jewel thefts. The hero, Derek Gorst, while not claiming to be other than what he seems, yet conceals the fact that he is the son of an elderly baronet who is also present in the house of mystery.

And so on. It seems that no British screenplay of the 1930s was complete unless at least one of its characters had a secret identity. As in comedy, masquerade and impersonation were very much the order of the day. The plots of the country house mystery were so interchangeable that nobody seemed to notice when they were reused under new titles. After making Neil Gordon's *The Shakespeare Murders* as *The Third Clue* in 1934, Fox successfully recycled the story as *The Claydon Treasure Mystery* only four years later.

Even by the early 1930s, the country-house mystery genre was becoming hackneyed, and scenarists were desperately struggling to find fresh variations. Just how desperately may be judged from *The Bioscope*'s review of Norman Lee's *The Strangler*, a 1932 offering from Pathe:

> With the frailest of stories, the author here endeavours to work up a thriller mystery, but without any marked success. The acting, probably due to poor direction, appears amateurish, and the dialogue is so commonplace as to border often on the ridiculous. In a country mansion a small group of people are gathered together to rehearse a play written by one of them. Two stage professionals are engaged, one of whom is revealed as a 'Yard' man, when the owner of the house, who is to act the

part of the dead man, is found in reality to have been strangled. Considerable cross-questioning and movements by mysterious parties lead nowhere, and in a most unconvincing finale the author confesses, then commits suicide. . . . Settings are confined to the rooms of the house, except for one or two storm-swept exteriors. *A fake gorilla and a wandering knife-throwing dago are included to add colour to the plot.*[34]

Fiercely independent, *The Bioscope* also acted like a good 'Yard' man. Before its ruthless strangulation at the hands of a KRS advertising boycott, it could usually be relied upon to sniff out and expose rank artificiality in the plots, characterisations and performances of quota pictures. It was particularly harsh on fanciful portraits of crooks and policemen, as its comments on Walter Summers' sinister thriller, *The House Opposite*, demonstrate:

> *Much Ado About Nothing* would perhaps be a more appropriate title for this almost plotless preamble connected with a set of 'dangerous' London crooks. . . . The hero we discover later to be a detective, though his facetious bearing, when not under the influence of drugs or a bludgeon, is as unlike that of a police officer as one could imagine. . . . Henry Kendall, who plays the part, cannot be said to enhance his reputation by it. Walter Summers, with an over-generous use of cobwebs in the empty house, bodies in cupboards and lurking shadows, has endeavoured to work up an atmosphere of mystery, but he has permitted his players, without exception, to overact.[35]

*The House Opposite* was the type of film that James Chapman has referred to as a 'shocker', that is a thriller (with origins in the Gothic romance) that had achieved mass popularity among readers of Victorian 'penny dreadfuls'.[36] Its emphasis on action and preference for the Gothic and macabre in its visual styling had made it highly suitable for the silent cinema; whereas the dialogue-based whodunit had been more appropriate to the stage. Its leading twentieth-century exponent had been Edgar Wallace, whose work was the cornerstone of British Lion's film productions. In the 1930s, Twickenham Studios borrowed much of the Gothic iconography and uncanny undertones of the shocker and grafted them onto the narrative structure of the whodunit, creating a distinctive and much-copied hybrid of wide appeal. Chapman has argued that the shocker was a distinctively British genre running counter to what would become a dominant realist aesthetic, but his claim that Hollywood failed to produce a direct equivalent is hard to sustain in the face of the strings of thriller serials manufactured by Monogram, Republic and others. In fact, Chapman acknowledges that Sax Rohmer's Fu Manchu, the prototype villain of the shocker, appeared only in American films in the 1930s and 1940s. The quota quickie could offer only a cheap knock-off in Sin Fang, who featured in a couple of 'yellow peril' pictures from Columbia, both directed by Tony Frenguelli: *Dr. Sin Fang* (1937) and *Chinatown Nights* (1938). The latter exercise in crude Orientalism provoked the following comment from a trade reviewer:

> The mainspring of the villainy and the venue of the plot are represented as having a Chinese origin: but we seldom seem to be out of a rather exotic film studio, and neither the plot nor the characters have any recognisable likeness to reality. Exhibitors will understand that this is a British quota picture of the usual 'quickie' type.[37]

Social relevance: the problems of bankruptcy were examined in Michael Powell's *The Brown Wallet* (1936)

Shockers made little attempt to represent the realities of crime for their audiences, but not all stories of criminal temptation were divorced from the harsh economic conditions of the time. A couple of Michael Powell's films – *Rynox* (1931) and *The Brown Wallet* (1936) – dealt with the effects of bankruptcy; as did Warners' poorly received *Head of the Family* (1933). All demonstrated the folly of resorting to crime to replace what had been lost. By the late 1930s, the occasional film attempted to deal more honestly with the sociology of crime. Lawrence Huntington's *Bad Boy* (1938), made for RKO, was, to judge from its trade reviews, a 'sincere' study of the causes of one man's criminality that avoided 'the usual sugary sentiment that is a feature of reformation dramas'.[38] Courtroom dramas were also a reliable staple of quota production, requiring few changes of set and containing an intrinsic element of suspense. The Boulting brothers, for example, had their first real success with the provocative court drama *Consider Your Verdict* (1938). However, devotees of battling barristers who sought out the promisingly titled *Crown Trial* (1938) would have been in for a surprise. This featurette from Exclusive was a bizarre mixture of classical Greek drama, modern wisecracks and a little slapstick, and was explicitly targeted at undergraduates. *Kinematograph Weekly* warned that, 'For students of Demosthenian oratory the trial scene may have a mild academic interest, but it is highly unlikely to be acceptable to any ordinary kinema audience.'[39]

## Song and dance

Andrew Sarris also included 'failed musical numbers' in his brief list of 'B' movie depressants, and this again may help to explain why, given the popularity of the genre, musicals were relatively rare as supporting features. Musicals and musical revues make up about 10 per cent of the total, whereas for first features, the percentage is close to 20. Stephen Guy has identified three subgenres of musical film in 1930s' British cinema: European operetta, music hall and musical comedy revue.[40] The romantic escapism of European operetta enjoyed a thirty-film cycle during the decade, but, with a rare exception such as *The Beggar Student* (1931), hardly any were second features. The second category relied on the talents of performers who had developed a following through stage appearances. Their 'turns' were often linked or framed by tenuous narratives. Some supporting features drew upon the English musical comedy tradition, which was closely associated with the West End stage, but most were happy to mix these generic strands in a carefree fashion, according to the material to hand.

Some early attempts to use song and dance in a low-budget production were not well received. MGM's *Romany Love* (1931), for instance, was condemned by the *CEA Film Report* as 'a poor, disjointed affair' with a 'silly' story, 'artificial' atmosphere and 'amateurish' treatment.[41] Pat Heale's single-set featurette for Paramount, 'a merry mix of music and mandarins' called *In a Lotus Garden* (1931) was summarily dismissed with the caustic comment: 'Some songs are rendered by none-too-attractive people'.[42] Geoffrey Benstead's *Stepping Stones* (1931) was given an equally rough passage by *The Bioscope*'s reviewer:

> This can hardly be classed as a film. . . . It is altogether without plot, and consists merely of the memories of an old Derby and Joan pictured in the flames and a comparison of the girl of the gay 'nineties with her sister of today. A group of singers dressed in the crinoline period, supply appropriate song and dance. . . . The old parties have a difference of opinion and we are switched over to a more or less up-to-date café, and witness the picture's first bit of life, a peppy performance by two clever step-dancers and a display by the Victoria Palace Girls. The acting of the old couple is singularly uninspired, while the sets are on mediocre lines. Lighting is none too good, and the camera work, which has allowed for no variation in angles, is amateurish.[43]

The review both demonstrates just how unsophisticated these early attempts at musical entertainment could be, and suggests how films of this period targeted the older viewer through nostalgia and discourses on social change. We can surmise that audiences might have been expected to sing along with the performers, just as they did in the music hall.

The lesson was quickly learned that successful musicals relied on star talent and the sort of high production values that second-feature budgets could not afford. Instead, some scenarios settled for timeless simplicity. Charles Barnett's *Wedding Eve* (1935), for example, consisted almost entirely of a pre-nuptial sing-song in a country pub. Although *Today's Cinema* considered it a 'useful second feature for the masses', *Kinematograph Weekly* did feel that this was scraping the bottom of the scenario barrel:

> Just a straggling parade of English radio turns, all of which are fast becoming hackneyed. The individual artists appear to enjoy themselves, but poor direction and painfully economic presentation

prevent them from conveying the same gay party spirit to the audience. The entertainment is not just dull, it is completely and hopelessly deficient.[44]

A rather warmer reception was given to those films which did little more than present a theatrical revue on screen. Revues, which are more numerous as second features than first, were often distributed by British, rather than American, renters. PDC's *The New Hotel* (1932), made at Cricklewood and directed by Bernerd Mainwaring, is an early example. Among the most successful were a series of Ace Films' featurettes, which allowed provincial audiences to sample the (nudeless) delights of the famous 'Revudeville' shows of London's Windmill Theatre. By 1937, the cycle of film musicals was beginning to run its course, and the supporting feature revues, like Viking Films' commercially successful *Shooting Stars*, were evidence of its decadent phase.[45] In contrast, expensively produced Ruritanian light operettas like *Glamorous Night* and *The Lilac Domino* (both 1937) were given a critical slating and often had to settle for second billing.[46] Their brand of musical romance was superseded by a series of films set in rural Ireland, and featuring traditional airs. Most were made by Donovan Pedelty's Crusader Films unit in Belfast, where they acquired first-feature status. The nature of their wholesome appeal may be gleaned from a letter to *Picturegoer* from a viewer in Scarborough, who congratulated all concerned with *West of Kerry* (1938), which, he wrote, 'develops with a pleasing lack of lewdness against a background of old-world Irish romance and scenery'.[47]

## Periwigs and postillions

In spite of the euphoria around the international success of *The Private Life of Henry VIII*, costume and historical subjects were generally shunned by the quota quickie producers. Costume films were expensive to make, and they were not particularly popular in working-class cinemas. Moreover, because so many quota quickies were independent productions, they were not able to reuse sets and costumes designed for the more costly pictures from a large studio. Thus, second features remained free of what Jeffrey Richards once termed the 'plethora of periwigs and postillions' that so angered critics who demanded greater contemporary realism in British pictures.[48] There were, of course, a few exceptions. Widgey Newman made an idiosyncratic film about Shakespeare, *The Immortal Gentleman* (1935) and a Robin Hood romp, *The Merry Men of Sherwood* (1932); while Paramount commissioned a flop about the Jacobite rebellion, *Flame in the Heather*. But really, the quota quickies showed interest in the costume cycle only when it was beginning to decay (and perhaps the costumes themselves could be recycled). MGM distributed *Auld Lang Syne* (1937), a Robert Burns biopic made partly in Scotland by James Fitzpatrick. Fox made *The Black Tulip* (1937), an historical adventure set in Holland. Julius Hagen made a few costume pictures as 'supers', but the more modest *The Vicar of Bray* (1937) seems to have played mainly as a supporting feature. George King's adaptation of *John Halifax, Gentleman* (1938) was expected to be a success, but turned out to be a disappointment when it became clear that actors accustomed to the contemporary settings of most supporting features did 'not appear to be at home in period costume'.[49]

The only really commercially successful costume films among the hundreds of British second features were George King's Tod Slaughter melodramas. The manager of the Embassy, Bolton, confirmed that his patrons liked 'old melodrama, especially in the cheap seats'.[50]

Critics were not always so keen. Even a sympathetic trade publication like *Today's Cinema* could recommend *Maria Marten* (1935) only for the 'unsophisticated' after delivering a roasting in its review.[51] Slaughter's films, like those based on music hall sketches, were another throwback to earlier forms of entertainment. The tendency of his films to target an older generation of cinemagoers was epitomised by MGM's *Darby and Joan* (1937), a melodrama of a blind girl, a rich man and his dissolute nephew, which was condemned by *Picturegoer* as 'hopelessly dated'.[52] Just as dated was Twickenham's romantic melodrama *The Rocks of Valpre*. Based on a book by the darling of the circulation libraries, Ethel M. Dell, nostalgia was laced into the very fabric of the story, which is filmed in flashback and ends with the aged heroine contemplating her lost love. *Today's Cinema* noted its old-fashioned quality, but believed there was still an audience for this type of sentimental treatment.[53] Indeed, there were many lost loves to be contemplated after World War I, and the film probably found a receptive audience among women of a certain age, just as Leslie Fuller's service comedies – *Not so Quiet on the Western Front* (1930), *Old Soldiers Never Die* (1931) and *Poor Old Bill* (1931) – appealed to the male survivors of the carnage.

## Searching for inspiration

As their name implies, 'second' features rarely broke new ground. They could even be re-makes of earlier films. For instance, 1935–6 saw a vogue for making British versions of French pictures, including Gainsborough's *First Offence* and Premier-Stafford's *Second Bureau* (one wonders if Teddington's *Third Time Unlucky*, the original title of Michael Powell's *Crown v. Stevens* [1935], might be a continuation of this numerical sequence, but it was a British original). More frequently, the themes of supporting features ran in cycles inspired by the success of more expensive and prestigious films, although the treatment of these themes could be radically different. The sequence of irreverent Leslie Fuller 'Old Bill' films, each recalling 'the lighter side of those dark days in 1914–19', offered humorous counterpoint to Lewis Milestone's harrowing epic *All Quiet on the Western Front* (1930).[54] Maintaining a more serious note, John Baxter directed a string of service reunion stories. The first of these, the generically titled *Reunion* (co-directed with Ivar Campbell), set the tone for the others: the simplest of narrative construction, the singing of the songs of the trenches, and a celebration of the value of self-sacrifice. It had, according to *The Times*, 'no pretensions either to technological refinements or to psychological subtlety', but was essentially 'a pamphlet written in broad, sentimental language that anyone can understand'.[55] A year later, Baxter was ploughing the same didactic furrow with *Lest We Forget*, described by its press book as a 'dignified and sincere story that teaches a lesson of comradeship, loyalty and devotion to duty' and 'shows that class distinctions and nationalities do not deter men from friendship'.

The film that *Reunion* supported at the Palace Theatre, London – Edmund Goulding's lavish *Grand Hotel* (1932) – inspired George Pearson's more modest and mawkish *Open All Night* (1934) ('Night life in a city where every smile may hide a breaking heart'). In Pearson's film, a Russian nobleman (Frank Vosper) has been reduced to working as a night porter at the aptly named Hotel Paragon. When he is further humiliated by being given his notice, he confesses to murder to save a guest, before taking his own life. This well-received Radio Pictures production used the same trope of multiple storylines, was filmed on one of the largest sets built at Twickenham, and was even proudly described in its publicity as 'An English Grand Hotel'.[56]

Sometimes a popular element in a Hollywood film would be extracted to form the basis of a British quickie. Oscar the penguin was a big enough hit in Radio's *The Penguin Pool Murder* (1932) for Harry Cohen and George King immediately to draft a similarly amusing bird into their Fox production *To Brighton with Gladys* (1932). Eliot Stannard's scenario from John Quin's story was ready only a few weeks after an 'interview' with Oscar appeared in *Film Pictorial*.[57] Less frequently, a rare international hit from a British studio might set a cycle of supporting features in motion. The aforementioned *Paris Plane*, for example, took off after the runaway success of *Rome Express* (1932), and the cycle was still rolling in 1935 when Herbert Smith delivered *Night Mail* and Twickenham followed up with the train crash thriller *The Last Journey*. On rare occasions, enterprising film-makers like John Paddy Carstairs and Anthony Havelock-Allan might set a cycle in motion with a low-budget film, as they did with their school drama for Paramount, *Holiday's End* (1937). Associated British and MGM followed up with the rather better-known *Housemaster* (1938) and *Goodbye, Mr. Chips* (1939), productions which could afford the schoolboy extras denied to Carstairs by his parsimonious budget (consequently, *Holiday's End* was set in the school vacation).[58]

As political tensions in Europe deepened and the war approached, espionage plots became more popular. The success of Hitchcock's *The 39 Steps* (1935) inspired a number of cheaper productions. An early example was George Pearson's thriller *The Secret Voice*, completed at the beginning of 1936. The plot centred on the attempt to steal the formula for synthetic petrol, 'a subject of first-class topical interest', according to Paramount's publicity. Pearson's last film, *The Fatal Hour* (1937), exemplified the trend. Billed as an 'original and exciting spy drama', this thriller has a nest of spies using that hackneyed den of iniquity the pin-table saloon as a front for their nefarious activities. The leader turns out to be a kindly old antique dealer (Edward Rigby), an entirely appropriate image of deceitful Englishness: 'He read *Alice in Wonderland* and had a prize Angora rabbit for a pet – yet he was the ruthless head of a gang of spies and crooks.'[59] His weapon of choice is an exploding clock, another uncannily apt symbol of the conflagration waiting to happen. *The 39 Steps* was doubtless also an inspiration for Reginald Denham's *The House of the Spaniard*, in which a group of Spanish revolutionaries use Liverpool as a base for a counterfeiting operation. But the long-faced and long-forgotten Peter Hadden playing a silly-ass adventurer was no Robert Donat, and the sub-Buchan script failed to generate any believability, despite extensive location filming.

Occasionally, quickies were made as direct lampoons of box-office hits like *Bring 'em Back Alive* (1932), which inspired the satire of jungle film-making, *Send 'em Back Half Dead* (1933). Made at Wembley, and condemned by *Picturegoer* as 'lamentably childish and obvious', the parody followed the anthropological investigations of some black explorers in London's East End.[60] Alternatively, a connection with a box-office hit such as *The Private Life of Henry VIII*, might be established via a title like Hammer's *The Public Life of Henry the Ninth* (1934). This film might be considered emblematic of the British second feature of the 1930s in the way it trades on a genre popularised by a more expensive product, giving it a contemporary setting, and exaggerating the element of broad comedy. It is also representative in the way in which it was designed as a vehicle for a popular personality whose celebrity had been established in another medium. According to *Today's Cinema*, the film was 'solely fashioned to exploit the gurgling gaieties of Leonard Henry, concert party star and idol of millions of radio fans'.[61]

The quickies generally focused on the contemporary, and sometimes liked to flaunt their awareness of fashion and topicality. MGM's *Alibi Inn* (1935), for example, was sold as 'A Modern Thriller' in which 'stories and settings from the front pages of today's newspapers form an integral part'. Using an original screenplay by Muriel Baker (Muriel Box), the film prided itself on its knowledge of the latest developments in recreation, crime and policing:

> The principal characters are a young girl whose father is the proprietor of a fashionable road-house, and two crooks who use high-powered cars for their 'getaways.' Modern methods of news-gathering are shown in many sequences, while the production also touches on the present day problem of unemployment.... *Alibi Inn* opens with a thrilling car chase through the heart of London, when the mobile police are on the track of two 'smash-and-grab' bandits, who escape by abandoning their stolen car. The action then switches to the luxurious road-house – one of those modern establishments that, in this petrol age, have replaced the coaching inns of a more leisurely epoch.[62]

Speed of production meant that themes could be highly topical. Fox's Edgar Wallace-style thriller *Dial 999* ('he answered the emergency call – and found romance') was written by Ernest Dudley and Lawrence Huntington in 1937, immediately after the new emergency number was introduced. The Jubilee celebrations for King George V were topically incorporated into the Paramount comedy, *Jubilee Window* (1935), an otherwise standard farce with the familiar ingredients of comical crooks, purloined pearls, hen-pecked husband and mad mix-ups, which was directed (apparently with little inspiration) by George Pearson.[63] *Doss House* (1933) was timed by its writer, the MGM executive Bert Ayres, to capitalise on the publication of George Orwell's *Down and Out in London and Paris*, and the association attracted publicity to the film well before its release.[64] British Lion's *Warn London*, a thriller about a German criminologist who adopts the path sinister when he is defrauded of his life's savings, was made in 1934 after the activities of a number of notorious swindlers had ruined thousands of people. But the plea to 'Warn London' against the menace of a German master criminal now seems a coded message about the danger of Hitler and the Nazi Party. International relations also formed the backdrop to Paramount's *Incident in Shanghai*, directed by John Paddy Carstairs at the end of 1937. The film included clips from contemporary newsreels of Japanese aggression in China, and was recommended for its 'first-class topical interest'.[65] However, film-makers had to be cautious not to be seen to be exploiting human tragedy. Fox's *The Last Barricade* (1938), directed by Alex Bryce, chose to use the Spanish Civil War as a setting for 'artless romantic melodrama' and was promptly castigated: 'The film merely dissipates topicality. There can be no half measures with such a stern theme as war.'[66] Occasionally, the quota quickie was so up to the minute that it got ahead of itself. Widgey Newman's comedy *On Velvet* (1938), distributed by Columbia, anticipated the arrival of commercial television by almost two decades. But Newman's gags, delivered by Wally Patch and Joe Hayman, were 'antique' rather than futuristic.[67] Unfortunately for these topical tales, the speed of production was not matched by that of distribution. It was usually six months before prints reached the provinces, and a film could remain in circulation for more than a year.

One might have expected a cinema overwhelmingly dedicated to the entertainment of domestic audiences to have drawn heavily on popular sporting activity for its subject matter. That this never really happened was again probably largely due to the gender-specific appeal of games like football and cricket. After the poorly received *The Great Game* (1930) and the Sidney Howard comedy *Up for the Cup* (1931), the only films about football were two that featured the Arsenal team: Anthony Asquith's *The Lucky Number* (1933) and Thorold Dickinson's *The Arsenal Stadium Mystery* (1939). Both were first features. Football was really only incidental to Asquith's romantic comedy, but a little more central to Dickinson's murder mystery, which managed to overcome what the censor considered the 'grave objection in this country to showing foul play taking place in English athletic and sporting events'.[68] Cricket featured in Paramount's hit *Badger's Green*, but Adrian Brunel's film failed to spawn any further white-flannelled foolery. The spirit of Hitchcock's celebrated pugilist drama *The Ring* (1928) lived on in Radio's *Mannequin* (1933) and *Fifty Shilling Boxer* (1937), an 'artless little story of a fairground boxer who trains up a young fighter'; but otherwise boxing remained a very minor cinematic attraction.[69] The fashionable craze for motor-racing spawned two second features in the summer of 1934, Columbia's *Eight Cylinder Love*, directed by Peter Saunders, and Associated British's incoherent *Death Drives Through* (1935). The latter was a thoroughly botched job by the American director Edward L. Cahn, but incorporated footage filmed on the Brooklands circuit. While admitting that the story was 'trite', *Today's Cinema* actually thought the film was 'quite well photographed' with 'at least one obviously authentic and exciting crash and some quite good skids'. Novelty will always compensate for other deficiencies, as the reviewer was prepared to acknowledge:

> Makers of track-racing films are fortunate that the public's knowledge of motor-racing is usually much flimsier than of most other sports, and that the pastime itself is usually sufficiently actionful to compensate for a measure of melodramatic ordinariness in the rest of the story.[70]

Although there was even a 1936 Fox comedy (*Highland Fling*) set at Scotland's Highland Games, the only sport to find a consistent place in the supporting feature was horse-racing. This may have been because it had a greater appeal to female filmgoers, or because the depiction of foul play was acceptable in the sport of kings, but most likely because horses and racing offered the opportunity to tick more audience appeal boxes than most subjects. A film like Fox's *A Hundred to One* (1932) could not only deliver discourses on a favourite theme of 1930s' film-making – luck – but also overcome a weak plot and win critical praise for its 'pleasing English countryside shots'.[71] This ability to deliver a sense of nationhood was always, potentially, the great redeeming quality of the quickie. It could bring dignity to the humblest of sports and pastimes. Thus, even the pub game, darts, could win praise as the subject for a feature film when it successfully evoked national sentiment. *Picture Show* found Radio's Maclean Rogers-directed *Darts Are Trumps* (1938), 'refreshing' because it was 'thoroughly English' and gave 'a vivid picture of typical suburban life'.[72]

## Monsters and zombies

Of course, the term 'B' movie now conjures up a vision of something cheap and campy with scream queens and bug-eyed monsters. This association rests largely on the cycle of SF/horror flicks generated in the USA in the 1950s, but not all the quota quickies of two decades before were more level-headed. The British Board of Film Censors (BBFC) was at pains to prevent the spread to British studios of unwholesome horror films like those made by Universal in the early

A director worth keeping an eye on: Brian Desmond Hurst's *The Tell Tale Heart* (1934)

1930s, but a few film-makers were infected.[73] Boris Karloff came back to England in 1933 to make *The Ghoul* for Gaumont-British, and returned periodically when any fresh macabre subject was planned by one of the larger production houses. However, more modest quota production was not without an occasional horror. Tod Slaughter's creepy melodramas were a staple of George King's output, Brian Desmond Hurst established a bubble reputation with the atmospheric *The Tell Tale Heart* (made for just over £3,000), and Widgey Newman also capitalised on the audience developed by films like *Frankenstein* (1931). When the BBFC banned Paramount's *Island of Lost Souls* (1932) Newman was brave or foolhardy enough to make his own mad-scientist movies *Castle Sinister* (1932) and *The Unholy Quest* (1934), both now sadly lost.[74] It was RKO's *King Kong* (1933) that created the most mayhem at the British box office, and it was inevitable that some opportunistic quota merchant would try his hand at a 'creature feature', undaunted by a minuscule budget for special effects. The surprise is that the shocker titled *The Secret of the Loch* (1934) was made at Ealing Studios, was co-scripted by Hitchcock's favourite scenarist, Charles Bennett, and was edited by David Lean. Although its makers have passed away, the film endures to sully the reputations of all involved, and is worthy of examination.

*The Secret of the Loch* was made by Bray Wyndham, an independent producer using Ealing's studios and technicians while Basil Dean sorted out his differences with RKO. It is therefore ironic that Ealing should produce a film that traded on the success of RKO's monster hit. Ealing's monster, however, was very British: the mythical denizen of Loch Ness. Made at the end

Creature feature: Underwater thrills in *The Secret of the Loch* (1934)

of a series of reported sightings of the beast in 1933–4, the picture was both topical and timely in the wake of news of, and cinematic interest in, prehistoric survivals. It was directed by Milton Rosmer, an established stage and silent screen actor, who went on to much more prestigious directorial assignments with Alexander Korda. *Picturegoer* devoted a whole page to the making of the film, looking forward to the performance of the revered founder of the Aldwych Theatre, Seymour Hicks.[75] When *The Secret of the Loch* actually surfaced for general release in time for Christmas 1934, it proved a huge disappointment to the magazine.[76] The BBFC generously awarded a 'U' certificate to attract the family audience. Perhaps the U in this instance stood for 'unclear', as no one associated with the film seems sure if they are making a comedy or a chiller, least of all the director. The performances are often exaggerated to parodic levels, and the characterisation and dialogue never strive for originality when there is a cliché to hand. The gallery of 'types' includes a demented scientist (Hicks), competitive newsmen, a flirtatious barmaid (the debut of Rosamund John), bumbling academics and the inevitable drunken Scotsmen. Connoisseurs of Ed Wood movies might appreciate the comically bad model shots and the final revelation of the secret of the Loch, which turns out to be a back-projected iguana (supposedly underwater). Seymour Hicks gives a performance more monstrous than Nessie's. He was knighted the following year. By the time Ealing's behemoth shuffled onto provincial screens, burdened by bad reviews, Loch Ness sightings and *King Kong* had become distant memories. Though it may have had ambitions to top the bill, it usually had to settle for something more modest.[77] It would be over twenty years before British cinema again dipped its toe into the murky waters of the monster movie.

Perhaps the trashiest of quota horrors was an obscure Paramount release called *Ouanga* (1934). Written, produced and directed by George Terwilliger, a veteran of over fifty American silent pictures, this rare excursion into supernatural horror somehow qualified as a quota release, in spite of the nationality of its director and some of its leading players. Probably inspired by Victor Halperin's *White Zombie* (1932), and a precursor to Tourneur's infinitely better-known *I Walked with a Zombie* (1943), the Paramount film was a steamy tale of voodoo and misplaced passion in the West Indies and 'starred' Ferdi Washington and Philip Brandon as neighbouring plantation owners, one black and one white. The theme of the film is the evil of miscegenation, and it enlists biblical support by naming the white planter and his British fiancée 'Adam and Eve' and representing the light-skinned voodoo priestess Klili (Washington) as a serpent in their Garden of Eden. The futility of attempting to pass for white and use magical powers against white colonials is demonstrated by Klili's death in the film's dénouement. The original intention had been to film in Haiti with authentic practitioners of the cult, but the unit offended its subjects and was obliged to relocate to Jamaica under what many believed to be a voodoo curse. This relocation to a British colony provided the basis for quota eligibility, which was just as well because the accursed film was initially rejected by America's Hays Office. When eventually released in the USA as *Crime of the Voodoo* and *Love Wanga*, it was advertised with the sensational tag line: 'Strange Loves of Queer People'. Its trade show in Britain was met with a critical reception more terrifying than any ju-ju cult. One character in the film dismisses voodoo as 'bally rot', and this phrase could also describe reviewers' impressions of *Ouanga*:

> The story, general treatment, acting and dialogue are so crude that the picture becomes positively laughable. . . . There is no need to dwell on the cast. The majority of the players have never been seen before, and, judging by their pitiful performances, it is unlikely that they will ever be seen again.[78]

*Ouanga* was indeed a story of human sacrifice – mostly of the cast by the critics. The dialogue is diabolical: 'I ain't scared of no voodoo if you is along, Big Boy,' says Susie the black maid (Bebe Joyce) to Adam's 'Yas-sir' servant (George Spink), who responds with, 'Ain't no black magic gonna get the best of this charcoal blonde!' *Ouanga* is certainly crude and artless, but it is not without historical significance. Not only is it one of the earliest British supernatural horror films to have survived, and the first to feature zombies, it is also, perhaps, the first British film to feature a substantial black cast (more than half of the principal players), albeit American actors.[79]

With the occasional exception of Tod Slaughter's pictures, critics did not look kindly on British excursions into the macabre. Vernon Sewell, one of British cinema's most consistent explorers of the uncanny, took his first steps into the realms of Grand Guignol with the MGM featurette *The Medium* (1934), José Levy's tale of a mad sculptor who murders his model and conceals the corpse in his studio (an idea later re-hashed by Sewell in his *Latin Quarter* [1945], and by Roger Corman in 1959's *Bucket of Blood*). Reviewers were quick to sharpen their scalpels:

A picture so poorly acted, so disconcertingly vague in its story outline, and so absurdly artificial in its Parisian atmosphere, that thrills fail to visit it. . . . Although the pseudo-highbrow may find 'the film' emotionally stimulating, there is little chance of the masses greeting it with enthusiasm.[80]

The horror genre rarely benefited from the critics' weakness for artlessness in films that often trod a thin line between what was perceived as either charming ingenuousness or incompetent bungling. Fox's aptly titled *The Perfect Flaw* (1934), for example, managed to stay on the right side of the line by appealing to a critical fondness for simplicity and directness: 'There is no attempt at subtlety, the film's modest strength rests on its likeable and disarming artlessness.'[81] Such artlessness was seen as a perfect flaw for 'popular and industrial halls'. So, while Warners' mystery *What Happened to Harkness?* (1934) was happily received as 'simple carefree diversion', a macabre film like *The Tell Tale Heart* or *The Medium* was deemed inappropriate as popular entertainment, and thought to be suitable only for decadent intellectuals.[82]

## Money, sex and social change

Emblazoned on the escutcheon that introduced Twickenham's Real Art productions was the motto, 'Looking Forward, Looking Back'. It summed up the double bind of much British cinema in the 1930s, which was expected to represent the powerful modernising forces shaping the country without losing sight of those traditional elements that really constituted 'Britishness' for so many. Discourses about the changing moral, social and economic order thus became recurrent underlying themes of the quota films of the 1930s, and were crucial to the way in which they constructed national identity. Sometimes these discourses surface as anxieties or uncertainties about class and social mobility, sometimes in relation to technological or moral threats to an established way of life.

Uncertainties surrounding social mobility were sometimes mapped onto the social and cultural divisions between the 'sophisticated' south of England and the 'unsophisticated' north. In Radio's well-received *The Right Age to Marry* (1935), produced at Nettlefold Studios by George Smith and directed by Maclean Rogers, comic actor Frank Pettingell plays Lomas Ramsden, a self-made cotton king who retires at fifty to the genteel resort of Hove, determined to enjoy the leisure he has previously denied himself. Unfortunately, Ramsden finds that he is a fish out of water in the pretentious society of the south coast, where the lifestyle expected of a gentleman of leisure remains 'a bit of a puzzle' to him. Symbolically, he is unseated by his horse at his first hunt and, without his protective housekeeper, he falls prey to a predatory society gold-digger. As if to confirm the folly of abandoning his honest northern roots for the airs and graces of the decadent south, his mill burns down. The business is uninsured because the Oxford-educated nephew whom Ramsden had installed as manager neglected to renew the premium. The self-made man is obliged to return north to toil again to build up his business and, when his socialite fiancée learns the extent of his losses, she catches the 'next train back to [southern] civilisation'. Bailed out of bankruptcy by an old friend and neighbour, Ramsden finally abandons all class pretensions and marries his faithful housekeeper. The film's tag line was 'From clogs to brass, and from brass to clogs'. Beyond the message that north is north and south is south, and never the twain shall meet, there is an implication that, in Ramsden's words, 'when a man's used to a thing, it doesn't do to break with it'. Ramsden discovers that, in spite of his wealth, his unsophisticated tastes and manners mean that attempts to be a 'real' gentleman can never be more than a form of class masquerade.

This theme of social masquerade is evident in many pictures of the period. In these films, usually comedies or romances, the protagonists experience what it is like to be treated as a member of a higher or lower class. While the films may offer mild social satire, it is the experience of differential treatment – enjoyed vicariously by the audience – that seems to be significant.[83] It might also be argued that the witnessing of convincing masquerade encouraged a belief in the possibility of social mobility for the viewer. In George Pearson's *Gentleman's Agreement*, for example, an unemployed man (Anthony Holles) changes places with a rich idler (Frederick Peisley) and discovers that he can be a successful businessman – although sadly it is the idler who wins the heart of Vivien Leigh. The little-booked RKO comedy *My Partner, Mr. Davis* (1936), also featured an out-of-work man masquerading as a businessman. Other class deceptions were to be found in two Warners' comedies: *High Society* (1932), in which Florence Desmond played a cockney maid posing as a moneyed woman; and *Too Many Wives*, in which Nora Swinburne played a maid impersonating her mistress. In Leslie Hiscott's better-booked *Bargain Basement*, a department store manager mistakes an ex-con for the heir of the shop's owner. Warners' rom-com *Too Many Millions* (1934) had a millionairess posing as a maid in order to court a penniless artist; while ABFD's *It Happened in Paris* (Carol Reed's 1935 directorial debut) had a rich American pose as a penniless artist to court an impoverished girl. Similarly, in Paramount's *Lancashire Luck* (1937) an aristocrat conceals his identity in case he alienates the mill girl for whom he has fallen. Fox's *Yes, Madam* (1933) – which premiered as a supporting film to *Silver Dollar* at the Empire, Leicester Square, and received plenty of provincial bookings – was a

Revenge is sweet: Allan Jeayes gets his comeuppance at the hands of George Curzon in *The Impassive Footman* (1932)

prime example of a plot in which a legacy is dependent on the recipient holding down a menial job for a specified period. Sometimes the films featured double masquerades, as in Michael Powell's hit Warners' comedy *Something Always Happens*, in which flat-broke Peter (Ian Hunter) poses as a car salesman and meets an heiress (Nancy O'Neil), who responds by pretending to be an ordinary working-class girl. The seaside, the quintessential liminal leisure space, was the perfect setting for this sort of pretence. In Fox's featurette *Holiday Lovers* (1932), an impecunious pair (Marjorie Pickard and George Vollaire) meet on a Brighton pier and court disaster by fooling each other into thinking they belong to the idle rich.

While we should not make too much of the transgressive potential of this theme of class masquerade, we should also not accept uncritically Stephen Shafer's interpretation of its conservative function as promoting 'the desirability of people staying in "natural" positions in which they seem to belong'.[84] When Shafer suggests that this is 'another potent, though unstated, argument for the *status quo* in society', he is following the standard interpretation of ideological effects in British cinema of the 1930s, which was established by Jeffrey Richards.[85] Alternatively, we might consider that class masquerade loosened the stays of the imagination as far as social stratification was concerned. Occasionally supporting features went even further and challenged the legitimacy of the social order. Perhaps the most striking example is *The Impassive Footman* (USA: *Woman in Bondage*), a Basil Dean film based on a play by Sapper. *Kinematograph Weekly* described it rather anodynely as 'a praiseworthy British effort' which should 'earn the plaudits of all types of audiences'; but, as a challenge to the *status quo*, it is rather more striking than that.[86] The film may be melodramatic and hopelessly stagey in its acting styles, but in its portrait of Marwood (Allan Jeayes), a selfish, domineering, hypochondriac magnate, and the alienation suffered by his wife and servant, it offers both feminist and socialist critiques of the dominant order. When we first see the eponymous footman (George Curzon) reading *The Decline and Fall of the Roman Empire* we know we are in for something a little more radical than usual, and the ending does not disappoint. The downtrodden servant finally becomes a dark avenger, hectoring his scheming and mendacious employer with a furious speech that provokes a fatal brain haemorrhage in the listener. The footman describes himself as 'Just one of the millions who went to that comic war and left everything behind', and criticises Marwood for preferring 'to stay at home and make money'. The footman's wife had been one of the secretaries ('over-worked and under-paid') employed by Marwood and then pressured into sexual favours when she assumed her husband had been killed. But the footman had survived, and returned to find his pregnant wife dying of 'shame and hunger' after being abandoned by her employer. Having exacted his revenge on behalf of all the people wronged by this 'very important fella', the previously stiff and impassive servant walks out of the house with a swagger and a smile.

Another surprisingly acerbic social critique was offered by *The Tenth Man* (1936), a less successful follow-up to Brian Desmond Hurst's hit drama *Ourselves Alone* (1936). In *The Tenth Man*, adapted from the play by W. Somerset Maugham, Hollywood reject, John Lodge, plays George Winter, a shady businessman-turned-politician who believes that nine out of ten people are fools who are easily conned, and that 'business must come first'. He is a megalomaniac who has 'no use for this world' unless he is 'sitting on top of it'. BIP's publicity described Winter as 'A Buccaneer of High Finance – A Bandit of the City, as ruthless and merciless in his struggle for riches as the Gold-hungry Pirates of old, stamping out Love and trampling on hearts in his insatiable lust for Wealth and Power'.[87] Vigorously directed by Hurst, the film was evidently designed to appeal to an American audience, and paints a portrait of electioneering which is every bit as cynical (if not as stylish) as *Citizen Kane*'s (1941). When gullible voters fall for Winter's lies and elect him, he declares it is 'a victory for English honesty, English plain-speaking, English integrity'; but his bubble is finally burst by that one man in ten who refuses to be corrupted.[88]

In the Twickenham production *Lord Edgware Dies*, dapper detective Poirot, asks his less intellectually gifted helper Captain Hastings (Richard Cooper) if he believes in heredity. Hastings replies immediately, 'You bet I do, that's how I got my money!' But inherited riches were often portrayed as the source of corruption or unhappiness in quota films. In Radio's *Windfall* (1935), based on a play by R. C. Sherriff and directed by George King, an ageing working man (Edward Rigby) inherits money, but he finds no satisfaction or meaning in a life of ease and luxury, and the lives of his family members are ruined. The film's tag line was 'A Fortune That Was a Misfortune'.[89] In a similarly plotted Leslie Fuller comedy, *Bill's Legacy* (1931), a bequest of £75,000, almost ruins the marriage of decorator Bill Smithers until he winds up broke again. The young couple (Derrick de Marney and Geraldine Fitzgerald) in Lawrence Huntington's Paramount rom-com *Café Mascot* (1936), speculate successfully with £1,000 left in a taxi, but 'eventually realise that happiness does not automatically follow in the train of riches'.[90] The previous year, Paramount's *Key to Harmony* (1935), concerned a penniless-but-happy Bohemian couple whose relationship is put under strain by sudden wealth and success. The press book described it as 'The striking story of a stage-struck girl who found love in an attic – and nearly lost it in a luxury flat.' The film set out to reverse the proverb about love departing when poverty appears by suggesting that the 'key to harmony' was to be found in neither material acquisitions nor social acclaim. It was a reassuring message for its hard-pressed audience, but one which, even in the 1930s, was well worn. *Film Weekly* felt that the constant refrain of the 'unimaginatively directed' *Windfall* – riches do not bring happiness – gave the picture 'an old fashioned air'.[91] Comments like this are an important counter to viewing film content as a simple reflection of contemporary attitudes. In the 1930s, the discourses of films were in continuous negotiation with wider societal discourses, just as they are today.

In accordance with a long tradition of Christian teaching, many of these films pointed to the incompatibility of money and the virtuous life. When wealthy parents over-indulged their children the result could be the kind of criminal disposition exhibited by the car thief played by John Mills in *First Offence*.[92] When the 'common man' tried to join his 'betters' by adopting their financial stratagems, the results were also unlikely to be satisfactory. In Fox's tellingly-titled comedy *Servants All* (1936), a butler (Robb Wilton) invests all his money in a dud company, and lives like a gentleman for a few days, before receiving a rude awakening. This might seem a classic example of the power of a dominant ideology in 1930s' cinema, but the cracks in the ideological edifice were already beginning to show by the time of the release of *Servants All*. Dismissing the entertainment value of a film containing 'poor' acting and direction, as well as 'atrocious dialogue', *Film Weekly* described *Servants All* as an 'old-fashioned comedy without a single redeeming feature' – including, one must assume, its message of 'know your place'.[93] Things were likely to work out more favourably when inheritance brought a title rather than simply riches, as in the popular Redd Davis romantic comedy *King of the Castle* (1936), in which a clerk

(Monty King) learns he is the rightful Lord of Drone Castle. The themes of title inheritance and class masquerade were combined in Twickenham's adaptation of a novel by Lady Troubridge, *His Grace Gives Notice* (1933). In this 'comedy drama of kitchens and coronets', directed by George Cooper, a footman (Arthur Margetson) discovers he is the heir to the Duchy of Marlow, and then pretends to be a servant again to save the woman he loves from a scheming Chicago gangster. The press book insisted that the whole scenario was 'typically English'. The acquisition of wealth and elevated social position conflicted with political beliefs in the well-received Radio comedy *If I Were Rich* (1936), in which a barber (Jack Melford) at first abandons his socialist convictions when he becomes an earl. However, he is unable to adjust to his new way of life, and is relieved when it is discovered that he has been given the title in error.[94]

Wealth compromised moral principles again in PDC's well-received *A Lucky Sweep* (1932), in which an anti-gambling chimney sweep (John Longden) wins the Irish Derby Sweepstake with a ticket bought in his name. In fact, luck in 1930s' quota films was a quality magically associated with the Irish. Warner Bros. exploited the association in their successful Teddington Studios production *Irish for Luck* (1936), which featured a very young Margaret Lockwood. The film's publicity hinted that the character of the Irish, forged during a 'dark and gloomy' history, might provide an ideal template for British viewers negotiating the privations of the 1930s' depression: '[T]he people of Ireland have two great qualities which enable them to reach good fortune in the end, and that is their never-failing optimism and cheerfulness.'[95] There was even a suggestion that the very act of viewing the film might act as a good luck charm. But luck was brief for its promising young director, Arthur Woods, who was killed in World War II. Paramount sponsored so many films with 'luck' in the title – *Lucky Days* (1935), *Lucky Loser* (1934), *Lucky Jade* (1937) – that it almost seemed that they were being used as company talismans. Certainly, the critical roasting given to most of their supporting features meant they needed all the luck they could muster. However, as the bathetic Sound City fantasy *Eyes of Fate* (1933) warned, luck could also be cursed. In this film, a man fortuitously acquires a copy of the next day's newspaper and uses it to back enough winning racehorses to make his fortune, only to finally read of his own death. Audiences could do without this sort of gloomy ending to a wish-fulfilment fantasy, and the *Eyes of Fate* did depressing business.[96] It was, however, emblematic of those films in which good fortune created problems which – as Shafer has calculated – surprisingly outnumbered stories in which luck produced unalloyed happiness by a ratio of three to two.[97]

If luck was the dominant theme of optimism in British supporting features, its pessimistic corollary was fear of public exposure. Blackmail and scandal provided the motor for countless plots. Private secrets seemed to lurk behind every public persona in a representation of the world that, in its emphasis on artifice, masquerade and pretence, mirrored the practices of film-making itself. Albert Bramble's last film, an adaptation of the popular stage play *Mrs. Dane's Defence* (1933), was a case in point. Described in its publicity as 'a woman's brave fight for her reputation', the film told the story of a widow (Joan Barry) who, as a young governess, had been seduced by her employer, provoking the suicide of his wife. In later life, this 'shadow from her past threatened to blot out her happiness'. Mrs Dane's battle with a scandal-mongering aunt is an eloquent evocation of an age before tabloid tittle-tattle, and of a moralistic social order in which respectability was worth more than riches, although *Picturegoer* thought the story already 'outmoded'.[98] Similarly, in Warners' *A Glimpse of Paradise* (1934), the wedding prospects of George Carney's screen

Keeping things on track: Norman Lee directs *Strip! Strip! Hooray!* (1932)

daughter (Eve Lister) are threatened by the revelation that her father is a vagrant, and she becomes a potential victim of blackmail. The plot of Paramount's popular, *The Barton Mystery* (1932), was driven by the attempt to save the reputation of a woman who had written compromising letters to a murdered philanderer; and Twickenham's adaptation of A. E. W. Mason's *House of the Arrow* (1930), concerned the unmasking of the notorious blackmailer known as 'The Scourge'.

Blackmail went hand in glove with social hypocrisy, and a number of films offered oblique comment on virtuous lives which might not be all they appeared. In fact, there was a short cycle of these films in 1932, possibly in response to a tightening of censorship in the film industry and beyond. Warners' *A Letter of Warning*, directed by John Daumery, suggested that a group of self-righteous church workers might have their own guilty secrets.[99] More pruriently, the BIP featurette *Strip! Strip! Hooray!* (1932) followed a reporter (Ken Douglas) as he investigated the activities at a sunbathing camp – 'something spicy for the jaded Sunday readers' – and exposed the moral hypocrisy of his prospective father-in-law, the President of the Wear More Clothes League (Albert Rayner). The plot, with its puritans, libertines and a young man on the make, would not have been out of place in a *Carry On* film; and nor would some of the dialogue: 'Any more nonsense and I'll pull your trousers off – I'll expose your villainy.' The script for the film that one critic called 'an excuse to exploit lightly-clad damsels', was the work of the future director of *The Wicked Lady* (1945), Leslie Arliss.[100] The same basic plot had already been used in the successful Fox comedy *Double Dealing* (1932).[101] In this film, Frank Pettingell played the pious chairman of a northern Watch Committee who is unmasked by his future son-in-law as a backer of a risqué revue. A similar theme was explored in another 1932 film, Pathe's sex comedy *Pyjamas Preferred*, in which the husband of a pillar of the Purity League secretly runs a notorious nightclub and is threatened with exposure by an old flame.[102]

Prurient curiosity was the unacknowledged appeal of many quota films of the period. Paramount's Rattigan-scripted *The Belles of St. Clements* 'an engaging story of life in a girls' school' featured 'lovely girls at work and at play'. Audiences were encouraged to 'See the great swimming and diving match between the Belles of St Clement's and the Eastfield beauties', and were thus assured a display of 'schoolgirl' flesh. 'Charming maidens', the press book promised, 'are seen working, playing, loving, laughing, swimming, diving, singing, dancing, "ragging" and pillow-fighting in a thoroughly convincing atmosphere.' However, the film's publicity was also at pains to point out that this was primarily the 'story of a schoolgirl's noble self-sacrifice for her friend', and that its director, Ivar Campbell, was a 'feminist': 'Mr Campbell is enthusiastic about women as film makers and artists. He considers that, generally speaking, they are more interested and receptive to new ideas than men.'[103] The story's moral uplift and Campbell's feminist credentials did not stop the censor slapping a cautious 'A' certificate on the film and thus confirming its risqué appeal. Radio Pictures' comedy *Handle with Care* (1935), directed by Redd Davis, swapped a girls' school for a 'Ladies Physical Culture Saloon', where a man on the run (Jack Hobbs) takes refuge from police pursuers. The fantasy of sexual plenitude, moderated by embarrassment, is all too obvious and would become a staple of 'B' comedy and science fiction for years to come. In this case, it is bolstered by a drug that turns weaklings into supermen. A ladies gymnasium also provided the venue for a 'leg show' in the near-the-knuckle MGM comedy *A Tight Corner* (1932), again starring Frank Pettingell.

Some scripts exploited public interest in liminal areas of social life and morality. In *The Water Gipsies*, the barge girl played by Ann Todd falls for a well-off young painter (Peter Hannen) and agrees to pose for him in something close to her birthday suit. While Ms Todd just about covers her embarrassment, the camera dwells lasciviously on a portrait of her with one breast fully exposed, in an example of nudity by proxy that is remarkable for the period. Carol Reed's first excursion into film direction, *It Happened in Paris*, was another racy study of love between an artist (John Loder) and his model (Nancy Burne) in Paris's Latin Quarter. The cover of the film's press book was adorned by a photograph of Miss Burne posing in her underwear, and (by way of legitimation) a line drawing of an artist's palette and brushes. The iconography of sexual freedom was less than subtle. The closest London could get to the exoticism of the Left Bank was Chelsea, an artist's quarter a little more accessible to the cameras of the Poverty Row production houses. We have already discovered that there was a lot of fuss about *Chelsea Life*, the quota quickie exposed in *Picturegoer*, but London's artist colony was already notorious for sexual laxity before Sidney Morgan used it as a background for his story. The merest mentions of an 'artist's model' and 'Gay Bohemian parties in a Chelsea studio' were sufficient to titillate audiences. 'They had very little money, but they saw a lot of life – Chelsea Life!' was the film's carefully coded tag line. One of the leading female roles in *Chelsea Life* was played by clergyman's daughter Anna Lee who was already a familiar face in exposés of 'the smart set' from a range of American renters including Radio (*Mannequin*) and Warner Bros. (*Mayfair Girl* [1933]). In George King's *Mayfair Girl* – 'a startling exposé of London's Bright Young Things' – a young American girl (Sally Blane) comes to London and joins a fast set of nightclub habitués. She ends up framed for a murder committed while she was insensible through alcohol. The film's ostensible aim was to teach a moral lesson to girls whose heads might be turned by the bright lights, but the interests of

Bright young things: the tired and emotional cast of *Mayfair Girl* (1933)

exploitation were not far below the surface: exhibitors were promised that the Mayfair set's 'wild parties, their sophisticated habits, are daringly presented in a manner that will hold any audience'.[104]

Paramount's *Faces* (1934), another Sidney Morgan film starring Anna Lee, was typical of the social morality of the 1930s' quota picture.[105] Based on a stage play by Patrick Ludlow and Walter Sondes, it was a familiar cautionary tale of an ambitious girl (Lee) who works in a West End beauty parlour and who is almost led astray by a philandering businessman, before returning to her ordinary devoted boyfriend (played by the future director, Harold French). The conventional message to the host of young women in the audience who might identify with Anna Lee was to beware of offers of rapid social advancement from unscrupulous men, and instead settle for a more modest life with a more loving and appropriate partner. The choice facing girls like Anna, insisted the film's tag line, was between 'honest and guilty love'. But as in so many films of the period, audiences were drawn to the message by promises of a glimpse into a vaguely exotic (and possibly erotic) world from which men, at least, were largely excluded. 'Should a woman tell her love troubles to her hairdresser?' asked one of the film's copy lines before promising to reveal 'Secrets of the Beauty Parlour!'[106]

The British pre-war programmer never sank to the salacious depths of the American exploitation film, but its makers and publicists were just as aware of the commercial value of the promise of titillation. Its school belles, fetching gymnasts, artists' models, department store mannequins and beautiful beauticians all occupied the space between the everyday and the out-of-reach, the known and the never-to-be-experienced, catering easily to female identification and male desire. They might flirt with danger, but they would invariably negotiate the territory of moral dilemma successfully. If the glimpses of the forbidden in any of these films raised a frisson of guilty desire, punishing expiation could always be sought in the iron morality of a film like Radio's *The Lash* (1934). In this Twickenham Studios adaptation of the crowd-pleasing stage play by Cyril Campion, John Mills played the sybarite son of a millionaire. He loves nightclubs and women and has seduced the wife of an aged and invalid friend of his father. The stern paterfamilias (Lyn Harding) first tries to pack his son off to Australia and finally, with the full blessing of the film-makers, sets about him with a bull whip. The result is not a further widening of the generation gap, but a reconciliation in which the son learns the error of his ways, and 'leaves for home on his father's arm, closer than they have ever been for some years'.[107] The publicity described the thrashing as 'an age-old cure for headstrong youth'. *Kinematograph Weekly*, commending its 'sound' moral lesson, suggested that 'the sentiments are not designed to appeal to the more sophisticated patron, but they are interpreted in a language which will thrill and appeal to the masses'.[108] *The Lash* again exemplifies the moral and philosophical tensions, so characteristic of the 1930s, between dominant discourses of tradition and the challenge posed by new leisure opportunities and libertarian impulses.

As often as not, these social tensions were played out within family relationships, and particularly within marriages. The dilemmas, uncertainties and moral imperatives of marriage are

'Headstrong youth': John Mills has the whip hand (temporarily) in Twickenham's *The Lash* (1934)

at the core of many quota films, and their press books indicate the way in which audiences were encouraged to extend the screen discourses into their own thoughts and discussions in a way that can best be described as agenda setting: 'Who should hold the purse strings, husband or wife? Or should it be a fifty–fifty partnership? Does a mean husband make a dishonest wife?' asked the publicists for *Purse Strings*, a Paramount film directed by Henry Edwards and starring Dorothy 'Chili' Bouchier. Sometimes these domestic quandaries took on a decidedly bizarre aspect. The questions posed by Paramount's *The Price of Wisdom* (1934) were: 'Should a man marry a girl who walks in her sleep, often screams for no reason at all, and sings negro spirituals while she carves a leg of mutton on the stairs?'

Fairly typical of films devoted to the trials of domesticity was Warners' *Leave It to Blanche* (1934), not least because it starred Henry Kendall, whose presence was almost obligatory for a quota picture that aspired to a place in one of the 'better-class' venues. Directed by Harold Young, an American associate of Alexander Korda, and scripted by another American, Roland Brown, the film was a comedy of errors about a golf widow who tries to revive her husband's (Kendall) interest by pretending to have an affair with a film actor (ironic, given the burgeoning size of Henry Kendall's fan base at the time).[109] The plot is indicative of the significance of cinema in its patrons' fantasy lives, and the picture offers a representation of the way in which the idea of film penetrated into the domestic environment. Sometimes domestic comedies

A marriage in need of a lift: Olive Blakeney gets carried away in Harold Young's *Leave It to Blanche* (1934)

would confront the politics of gender more directly, although few would now win the approval of feminist critics. Fox's well-received *Virginia's Husband* (1934), directed by the doughty Maclean Rogers and based on a novel by Florence Kilpatrick, gently mocked the hypocrisy of the attractive young leader of the 'Women's League of Liberty' (Dorothy Boyd), who pretends to have a husband in order to secure the financial support of her aunt. 'Amusing adventures with an inconsistent Amazon,' declared the film's tag line. 'It is the artless honesty of its humour that makes it so pleasantly entertaining,' commented *Kinematograph Weekly*.[110] Maclean Rogers' *Merely Mr. Hawkins* (made this time for RKO in 1938) was another blast against the monstrous regiment of women. Described as an 'accurate commentary on lower middle-class domesticity', its story offered hope to members of the 'Hen-pecked Husband's League' when a domineering wife (Sybil Grove) is humbled by a con man, leaving husband Eliot Makeham with a little more self-respect.[111]

## Old faithfuls and new fangles

Films depicting threats to an established way of life from new technology or patterns of consumption were often unashamedly sentimental, and tuned to the structures of feeling of older audiences. The title of Radio's *Old Faithful* (1935), again directed by Maclean Rogers (who would himself become an 'old faithful' of the British 'B's), is indicative of this approach. Horace Hodges played an ageing cockney driver of a horse-drawn hansom cab who discovers that his daughter has fallen for the driver of a motorised taxi. Horace the hansom man is put out of business by the death of his horse, but the loss of his 'old faithful' is compensated for by the love of a good woman (his landlady). Times must change, the film seems to say, but there is virtue in an emotional attachment to the past. *Kinematograph Weekly*'s comments on the film are revealing:

> The plot is old-fashioned and obvious. The entertainment rests on the quiet commentary on working-class life and the clever and amusing character cameos. It is the domestic side of the play that carries it, and this is strengthened by bright repartee, couched in a cockney vein. The producer saves himself and the picture by imparting that friendly, homely touch that means so much to the masses, and so surely disarms criticism.[112]

The pleasures for the audience were thus in recognition and reassurance, delivered with homely humour. The formula was tried and tested, and considered virtually beyond criticism. Maclean Rogers returned to the theme of displacement by technology in another Radio-distributed film, the well-received *The Heirloom Mystery* (1936). Edward Rigby played a craftsman whose honesty is challenged when his work is threatened by cheap mass-produced furniture. *Picturegoer* was pleased to report that the picture drew 'a sound moral that the craftsman should be proud of his craft'.[113]

Two of the leading exponents of the theme of redundancy, hardship and displacement, handled with reassurance and homely humour, were John Baxter and his regular scriptwriter, the MGM executive Bert Ayres. Edward Dryhurst described *Commissionaire* (1933), a film he scripted and directed for MGM from a story by Ayres, as 'mawkish and jingoistic . . . patriotic, flag-waving chauvinism'.[114] Ayres was one of the most red-white-and-blue of the colourful characters flushed out by the Quota Act. That he was certainly a man with an eye for the main

Horse power: A trade advertisement for the nostalgic *Old Faithful* (1935). Author's collection

chance is evidenced by his willingness to commission his own scripts; but he was also a fervent patriot who had fought in the Battle of the Somme and who had sympathy with the common man. Somehow he managed the contradictions of commissioning quota films for an American multinational, and promoting a sentimental depiction of an England in the grip of brutalising forces. Both Baxter and Ayres saw cinema as a forum for raising issues and giving a voice to the powerless; and Ayres' dialogue could be daringly political. In *The Real Bloke* (1935), for instance, the issue of the redundancy created by mechanisation is highlighted by the case of Bill (George Carney) a navvy dismissed for complaining about pneumatic drills. Having reassured a trauma-tised shopkeeper, who believes that the drilling will drive him to an early grave, that 'we're navvies, not Nazis', Bill admits that the automatic drills remind him of machine guns because 'The blokes who make the money from them don't 'ave to use 'em.'[115] Ayres' efforts lent credi-bility to the notion that the pound-a-foot merchants, served by British technicians and work-ing in characteristically British idioms, were closer to the essence of a national cinema than their more cosmopolitan brothers at Denham, Pinewood or even Elstree. Through Ayres, MGM – the arch villain in Rachael Low's account of quota production – did as much as anyone to put the ordinary lives of the country's hard-pressed poor on screen.

'Navvies, not Nazis': mechanisation shakes things up in John Baxter's *A Real Bloke* (1935)

In a pair of films – *Song of the Plough* (1933) and *Song of the Road* (1937) – John Baxter used the device of the relationship between a man and a working animal to symbolise the affective bonds that had humanised the workplace in a more caring and less rapacious age. For maximum effect, Baxter placed his characters in a countryside where the 'natural' way of things was being challenged by economic strictures and technological change. Frequently in quota films like these, the moral order under threat from new ideas and practices is represented by village life in opposition to city corruption. In Bernerd Mainwaring's *Old Roses*, traditional life is represented by the eponymous hero (Horace Hodges again), 'a lovable old character living in a peaceful little village', obsessed with his garden. But the tranquillity of his life and his community is threatened by a ruthless blackmailer and a landowner who wants to drive an arterial road through the village. Fox's publicity suggested that the way these threats are overcome would make essential viewing for 'all who love the beautiful simplicity of the rural existence', which the film presented, complete with gypsies and a poacher. Clearly the urbane sophisticates at *Kinematograph Weekly* could not be counted among the film's target audience: the journal's reviewer dismissed *Old Roses* as 'just a pretty-pretty quota feature for small halls', describing its plot as 'naïve' and 'old-fashioned', its dialogue as 'trite', and its sentiment as 'sugary'.[116] The hard-nosed *Observer* critic, Caroline Lejeune, had been just as severe on the one-man-and-his-dog storyline of *Song of the Plough*, a film shot in difficult conditions on Sussex farmland. She advised MGM to ditch the thin narrative and unreal portraits of 'country yokelry' and cut the picture down to a one-reel travelogue of Sussex.[117] Audiences, even in the Empire, Leicester Square, turned out to be more sympathetic to Baxter's project, and the weight of letters supporting the film in Lejeune's mailbag eventually obliged her to recant and accept its virtues.[118] *Song of the Plough* clearly managed to yoke the kind of homage to the English countryside that would become such a feature of British Transport Films, to the sort of theatrical melodrama that could still grip the public imagination. The result effectively mobilised sentiment for a mythic disappearing Britain – a green and pleasant pasture being submerged under the sprawl of slumland and Metroland. This might not have been the realistic depiction of Britain craved by Lejeune, but as a way of *imagining* the nation it was in touch with audience desires. J. B. Priestley once observed that, 'It is when an enduring and completely satisfying life in the country is on its way out that it is presented with pastoral effects and Arcadian highlights', and in the 1930s the rural economy was already in long-term decline.[119] Commenting on the enduring popularity of *Song of the Plough*, which one cinema had booked seventeen times, Baxter was typically self-effacing:

> It is not for me to explain why the effect should be so marked, but the times were difficult and I think audiences found some relief in the beauty of the countryside and the character of the people in meeting and overcoming their problems.[120]

Another classic evocation of the village as emblematic of the settled nation is George King's *Silver Top* (1938), a 'human story of a crook's regeneration'. The moral regeneration is accomplished by the love of a vicar's daughter and a kindly village shopkeeper (Marie Wright) who has been targeted by city criminals because she has recently received a large inheritance. The ideological disposition of *Silver Top* is very much in keeping with Napper's argument that the thematic concerns of the quota quickies dramatised 'fears of a threat to indigenous cultural values' – the threat being bound up with 'the modernity, classlessness and instability implied by the impetus towards social mobility which was an increasingly visible aspect of Britain in the 1930s'.[121] In *Silver Top*, the initial disruption to village life comes in the form of a car crash which delivers a 'fast' young female gangster into the care of the shopkeeper – a representative of the 'nation of shopkeepers'. That her shop is emblematic of age, diversity and homely tradition, is evident in its description in the film's press book:

> The almost unbelievable jumbling up of unrelated things – as a rule diametrical opposites – which seems to be the guiding principle of old-fashioned village general stores was faithfully adhered to by the property man in *Silver Top*. . . . Many of the scenes take place in this emporium, which besides being practically the universal provider of the needs of the inhabitants, is also a centre for the exchange of communal gossip. . . . From the parlour window could be seen the winding village street, the church and an AA box – *practically the only sign of modernity in the picture.* (my emphasis)

If the symbolism of cultural conservatism is pretty obvious in *Silver Top*, it is unashamedly explicit in one of the most popular of the quota quickies, Paramount's adaptation of R. C. Sherriff's play *Badger's Green*. *Kinematograph Weekly* was impressed by the way in which its affectionate satire on the 'narrowness of village life' was given the cinematic scope denied to the play on stage.[122] *Badger's Green* is the story of a small community, largely controlled by the benevolent despotism of three old residents, and an outsider who arrives with the idea of developing the sleepy village into a place of importance. Resistance to this transformation is centred on the local cricket club, which is eventually obliged to play a match against the developer's team to decide the future of the village. The film contains footage of an England vs Australia test match at Lords but, as the press book put it, the cricketers of Badger's Green 'were not fighting for the Ashes, but for the village they loved and wanted to preserve in all its old-world charm'. Reviewers were particularly impressed by what *Kinematograph Weekly* called 'a charming idyll of the English countryside, packed with human interest, wholesome sentiment, and delicious fun'.[123] Filmed partly on location at Kings Langley, Buckinghamshire, the English life depicted, of course, was both stable and rural, a society in which the place was secure and 'places' were known. The game chosen to symbolise that way of life, cricket, is also one in which everyone knows their position – on the field and in the batting order. The village 'types' were presented with no apologies for conventional characterisation: the elderly doctor, the blustering retired major, the jolly publican and the brawny blacksmith who provided the spearhead of the team's bowling attack. Confronted by so reassuring a picture in a cinema culture in which characters were constantly masquerading as someone they were never intended to be, the *Picturegoer* reviewer was moved to say that 'After seeing the picture one feels that one has been out in the open country for an hour – it is a very refreshing feeling.'[124] It is not too difficult to see *Badger's Green* as an allegory of the British film industry. Like the valiant village cricket team, it was struggling against the odds to protect English cultural values against money-driven, homogenising imperialism. Hollywood, like the developer, had superior know-how and resources, but was obliged by the Quota Act to seek partnership and compromise.

It would be a mistake, however, to assume that all audiences were dewy-eyed about small-town life. Urban opposition surfaced in the following letter to *Picturegoer*:

> I'm all against British village life being filmed. Whilst the opportunities given for showing us beautiful scenery are tremendous, the fact still remains that 'Bai gum' and haystacks cannot compete with Hollywood's slick wise-cracks and gangsters' hide-outs. British films want speeding up. The perambulations of the village doctor and the ringing bells of the village church will apply the brake instead of touching the accelerator. The promise that we shall be given more opportunities for seeing rural Britain in British films may send a small minority into ecstasies, but I think that the majority of us will still dive into the cinema which offers us that laughter-raising, spine-tickling, big-town fare.[125]

The ambivalent attitude of urbanites towards all things rural was caught in Paramount's *Lancashire Luck*, efficiently handled by Henry Cass on his first directorial outing. Mrs Lovejoy (Muriel George), wife of a city carpenter (George Carney), wins the football pools and sets up a family catering and garage business on the country estate of cash-strapped aristocrat Sir Gerald Maydew (George Galleon). The Lovejoys are 'sick of the town and everything in it', including unemployment and monotonous factory work. Initially, they take to the country 'like ducks to water', but they soon discover that rural life is no paradise. They encounter the class prejudice of Sir Gerald's waspish mother (Margaret Damer), president of the local 'Society for the Preservation of Merrie England', who disrupts the Lovejoys' trade by closing the local woods to visitors and prosecuting young Joe Lovejoy (Nigel Stock) for poaching when he is framed by a local

'Don't trust them toffs': George Carney tries the country life with film debutante Wendy Hiller in *Lancashire Luck* (1937)

villain. The suspicions of Lovejoy senior – 'I don't trust them toffs and never will; it's all shop window with them, and nothing inside' – appear to be confirmed until Sir Gerald, who has fallen for the daughter of the family (Wendy Hiller in her first screen role), comes to the Lovejoys' rescue.

*Lancashire Luck* makes much of its class contrasts. George Carney is the epitome of the working man, drinking his tea from a saucer and carving a loaf in a bowler hat, pipe between his teeth. Margaret Damer's Lady Mayhew, on the other hand, is a ruthless snob who polices her sensitive son's manners and thinks of town girls like Lovejoy's daughter as 'common sluts'.[126] The Lady of the Manor and the poacher Black John are the serpents in the Lovejoys' Garden of Eden and, for a while, convince them that they 'don't belong to the country at all'. But the film's ultimate message, one which was likely to go down well with its primarily urban audiences, is that 'It takes a townsman to get the best out of the country'. The city carpenter puts his knowledge of wood to profitable use by going into partnership in a forestry business with his future son-in-law, the Lord of the Manor – a union of working-class know-how and progressive aristocratic thinking.[127]

That the fancy needs the plain apparently was always so, because Twickenham's *Vicar of Bray* carries a similar message. In this farrago of bad wigs and worse history, set in the seventeenth century and made in the same year as *Lancashire Luck*, Stanley Holloway plays the vicar of a hamlet near Dublin. We should perhaps not dwell on the unlikelihood of such a solidly Protestant settlement in so Catholic a country, or of his being plucked from rural obscurity to be tutor to the wayward son of Charles I, because it is the qualities of the character that are the keynote of the film.[128] The Vicar is an embodiment of the spirit of humanism and compassion that transcends political differences and temporary conditions. He is a force for integration and consensus, which never fails to quell and seduce the forces of conflict and dissent. The grace, conviviality and roguish good humour of this clergyman who is 'well-read but not bookish' and 'can drain a bowl of wine with the best of us', is equally irresistible to the haughty King Charles, his sybarite son and the Puritan Oliver Cromwell. His motto is 'Whatsoever king may reign, I'll still be the Vicar of Bray', and, in the politically divided 1930s he represents a longed-for time when 'all old wounds will be healed and all old differences forgotten'. 'It's peace and goodwill this old country wants,' asserts Holloway, 'and away with all the old feuds.' The day may still come, the film suggests, when fractious city-dwellers will learn the lessons of fellowship and harmony being taught in the country parishes.

While the threat to the rural idyll in dramas like *Badger's Green* and *Silver Top* is mostly external, the disruption of the established social order in the thriller is frequently internal. In the inter-war country-house detective story, murder is a symptom of the tensions and insecurities of a ruling class beginning to give ground under pressure. A film like Twickenham's *The Shadow* is redolent with paranoia. Its tone is noir and claustrophobic and its action is almost exclusively confined to a single country mansion shrouded in a fog that makes any departure problematic.[129] The mansion has been infiltrated by a ruthless blackmailer and murderer known to Scotland Yard as 'The Shadow', provoking the lady of the house to declare 'We shall all be murdered in our beds.' The killer might be almost any of Sir Richard's guests, including a gatecrashing couple – the female half of which is described disparagingly by the family retainer as 'a very

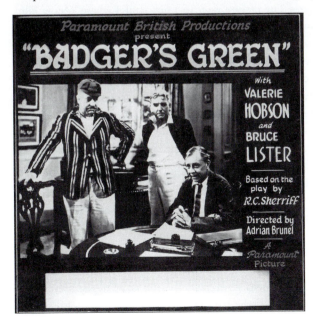

Cultural conservatism: David Horne, Frank Moore and Sebastian Smith are depicted in this glass advertising slide for *Badger's Green*. Author's collection

modern miss' – with designs on the family jewels. A certain amount of comedy relief is provided by the 'silly-ass' antics of Henry Kendall's character, but discomfiture returns when he is revealed as the criminal mastermind, the class traitor within. Cheap and derivative it may be, but *The Shadow* tapped a vein of anxiety running through the old moneyed families and into the aspiring middle classes.

If the core of that threat was, as Napper argues, modernity, then one of its key signifiers was, paradoxically, the medium of potential reassurance itself: the cinema. Certainly, there is a significant difference between the depiction of a more traditional form of entertainment, the music hall, and that of the cinema. In sentimental films like those of John Baxter, the music-hall style of entertainment is nostalgically reconstructed as a world of community, fellowship and warm-heartedness that is rapidly being swept away on a tide of commercialism. The spirit of togetherness and mutual support that music hall represents is seen by Baxter as vitally needed in the troubled times of the 1930s. As a transmitter of humane values of kindness and understanding, music hall has the advantage of being an unmediated form of communication. It contrasts favourably with the mediated, more alienating and atomising effects of the film *business*. So often in Baxter's stories, music-hall performances actually raise money for (diegetic) audience members while, ironically, the film being watched actually relieves the real (extra-diegetic) audience of its coins. While music-hall performers are depicted as honoured members of the working-class community, people 'like us'; film *stars* are seen as distant, aloof and 'other'. They are concerned, perhaps, less with performance and public service than with money and the opportunities for conspicuous consumption and 'glamour' that it offers. When Baxter decided to depict the cinema, the result was the featurette *Screen Struck* (1937), which he produced with his partner, John Barter. The film was directed by Lawrence Huntington and – bravely – distributed by MGM. Bravely, because it appears to have been a satire on the whole business of quota quickies. Ironically, the idea for the film probably came from within MGM itself, as the screenplay was co-written by Bert Ayres. The picture is set in a film studio where 'Quota Film Productions' is under the direction of an American (Julian Vedey) keen to make movies about an English way of life of which he is woefully ignorant. Burlesque, it may have been, but its comments on the clichés and cost-cutting of quota production were uncomfortably truthful.

For those stuck on the quota treadmill, making films about the British way of life was more like a life sentence. Some, like George King, occasionally indulged their fantasy lives as dashing swashbucklers. King made *Adventure Limited* (1934) for Paramount, in which a group of devil-may-care adventurers attempt to rescue an imprisoned South American president by posing as a film production company. Of course, the real film unit never ventured further than Elstree, but they could dream.[130] Film stars, or the impersonation of stars, were fairly common motifs in low-budget film-making. Some pictures, such as Warners' *Little Miss Nobody* and Louis Blattner's *My Lucky Star* (both 1933) made for Gaumont-British, unashamedly exploited the fantasies of the screen-struck young women in their audience. The latter's protagonist (Florence Desmond) is a 'gofer' for a fashion house who achieves the stardom and romance she craves almost accidentally when she is sent on an errand to a film studio. Occasionally, film production would take 'centre stage'. In 1931, George King's *Deadlock* explored the idea of a murder committed during the filming of a crime picture. In the dénouement, it was random shots taken by the film camera which revealed the truth.[131] Four years later, Leslie Hiscott revisited the theme with *Death on the Set*, made on Julius Hagen's night shift for distribution by Universal. The film takes the self-referentiality that was not uncommon in films of the period, to an extreme as it actually shows a picture like itself in the process of creation, using Twickenham Studios themselves as its sets. It is a far from flattering portrait of film-makers. The actors are shown as shallow, vain and barely competent. The leading lady is a real 'Lady' as her glamour has netted an old-but-titled husband whom she has turned into a cuckold by her affair with the director. The director, himself (Henry Kendall), is a bullying martinet who will murder to make his life easier. He exploits and appears to despise his actors, and his interest in the creative process goes little beyond getting it over with as quickly as possible. His life, like his work, centres on the manipulation of other people. Unfazed, *Today's Cinema* blithely pronounced the film 'Good entertainment for the masses'.[132]

The contrasting worlds of the English country estate and American film-making were brought together in the Twickenham comedy *Annie, Leave the Room!* (1935), also directed by Hiscott and distributed by Universal. The film was based on a West End play by Norman Cannon and depicted, in the words of its press book, 'The mirthful adventures of movie-makers at the ancestral home of the penniless, picture-struck Lord Spendlove'. The impoverished peer (Morton Selten) sees the offer from a Hollywood company to rent his mansion as a location as a way of gaining independence from his domineering mother-in-law (Eva Moore) and launching a career as a film star. Unfortunately, it is his gormless maid, Annie (Davina Craig), who ends up with the studio contract, while his mother-in-law turns out to be the vice-president of the film company. *Annie, Leave the Room!* is a striking fable of the seduction of English class tradition by American popular culture. The US-dominated film world is imagined as a saviour from financial failure and social repression, liberating the potential within the 'Old Country', both for the film's protagonists and for indigenous production houses like Twickenham. As well as supplying a valuable glimpse of contemporary film production techniques, it might easily be read as an allegory of the Quota Act itself, with Hollywood businesses beginning to make films in England and (perhaps reluctantly) helping the cash-strapped and starry-eyed home industry back to its feet through a form of partnership. It is tempting to read allegories of the film industry in a number of other quota quickies. Radio's *Easy Riches* (1938), an apparently 'homespun' and 'unsophisticated' story directed by Maclean Rogers after the production finance crisis of 1936, has a title that invites allegorical interpretation.[133] And lo and behold, we find Gus McNaughton and George Carey playing rivals in the building business. Carey wins the contract to supply bricks for the new town hall, but falls prey to the wiles of a plausible foreign crook financier (Peter Gawthorne) with a grandiose scheme for a garden city. The plot might easily allude to the over-reaching and dubious financing of British film. Brock Williams' script for *Hello, Sweetheart* (1935) satirised the murky business of film finance more directly. That he could get away with casting the American characters as swindlers at least shows that his employers, Warner Bros., had a sense of humour.

While film-*making* was represented largely as a powerful modernising force in these pictures, film *exhibition* was the subject of more contradictory discourses. The super cinema was clearly identified with modern consumption, but the small, independent picture house could stand for honest old ways under threat from ruthless new methods. Paramount's *Pay-Box Adventure* (1936), the last film directed by W. P. Kellino, was the modest 1930s' example of a theme that would be explored to greater effect by *The Smallest Show on Earth* (1957). Based on an original story by

First step to stardom: Vivien Leigh
in *The Village Squire* (1935)

W. Gerald Elliott, the now-lost *Pay-Box Adventure* related the story of a struggling small-town cinema, run by a staff that is 'one big happy family'.[134] The picture house's patrons, however, are being poached by the new super cinema in the neighbouring town. The names of the rival picture houses – the Arcadia and the Palace – nicely evoke the challenge to the rural idyll by metropolitan glamour. In an effort to save the Arcadia, its manager (Billy Watts) goes into partnership with its owner (Molly Hamley-Clifford), hoping to sell the cinema to the 'Inter-Continental' circuit. This they finally achieve, in spite of the machinations of their rapacious and unscrupulous lawyer (Eric Fawcett). The action mostly takes place in the foyer of the Arcadia, where the commissionaire (played by music-hall comedian, Syd Crossley) organises amusing stunts to pull in customers. While ostensibly about the plight of the independent exhibitor trapped in the vice of circuit expansion, the film manages to resolve the differences between small showman and large combine by introducing a third party who is the 'real' villain of the piece. The solicitor is given the characteristics which might otherwise have been associated with the circuit controllers. Distaste at this trite resolution of fundamental conflicts within its readership may have influenced the unusually savage attack on the picture mounted by *Kinematograph Weekly*, which listed the film's points of appeal as 'none':

> The Quota Act has in its time been responsible for many sins in celluloid, but few greater than this, a preposterous drama crudely depicting the ups and downs of a small kinema proprietress, hemmed in by circuit opposition. From first to last it is pitiful: the film is, in fact of no earthly use to the

average exhibitor. Billy Watts is a poor example of managerial efficiency as Jimmy. Marjorie Corbett would never last a day in an up-to-date hall as the cashier, Mary. While Mary [sic] Hamley-Clifford more than deserves her share of bad luck as Mrs Bartlett, the proprietress. . . . Although the character drawing in this picture is a joke, the biggest joke of all is the story treatment. Nothing intelligent ever happens, and that which does is frequently beyond normal comprehension. Unable to conceal its crudities behind topicality and trade technicalities, the drama must be dismissed as useless.[135]

The worlds of rural tradition and cinema modernity were also brought into direct opposition in Reginald Denham's Paramount quickie *The Village Squire*, the picture that introduced Vivien Leigh to the filmgoing public. The plot concerns a Hollywood star (Leslie Perrins) holidaying incognito with his sister (Leigh) in an English village where the ultra-conservative Squire (David Horne) 'hates modern inventions, particularly films'. The Hollywood actor and the English landowner find common ground in a mutual admiration for Shakespeare, but the Squire is distraught when the star falls for his daughter (Moira Lynd). All, however, are reconciled when the star saves an amateur production of *Macbeth*, staged as a fund-raiser for a local hospital. Thus the film ultimately celebrates a marriage between the representatives of the old and the new. *The Cinema* found it 'rather refreshing entertainment' and warmly recommended it to exhibitors as 'characteristically British'.[136]

## Notes

1. *The Bioscope*, 27 January 1932, p. 19.
2. Edward Wood, 'Happy Ever After?', *Picture Show*, 18 April 1927, p. 15.
3. Arthur Dent, 'Appealing to the Ninepennies', *Kinematograph Weekly*, 14 January 1937, p. 34.
4. Ibid. There was certainly support for this view from the Mass-Observation's survey of Bolton cinemagoers: 'When I go to the pictures I go to be entertained. . . . I know far more about my own problems than film producers do or ever will do, so that when I go to the pictures I don't want to see these problems solved (to the satisfaction of the producers) in what are called true to life pictures. I like seeing historical romances . . . Failing this, I like Musical Comedies or a really good Detective Picture because they take my mind off everyday things.' Bolton cinemagoer Mrs E. Skellen, aged 27, Mass-Observation Cinema-going in Worktown questionnaire 1937, quoted in Jeffrey Richards and Dorothy Sheridan (eds), *Mass-Observation at the Movies* (London: Routledge, 1987), p. 121. A survey of exhibitor opinion in early 1937 also revealed a belief that the family audience craved: 'Love, life and laughter with serious interludes'; 'a simple blending of pathos and humour'; and 'romantic films with a sensible story, "not too true life", though dealing with people like themselves whose lives they can understand and whose reactions they can appreciate'. The desire was for 'something they need not think about, something that will catch their eye, tickle their fancy but not trouble their mind'. A happy ending was thought essential. 'Conflicting Tastes of British Film-goers', *World Film News*, February 1937, p. 7. The demand for 'escapist' entertainment in the period is discussed more fully in Stephen Shafer, *British Popular Films 1929–1939: The Cinema of Reassurance* (London: Routledge, 1997), pp. 44–55.
5. 'The spectator watches the party of youngsters exploring the countryside . . . There is much picturesque charm in the districts visited, Gilwell Park, Romney Marsh, Folkstone, with its fishing

boats, and Lympne with up-to-date aeroplanes. Many beautiful cloud effects are introduced, Stanley Rodwell deserving warm praise for his artistic photography. One of the merits of the picture is the absence of acting in the ordinary sense of the word: the boys while in camp, and engaged in the week's "hike", moving about as unconcernedly as though cameras did not exist.' *The Bioscope*, 2 July 1930, p. 29.

6.   *Kinematograph Weekly*, 17 November 1938.

7.   The majority of the film's bookings in Leicester was as a first feature.

8.   *Kinematograph Weekly*, 28 September 1933.

9.   *Down Our Street* press book. This early exercise in social realism was praised by *Film Pictorial* for declining to show 'Britain's painted and powdered face, made to look pretty and beautiful for those who can't see beneath the skin'. 17 September 1932, p. 20.

10.   John Baxter, 'Stepping Stones', unpublished manuscript, BFI Special Collections, p. 16.

11.   The table employs the genre classifications used in Denis Gifford, *The British Film Catalogue 1895–1985* (Oxford: David and Charles, 1986). These must be treated with some caution, because the films were rarely generically pure. What was being classified, more often than not, was the dominant generic element in a hybrid picture. Gifford's categorisations, however, have been used to enable us to compare the relative sizes of genres within second-feature production with those of British films as a whole.

12.   Andrew Sarris, 'Beatitudes of B Pictures', in Todd McCarthy and Charles Flynn (eds), *Kings of the Bs: Working within the Hollywood System* (New York: E. P. Dutton, 1975), p. 49.

13.   A detailed statistical breakdown is supplied in Shafer, *British Popular Films*, p. 22.

14.   David Sutton, *A Chorus of Raspberries: British Film Comedy 1929–1939* (Exeter: Exeter University Press, 2000), p. 101.

15.   Ibid., p. 206.

16.   *Kinematograph Weekly*, 14 March 1935.

17.   *Picturegoer*, 27 August 1938, p. 22.

18.   Andy Medhurst, 'Music Hall and British Cinema', in Charles Barr (ed.), *All Our Yesterdays: 90 Years of British Cinema* (London: BFI, 1986), p. 185.

19.   John Grierson, 'The Fate of British Films', *The Fortnightly*, July 1937.

20.   *Kinematograph Weekly*, 5 September 1935, np.

21.   For a discussion of Old Mother Riley and cross-dressing in comedy see Marcia Landy, *British Genres: Cinema and Society 1930–1960* (Oxford: Princeton University Press, 1991), pp. 354–7.

22.   *The Bioscope*, 23 March 1932, p. 22.

23.   Evidence from Leicester and the lavishness of some of the *Josser* press books suggest first-feature status, but cinemas in 'better-class' neighbourhoods might easily have booked Lotinga's films as supporting features (if at all). For example, the small Scala Cinema in Oxford booked *Dr. Josser, K.C.* (1931) as a second feature.

24.   *The Bioscope*, 11 February 1931, p. 43.

25.   *The Bioscope*, 4 February 1931.

26.   A detailed statistical breakdown is supplied in Shafer, *British Popular Films*, p. 26.

27.   *CEA Report* 617, 3 January 1931. Warners' *Double or Quits* (1938), directed by American Roy William Neill, was one of the few British gangster pictures that was thought 'a first-rate copy of the real thing'. *Kinematograph Weekly*, 31 March 1938, p. 47.

28. *Kinematograph Weekly*, 7 November 1935, p. 31.

29. *Kinematograph Weekly*, 5 March 1936.

30. *Kinematograph Weekly*, 27 September 1934, p. 27.

31. *Picturegoer*, 19 August 1939, p. 22.

32. At least 60 per cent of patrons in the 1930s were women. Nicholas Hiley, 'Let's Go to the Pictures: The British Cinema Audience in the 1920s and 1930s', *Journal of Popular British Cinema* no 2, 1999, p. 47. See also Ross McKibbin, *Classes and Cultures: England 1918–1951* (Oxford: Oxford University Press, 1998), p. 421. As Sound City's Norman Loudon put it: 'women today are such an essential element at the box-office'. *Picturegoer*, 6 May 1933, p. 13.

33. *CEA Film Report*, 1 August 1931.

34. *The Bioscope*, 23 March 1932, p. 23, my emphasis.

35. Ibid.

36. James Chapman, 'Celluloid Shockers', in Jeffrey Richards (ed.), *The Unknown 1930s: An Alternative History of British Cinema 1929–1939* (London: I. B. Tauris, 1998), pp. 75–97.

37. *Kinematograph Weekly*, 31 March 1938, p. 27.

38. *Kinematograph Weekly*, 10 March 1938, p. 23. The decadence of the genre by the late 1930s was confirmed by a couple of lampoons produced at Teddington and starring Claude Hulbert as a 'nit-wit detective on the trail of master criminals', *The Vulture* (1937) and *The Viper* (1938).

39. *Kinematograph Weekly*, 7 April 1938, p. 28.

40. Stephen Guy, 'Calling All Stars: Musical Films in a Musical Decade', in Jeffrey Richards (ed.), *The Unknown 1930s*, pp. 99–120.

41. *CEA Film Report*, 28 February 1931. *The Bioscope*'s review summed it up as 'Feeble story of a gipsy girl's love affairs. Much music. Tuneful singing. Ordinary dancing. Poor production.' 25 February 1931, p. 53.

42. *CEA Film Report*, 28 February 1931. Concurring, *The Bioscope* noted that it was difficult to tell 'whether the producer intended his subject as burlesque or romance'. 25 February 1931, p. 54.

43. *The Bioscope*, 24 June 1931, p. 25.

44. *Kinematograph Weekly*, 28 February 1935, p. 27; *Today's Cinema*, 22 February 1935, p. 8.

45. For exhibitor opinion on the waning popularity of musicals see 'Conflicting Tastes of British Film-goers', *World Film News*, February 1937, p. 6.

46. *Picturegoer* (20 November 1937, p. 31) dismissed *Glamorous Night* as 'very unconvincing', and complained that the story value and humorous content of *The Lilac Domino* were respectively 'negligible' and 'exceptionally weak'. 20 November 1937, p. 31, and 14 December 1937, p. 24.

47. Letter from Sidney T. Woodmansey of Scarborough, *Picturegoer*, 16 September 1938, p. 8.

48. Jeffrey Richards, *The Age of the Dream Palace: Cinema and Society in Britain, 1930–1939* (London: Routledge, 1984), p. 258.

49. *Picturegoer*, 9 July 1938, p. 26.

50. Worktown Box 29E, Mass-Observation Archive, quoted in Richards and Sheridan, *Mass Observation at the Movies* p. 30.

51. *Today's Cinema*, 6 April 1935, p. 4. King had less success with the Slaughter-less historical, *John Halifax Gentleman*, which *Kinematograph Weekly* dismissed as a 'costume piece made to modest quota measurements'. 24 March 1938, p. 41.

52. *Picturegoer*, 24 July 1937, p. 31.

53.   *Today's Cinema*, 17 January 1935, p. 6.

54.   *Old Soldiers Never Die* press book.

55.   *The Times*, 29 December 1932.

56.   *Open All Night* press book. The film, which mirrored George Pearson's own fall from grace, is favourably reviewed in *Kinematograph Weekly*, 25 October 1934, p. 33, and discussed in more detail in Kenton Bamford, *Distorted Images: British National Identity and Film in the 1920s* (London: I. B. Tauris, 1999), pp. 173–4.

57.   'Squark! Says Hollywood's Newest Star', *Film Pictorial*, 3 December 1932, p. 27.

58.   John Paddy Carstairs, 'Thanks for the Remittance', *Film Pictorial*, 31 December 1938.

59.   *The Fatal Hour* press book.

60.   *Picturegoer*, 22 July 1933.

61.   *Today's Cinema*, 31 January 1935, p. 14.

62.   *Alibi Inn* press book.

63.   'The production is hardly up to the standard one expects from George Pearson.' *Kinematograph Weekly,* 27 June 1935.

64.   Geoff Brown and Tony Aldgate, *The Common Touch: The Films of John Baxter* (London: BFI, 1989), pp. 29–30.

65.   *Kinematograph Weekly*, 27 January 1938, p. 27.

66.   *Kinematograph Weekly*, 31 March 1938, p. 39.

67.   *Kinematograph Weekly*, 17 March 1938, p. 34. Lionel Collier also criticised the film as desperately 'dated' in its humour and approach. *Picturegoer*, 24 September 1938, p. 30.

68.   BBFC Scenario 105, *Speed King* (*Money for Speed*), 19 December 1932.

69.   *Picturegoer*, 25 September 1937. The boxing match in *Mannequin* was described by *Film Pictorial* (5 May 1934, p. 23) as 'farcical in its artificiality'.

70.   *Today's Cinema*, 26 February 1935, p. 8. The film is unlikely to receive many television screenings these days as one of the protagonists (a white mechanic) has the unfortunate nickname 'Nigger'.

71.   *Picturegoer*, 4 March 1933. For a discussion of the lack of British sports films see Gene Gerrard, 'Where Are Our Sports Films', *Picturegoer*, 1 June 1935, p. 15. See also, Simon Rowson's comments on sports films in Cmd. 5320: 1272.

72.   *Picture Show*, 9 July 1938, p. 19.

73.   Ian Conrich, 'Horrific Films and 1930s' British Cinema', in Steve Chibnall and Julian Petley (eds), *British Horror Cinema* (London: Routledge, 2001), pp. 58–70.

74.   Not that contemporary critics would have mourned their loss. It was thought that the 'eerie atmosphere' of *Castle Sinister* might 'raise the hair of not too discriminating patrons' but the story was 'unconvincing', the production 'weak' and the action 'decidedly jerky'. *Kinematograph Weekly,* 7 April 1932, p. 33. *The Bioscope* (6 April 1932, p. 12) agreed that it was 'so theatrically staged, poorly mounted and lighted, and acted with such amateurism that it never for a moment convinces'.

75.   *Picturegoer*, 7 April 1934, p. 30.

76.   *Picturegoer*, 1 December 1934.

77.   The film had three bookings over two months in Leicester, none of them as a first feature.

78.   *Kinematograph Weekly*, 13 August 1934.

79.  *Ouanga* is often classified as American in reference works. Its production is discussed in George E.
     Turner and Michael H. Price, *Forgotten Horrors* (Eclipse, 1986). It survives in its abbreviated fifty-
     six-minute American version only. The British version ran to sixty-eight minutes.

80.  *Kinematograph Weekly*, 27 September 1934, p. 27.

81.  *Kinematograph Weekly*, 5 July 1934.

82.  *Kinematograph Weekly*, 23 August 1934.

83.  Stephen Shafer devotes two chapters to this theme of 'mistaken identities', calculating that
     almost one in seven quota films of the 1930s contained working-class characters who either
     become, impersonate, or are mistaken for people of a higher social status. *British Popular Films*,
     pp. 84–5.

84.  Ibid., p. 60.

85.  Richards, *The Age of the Dream Palace*.

86.  *Kinematograph Weekly*, 30 June 1932, p. 35.

87.  *Film Weekly*, 7 November 1936, p. 46.

88.  A letter from E. L. Parker of Brighton to *Film Weekly* (6 February 1937, p. 14) cited *The Tenth Man*
     as the sort of programme picture that the British industry needed to counterbalance expensive
     'supers'.

89.  *Windfall* press book. This source confirms that the picture was directed by George King rather
     than Frederick Hayward, who is credited by Rachael Low (*The History of the British Film,
     1929–1939: Film Making in 1930s Britain* [London: Allen and Unwin, 1985], p. 410).

90.  *Café Mascot* press book.

91.  *Film Weekly*, 23 November 1935, p. 77.

92.  For a discussion of Mills, 'man-making' and nationality in this film, see Gill Plain, *John Mills and
     British Cinema* (Edinburgh: Edinburgh University Press, 2006), pp. 45–50.

93.  *Film Weekly*, 18 June 1936, p. 37.

94.  See Shafer, *British Popular Films*, pp. 77–8 for a more detailed discussion of the film and its critical
     reception.

95.  *Irish for Luck* press book.

96.  It had no bookings in Leicester, for example. René Clair used a similar plot for *It Happened
     Tomorrow* (1944).

97.  Shafer, *British Popular Films*, pp. 180–1.

98.  *Picturegoer*, 5 May 1934.

99.  John Daumery was a cameraman with the Belgium Army during World War I. After working for
     Warners and Paramount, he had just begun directing for BIP when he died in May 1934.

100. *Kinematograph Weekly*, 30 June 1932, p. 35.

101. *Double Dealing* received four bookings in Leicester.

102. Political hypocrisy was also lampooned in Warners' *Hyde Park* (1934), in which George Carney
     took the role of an insincere socialist orator.

103. *The Belles of St. Clements* press book.

104. *Mayfair Girl* press book.

105. The film won Anna Lee a contract with Gaumont-British. She married director Robert
     Stevenson and enjoyed a relatively successful career in Hollywood. See Kathleen Portlock, 'The
     Adventures of Anna Lee', *Picturegoer*, 14 November 1936, p. 15.

106. Similarly, the publicity for the MGM thriller, *Alibi Inn*, posed the question, 'What happens to the winners of beauty competitions?'

107. *The Lash* press book. Director Henry Edwards was apparently so fearful that Mills might be seriously injured in this assault that he shot the whipping scene after the rest of the film was safely in the can.

108. *Kinematograph Weekly*, 10 May 1934.

109. Harold Young directed Korda's *The Scarlet Pimpernel* (1934) before returning to 'B' features in the USA.

110. *Kinematograph Weekly*, 13 September 1934.

111. *Kinematograph Weekly*, 3 February 1938, p. 31.

112. *Kinematograph Weekly*, 5 September 1935, p. 30.

113. *Picturegoer*, 3 April 1937, p. 30.

114. Edward Dryhurst, *Gilt Off the Gingerbread* (London: Bachman & Turner, 1987), p. 184.

115. The shooting script for *A Real Bloke* is printed in Brown and Aldgate, *The Common Touch*, pp. 128–63. The issue of adapting to mechanisation had been aired by Stanley Baldwin in his speech to the Tory Party Conference in 1934.

116. *Kinematograph Weekly*, 1 August 1935.

117. *Observer*, 4 February 1934.

118. One woman who saw the film at the Empire wrote to the scriptwriter, Reginald Pound, to say that it was 'a lovely, lovely film' and 'such a great relief from those American films always shown at this cinema'. Brown and Aldgate, *The Common Touch*, p. 35. Similarly, Mrs Muriel Violet King wrote to *Film Pictorial* (8 September 1934, p. 30) to announce that *Song of the Plough* had 'crammed' her local cinema at Crofton Park, SE4, because the picture offered a wonderful moral contrast to Hollywood's products that appealed to 'the intellectually underdeveloped who appreciate undressing and bedroom scenes': 'The glorious English scenery, set to perfect music, was a thousand times preferable to any American "wise-cracker".'

119. J. B. Priestley, *The English* (London: Heinemann, 1973), p. 46.

120. Baxter, 'Stepping Stones', pp. 17–18.

121. Lawrence Napper, 'A Despicable Tradition? Quota Quickies in the 1930s', in Robert Murphy (ed.), *The British Cinema Book* (London: BFI, 1997), p. 49.

122. *Kinematograph Weekly*, 20 September 1934. *The Cinema* described this 'wholesome entertainment' as a 'triumph of scenario, treatment and characterization, incisive and witty direction'. Quoted by Adrian Brunel in a letter to Michael Balcon, 30 July 1936, BFI Special Collections, MEB D/16.

123. Ibid.

124. *Picturegoer*, 9 March 1935, p. 24.

125. Letter from E. A. Humphreys of Birmingham, *Picturegoer*, 24 July 1937.

126. Wendy Hiller may have been born in neighbouring Cheshire, but she makes a pretty weak stab at a Lancashire accent. However, this difficulty with accents did not stop her going straight into the lead role of a cockney flower girl in *Pygmalion*.

127. *Lancashire Luck* was one of the first film productions to be covered by television when BBC cameras visited Pinewood during its making. Press book.

128. Fidelity to historical truth is again traduced by making Prince Charles' lover an actress, at a time when women were barred from the legitimate theatre.

129.  The complete absence of natural light in the film indicates that *The Shadow* was shot on
      Twickenham's night shift. The film apparently played as a main feature at some cinemas, but not in
      Leicester.
130.  *Kinematograph Weekly*, 25 October 1934, p. 32 commented poignantly: 'The settings, mostly
      confined to interiors, are very studio, and the camera work is static.'
131.  With a distinguished cast and an eighty-four-minute running time, Butcher's had intended
      *Deadlock* as a first feature, but it was still booked at some venues as a supporting attraction.
132.  *Today's Cinema*, 2 March 1935, p. 4. Twickenham's *Lord Edgware Dies* features another 'vain and
      spoilt', faithless actress (Jane Carr) married to a peer. The modernity of Lady Edgware is
      emphasised by her wearing of trousers, the décor of her town apartment and, most of all, by her
      nationality: American. Her relationship to her husband is blatantly homicidal: 'If we were in
      Chicago,' she remarks, 'I could get him bumped off quite easily.' In England, however, she is forced
      to do it herself after creating an ingenious and ironic alibi.
133.  *Kinematograph Weekly*, 13 January 1938, p. 27.
134.  *Pay-Box Adventure* press book.
135.  *Kinematograph Weekly*, 18 June 1936, p. 28. The theme of independent businesses being engulfed by
      the large multiple had been introduced the previous year by John Baxter in *The Small Man*, which
      sought to show what could be achieved by independents banding together and confronting their
      antagonists.
136.  *The Cinema*, 17 April 1935, p. 12.

# 5

# Cuts to the Quickies

The criterion for the exhibition of 'dirt' – horrid but expressive word – should be whether it is witty or artistic, for it can well be both. A little tabasco sauce effects an enormous improvement in many otherwise slightly dull dishes. The difficulty seems to be that we British are not usually a witty or artistic race . . . It is, therefore, perhaps better for our well-being that we should take our dishes plainly boiled, with very little in the way of spicy condiments.

Letter to *Film Weekly*[1]

While the content of British supporting features was primarily shaped by budgets and the conventional wisdom of the cinema trade, each film had also to pass the scrutiny of the British Board of Film Censors. Work on the paternalistic operation of the BBFC in the 1930s has revealed that, although the Board took a strict and doctrinaire view in matters of moral laxity, it was also subject to conservative pressures applied by bodies such as the National Council for Public Morals, the London Public Morality Council, the Mothers' Union and the National Council of Women. The Board's decisions were also potentially subject to the attentions of local watch committees not known for their liberal predilections. The combined effect of this network of moral conservatism was to effectively stifle any frank discussion of matters sexual and political, sanitise all depictions of crime and violence, and protect all established institutions from forceful criticism.[2]

## Cut Shortt

At the beginning of 1931, the new president of the BBFC, former Home Secretary, Edward Shortt, fired off a circular to film producers warning them that the Board would not tolerate the new trend towards 'grossly brutal and sordid themes'.[3] This initiative was chiefly provoked by Hollywood pictures that had brazenly flouted the Hays Code guidelines, but, as if to emphasise that the warning applied just as much to British film-makers, the Board took the rare step of refusing a certificate to a would-be quota picture called *Night Shadows*, condemning it as 'squalid, sordid and totally unfit for public exhibition'. The offending film, which was adapted by the young Sidney Gilliat from a play by Louis Lemarchand and directed by Albert de Courville, had been made in two weeks at Walton for Fox.[4] However, according to Vernon Sewell, who was a Walton technician at the time, the studios' blind owner, Archibald Nettlefold, had no knowledge of the project. The man responsible for sanctioning the production of this forty-five-minute Marseilles waterfront shocker in which a sailor dances 'with a dead whore' was the studio manager, Bill Lott.[5] It got him the sack, and must have been deeply embarrassing for all concerned, although Gilliat, who had just had his first screenplay credit on another racy French drama, Gaumont's *A Gentleman of Paris* (1931), managed to keep his name off this one.[6]

The solution offered to cautious film-makers eager to avoid the fate of *Night Shadows* and the incurring of expenses on unacceptable projects was to submit treatments and scenarios for approval, prior to production. The examiners who sat in judgment of these scenarios were Colonel J. C. Hanna and (from April 1934) Miss N. Shortt, the president's daughter. The pair are described by Jeffrey Richards as 'a rather tetchy retired army officer and a sheltered upper-class spinster'.[7] The number of producers taking advantage of this service rose steadily during the decade, but the first submissions came from established British studios, and particularly from Gainsborough, whose proposal for a film based on the life of a French spy seduced by a priest at a tender age became the first victim of script-vetting.[8]

The first of the quota quickie merchants to submit a scenario was Langham Productions in July 1931. The property was the innocuous *A Safe affair* (even its generic title *Gay Adventure Number 1* would have raised no eyebrows at the time), a Douglas Hoare story about the papers of a Russian countess, which was made for MGM distribution.[9] It sailed through, and Twickenham Studios quickly followed the lead, presenting their first scenario, *Jack O'Lantern*, in September. As *Condemned to Death*, it was eventually passed by the BBFC with one small cut at the end of the year.[10] Twickenham ran into its first problem with the synopsis for *Sir Richard Meets a Fairy*, which was regarded as 'somewhat daring and unusual and would require very delicate handling'.[11] When submitted the following year as a full scenario, it ran into problems over the idea of a 'collusive divorce', a means of circumventing the strict matrimonial laws of the period, commonly practised by the wealthy, but unsuitable for the plot of a popular feature.[12]

By the beginning of 1932, there had been only forty-one submissions. The American renters were particularly slow to become involved, regarding it as the responsibility of the production companies to acquire clearance for their scripts. Some producers, in turn, left it to their scenarists. For example, the adaptation of Douglas Newton's *Sookey*, which was to be made by George King for United Artists as *Self-Made Lady* (1931), was submitted by its adaptor, Billie Bristow.[13] By the middle of 1932, Paramount, MGM, Radio, and Warner Bros. had begun to submit the odd scenario. The first from Warners-British eventually became the featurette *Her Night Out*, but it was initially submitted as *Alone at Last* by Scott Darling, and was greeted with a hostile response: 'The whole story is fantastic and very unreal. Two of the principal characters are prostitutes. There is a good deal of drinking and a certain number of scenes of ladies in various stages of undress. We do not consider that the film, if completed on these lines, would receive our certificate.'[14] The whole thing was toned down and finally passed with an 'A' certificate after further deletions in March 1933. Warners' next submission, *Little Fella* (1932), a comedy in which a baby plays cupid to a girl and a major, was considered 'harmless' apart from a few snatches of suggestive dialogue and a shot of the baby's bum.[15] Fox's first submission, on the same day as *Little Fella*, was a much bigger headache. *The Masquerade*, a play by J. H. Booth featuring a drug addict, was deemed unacceptable unless alcohol was substituted for dope.[16] Twickenham also ran foul of the dope ban when it submitted a scenario for a comedy provocatively titled *It Looks Like Snow* (although Colonel Hanna may not have realised that 'snow' was a slang term for

Misconduct? Binnie Barnes (left) and Jane Carr share a bed in *A Taxi to Paradise* (1933)

cocaine). The prohibited substance was to be hidden inside some golf clubs. Astonishingly, sac-charin was suggested as a substitute.[17] Julius Hagen decided to shelve the project, but managed to get away with portraying a doctor as a drug fiend in *A Shot in the Dark* (1933), perhaps because he is warned by the film's clergyman sleuth (O. B. Clarence) 'You know that stuff's no good to you, leave it alone.'

Sometimes the titles of scenarios did cause the censor qualms. *Misconduct*, a farce submitted by George Smith, was thought 'unpleasant' and was changed to *A Taxi to Paradise*, and was a hit for Adrian Brunel and Fox.[18] *To Brighton with a Bird*, the original title of the George-King-directed and Harry-Cohen-produced comedy about a penguin's visit to the seaside, could not be allowed; but *To Brighton with Gladys* was deemed less suggestive. However, warnings were issued about showing the penguin drunk and displaying the leading lady's 'under raiment'.[19] The latter warning was repeated in relation to the 'unnecessary display of cami-knickers' in Brock Williams' script for the Warners' comedy *Double Trouble* (re-titled *Double Wedding* [1933]).[20] Leav-ing a story untitled would not necessarily ensure an easier passage across Colonel Hanna's desk. Warners really should have known better than to submit the tale of Grace, a typist who is raped, stabs her violator and gives birth in prison. The response was predictable: 'I am strongly of the opinion that this story is unsuitable for exhibition in this country.' Objection was taken to the character of Grace's fellow typist, Jenny: 'Her secretarial duties are just something on the side. Her real profession has a much greater place in history.' There were also problems with depicting pregnancy: 'We consider the whole theme of impending motherhood to be too intimate and delicate a subject for showing in detail on the screen.'[21]

## Unwholesome smut

'Sex pictures', mainly from Hollywood studios, caused considerable disquiet at the Board in the early 1930s, provoking Edward Shortt to warn the British trade against emulation:

> The Board has always taken exception to stories in which the main theme is either lust or the development of erotic passions, but the president has come to the definite conclusion that more drastic action will have to be taken with regard to such films in the future.[22]

By the summer of 1932, Shortt was pleased to note that his warning had been heeded.[23] For the most part, there was very little pressure from the cinema trade for the relaxation of censorship. Vice-president of the CEA, James Welsh, approved of the contemporary regime of censorship because it constituted 'a definite barrier to the showing of films that would debase our screens and finally bring ruin to the industry'.[24] Trade periodicals, far from campaigning against the censorship of the artist, sometimes criticised the Board for being too lenient and film-makers for being too outspoken. For example, reviewing MGM's *Come into My Parlour*, *The Bioscope* commented that, 'The opening bedroom scene in which the censor's forbearance must have

More than a glimpse of stocking: Marguerite Allan and Camilla Horn in *Matinee Idol* (1933)

been stretched to its limit, and another vulgar interpolation might well have been omitted.'[25] The doyen of trade journalists, P. L. Mannock, was far from a lone voice when he appealed, early in 1932, for 'More Wholesome Product' from British studios. A reputation for wholesomeness, he argued, would give British pictures a competitive edge over foreign competition, adding: 'Who on earth would really lament the decline of the sex picture, or a slump in some of the forms of screen "humour" which are very little removed from sheer dirt?'[26] *Picturegoer's* reviewer, Lionel Collier, sometimes warned his readers of smutty humour, remarking of Radio's *Annie, Leave the Room!* 'The dialogue tends to go too near the bounds of decency at times, and one crack definitely oversteps the mark.'[27] Even 'low' comics like the Geordie comedian, Albert Burdon, were mindful of the public reaction to 'blue jokes':

> The healthy minded public . . . wants real honest-to-goodness fun to laugh at, not innuendoes to snigger at. . . . Suggestiveness may create a diversion in the smoke-room, but it is not real humour or it would not require the spicy trimmings. Unclean humour does not find favour with a whole audience, and a joke which delights some and makes others feel uncomfortable is much better left uncracked.[28]

Exhibitors were no more liberal. In September 1931, *The Bioscope* published two letters from northern exhibitors complaining about the use of profanities and 'cheap and vulgar raspberries' in British films.[29] Five years later, a letter to *Picturegoer* from the North of England was still registering 'the strongest possible protest against the cheap vulgarity so evident in many of the British-made films on view at present'. William Beaudine's Wardour musical *Two Hearts in Harmony* (1935) was the prime offender, but objection was also taken to Twickenham's superior programmer, *The Last Journey*, in which the part of the Frenchman was considered 'unnecessary apart from the vulgar incidents'. The writer had asked the cinema's manager if 'this sort of thing is appreciated down South', but was assured that 'it was depreciated all over the country'.[30] There was evidence for his view in a missive fired off to *Picturegoer* from London's Finsbury Park, wondering if 'the censors were awake' when they passed the 'appallingly vulgar film' *Aren't Men Beasts* (1937), and pointing out that 'the sight of elderly men disarranging a young lady's clothing is not funny'.[31]

For a large segment of the audience, part of the 'national value' of British films was their sexual probity. In June 1933, for example, Joan Allen wrote to *Picture Show* from Grays, Essex:

> I should like to say a few words in praise of British films, and of the Jack Payne film, *Say It with Music*, in particular. . . . There was no sordid sex business, and the humour was clean and wholesome. . . . It is my firm belief that such films are equally as popular as sex-appeal ones.[32]

Sin, in the Puritan imagination, tends to emanate from the nether regions, and might thus be expected to reside at the bottom of a double bill. Miss M. Brown of London certainly seemed to think so when she wrote to *Picturegoer* early in 1933. Her letter is an excellent example of the way in which the moral and pecuniary components of vulgarity could be easily conflated:

> Showing a distinctly vulgar picture in the same programme as one of real merit is bad policy. One such recently shown was revolting. A perfect programme to me would be a first-class picture featur-

ing Colman, Veidt, or any other distinguished and fastidious actor, a Walt Disney comedy, news, and a travel picture with beautiful scenery.[33]

There were some signs in the films themselves, however, that there was resentment in the production industry towards censorious intervention. As already noted, in 1932 there was a spate of films that ridiculed moral entrepreneurship and hypocrisy, possibly in response to the petition, drawn up by the self-appointed Birmingham Cinema Enquiry Committee, against 'the harmful and undesirable nature of many films'.[34] Not surprisingly, these scenarios were generally not submitted to the BBFC for prior approval. The films in question treated those who would ban depictions of sexuality as figures of fun rather than as threats to artistic freedom and open discourse, but a few liberal-minded souls did write to the trade press to advocate a relaxing of censorship in the interests of frank discussion of human relations:

> The cinema as an adult entertainment should not have to undergo such strict censorship. Victorianism ought to have died out long ago, but apparently traces of it still linger among our Board of Censors. . . . It is only by depicting realities that we shall bring to the screen a greater understanding of the difficulties that beset modern life. . . . Ignorance is not a virtue, but a sin. If the cinema, the only medium that can successfully reach the masses, has not the courage to picture life as we should know it, if only to increase our sympathy for human nature, then the everyday person will be subject to all temptations and adversities without the knowledge capable of averting catastrophes. . . . Wit of the keenest variety must inevitably contain a subtle underflow, and filmgoers who cannot swallow a little 'honest vulgarity' (to quote George Robey) should not visit the cinema.[35]

Appeals like this were largely in vain because the fear that any section of the population might not visit the cinema was in the forefront of the trade's support for the dominant regime of censorship.

Among the American renters, Warners encountered more censorship problems than most, and a number of submissions were judged to be sailing close to the wind. Hanna considered the controversial *Mayfair Girl* 'not exactly a Sunday School tale', for instance, but he could find no 'objectionable sex angle' apart from a spanking scene, which was eventually excised from the final cut.[36] With *Smithy* (1933, submitted as *The Man with a Million*) Warners learned that the Board would not tolerate any ambiguity in the depiction of sexual relationships, let alone any suggestion of pre-marital intercourse: 'The fade out at the end of scene 132 is the conventional method of indicating that these two people remained together. . . . This should be avoided by adding a good-bye scene, definitely establishing the fact that no impropriety took place.'[37] Hanna's suggestion was adopted. *Other Men's Women* was another dubious tale of a young man with a past whose attempts to recover compromising letters from a blackmailing innkeeper result in a murder and 'a mix-up of bedrooms'. Hanna condemned it as a 'bad story' with 'dialogue and scenes most suggestive and prohibitive', and strongly advised against its filming.[38] This time, however, Warners stuck to their guns, and, with a little doctoring of Randall Faye's screenplay, the film was made as *Murder at the Inn* (1934) and given an 'A' certificate. But all thoughts Warner Bros. had of adapting A. P. Herbert's novel *Holy Deadlock* were temporarily banished when the

Board rejected it as 'propaganda against the existing Divorce Laws'.[39] Warners might have forever held their peace, but four years later, a script for *Holy Deadlock* was finally approved. Unfortunately, it never made it up the production aisle.

When Warners submitted *Call Me Mame* (1933), a low comedy containing a character described as 'rather on the lines of a "Nancy"', the Board made it clear that the suggestion of homosexuality was not permissible (and neither, remarkably, was a scene of a small boy saying his prayers).[40] However, what constituted a suggestion of homosexuality seemed to be fairly liberally interpreted. Obviously, a title like British Lion's *Gay Love* did not mean then what it does today, but there were numerous examples of the passing of dialogue that would now readily be taken as evidence of a gay subtext to the narrative.[41] In Twickenham's *Tangled Evidence*, for instance, Underhill, the unmarried Colonel's 'most intimate friend' and murderer tells one of the Colonel's nieces: 'I was very fond of your uncle. He was a queer old fellow, but there was something lovable about him when you got to know him.' No wonder that scenarist H. Fowler Mear felt it necessary to establish from the outset Underhill's status as a man engaged to be married. The reassuring indication of heterosexuality is this information's only relevance to the story. However, we may still have our suspicions about the inclinations of the Colonel's shrill, sly, and misogynistic librarian. Similarly, even allowing for the level of effeminacy sanctioned by contemporary codes of upper-class masculinity, the killer (Ernest Thesiger) in Michael Powell's *The*

'We'll all be fairies together!': Sun worshippers in *Strip! Strip! Hooray!*

*Night of the Party* (1933) appears unmistakably homosexual – apart from the obligatory wife he is given. Even more explicitly, BIP's sunbathing comedy *Strip! Strip! Hooray!* contains the immortal and uncensored line 'We'll all be fairies together!'

Unlike Warners, Fox submitted very few scenarios, but when it sent two in the summer of 1934, they ran into trouble with the new girl at the Board, Miss Shortt. Colonel Hanna had only a few routine objections to the script of the bizarre fantasy *Lucky Star* (eventually made as *Once in a New Moon* [1934]) – references to 'birth control', the word 'lousy' – but Miss Shortt was appalled by the script's 'class controversy'. The controversy involved the election of a socialist postmaster as mayor of a village (shortly before he is launched into space by a stellar collision). Miss Shortt was also suspicious of the remark 'Plenty of no9's, Doctor', confessing 'I do not know what it means, but coming from an ex-Sergeant Major, I fear the worst!'[42] On reading Fox's script for the low comedy *Josser on the Farm* (1934), Miss Shortt thought 'very little of it suitable for production'. The battle-hardened Colonel Hanna, on the other hand, thought this film in the *Josser* series 'not so coarse as usual', and acceptable apart from the 'first night' scenes and the potential display of 'bedroom crockery'. Two months later, the completed film was given an 'A' certificate after a few deletions.[43] This sort of comedy was not really to the Board's liking, especially when it involved inappropriate professions. Lupino Lane was advised that a comic undertaker in a 'vulgar slapstick comedy' like *Who's Your Father?* (1934) was in very poor taste, and the character's occupation should be changed.[44]

By the summer of 1933, the Board was becoming concerned that the vogue for bawdy period drama might open the floodgates to a wave of licentious costumers. When Sound City submitted plans for their 'super' production *Captain Blood*, Hanna warned that: 'Manners and conversation 250 years ago were much freer and more outspoken than today, and if reproduced with historical accuracy might easily fail to pass our modern standard.'[45] Here, then was yet another reason for quickie producers to avoid historical subjects. Sound City's more contemporary (and Navy-sponsored) *White Ensign* (1933) was given an easier passage with few objections raised, apart from a spanking scene and the use of the word 'constipated', and was eventually passed with a 'U' certificate.[46] In later submissions, Sound City also discovered that they should not employ the words and phrases: 'tart', 'My God' (*The By-Pass to Happiness*), 'raspberry' (*Menace*) and 'nuts' (*Radio Pirates* aka *Money in the Air*).[47] From *Designing Woman* (submitted as *What Shall It Profit a Woman*) they were asked to delete 'You like them young and toothsome, don't you? I've seen your new typist, you dirty old man' and, 'Don't be so beastly virginal.'[48] But with a little more subtlety, the odd utterance suitable for a Donald McGill postcard could be smuggled through. A gossipy telephonist in the dire crime comedy *The Avenging Hand* (1936), for example, was allowed gratuitously to say: 'My mother said to me "Did he treat you as a gentleman should?", and I said "Yes, but I think I can break him of that."'

Associated Sound Film Industries ran into problems with *The Fear Ship* (originally submitted as *The Second Mate*) over the depiction of drunkenness and the suggestion of sexual assault. Among the objections to dialogue in this film were: 'lousy', 'tonight's the night', and 'You shouldn't go without anything that makes life worth living'.[49] Triumph Films, searching for a suitable subject for the first quota production at the new Riverside Studios at Hammersmith, quickly dropped *The Shadow on the Blind* when Colonel Hanna advised that it was not 'an attractive subject for a film' and should be 'left alone'. The synopsis sketched the story of an adulterous couple who witness the murder of a titled lady, and the dilemma they face in admitting their presence to the authorities.[50] Triumph made a couple of comedies instead.

## Sensitive spots

Most censorial interventions in quota quickie production were concerned with matters of taste and sexual decorum, rather than the discussion and depiction of class and international relations or social institutions. John Baxter's films dealing with the tribulations of ex-servicemen and industrial workers, for example, were not deemed controversial, and passed largely without adverse comment from the Board.[51] However, the BBFC was so sensitive to the criticism of foreign regimes and 'the creeping of politics into films' that it was in some ways easier to set espionage plots in distant history.[52] The classic example from higher-budget film-making is *The Scarlet Pimpernel* (1934), but Poverty Row production had its equivalents. Thus Donovan Pedelty dispatched his English secret service agent, Colonel Stafford, to the Scottish highlands to spy on eighteenth-century Jacobites in Paramount's *Flame in the Heather*. Clergymen were another protected species. *Film Pictorial* reported that the censor had suggested that the adaptation of R. M. Raleigh's novel about a meek curate who believes he has murdered his domineering bishop should substitute an Imperial army setting for the ecclesiastical original.[53] The bishop should be made a general, and the curate a colonel (like Hanna). H. Fowler Mear's script for the Twickenham production of *Excess Baggage* (1933) duly obliged, with Frank Pettingell as a peppery major-general and Claud Allister as his sensitive colonel.

The depiction of crime and the penal system was another sensitive area, and the Board generally took a very cautious approach. When quota producer, Harry Cohen, submitted the synopsis for a gangster thriller, *The Mail Boy Murder*, for instance, Colonel Hanna made sure this libel on his fair land was taken no further: 'A very lurid, fantastic story which is rendered all the more impossible because the venue is laid in England. . . . We do not encourage the exhibition of films showing armed gangsters operating in England.'[54] Cohen's occasional partner, Bray Wyndham, received a similar response when he submitted John Quinn's scenario for his thriller *Tiger Bay* (1933). This was particularly incendiary material because the eponymous bay was really Limehouse, a polyglot district of London's dockland, which had become notorious over the previous two decades as a magnet for dissolute debutantes and flappers in search of an opium den. The BBFC were determined to prevent film-makers profiting from such notoriety, and tried to nip the project in the bud:

> The whole story is an exact replica of the worst type of American gangster films with the scene laid in London, amidst very low and sordid surroundings. The minor characters are drunken sailors and prostitutes of every race and colour. The dialogue savours strongly of American phrases and is not infrequently coarse. I do not consider that a film on these lines would be suitable for exhibition in this country, nor can I suggest any modifications which would make it acceptable.[55]

But Wyndham had already cast Anna May Wong as his leading lady and was not to be deterred. After discussions between the resourceful publicist and script editor, Billie Bristow, and a representative of the Board, fresh plans were submitted. These involved shifting the location to a South American port, removing all drunks, prostitutes and usage of firearms and the cleansing of the dialogue.[56] The plans proved successful, but it was clearly too late to change the trade

Incendiary material: Anna May Wong, Rene Ray and the suggestion of inter-racial lesbian desire in *Tiger Bay* (1933)

announcements of the film, which described it as 'an original story of British dockland and the glamorous East'. It was also too late to make major alterations to the casting. Hence the exotic dockside nightclub is run by a manageress who is more Blackpool landlady than Guianan chatelaine, and terrorised by a gang of cockney protection racketeers. Six weeks after its scenario was first submitted, the completed film, edited by David Lean, was passed 'A' with only minor deletions. Perhaps predictably, nobody seemed to notice the strong suggestion of lesbian desire in the way in which Lui Chang (Anna May Wong) relates to Letty (Rene Ray), the girl she had saved from Chinese insurgents. At the end of the film Lui Chang kills the man who has abducted her ward and, faced with jail, commits suicide declaring, 'Letty could never be happy knowing I was in prison.' But Lui's yearning, empty arms suggest that she cannot be happy knowing that Letty has fallen for Michael (Lawrence Grosmith), the young adventurer who has come to Tiger Bay in search of romance ('Do you think that a man or girl has to have clean feet before they can be romantic?').[57]

What is particularly interesting about the censorship of *Tiger Bay* is the way in which it transformed a story rooted in (admittedly sensational) social reality into fantastical and unconvincing fiction. The character Lui Chang had real-life referents: Brilliant Chang, Limehouse's most notorious drug trafficker in the 1920s, and Annie Lai, a Limehouse prostitute and drug dealer who recorded a series of oral history interviews in the 1980s.[58] Verisimilitude, of course, was no defence as far as the Board was concerned. No suggestions for the serious depiction of life in British prisons got past the Board, and most producers were sensible not even to attempt a scenario. At the end of 1934, Screen Services and Gaumont-British submitted two novels – Stuart Morton's *The Hangman's Guests* and Margaret Wilson's *Dark Duty*, respectively – but both were considered 'unsuitable for exhibition on the screen'. Wilson's book was thought to be 'propaganda against our prison system'.[59]

The protection of the public from the realistic depiction of British impropriety and illegality was not appreciated by all of those so protected. One reader wrote to *Picturegoer* to express frustration at the sanitised view of the country propagated in films:

> England may be a more law-abiding country than America, but I fail to see why filmdom should make it so stodgy and uninteresting. After all, even this country is not perfect – except in films. Let us have some film-heroes; and let our villains be of the deepest dye, undiluted by too much patriotism.[60]

The magazine replied that it would like to see the exposure of 'rackets and corruption' in British public life; but neglected to mention that the censor would never allow it.

*Picturegoer* was more guarded about the desirability of allowing horrific material to be viewed. It was in favour of the protection of children and young people via the 'H' Certificate, and welcomed the powers of exclusion granted to the certificate in 1937.[61] Given the BBFC's well-publicised aversion to horror films, the producers of pictures like *Ouanga* and *The Medium* (1934) might have anticipated a harrowing time for their scenarios. In fact, the script of *Ouanga*, submitted by Paramount as *Drums in the Night*, caused some disquiet because of its depiction of Christian symbols in voodoo ceremonies, but, nine months later, the completed film was passed with only two significant deletions.[62] Clearly, the Board was not too bothered about the overtly racist attitudes expressed in the film. For example, after priestess Klili is rejected by her erstwhile beau, Adam, in favour of his respectable new fiancée, Eve Langley (Marie Paxton), with the words 'You belong with your kind', she is 'counselled' by her black suitor, LeStrange (Sheldon Leonard):

> Klili: If I can't have him, no one else will!
> LeStrange: You're wrong. He's going to marry Miss Langley, she's his kind, she's white.
> Klili: You think so? I'm white too, as white as she is.
> LeStrange: You're not, you're black . . . Klili, forget this madness, your white skin doesn't change what's inside you, you're black. You belong to us, to me.
> Klili: . . . I hate you, you black scum!

*The Medium* was first submitted as *The Model* by Vernon Sewell's Film Tests Ltd. Colonel Hanna thought it 'a gruesome little tale' and remarked on its similarities to the recently passed *The Wax Museum*. However, although he cautioned that the 'unpleasant details' would require careful handling, he did not think the subject was 'prohibitive'.[63] An amended scenario as *The Medium* was resubmitted by Sewell's friend, Michael Powell, but received a similar response from the Board.[64] Sewell pressed ahead, and the film was eventually given an 'A' certificate and the additional classification 'Horrific'. Film Tests had already submitted the synopsis for another macabre tale, *Riverside Morgue*. Written by Donovan Pedelty and John Paddy Carstairs, it was the story of a reporter who hides in a morgue to catch some jewel smugglers. When two bodies are deposited, one comes to life and rips open the other to retrieve a diamond. Colonel Hanna's response was unambiguous:

> Though the scene is laid in London, the story is obviously of American origin, both from dialogue and treatment . . . The story is fantastic and, of course, could not happen in England. The main interest is the weird and gruesome scene in the Morgue, which is described with a wealth of detail that makes it easy to visualize. I have no hesitation in reporting that I consider the story very undesirable, and extremely unlikely to obtain our certificate, even if the details are considerably altered.[65]

Clearly, *The Medium* was the sounder financial proposition.

An adverse report from the Board could sometimes result in the option on a property being sold on to another producer. For example, Nettlefold passed on the rights to the play *The Lash* (1934) to Julius Hagen at Twickenham, after Colonel Hanna advised caution in its adaptation for the screen.[66] Hagen, himself, only submitted scenarios very sparingly, presumably when he thought they contained controversial elements. *Anything Might Happen* (1934) was given a clean bill of health, provided there were no references to 'dope'; but the script of the stage play *Recipe for Murder* caused considerable soul-searching because of its depiction of a 'particularly unpleasant' form of blackmail and the collusion in criminal activity of a doctor.[67]

Colonel Hanna and Miss Shortt ran a universally tight ship at the BBFC in the 1930s. There is little evidence in the scenario reports to suggest that they gave greater latitude to film-makers with a reputation for artistic integrity, in the way post-war censors were more inclined to do. Nor was any allowance for the needs of artistic freedom apparently demanded by film-makers who, when it came to controversial subject matter, lived more in hope than expectation of censorial leniency. With the exception of one or two renegade spirits like Graham Greene, critics largely colluded with the Board, while producers, distributors and exhibitors feared the effect on the family audience of any significant trend towards screen permissiveness. It was left to a few progressive cinemagoers, like D. G. Maitland of Newcastle-upon-Tyne to express the kind of views that are now commonplace:

> For how long are picturegoers to be thought of as weak-minded imbeciles affected for the worse by anything 'unwholesome'? The screen should not try to be 'wholesome and dignified'. The screen is an art, albeit a young one. It should try to be great art and let the wholesome and dignified stuff take care of itself.[68]

## Notes

1. Letter from 'Hibernian' of Tunbridge Wells, *Film Weekly*, 19 January 1935, pp. 96–7.
2. Jeffrey Richards, 'The British Board of Film Censors and Content Control in the 1930s', *Historical Journal of Film, Radio and Television* vol. 1 no. 2, 1981, pp. 95–116, and vol. 2 no. 1, 1982, pp. 39–48. See also Jeffrey Richards, *The Age of the Dream Palace: Cinema and Society in Britain, 1930–1939* (London: Routledge, 1984); James C. Robertson, *The Hidden Cinema: British Film Censorship in Action 1913–1972* (London: Routledge, 1989), pp. 40–73.

3. Linda Wood (ed.), *British Films 1927–1939* (London: BFI, 1986), p. 22. A BBFC questionnaire issued to 603 film licensing authorities at around the same time, revealed very little public disquiet about this 'new trend'. Only twenty-one authorities had received any complaints about films screened. Jeffrey Richards, 'The Cinema and Cinema-going in Birmingham in the 1930s', in J. K. Walton and J. Walvin (eds), *Leisure in Britain 1780–1939* (Manchester: Manchester University Press, 1983), pp. 31–52.

4. Gilliat had already worked at Walton as a joke writer, actor and assistant director. After moving to Gaumont-British, he ghosted *Night Shadows* for Harry Fowler Mear for a meagre £10. Geoff Brown, *Launder and Gilliat* (London: BFI, 1977), p. 42.

5. Vernon Sewell interview, BECTU Oral History Project, Interview 329, 7 July 1994.

6. The film also virtually ended the career of silent star Estelle Brody. David Quinlan, *British Sound Films: The Studio Years 1928–1959* (London: Batsford, 1984), p. 121.

7. Richards, *The Age of the Dream Palace*, p. 108.

8. Scenario 2, *Portrait of a Spy*, 28 November 1930. Scenario reports are held in the BFI Special Collections.

9. Scenario 23, 6 July 1931.

10. Scenario 28, 7 September 1931.

11. Scenario 47, 19 January 1932.

12. Scenario 124, 6 February 1933.

13. Scenario 37, 11 December 1931. Although a George King production, the film played as a first feature at London's Dominion.

14. Scenario 77, 19 July 1932.

15. Scenario 78, 26 July 1932.

16. Scenario 79, 26 July 1932.

17. Scenario 112, 12 January 1933. The prohibition on the depiction of drug-taking was largely the result of controversy stirred up by two films which exploited notorious real-life examples of death from overdoses: the British picture *Cocaine* (1922) and the American film *Human Wreckage* (1924). Marek Kohn, *Dope Girls: The Birth of the British Drug Underground* (London: Lawrence and Wishart, 1992), Chapter 8.

18. Scenario 92, 20 October 1932.

19. Scenario 107, 22 December 1932.

20. Scenario 109, 3 January 1933.

21. Scenario 129, 21 January 1933.

22. *Kinematograph Weekly*, 18 February 1932, p. 21. Censorship remained a live issue in magazines like *Film Weekly* throughout the spring of 1932.

23. *Kinematograph Weekly*, 9 June 1932, p. 21.

24. Ibid.

25. *The Bioscope*, 30 March 1932, p. 17.

26. *Kinematograph Weekly*, 28 January 1932, p. 42.

27. *Picturegoer*, 13 July 1935, p. 28.

28. Albert Burdon, 'Humour the Public Wants', *Film Weekly*, 12 January 1934, p. 10.

29. *The Bioscope*, 2 September 1931, p. 25.

30. Letter from J. Stevens of Liverpool, *Picturegoer*, 4 July 1936, p. 30.

31. Letter from A. M. Russell of Finsbury Park, *Picturegoer*, 3 July 1937, p. 36.

32. Letter from Joan Allen, Grays, Essex, *Picture Show*, 3 June 1933, p. 4.

33. Letter from [Miss] M. Brown of London, *Picturegoer*, 20 January 1933.

34. The activities of this Committee are discussed in Richards, 'The Cinema and Cinema-going in Birmingham'.

35. Letter to *The Cinema* from Gladys I. Horner of Westcliff-on-Sea, Essex, 7 March 1934, p. 19.

36. Scenario 160, 30 May 1933.

37. Scenario 188, 20 September 1933.

38. Scenario 219, 21 September 1933.

39. Scenario 366, 11 December 1934.

40. Scenario 144, 20 March 1932.

41. Stephen Bourne, *Brief Encounters: Lesbians and Gays in British Cinema 1930–1971* (London: Cassell, 1996), has identified a number of gay subtexts in British films of the period, including *Journey's End* (1930), *Murder* (1930), *Soldiers of the King* (1933) and *Jury's Evidence* (1936).

42. Scenario 315, 9 July 1934.

43. Scenario 324, 16 August 1934.

44. Scenario 329, 4 September 1934.

45. Scenario 177, 25 June 1933.

46. Scenario 232, 13 November 1933.

47. Scenarios 258, 19 January 1934; 285, 5 April 1934; and 293, 30 April 1934 respectively. There were also concerns that *Money in the Air* might compromise 'the dignity of Scotland Yard'.

48. Scenario 247, 12 December 1933.

49. Scenario 182, 4 July 1933.

50. Scenario 249, 21 December 1933.

51. See the Board's comments on *The Navvy*, Scenario 364, 4 December 1934, for instance.

52. 'Censor on Improved Standards', *Kinematograph Weekly*, 25 June 1936, p. 7.

53. *Film Pictorial*, 4 March 1933, p. 13.

54. Scenario 153, 28 April 1933.

55. Scenario 173, 14 June 1933.

56. Apparently the line that described modern literature as 'the product of effeminate Jews who have to dip their pens in disinfectant before writing', was considered acceptable.

57. Stephen Bourne (*Brief Encounters*, p. 22) does note the strong suggestion of lesbian desire. The larger posters to promote the film depicted the two women entwined in each other's arms.

58. Annie Lai, Bob Little and Pippa Little, 'Chinatown Annie: The East End Opium Trade 1920–35: The Story of a Woman Opium Dealer', *Oral History Journal* vol.14 no.1, Spring 1986, pp. 18–30.

59. Scenarios 368, 14 December 1934, and 373, 27 December 1934.

60. Letter to *Picturegoer* from E. A. Humphreys of Birmingham, 17 November 1934.

61. *Picturegoer*, 16 January 1937, p. 7.

62. Scenario 200, 10 August 1933.

63. Scenario 225, 17 October 1933.

64. Scenario 248, 14 December 1933.

65. Scenario 246, 12 December 1933.

66. Scenario 244, 4 December 1933.

67. Scenarios 267, 6 February 1934; 314, 28 June 1934.

68. Letter from D. G. Maitland of Newcastle-upon-Tyne, *Picturegoer*, 27 July 1935, p. 34.

# 6

# Also Showing . . .

Upon entering one of the best known kinemas in Manchester, I was amazed to see flashed upon the screen a lengthy apology for a British quota film which had been shown the week before. . . . The manager apologised for inflicting upon the public a British film of that calibre, and asked the public's forbearance. It ended 'We know that you cannot enjoy such films, but for the sake of patriotism we crave your indulgence for them.'

Letter to *Picturegoer*[1]

The rosy nostalgia with which cinemagoing has been remembered has obscured just how difficult and stressful the business of film exhibition was for many in the 1930s. Once the initial euphoria around the arrival of the talkies and the boom in British production abated, the hard financial realities of trying to run profitable businesses in the teeth of an economic depression began to assert themselves. First there was the expense of converting theatres for sound. Then distributors increased the rental charges for the new talking pictures. In August 1931 Britain went on the Gold Standard with the (indirect) consequence that disposable income was reduced for many patrons, particularly in the North of England. In October, the situation was exacerbated by the reduction of unemployment pay and a subsequent decrease in cinema attendances. The exhibitors' profits were further squeezed by the re-imposition of Entertainment Tax on seats of 6d and under.[2] The small, independent cinemas were hardest hit. As the manager of the Rialto in York put it: 'Many independents have been keeping a stiff upper lip for so long that it is so out of all proportion to the rest of their physiognomy that [one might soon] be able to post a twelve sheet and two double crowns on it.'[3] In 1933 there were 1,200 cinemas which took no more than £8 daily.[4] Increasingly, these struggling halls faced formidable competition from the 'super' cinemas being built by the large circuits.[5] The supers could expect much better deals from the renters, paying a lower proportion of their takings for film hire.[6] Rather than a response to the increasing popularity of cinemagoing, as one recent study has erroneously suggested, the building boom was initially stimulated by increased competition for a dwindling audience, and the drive towards duopolistic control by the two major circuits.[7] The over-provision of cinema seats became a perennial concern of the 1930s. In these circumstances the cost of renting supporting features could become the straw that could break the camel's back.

## Two's a crowd

> Why should the most patient audiences in the world suffer these hours of boredom, wedged mali-
> ciously between the news reel and the main feature?
>
> Letter to Picturegoer[8]

After taking cinema programming by storm in 1931, the utility of the double feature was now
seriously in question. When an American survey indicated that second features were unpopular,
the editor of *Picturegoer* suggested that, if his mailbag was anything to go by, they were also
unpopular in Britain, and sometimes necessitated cuts to the main feature to accommodate their
running time. Furthermore: 'it almost invariably happens that the two pictures that are shown
do not belong to the same kind of audience. And far too many exhibitors use cheap "quickies"
as their second feature'.[9] The over-production of films to fill double-bill programmes, the magazine believed, was causing quality to suffer. The abolition of the two-picture programme was
repeatedly advocated by MGM's Sam Eckman, the president of the KRS, and by other influential figures such as David Ostrer of Gaumont-British, who maintained that 'the second feature
was frequently of little importance' and would soon be swept away on a tide of longer films.[10]
John Downing, publicity manager at B&D Studios, called for 'the elimination of the limping
second feature' as the 'best thing that could happen to the film business'.[11] Hollywood studio
president, Hal Roach, agreed that the 'evil' double bill cut profits and bored patrons.[12]

   The popularity of the double bill had an immediate effect on short films, making their production, in the view of some of the larger studios 'commercially impossible'.[13] This squeeze on
the shorts came at precisely the time that the British documentary movement was in flower. The
building criticism of low-budget quota pictures gave producers of these actuality films an opportunity to express their discomfort. Films depicting 'wholly or mainly news and current events'
or 'an industrial process' were denied automatic quota status under the Act; and it was hardly
surprising when some actuality film-makers began to question the status given to their products
when 'the Act is giving every day a commercial value to certain fiction films, which, without
the Act, would . . . be nothing more than so much wasted celluloid'.[14] Among the most outspoken of critics was Bruce Woolfe, the managing director of Gaumont-British Instructional
Ltd. Woolfe condemned the double-feature programme as 'a concession to half-wits' who were
more concerned about the length of a programme than about the quality, and accused it of
almost driving the short film off the market.[15]

   These views received support from some exhibitors. One blamed falling attendances in part
on the double bill because 'It so often happens that if one feature in a double programme is
good, the other is poor, and the whole programme is reduced to a mediocre level.'[16] But the
advocacy of a return to a single feature and full supporting programme was more often met with
opposition from showmen who realised that they would struggle to fulfil their quota obligations,
and feared competition from those who chose to maintain a full three-hour programme. The
public, it was argued, demanded value for money. Simon Rowson's researches strongly supported
this view, suggesting that in 1934 more than 85 per cent of cinemagoers wanted a programme
of three hours or more.[17] So did Sidney Bernstein's questionnaire survey of 159,000 cinemagoers, which showed almost 80 per cent in favour of two-feature programmes, preferably con-

sisting of films of contrasting genres. The highest level of support for the double bill was among women.[18] There was even a demand from some sections of the audience for a packaged double-feature programme. This would ensure, argued a letter to *Film Pictorial*, that patrons would not discover, when 'lured' by the main attraction, that they had already seen the supporting feature with another film elsewhere.[19] The Mass Observation survey of cinemagoers carried out in Bolton, suggested little opposition to the double bill, *per se*. Of 559 respondents, only nine called for an end to the double-feature programme, while almost as many (seven) preferred it to a main feature with full supporting programme. For instance, twenty-eight-year-old Mrs Lofts, a supporter of British films, thought 'double-feature programmes are better than one big film and a lot of scrappy little American comedies'.[20] Dissatisfaction with the double feature was largely with the lack of variety created by programming two films of similar type.[21]

Opposition to the double-feature programme was represented by H. A. Whatly of Birmingham who wrote to *Picturegoer* to advocate a one-and-a-half-hour programme with only a news reel or cartoon to support the big feature, so that 'the second-rate feature pictures and shorts that are found in 80 per cent of the kinema shows' could be avoided.[22] Another reader offered his own solution to 'the ordeal of watching a long supporting film', consisting of 'the uttermost depths of weak acting, clumsy production, and slow movement': 'I suggest that a new type of censor be created; one empowered to reject films if they are unworthy of the public; and further, that he be elected from the leading newspaper and magazine critics.'[23] However, the letter does not point the accusing finger directly at British films, and indeed a subsequent letter identified the offending pictures as 'American sob-stuff or comedy'.[24] Further missives on the 'double-feature controversy' swelled the magazine's mailbag, but none of the selection printed in the issue of 20 January 1934 singles out British 'B' features. The target was more often American vulgarity.[25]

Some showmen were even prepared to steal a march on their competitors by introducing a three-feature programme. Paramount tried this practice in the half-dozen cinemas it owned as a means of dealing with the lack of bookings for its supporting features. But, as the depression deepened, the CEA and the KRS acted jointly to save the exhibitor money by outlawing the hiring of three films for the same bill.[26] The maximum running time for a programme was set at three-and-a-quarter hours, effectively institutionalising the double bill. As the Quota Act enjoyed its tenth birthday, Arthur Moss, the general manager of Associated British Cinemas, ruefully confirmed what 'every experienced exhibitor knows' that 'the public has become accustomed to the two-feature programme and now demands it'.[27]

Part of the opposition to the double feature can be traced to the suspicion of 'block booking', the practice which Rachael Low would later seize upon as evidence of the perfidy of the American renters. The idea that exhibitors were coerced into taking quota films probably originated with the complaints of the CEA's London and Home Counties Branch in the summer of 1934 that American renters were no longer satisfied with making poor-quality footage and leaving it on the shelf, but 'were now compelling exhibitors to take it in order to book some better American product'.[28] While there may have been the odd instance of this occurring, its incidence was likely to have been exaggerated as useful propaganda by London exhibitors whose patrons were notorious for their antipathy to British films. In fact, the 'gentlemen's agreements' between renters and exhibitors were more mutually acceptable than Low suggests. The blocked programme, after all, allowed the exhibitor to fulfil quota obligations with a minimum of effort and paperwork, while providing a desirable Hollywood feature attraction. Certainly, the evidence given to the Moyne Committee overwhelmingly supports the idea that package deals on films were freely agreed and mutually beneficial. CEA president T. H. Fligelstone stated categorically that no American renter had ever obliged him to take a quota film in return for being allowed to book a Hollywood picture, adding: 'They do not come with a pistol to your head and say, "Take so-and-so".'[29] The cinematographer, Desmond Dickinson, explained that quota films were often used as booking-deal clinchers, at little cost to the exhibitor:

> It is not the renter who says the exhibitor must have the [quota] picture, but it is the exhibitor who says he cannot afford the amount of money asked for the big foreign special star picture. So the renter says, 'You can have an English picture with it for nothing'.[30]

John Maxwell for the renters made it clear that he 'had never met a case of a renter insisting on his exhibitor taking the poor pictures', and that British distributors used similar tactics based on 'verbal understandings' to book their main attractions at the best possible percentage of box-office receipts.[31] The use of these package deals, then, was a standard part of film acquisition. The real problem for the small exhibitor was not 'block booking', but 'barring', as we shall see.

## Behind the bars

> The better the picture, the more it is barred.
>
> Captain Richard Norton, producer for Paramount[32]

When it came to film exhibition, size was everything in the 1930s. In truth, the quota was a problem for the independent exhibitor only. Among the independents, the quickies were of greatest concern to the smaller houses, especially 'in towns served by the large circuits who already show their own product'.[33] The large concerns received the quality films, while their smaller brothers had to make do with the dross. As one exhibitor put it: 'Gaumont, B&D, BIP and London Films have put out some masterly paybox films, but the independent exhibitors do not get them.'[34] Thus, the problem of the quality of the British supporting feature was contingent upon prevailing exhibition practices and the reluctance, or inability, of the independent exhibitors to organise themselves into circuits with allied production houses. Certainly, they were not helped by a KRS policy that militated against exhibitors forming a booking combine. As one northern manager summed up the situation:

> The Quota Act operated very unfairly against the small independent exhibitors. There was nothing available for an independent exhibitor that was worth showing after the big circuit houses got what they wanted. An independent might be a first-run house in his district, but he was not a first-run house when it came to British films.[35]

Industry observers were in little doubt that the problems of restrictive distribution practices – often involving the 'barring' of films to competitors in close geographical proximity – and the poor quality of quota films available to small exhibitors were inextricably linked. For example, writing a review of the year's films in the same issue of *Kinematograph Weekly* in which so many cinema managers had sung the praises of British films, P. L. Mannock selected only forty-five of 113 quota pictures registered in 1930 as 'presentable entertainment comparable with the average ordinary programme picture of America'. But the 'big kinema circuits' had to shoulder some of the blame for this situation because:

> The best product of Elstree, Shepherd's Bush and Islington is barred from first runs outside Gaumont-British and ABC. This means that the majority of British showmen cannot show the best British pictures. What they do show confirms millions of patrons in their belief that all British films are mediocre. . . . The relaxation of the 'bar' seems hopeless, but is it impossible? Failing some move in this direction, I should like to see a first-class independent production company or two established to supply the independent British exhibitor with the good films he cannot get to-day.[36]

Thus, the exploitation by American renters was only possible because of the denial of bigger-budget British films by the British-owned circuits. The major British film producer/exhibitors can, therefore be seen to have had a vested interest in the continued production of poor-quality quickies, which their own houses had no need to screen. From their point of view, the quickies offered poor competition and helped to build their own revenues. As John Maxwell, chairman of BIP, admitted, the pictures produced by the American renters 'have been so bad that they did not compete with us'. On the other hand, he was prepared to concede that any large increase in the 'worthwhile' pictures made by these companies 'would be seriously injurious to the fortunes of the purely British producing companies'.[37] The criticism of the quickies reflected well on his own 'quality' productions, and his only worry was that the bad reputation of the quickies might be infectious.

P. L. Mannock understood the complexities of the problem better than most. He pointed out that the scramble to increase quality by reducing quantity was not wholly compatible with the rising quantitative demands of the quota. British production was already less than 10 per cent above the minimum requirement to service an exhibition system that consumed product at a frightening rate, and a distribution system burdened by restrictive practices:

> In fact, the position that exists is the one and only reason why any shoddy quota 'quickie' gets any bookings at all. There is no wide choice for the ordinary individual showman: and the smaller independent halls are all in a cleft stick over British films. Even lesser circuits cannot get enough good British pictures. They could if more were made. In my opinion, the situation is made more irksome because one or two of our major companies . . . have made fewer and costlier films, not always with the best judgement as regards subjects.[38]

Adding insult to injury, as far as the small exhibitors were concerned, Arthur Jarrett, the film-booker for the 350-cinema Gaumont-British chain, took a page of *Picturegoer* to attack the only British films available to many of his competitors:

> The deluge of so-called 'Quota Quickies' . . . has, by lowering and distorting the standard of British talkies, done a tremendous amount of harm to production in the past months. Anyone who goes

into a kinema and sees one of these cheaply produced pictures, made solely to circumvent the letter of the law, must get a completely erroneous value of British films.[39]

This concern with the quality of quota pictures might seem surprising at a time when the overall percentage of British films being shown in cinemas far exceeded quota obligations. But, the reception of British films varied enormously across the country and within districts.

## Regional reels

> Some people like spinach, and others do not. Some districts like British films, others do not.
>
> T. H. Fligelstone, CEA president[40]

Englishness was an issue for all British films. In some areas of the UK it was a bigger issue than the quality of the picture. Thus, the president of the CEA could assert that, in some districts, British films were simply not acceptable, 'however good they are'.[41] This prejudice was unevenly distributed across the country, and was concentrated in the largest metropolitan districts of England, and industrial areas of Scotland. These districts were 'resentful' of the Englishness in British films, either because it was culturally alien, associated with a dominant class, or because of a strong identification with the aesthetics of Hollywood films and the lifestyles depicted by them. In any case, this attitude created considerable problems for exhibitors burdened with quota obligations when the showing of a British picture could mean a 25–35 per cent drop in takings. Consequently, the CEA felt justified in warning the Board of Trade: 'We are prepared to be patriotic, but do not drive us too hard.'[42] Quota quickies bore the brunt of anti-English prejudice, because exhibitors in hostile areas were less likely to risk British first features and preferred to smuggle their quota past their patrons in the form of supporting features.

It was always hard for English films to find modes of representation that were appropriate for Scottish audiences. In 1930, considerable publicity was given to the correspondence between the Board of Trade and a Glasgow exhibitor who complained that legal compulsion obliged him to book bad British films, because better ones were reserved by the leading producers for their own circuit cinemas. Richard Williamson estimated that his Eastern Picture House had lost from £16–82 per week running inferior British films, and reported that only one London production had avoided getting 'the bird'.[43] In 1932, one leading exhibitor warned that, 'British producers are drifting into a narrow groove of a type of picture similar to the average London West End play, mostly society drama or farce. This is quite unsuitable for the popular working-class type of hall.'[44] The belief grew among exhibitors that many London-produced pictures were suitable for showing only in 'high-class halls'. The reminiscences of one Scots cinemagoer of the period corroborate the idea that English class representations were barriers to enjoyment: 'British films did not make much impression on us working-class people. The people on the screen seemed always to be dressed in bow-ties, dickies and evening dress. Their language was so la-di-dah, we thought they came from another world.'[45] But when films about ordinary Londoners were shown, Scottish readers of *Film Weekly* complained that the cockney dialect was unintelligible.[46] By comparison, Hollywood pictures benefited from their exoticism as another filmgoer recalled:

I never really liked British films. They reflected our own lives too much. The actors dressed like us, the houses were similar to our own. There was no escapism. The American films offered glamour and excitement, sheer fantasy – ordinary people had lovely clothes and hairstyles, and lived in beautiful houses.[47]

Early in 1935, Arthur Jarrett of Gaumont-British claimed that English films were steadily growing in popularity in Scotland, particularly in Edinburgh and Aberdeen, and he was given some support by the chairman of the East of Scotland branch of the CEA, who hailed the national cinema as a potential cultural saviour:

It is certain that with more good British films, British scenery, and the English language as it should be spoken, that portion of the public who resent all the slang Americanisms and hackneyed triangle themes, delivered with a nasal articulation, will be again gathered into the folds of the kinemas.[48]

But by 1936, opposition was more evident. The Scottish CEA, for example, campaigned for the reduction of the exhibitors' quota to 10 per cent.[49] In 1938, the principal of one of the largest Scottish independent circuits, Herbert Green, summed up audience antipathy to English films as: 'British pictures have come to mean thin houses.' Green further suggested that, thanks to Oxford accents and the 'West End complex', the desertion from quota programmes had become so general that many exhibitors had begun to 'hide the fact that they have a British film'.[50] Consequently, the authorities could take such a lenient view of quota shortfalls that it almost seemed like collusion in the circumvention of the law. In 1938, when Mrs Readshaw of the Picture House, Bonnyrigg, was prosecuted at Edinburgh Sheriff Court, she was defended by the secretary of the local CEA. She told the court that her patrons liked films with Gracie Fields and George Formby, but did not seem to care for some of the other English stars. Mrs Readshaw's daughter, who managed the cinema, added that some of the quota quickies were very bad and she always had trouble with her patrons when they were shown. The Sheriff told her that he sympathised with her 'very much indeed', and imposed a nominal fine of £1.[51] Remarkably, however, most Scottish cinemas not only met their quota, but exceeded it. In the exhibitors' quota year 1934–5, Scottish cinemas showed almost as high a percentage of British films as English exhibitors: nearly double the required figure at 28.2 per cent.[52]

Problems concerned with class and regionalism in audience responses to British pictures were also evident in the North West of England. Lancashire exhibitor, Stanley Grimshaw, for example, complained that, while Hollywood produced 'films for all classes', British features 'introduce the la-de-da manner of speech, the Oxford accent, which people in working-class districts will not stand for. In fact, they laugh it off. What are wanted are more films of the Sidney Howard and Leslie Fuller stamp.'[53] However, this message seems to have taken a long time to get through to American renters in Britain, although warning signs were quickly evident. For instance, when First National distributed Guy Newall's cross-dressing caper *The Other Mrs. Phipps* (1931), they were cautioned by *The Bioscope* that its star, the 'silly-ass' actor Richard Cooper, would receive a rough ride from working-class audiences: 'With the better-class audiences his affected talk may get over, though it is pretty certain that it will run the risk of being soundly "razzed" by industrial patrons.'[54] The sound of the derisive raspberry was almost audible when another northern exhibitor, Alfred Snape, addressed the renters directly. Describing them as those who 'make us buy liver and lights and offal to get a fillet steak and then overcharge us for the lot', he accused them of being out of touch with ordinary people:

> You are catering too much for high-brows. Too much costume stuff – too much operatic stuff – too much high-falutin'-tennis-club-garden-party, empty-headed, noodle and nincompoop stuff that the man-in-the-street doesn't understand. Too much dialogue; Shakespeare, Dickens, grand opera and historical stuff. Too many Ruritanian empires and thrones to be saved, or taken, by dictators and young English and American heroes. . . . You are listening too much to educationists and reformers and highbrows and 'uplift' people. Our patrons don't want any of this – they want *entertainment*![55]

The Bolton Mass-Observation survey suggested an overall preference of audiences in all types of cinemas for American over British films. Sixty-three per cent preferred American films, 18 per cent British, while 19 per cent thought them about the same value. Support for the British product was slightly higher among women (who were under-represented among the respondents), and lowest among patrons of the least prestigious cinema. Among those that chose to comment further on their preference: 'The overwhelming complaint was that there was not enough action in British films. They were dull and lifeless. The settings were restricted and poverty stricken. The acting was stiff and artificial.'[56] Fifteen-year-old Arthur Walker summed up the feelings of many young, working-class patrons when he complained that actors in British films 'always seem to talk soft instead of ordinary' and that the national cinema was 'no good for Gangsters or mystery like American pictures'.[57] Laying the blame for poor cinematic performance squarely at the door of British directors, twenty-one-year-old James Glazebrook also believed that the key to the success of Hollywood films was that 'they give the public what they want, not what *they* want to give us'.[58] Clearly, class resentment found a focus in opposition to a bourgeois British cinema and the sort of film scenarios that another complainant dismissed as 'a lot of nincompoops in evening dress drinking champagne'.[59] Judging by these comments, cinemagoers believed that the brickbats regularly hurled by critics and independent exhibitors exclusively at British supporting features might just as well be tossed at British cinema as a whole. In fact, not one of the respondents used the phrase 'quota quickies' and only one comment, from twenty-year-old Harold Walker, can be interpreted as explicitly criticising British second features: 'American films are far superior to British on every point: acting, direction, production, humour, yes everything! (If I'm not mistaken, *you know it!*) As for your cheaply made "Quota" films – well!'[60] Respondents complained more about American shorts, cinema advertising, cuts made to release prints by exhibitors and too many serious, depressing and violent films.

Rather paradoxically, however, the biggest critics of the London-based cinema were the metropolitans themselves. West End exhibitors were the most reluctant to play the films produced just down the road, particularly if they had been made cheaply.[61] As early as 1931, a small independent exhibitor in London wrote to *The Bioscope* to complain that:

> I have lost money on nearly all the British pictures I have shown. Every time I have put on a Quota film my takings have dropped and on many occasions regular patrons have asked whether a coming

attraction was British or not, and when I have said it was they have replied that they would stay away from the theatre that week.[62]

Because the big circuits monopolised the only decent indigenous films, he argued, the situation would not change until the production of British pictures exceeded the exhibitors' quota by three to one. Ben Jay purchased the 400–seat Mile End cinema in July 1931, for £1,000, and spent £2,400 on talkie equipment, in addition to having the premises refurbished. He struggled on for four years, but, as he told the court during his prosecution for failing to meet his exhibition quota, whenever he showed British films he showed them to empty houses.[63] Another East End exhibitor was quoted as saying his customers would not stand British pictures 'at any price':

> When we have one in the programme, many of our patrons come in late or early to avoid seeing the British picture. Any good adventure or gangster film will pack the house, though often a poor British second feature will affect the takings considerably.[64]

The problems with quota films, as far as this type of working-class audience was concerned, were clearly stated by another East End cinema manager: 'British pictures are disliked because the acting is wooden, because the actors and actresses talk "society fashion" and because they are too slow.'[65] The MP, Sir Arnold Wilson, articulating the widespread prejudice of his day, had an alternative explanation. Sir Arnold, preferred to blame 'Jewish elements' with 'a natural antipathy to the British outlook', an idea vigorously resisted by the CEA.[66]

But, rather than the vilification they received in the cosmopolitan East End of London, it was the controversy surrounding their exhibition in the swankier cinemas of the West End that fixed the reputation of the quota quickies. It was here that the British supporting feature was at its most visible to newspaper critics as well as workers and executives in the London-based film industry. It was here, too, that the legend of the 'charlady epic' was born.[67] There is an abiding myth that quota quickies were hardly shown in cinemas, at least when there was an audience present. The myth has been propagated by some of the leading figures and commentators in the industry, notably Michael Balcon.[68] Looking back in 1960, for example, the critic and film business insider, Ernest Betts, wrote:

> The American companies made cheap quickies to fulfil the letter of the law, and in many cases didn't even trouble to show them. British producers made quickies, but unfortunately showed them, thus throwing the industry into disrepute, for they were quite worthless. Moreover, these films were shown at cinemas in the early morning when the charladies were at work, the public never saw them at all.[69]

The distinguished director and cinematographer Ronald Neame has, more recently, suggested that this practice was universal:

> They [American Renters] opened the theatre at eight o'clock in the morning (by the theatre I mean everywhere in the country). The theatres opened at eight o'clock, and the British film was run from eight to nine thirty, to the cleaners. And then at around about nine thirty, they ran it again.

British film quota in the Dominions and Colonies, but, as a consequence of the report of the Colonial Films Committee in 1929, settled for a re-vamped system of distribution. The British United Film Producers Company was established to distribute the products of British studios to the Empire, particularly to the West Indies and West Africa.

The racial assumptions and distinctions of imperial rule were explicit in the discussion of film distribution in the Colonies. In a Minority Report dissenting from the Colonial Films Committee Report, Sir Hesketh Bell emphasised the following:

> Although we know that a vast deal of harm can be done even to civilised persons by the display of bad pictures, the injury which can be done to primitive people by the exhibition of demoralis-ing films, representing criminal and immodest actions by white men and women, can hardly be exaggerated. The success of our government of subject races depends almost entirely on the degree of respect which we can inspire. Incalculable is the damage that has already been done to the pres-tige of Europeans in India and the Far East through the widespread exhibition of ultra-sensational and disreputable pictures, and it behoves us, therefore, *while there is still time*, to see that the same harm shall not be repeated in our Tropical African Empire.[137]

But similar ideas were expressed even in a liberally minded report like *The Film in National Life* (which recommended the establishment of the BFI):

> The backward races within the Empire can gain more and suffer more from the film than the soph-isticated European, because to them the power of the visual medium is intensified. The conception of white civilisation which they are receiving from third-rate melodrama is an international menace.[138]

However, as far as British supporting features was concerned, distribution in Africa was prob-ably never significant as many of its cinemas were in far-flung rural locations where audiences expected no more than one feature per programme.[139]

Australia was by far the most important Empire market for British films, not least because distribution and exhibition in the second largest market – Canada – was dominated by Ameri-can interests.[140] Distribution returns from Australia were likely to be higher than from the whole of the rest of the Empire. The number of cinemas in Britain and the Empire is given in Table 6.2.

The distribution of British films in Australasia was primarily the province of British Dominions Films Ltd (Australia), known as BDF. With the arrival of sound films, the prejudice created by previous dumping practices began to be overcome, although films that were too parochially British – such as the soccer film, *The Great Game* and the *Josser* comedies – were still not appreciated.[142] As *The Bioscope* pointed out, the progress of British films in Australia was handicapped by producers' cautious approach to publicity at a time when a concerted campaign was called for.[143] In spite of this, many British films played in Australia, including some sup-porting features. Programmers from BIP and Gaumont usually gained distribution, Julius Hagen was particularly adept at selling his products abroad, and early modest productions for Fox *Immediate Possession* and *The Wrong Mr Perkins* were both distributed in South Africa and Aus-

**Table 6.2** Distribution of cinemas in Britain and the Empire[141]

| Country | Number of cinemas |
|---|---|
| Great Britain and Ireland | 4,705 |
| Australia | 1,334 |
| Canada | 862 |
| New Zealand | 435 |
| India | 308 |
| South Africa | 200 |
| Malay States | 57 |
| Ceylon | 18 |
| Trinidad | 17 |
| Bermudas | 9 |
| **Total** | 7,945 |

tralia. Fox's distribution channels in Australia were particularly robust, and further research may well reveal that much of their Wembley output played in Sydney and beyond. In 1931, the Lyceum cinema in Sydney turned itself over entirely to British pictures under the slogan 'British Voices for British People'.[144] By 1934 Melbourne had three cinemas dedicated entirely to British pictures, and some, like *Jack's the Boy* (1932) were held over for runs in excess of twenty weeks.[145] The percentage of British films being shown in Australia had trebled, causing *Picturegoer* to comment:

> Australia, indeed would seem to be more patriotic in its picturegoing than we are ourselves. . . . A recent merger between the General Theatres Corporation and Fuller's Theatres has resulted in the establishment of a circuit of 214 kinemas pledged to a policy of all-British programmes. . . . in more than one case, a British film has in Australia and New Zealand alone made a sufficiently large net profit to return to England more than the entire cost of production. . . . In 1933, the Dominion took 112 of our feature films – something like six times as many as the whole of Europe and America combined.[146]

S. F. Doyle, the controller of the largest metropolitan circuit in Australia, told the British trade that 'Themes of Empire prestige and development never fail to get a ready response from Australians, especially when the plot is fast moving and excitement abounds. Those are qualities that appeal to the virile Australian.' In addition, audiences were fond of plenty of outdoor locations and comedy, although low comedy of the *Josser* variety was not popular. They generally shunned costume and period films ('Australians lack the love of pageantry'), operatic singing, heavy dialect speech and hackneyed backstage musical comedies. However, gender-bending did seem to be acceptable: the Dolly Hass comedy *Girls Will Be Boys* created such a stir as a second feature that it was raised to first-feature status.[147]

Predictably, the bar to further expansion was the much-maligned quota quickie. A report by the Australian censor revealed that, in 1934, 27 per cent of long films distributed in the country were British, and this would have been higher but for 'a certain proportion of cheap and nasty "quickies" made to comply with quota regulations'.[148] The Australian rejection of shoddy British product renewed fears of the deleterious effects of substandard pictures on international prestige. Indeed, it was responsible for provoking *Today's Cinema*'s 'Open Letter to Quota Quickie Purveyors', which began:

> Gentlemen, The letter published in our columns recently from Mr Ernest Turnbull, managing director of British Dominions Films of Melbourne, raises a very important aspect of the quota quickie problem. It shows that in markets such as Australia, where British films are very much more 'up against it' than here, the quota quickie is doing almost incalculable harm in lowering their prestige. In other words, the quota quickie, always bad film art, has now become short-sighted commercial policy.[149]

In 1936, BDF combined with Fox and Hoyt's Theatres to form Dominions Film Distributors, initially to handle the products of Gaumont-British, Gainsborough, B&D, Fox-British and Twickenham. BDF's head, Ernest Turnbull, announced that a 'clearing house system' would be put in place to ensure that only quality films would be distributed: 'The "Quota Quickie" or the junk British film had done more to damage the prestige of British films in the Dominions than any other cause.'[150] While this might have been the case in Australia, many parts of the Empire were unlikely ever to have seen a British quickie. Distribution to the West Indies and West Africa, for example, was effectively under the control of Gaumont-British, a firm that rarely soiled its hands with such stuff.[151] New Zealand was also largely quickie-free. Although New Zealand instituted its own Quota Act in 1929 and, by 1933, 200 of 468 features imported were British (four times as many as Canada took), it was all of little assistance to British supporting features because New Zealand cinemas were very slow to embrace the two-feature programme.[152]

## Notes

1. Letter from Jean T. Lappa of Salford, *Picturegoer*, 17 August 1935, p. 30.
2. For an account of exhibitors' privations in 1931 see the CEA annual report in *The Bioscope*, 9 March 1932, pp. 16–17.
3. Letter to *The Bioscope*, 16 September 1931, p. 31.
4. Annual Report, KRS, 1934.
5. Margaret Dickinson and Sarah Street, *Cinema and State: The Film Industry and the British Government 1927–84* (London: BFI, 1985), p. 36.
6. Rachael Low, *The History of the British Film, 1929–1939* (London: Allen and Unwin, 1985), p. 3.
7. The study of Nottingham – Mark Jancovich and Lucy Faire, *The Place of the Audience: Cultural Geographies of Film Consumption* (London: BFI, 2003), p. 86 – asserts that the late 1920s and 1930s 'saw the highpoint in cinema attendance'. Attendances, in fact, were higher in the mid-1920s and

mid-1940s. There was widespread concern in the trade about *falling* attendances in the early
1930s. See *The Cinema*, 7 March 1934, p. 3.

8.   Letter from John MacConnell of Golders Green, London, *Picturegoer*, 4 November 1933.

9.   *Picturegoer*, 20 May 1933, p. 5. See also support for these views on the magazine's letters page 15
     July 1933, and the letter from P. Wheeler of Finchley suggesting that longer first features might
     save audiences from 'the irritation and boredom of having to sit through mediocre second
     features', *Film Weekly*, 23 September 1932, p. 22.

10.  See 'Common Sense in Programme Building', *Kinematograph Weekly*, 13 April 1933, p. 4; Cmd.
     5320: 1039; and 'Two-Feature Programme Condemned', *Kinematograph Weekly*, 7 May 1936,
     p. 30.

11.  *The Cinema*, 2 January 1935, p. 21.

12.  Ibid., p. 37.

13.  Cmd. 5320: 1038, evidence of Sam Eckman.

14.  C. H. Dand quoted in 'The Advisory Committee Is Asked a few Questions', *Kinematograph Weekly*,
     23 November 1933, p. 4. His rhetoric concealed the fact that short non-fiction films could be, and
     were, registered for quota on the judgment of the Advisory Committee that they possessed
     'special exhibition value'. Forty-six were registered in the quota year ending March 1936.
     Cmd. 5320: 30 and 43.

15.  'Quota "Quickies" for Half-wits', *Kinematograph Weekly*, 15 October 1936, p. 30.

16.  A. Favell, 'Scrap the Two-Feature Programme', *Kinematograph Weekly*, 11 January 1934.

17.  Simon Rowson, 'A Statistical Survey of the Cinema Industry in Great Britain in 1934', *Journal of
     the Royal Statistical Society* no. 99, 1936, p. 114.

18.  'Patrons' Likes and Dislikes', *Kinematograph Weekly*, 24 June 1937, p. 21. For a discussion of the
     Bernstein questionnaires 1929–37, see Caroline Moorehead, *Sidney Bernstein: A Biography*
     (London: Jonathan Cape, 1984), pp. 50–1.

19.  Letter from Emlyn Price of Merthyr Tydfil, *Film Pictorial*, 10 September 1932, p. 28. Rival
     magazine, *Film Weekly*, had championed the idea of renters supplying an appropriate supporting
     feature for their main attraction as early as the end of 1931: 'the cinema-owner's problem would
     be automatically solved, and the filmgoer would benefit by seeing a well-arranged double
     programme'.
     (12 December 1931, p. 3).

20.  Richards and Sheridan, *Mass Observation at the Movies*, (London: Routledge, 1987) p. 73. See, also,
     the comments by sixty-year-old M. E. Hutchinson on p. 70, thirty-four-year-old E. Dalley on p.
     97 and twenty-eight-year-old Mrs Irene Berry on p. 121.

21.  As seventeen-year-old Florence Cocker put it: 'When two long films are shown on the same
     programme, they should be totally different.' Ibid., p. 71.

22.  Letter from H. A. Whatly of Birmingham, *Picturegoer*, 19 January 1935, p. 30.

23.  Letter from John MacConnell, ibid..

24.  Letter from Dorothy H. Johnson of Sunderland, *Picturegoer*, 30 December 1933.

25.  There were also complaints from some filmgoers, concerned that, for provincial bookings, the
     running time of major Hollywood features was being cut down to accommodate a supporting
     feature. See, for example, the letter from Cecil A. Kitson, London W2, *Film Pictorial*, 30 September
     1933, p. 54.

26.  *Kinematograph Weekly*, 20 April 1933. However, there were complaints from independent exhibitors that the rule was not being enforced for many of the large circuit cinemas. 'Renters Ignore 3¼ Hours Programme Policy', *Kinematograph Weekly*, 6 September 1934, p. 7.

27.  'It All Comes Back to the Films', *Kinematograph Weekly*, 13 January 1938, p. 43.

28.  *Kinematograph Weekly*, 14 June 1934.

29.  Cmd. 5320: 704–5.

30.  Ibid.: 627. However, Dickinson did point out that this arrangement would not benefit any British producer who might have a profit-sharing deal with his distributor.

31.  Ibid.: 1043 and 1008. The Film Producers' Group also admitted that British renters used 'gentlemen's agreements', but this did not prevent it from implying an element of coercion when it argued that block booking was mainly responsible for a situation in which exhibitors were 'forced to take the British quickies'. Ibid.: 166 and 16.

32.  Cmd. 5320: 193.

33.  'Films Act Revision Demanded' *Kinematograph Weekly* 19 July 1934, p. 7.

34.  Letter from Richard Williamson of the Park Cinema, Dennistown, *Kinematograph Weekly*, 6 April 1934.

35.  John Claughton, reported in *Kinematograph Weekly,* 28 June 1934, p. 7. This issue was raised in Parliament as early as November 1930, when the Board of Trade was made aware of the way combines were 'monopolising all the good British films and consequently forcing the small independent exhibitors right out'. *Kinematograph Weekly*, 6 November 1930, p. 29.

36.  *Kinematograph Weekly*, 8 January 1931, p. 99. Mannock later calculated that roughly half of the nation's cinemas were barred from booking half of all British productions (including most of the quality pictures) on their first run. *Kinematograph Weekly*, 10 January 1935, p. 143.

37.  Cmd. 5320: 989, and Memorandum by John Maxwell on behalf of the KRS, para. 12. Basil Dean, on the other hand, thought that the American-financed quota quickies constituted unfair competition at the lower end of the market because they were not expected to recoup their costs. Dean's company, ATP, had lost almost £100,000 in the previous year. 'Basil Dean Urges Separate Quota', *Kinematograph Weekly*, 6 January 1938, p. 7.

38.  *Kinematograph Weekly*, 10 January 1935, p. 143.

39.  Arthur Jarrett, 'We Don't Want the Quota Act', *Picturegoer*, 5 May 1934.

40.  Cmd. 5320: 644.

41.  Ibid.: 645.

42.  Ibid.: 696–7 and 657.

43.  See, for example, *The Bioscope*, 20 August 1930, p. 19.

44.  Louis D. Dickson, ex-president of the CEA Scottish Branch, *The Cinema*, 2 January 1935, p. 37. See also 'British Films: Scotland's Complaint', *Kinematograph Weekly*, 3 November 1932, p. 26. The Englishness of British films did not always seem to be a particular problem for audiences in Wales, as H. Victor Davis, Chairman of the South Wales branch of the CEA confessed: 'It has been cheering to those of us who are exhibiting films in the industrial areas of South Wales to note the quick appreciation and depth of enjoyment of the working classes in regard to British pictures.' *The Cinema,* 2 January 1935, p. 37.

45.  Walter Watt, in Andrew Martin, *Going to the Pictures: Scottish Memories of Cinema* (Edinburgh: National Museum of Scotland, 2000), p. 33.

46.  *Film Weekly*, 29 April 1932, p. 66.

47.  Christine Paul, in Martin, *Going to the Pictures*, p. 33.

48.  A. S. Albin, *The Cinema*, 2 January 1935, p. 3

49.  *Kinematograph Weekly*, 23 April 1936, p. 11.

50.  'British Producers – Listen to the British Public', *Kinematograph Weekly*, 13 January 1938, p. 45.

51.  *Kinematograph Weekly*, 20 October 1938, p. 23.

52.  Cmd. 5320: 62.

53.  'Lancs Public Laughs off Quota Quickies', *Kinematograph Weekly*, 18 July 1935, p. 15.

54.  *The Bioscope*, 6 January 1932, p. 79.

55.  Alfred Snape, 'Adjustments That Are Long Overdue', *Kinematograph Weekly*, 9 January 1936, p. 39.

56.  Richards and Sheridan, *Mass Observation at the Movies*, p. 39.

57.  Ibid., p. 43.

58.  Ibid., p. 86.

59.  Twenty-year-old Samuel Hodson. Ibid., p. 85. However, ten respondents thought British films were improving, the individual film most often mentioned favourably was *Victoria the Great* (1937), and American accents and slang received far more criticism than Oxford accents in British pictures.

60.  Ibid., p. 83. However, twenty-eight-year-old James Broadbent may also have had quota quickies in mind when he complained about 'cheap, pointless films, employing half a dozen actors and two rooms, slow-moving dialogue, with a very uncertain climax'. Ibid., p. 63.

61.  Shirley Simpson at the Regal, Marble Arch, was something of an exception, anticipating a time when any cinema should be able to run profitably 'almost exclusively on British films'. *Kinematograph Weekly*, 6 November 1930, p. 29.

62.  *The Bioscope*, 9 September 1931, p. 26.

63.  *Kinematograph Weekly*, 9 April 1936, p. 26.

64.  *World Film News*, January 1937, p. 9.

65.  Ibid.

66.  Cmd. 5320: 794–8. Significantly, perhaps, Sir Arnold thought it might be a good idea for the American renters to import German films. Ibid.: 1073–6.

67.  Colin Belfrage suggests that the phrase 'Charlady epics' was in common use. *All Is Grist*, p. 108.

68.  Michael Balcon, *Michael Balcon Presents . . . A Lifetime in British Films* (London: Hutchinson, 1969), p. 93.

69.  Ernest Betts, *Inside Pictures* (London: Cresset Press, 1960), pp. 6–7. Betts' comments beg the question: if the films were hardly seen, how could they bring the industry into disrepute?

70.  Interviewed by Matthew Sweet, NFT, 19 October 2003, www.bfi.org.uk/showing/nft/inter views/neame/; see also Ronald Neame, *Straight from the Horse's Mouth* (Lanham, MD and Oxford: Scarecrow Press, 2003), p. 35.

71.  Eric Cross interview, BECTU Oral History Project, Interview 1, 6 March 1987.

72.  *The Era*, 10 July 1935.

73.  John R. Broadly, 'A Life in Leeds Cinemas', *Picture House*, 11, 1987, p. 12. Edward Dryhurst, *Gilt Off the Gingerbread* (London: Bachman & Turner, 1987), p. 180.

74.  Cmd. 5320: 1079, 1090 and 1093. According to Allen Eyles, 'The Empire That Was, 1928–61', *Picture House* 13, 1989, the Empire showed 76 British films between November 1928 and March 1938, of which 67 played as second features. However, Eyles' data may not include all British

supporting features shown before 1933. Neither *The Woman from China*, nor *Reunion* appear in his listing, although both are believed to have been screened at the Empire.

75. *Kinematograph Year Book 1938* (London: Kinematograph Publications, 1937), p. 216. There had also been isolated prosecutions of two cinemas in the South of England, which had experimented with showing British films in the mornings at reduced admission prices. Cmd. 5320: 228.

76. Jack Rockett interview, BECTU Oral History Project, Interview 54, 22 August 1988.

77. Cmd. 5320: 97–102.

78. *Kinematograph Year Book 1938*, p. 216.

79. John Mills, *Up in the Clouds, Gentlemen Please* (Harmondsworth: Penguin, 1981), p. 179. Mills' recollections of the date and the main feature are a little off beam.

80. John Paddy Carstairs, *Movie Merry-Go-Round* (London: Newnes, 1937), p. 170.

81. Adrian Brunel, *Nice Work: Thirty Years in British Films* (London: Forbes Robinson, 1949), pp. 167–8.

82. Cmd. 5320: 897.

83. Randolph E. Richards, *Kinematograph Weekly*, 10 November 1932, p. 36.

84. Arthur Jarrett, 'We Don't Want the Quota Act'.

85. *Picturegoer*, British Films Supplement, 13 July 1935.

86. *The House of Unrest* press book. The profitability of British renters depended on maximising bookings for their pictures, and sometimes all the publicity stops would be pulled out to try to lift their product above second-feature status. In 1931, after enthusiastic trade reviews, Stoll and PDC produced a *Bioscope* supplement to promote the courtroom drama *Other People's Sins*. The director, Sinclair Hill, and his stars Horace Hodges and Anne Grey, contributed articles which were accompanied by messages of congratulations from all quarters. Promotional materials were lavish, to judge from the description supplied by PDC Advertising Manager, F. G. Cobb: 'We will try our utmost to provide the "live" showman with the most helpful exploitation book yet published in connection with a British picture. The full range of posters will include every size from double crown to 48–sheet . . . All posters and other advertising material will be offered to exhibitors at "Bargain Prices". . . . Other advertising accessories in the course of preparation include Programme Blocks, Advertising Blocks, 10x8in. Black and White Stills, 11x14in. Display Cards, Oil Paintings, Throwaways, Window Cards, Linen Banners and Double Crown Display Panels.' *The Bioscope*, 4 March 1931, p. 55. All this endeavour could not prevent *Other People's Sins* being booked as a supporting feature at Leicester's first-run venue, the City cinema, but it did earn the film top billing at the rather less prestigious second-run High Street cinema, more than three months later.

87. Contemporary reviews in the trade press were kind to this fanciful tale of a mad scientist who attempts to resurrect an embalmed crusader, but they hardly justified the superlatives used in its marketing. *Kinematograph Weekly* reported: 'R. Lottinga's [a Newman pseudonym] direction is seen at its best in the final scenes, in which eeriness and suspense are well attained. Earlier incidents move somewhat slowly . . . Photography is satisfactory.' Quoted in *The Unholy Quest* press book.

88. In typically flamboyant style, Newman even took the front page of *Today's Cinema* (23 March 1935) to ballyhoo his film. The magazine's reviewer responded by assuring readers that *The Immortal Gentleman* was 'no mere quota quickie', but instead was 'a sincere and courageous attempt to present the more beloved passages of the immortal bard in a fashion thus far foreign to

them'. Any idea that the reviewer might have tongue firmly in cheek was dispelled by the assertion that the piece was 'sensitively played, effectively staged and meticulously faithful as to its period detail and general atmosphere'. *Today's Cinema*, 27 March 1935, p. 14.

89.   *Head of the Family* press book. The copy apparently did little to enhance its booking prospects.

90.   *Kinematograph Weekly*, 23 April 1936, p. 2. The films were: *Blind Man's Bluff*, *Wedding Group*, *Find the Lady*, *Highland Fling* and *Rhythm in the Air*.

91.   Lawrence Napper, 'A Despicable Tradition? Quota Quickies in the 1930s', in Robert Murphy (ed.), *The British Cinema Book* (London: BFI, 1997) p. 46.

92.   Ibid., p. 49

93.   Richards and Sheridan, *Mass Observation at the Movies*, p. 131.

94.   The film and its critical reception are discussed at greater length in Stephen Shafer, *British Popular Films 1929–1939: The Cinema of Reassurance* (London: Routledge, 1997), pp. 190–2.

95.   Quoted in Jeanne Carswell and Tracy Roberts (eds), *Cinema in Coalville* (Coalville: Coalville Publishing, 1991), np.

96.   'What the Patron Wants?', *Kinematograph Weekly*, 17 October 1935, p. 1. For a discussion of the tastes of middle-class, working-class and family audiences see Jeffrey Richards, *The Age of the Dream Palace: Cinema and Society in Britain, 1930–1939* (London: Routledge, 1984), pp. 24–30.

97.   *Kinematograph Weekly*, 2 February 1933.

98.   *Kinematograph Weekly*, 18 April 1935.

99.   *Kinematograph Weekly*, 26 July 1934. See also *The Bioscope* editorial on appropriate accents and speech in films, 12 August 1931, p. 1.

100.  See, for example *Kinematograph Weekly's* review of *Josser on the Farm*, as Lotinga finally began to take his place as a star of second features. 8 November 1934.

101.  Worktown Box 29E, Mass-Observation Archive, Richards and Sheridan, *Mass Observation at the Movies*, p. 30.

102.  *Kinematograph Weekly*, 9 February 1933.

103.  *Kinematograph Weekly*, 2 March 1933, p. 21.

104.  *Kinematograph Weekly*, 14 June 1934, p. 6.

105.  Richards and Sheridan, *Mass Observation at the Movies*, pp. 34–6. Curiously, the questionnaire did not include 'comedy' as a category, only 'slapstick comedies', which few cinemagoers were prepared to admit liking. However, when asked what they wanted to see more of in films, the overwhelming response was 'more humour', particularly among patrons of the more modest halls. Ibid., pp. 36–8. On the popularity of different types of films in Bolton, see John Sedgwick, *Popular Filmgoing in 1930s Britain* (Exeter: Exeter University Press, 2000), pp. 102–42.

106.  'Give Us Full-blooded Human British Films', *Kinematograph Weekly*, 9 January 1936, p. 45.

107.  *Kinematograph Weekly* (16 April 1936, p. 22) condemned *Eliza* as an: 'Old-fashioned commonplace, farcical comedy, too far behind the times in its humour, trite in its dialogue and colourless in its interpretation', and Betty Balfour, as 'hopelessly out of her element'. See also Bamford, *Distorted Images*, p. 156.

108.  *The Cinema*, 2 January 1935, p. 132.

109.  *Kinematograph Weekly*, 16 April 1936.

110.  'What the Patron Wants?', p. 1.

111.  *Kinematograph Weekly*, 25 April 1936, p. 31.

112. See Sedgwick, *Popular Filmgoing in 1930s Britain*, pp. 89–100.

113. Ibid., p. 109.

114. *The Bioscope*, 6 August 1930, p. 15.

115. *Kinematograph Weekly*, 6 November 1930, p. 29.

116. *Kinematograph Weekly*, 25 September 1930, p. 49.

117. *Kinematograph Weekly*, 18 July 1935, p. 15 and 20 February 1936, p. 1. See also Cmd. 5320: 63.

118. Ibid.

119. Cmd. 5320: 52.

120. His statement in mitigation was a familiar one: He had 'great difficulty in getting suitable British films as our audiences will not stand for them at any price. Also I have had to run them after our opposition, which belongs to the two big combines. . . . We are fighting a losing battle all the time.' 'Liverpool Quota Case', *Kinematograph Weekly*, 16 July 1936, p. 16.

121. *Kinematograph Weekly*, 3 October 1935, p. 35.

122. *Kinematograph Weekly*, 26 September 1935, p. 41.

123. 'Quota Default Figures', *Kinematograph Weekly*, 28 January 1937, p. 3.

124. 'Liverpool Quota Case', *Kinematograph Weekly*, 16 July 1936, p. 16.

125. 'Attack on Quality of British Pictures', *Kinematograph Weekly*, 28 June 1934, p. 13.

126. *Kinematograph Weekly*, 24 June 1937, p. 5.

127. *Kinematograph Weekly*, 16 March 1939, p. 3.

128. Cmd. 5320: 1031.

129. Ibid.: 292.

130. *The Bioscope*, 20 May 1931, p. 19.

131. These figures derive from a number of sources, including Sarah Street, *Transatlantic Crossings: British Feature Films in the USA* (London: Continuum, 2002); Anthony Slide, *Banned in the USA: British Films in the United States and Their Censorship 1933–60* (London: I.B. Tauris, 1998); as well as listings of alternative American titles in various reference works; and surviving material evidence in the form of posters or press books.

132. Paramount did distribute its hit Korda production *Service for Ladies* as *Reserved for Ladies* in 1932.

133. The acceptance of *Honours Easy* for distribution in the USA may have been helped by the reputation of its Irish-American director Herbert Brenon, and the presence in the cast of Patric Knowles, already a Hollywood actor.

134. In a letter dated 10 March 1931, Radio's Lee Marcus had admitted that the quota pictures that he encouraged Dean to produce were unlikely to receive distribution in the USA. Basil Dean Collection, 4/2/11, BFI. See also Street, *Transatlantic Crossings*, pp. 83–4.

135. Slide, *Banned in the USA*, Appendices.

136. Stuart F. Doyle, 'Boom for British Films', *Kinematograph Weekly*, 15 October 1931, p. 26.

137. Cmd. 3630 (1930), Minority Report. As one of the Tanganyikan censors argued: 'It is quite impossible to expect the native, in his present stage of mental development, to achieve a perfectly balanced opinion of all that he sees – even in representations on the screen. As far as European interests are concerned, and where five thousand whites live amongst a native population of four and a half million, it is necessary and desirable that the white man's and white woman's prestige should be maintained at a high level. Nothing seriously derogatory to that should be shown to

uninstructed native audiences.' 'Colonial Censorship: Why Certain Films Are Banned',
*Kinematograph Weekly*, 19 May 1932.

138.   The Commission on Educational and Cultural Films, *The Film in National Life* (London: Allen
       and Unwin, 1932), para 189.

139.   See, for example, the letters to *Picturegoer*, 16 October 1937, p. 28.

140.   Cmd. 5320: 83. By mid-1932, about one British film each week was being 'widely shown' in
       Canada. *Film Weekly*, 26 August 1932, p. 5.

141.   Table adapted from the Appendix to Simon Rowson's evidence to the Moyne Committee.

142.   Doyle, 'Boom for British Films'.

143.   *The Bioscope*, 7 January 1931, Editorial, p. 1.

144.   *The Bioscope*, 18 November 1931, p. 14.

145.   Letter from N. Meale of Sydney, Australia, *Film Weekly*, 4 May 1934, p. 69.

146.   *Picturegoer*, British Films Supplement, 13 July 1935.

147.   'British Films the Dominions Want', *Kinematograph Weekly*, 2 April 1936, p. 5.

148.   *Today's Cinema*, 23 March 1935, p. 1.

149.   *Today's Cinema*, 12 January 1935, p. 3.

150.   *Kinematograph Weekly*, 23 April 1936, p. 5.

151.   Cmd. 5320: 90.

152.   Ibid: 372.

# 7

# Case Study: Film Exhibition

## A Quickie at the Local: British Supporting Features in Leicester

> If you don't have to sit through this to see another picture, I should advise giving it a miss.
>
> Review of Warners-British's *Father and Son* (1934) in *Picture Show*[1]

In 1930 Leicester was a city of above-average affluence, insulated from the worst effects of the depression by its expanding staple industries of knitwear, hosiery and footwear manufacture and its developing expertise in light engineering. Printing, food processing and retailing were also significant industries in the city's diverse portfolio of trades. Visiting journalists, such as J. B. Priestley, noted a general air of prosperity.[2] In 1936, the League of Nations listed Leicester as the 'second most prosperous city in Europe', based on average household income. This figure was helped by high rates of female employment, but it should not disguise the fact that, like most areas of the country in the early 1930s, Leicester also had an unemployment problem. Unlike many areas of the North, however, it was not longterm and chronic. In 1932, unemployment peaked at 16,000, some 10 per cent of the workforce, and remained mostly over 10,000 until World War II. The relative poverty of the unemployed was exacerbated by the high wages paid to those working in the booming hosiery industry.[3]

By the early 1930s, Leicester had twenty cinemas serving a population of a little under 240,000. Thus, there was one cinema for every 12,000 inhabitants, a little above the exhibitors' standard ratio of 1:10,000. The cinemas might be roughly classified as city centre, inner city and suburban.[4]

The city centre had three large 'picture palaces', all constructed or refurbished in the previous six years, and catering to a variety of income groups, zoned according to admission price. The 2,000–seat Picture House had been built in 1910 in a prime position between the main (Granby) street and the town hall square for Provincial Cinematograph Theatres, which became part of the Gaumont empire in 1929. Further down the street was the similar-sized and the newly refurbished Princes cinema, leased to the ABC circuit. Largest of all was the newly built City cinema on the market place, with 2,300 seats. It was also part of the Gaumont circuit. In addition, there were three other less prestigious city-centre cinemas that mainly served a working-class clientele. The small and ageing Floral Hall and adjoining Palace Theatre were owned by the Stoll group. The Palace mixed film and live entertainment, while the Floral Hall proudly exhibited a relatively high proportion of British films under the rubric of 'A Fine British Production'. The similar-sized independent High Street cinema was the last to convert to sound, projecting silent films until it was re-branded as the Arcadia in May 1931.

Leicester's inner city contained a number of small and medium-sized neighbourhood cinemas showing mainly second-run films to a local catchment area. The 750-seat Hippodrome, situated in one of the most deprived areas, doubled as a music hall and relied on neighbourhood posters and word-of-mouth for its audiences. So too did the nearby Star (500 seats), a more modern auditorium, but with a reputation as a 'flea pit'. To the north east of the city's central clock tower was the Belgrave (720 seats), which operated almost as a leisure extension of a large hosiery works situated opposite. Not far from the Belgrave was the larger Coliseum, an unpretentious barn of a building, which was replaced by a new construction in the mid-1930s. It was part of the H. D. Moorhouse circuit, which included the inner-city Sovereign (900 seats) and Olympia (1,500 seats), and the more suburban Shaftsbury (830 seats) respectively in the north, west and east of the city. Also in the eastern quarter of the city was the Melbourne, which became part of the ABC circuit in 1931. Lower down the pecking order were two smaller neighbourhood cinemas, the Imperial (460 seats and under the same ownership as the Star) and the Picturedrome (420 seats), a converted Wesleyan Mission Hall that changed hands quite frequently. Neither cinema went to the expense of newspaper advertisements. The west end of Leicester had two large picture houses: the Tudor and the Westleigh. The southern and most prosperous quarter of the city was largely devoid of cinemas. There was only the 1,200-seat Aylestone, built on the edge of the new Saffron Lane council estate, and part of a Birmingham-based chain.

The decade's cinema building boom added three modern picture palaces at the termini of major tram routes out of the city: the sister cinemas the Roxy at the western terminus, and the Knighton at the southern, and the Trocadero cine-variety and leisure complex at the eastern terminus. The 'Troc' was absorbed by the ABC circuit in 1938. There were also two new city-centre super cinemas built in 1937 and 1938 – the Savoy for the ABC circuit; and the Odeon – and two smart new picture palaces, the Carlton and the Fosse, built in the middle of the decade to serve the relatively genteel garden suburbs and council estates growing on the eastern and western fringes. In addition, the Stoll Palace Variety Theatre was converted to a large city-centre cinema in 1931, and in 1936, a new inner-city cinema, the Regal, was erected close to the Royal Infirmary. Finally, new cinemas began to spring up in the outer ring of Leicester suburbs: the Lawn at Birstall, the Magna and the Ritz at Wigston, the Savoy at Syston and Ansty, the Regent at Ansty, the Oadby and the tiny Majestic at Ratby.

Outside of the two large ABC and Gaumont circuits, exhibition in Leicester was dominated by a small number of cinema-owning families.

1. The Manchester-based H. D. Moorhouse circuit owned the Coliseum, Shaftsbury, Sovereign and Olympic.
2. Arthur and Edith Black owned most of Leicester's inner-city cinemas in the 1930s: the Tudor, Belgrave, Hippodrome and later the Regal.
3. Alfred Mynard, who had been a film exhibitor since before World War I, owned the Imperial, Star and, for a period, the Picturedrome. Mynard developed his own system of sound reproduction, which he installed in his cinemas and leased to other Midlands' picture houses.
4. George Scarborough, Leicester's leading showman in the 1930s, and his partners controlled a chain of cinemas from their head office at the Evington. Originally in the footwear trade,

**Table 7.1** Leicester cinemas 1931–7

| Zone | Cinema | Opened | Circuit | Seats |
|---|---|---|---|---|
| **City centre** | Picture House | 1910/24 | GB | 1626 |
| | City | 1924 | GB | 2023 |
| | Floral Hall | 1910 | Stoll | 900 |
| | Palace | 1931 | Stoll | 1883 |
| | Princes | 1930 | ABC | 1170 |
| | Savoy | 1937 | ABC | 2424 |
| | Arcadia | 1931 (1910) | Scarborough | 720 |
| **Inner city** | Belgrave | 1913 | Black | 760 |
| | Tudor | 1914 | Black | 1250 |
| | Regal | 1936 | Black | 1080 |
| | Hippodrome | 1922 | Black | 750 |
| | Imperial | 1912 | Mynard | 700 |
| | Star | 1914 | Mynard | 800 |
| | Picturedrome | 1912 | Various | 420 |
| | Sovereign | 1919 | Moorehouse | 800 |
| | Olympia | 1913 | Moorehouse | 800 |
| | Melbourne | 1920 | ABC | 944 |
| **Suburban** | Evington | 1916 | Scarborough | 978 |
| | Westleigh | 1926 | Scarborough | 1334 |
| | Carlton | 1934 | Scarborough | 1304 |
| | Knighton | 1934 | Scarborough | 1291 |
| | Roxy | 1936 | Scarborough | 1800 |
| | Fosse | 1936 | Scarborough | 998 |
| | Shaftsbury | 1914 | Moorehouse | 830 |
| | Coliseum | 1933 | Moorehouse | 1552 |
| | Aylestone | 1926 | Birmingham | 1206 |
| | Trocadero | 1931 | Independent | 2131 |

Scarborough had been part of the consortium of businessmen that founded the Evington cinema in 1916 and he soon acquired a controlling interest. His booking manager was Charles West, who had been involved in film exhibition in the city since 1909. The Scarborough Group assiduously followed the city's housing changes in the 1930s, erecting cinemas close to new areas of population as the council and private developers expanded their building programmes, consequent upon slum clearance in the inner city. The group also owned the two cinemas in Melton Mowbray, the Regal and the Picture House. All were booked by Charles West at the Evington. The Scarborough cinemas constitute a 'hidden' circuit, unbranded, apparently independently owned, and identifiable as a chain only by their central booking policy. George Scarborough was chairman of the local CEA and a member of the CEA general council from the mid-1920s. He became president of the Association in 1946, continuing to take an active interest in film exhibition until his death in 1972.

5. The Cockcroft company owned a number of cinemas in Leicester's suburbs: the Oadby, the Magna (Wigston), the Ritz (South Wigston), the Lawn (Birstall) and, before selling it on to George Scarborough, the Fosse in Leicester's west end.

Thus, when the operation of the second Cinematograph Films Act began in 1938, Leicester had twenty-eight cinemas with a further eight in its immediate suburbs.[5] Only six of these were part of the major circuits, although none were single independents apart from the Hippodrome, and this was soon to close. Twelve of these picture houses were large (over 1,200

**Table 7.2** British supporting features (BSF) booked in Leicester 1928–37

| Year | 1928 | 1929 | 1930 | 1931 | 1932 | 1933 | 1934 | 1935 | 1936 | 1937 | Total |
|---|---|---|---|---|---|---|---|---|---|---|---|
| Total BSF | 29 | 20 | 50 | 65 | 78 | 108 | 108 | 92 | 109 | 112 | 771 |
| Booked in Leicester (%) | 18 (62.1) | 7 (35.0) | 29 (58.0) | 40 (60.1) | 50 (64.9) | 77 (71.3) | 70 (64.8) | 60 (65.2) | 64 (58.7) | 72 (64.2) | 487 (63.2) |
| Total number of bookings | 33 | 13 | 45 | 81 | 125 | 218 | 180 | 240 | 258 | 299 | 1492 |
| Average bookings per film | 1.8 | 1.8 | 1.6 | 2.0 | 2.5 | 2.8 | 2.6 | 4.0 | 4.0 | 4.2 | 3.1 |
| Cinemas advertising | | | | 13 | | | | | | 23 | |

**Table 7.3** British supporting features (BSF) booked in Leicester 1928–37: by nationality of renter

| Year | British renters | | | US Renters | | | All renters | | |
|------|------------------|-------------------|---------------------|------------------|-------------------|---------------------|------------------|-------------------|---------------------|
|      | BSF produced | Screened in Leicester | Bookings in Leicester | BSF produced | Screened in Leicester | Bookings in Leicester | BSF produced | Screened in Leicester | Bookings in Leicester |
| 1928 | 25 | 18 | 31 | 4 | 2 | 2 | 29 | 20 | 33 |
| 1929 | 14 | 3 | 5 | 6 | 3 | 5 | 20 | 6 | 10 |
| 1930 | 29 | 18 | 29 | 21 | 11 | 16 | 50 | 29 | 45 |
| 1931 | 39 | 22 | 49 | 27 | 19 | 35 | 66 | 41 | 84 |
| 1932 | 18 | 9 | 15 | 60 | 41 | 110 | 78 | 50 | 125 |
| 1933 | 27 | 21 | 63 | 81 | 56 | 155 | 108 | 77 | 218 |
| 1934 | 23 | 11 | 31 | 85 | 59 | 149 | 108 | 70 | 180 |
| 1935 | 29 | 19 | 80 | 63 | 41 | 160 | 92 | 60 | 240 |
| 1936 | 34 | 24 | 91 | 74 | 40 | 167 | 109 | 64 | 258 |
| 1937 | 30 | 14 | 67 | 82 | 58 | 232 | 112 | 71 | 295 |
| 1928–31 | 268 | 159 | 461 | 503 | 328 | 1031 | 771 | 487 | 1492 |

seats), ten medium-sized (800–1,200 seats) and six small (under 800 seats). When it comes to quantifying the number of British supporting features shown in the city, these small cinemas are significant. Isolated from the major circuits, they were mainly at the bottom of the pecking order as far as bookings were concerned and were therefore the most likely houses to book quota quickies. But unfortunately, the majority of these small houses did not advertise their programmes in the local press, and so we have no way of knowing which films they booked. Therefore, the figures for the exhibition of supporting features in Leicester necessarily exclude films screened at the Imperial, Star, Hippodrome and Picturedrome cinemas. Had it been possible to include their programmes, the total number of screenings of British second features would have been increased by as much as 20 per cent.

The data on exhibition presented in the following tables are derived from a study of cinema advertisements appearing in the *Leicester Mercury*. While the 'super' cinemas in the city centre changed their programme weekly, the others normally screened a completely new programme every Monday and Thursday unless, exceptionally, a film was expected to be so popular that it was booked for an entire week. The Monday and Thursday editions were used to sample ten years of the *Mercury's* entertainments page.[6] Outside the city centre, picture houses catered mainly for a regular clientele of local inhabitants.

Approximately two-thirds of BSFs were booked in Leicester. Sixty-four per cent is a minimum figure, which might have risen to around 75 per cent if the four cinemas that did not advertise their programmes in the local paper could have been included. On average, every BSF produced could expect two bookings in Leicester. The number of Leicester bookings increased by 650 per cent between 1930 and 1937, while the average number of bookings per film increased by 260 per cent. The peak year for quota quickies in the city was 1933 when, given the lag between production and provincial exhibition, the vast majority of available supporting features were given a screening, and the number of bookings was almost twice as many as in the previous year.

As can be seen in Table 7.3, in the first year of the Quota Act, only one in ten BSFs booked in Leicester was supplied by an American renter. By the last year of the Act, the American firms were distributing eight out of ten. After losing considerable ground up to 1935, British renters staged a creditable recovery over the next two years before being overwhelmed in 1937.

**Table 7.4** British supporting features booked in Leicester 1932–7 by American Renters Bookings % (actual figures in brackets)

| Renter | 0 | 1–3 | 4+ | Total bookings | Films | Booking ratio |
|--------|-----|------|------|------|------|------|
| Radio | 14.7 (11) | 42.2 (30) | 45.9 (34) | 260 | 75 | 3.47 |
| WB | 29.9 (26) | 28.7 (25) | 41.4 (36) | 228 | 87 | 2.62 |
| MGM | 21.5 (14) | 55.4 (36) | 23.1 (15) | 161 | 65 | 2.48 |
| Fox | 25.0 (18) | 45.8 (33) | 29.2 (21) | 171 | 72 | 2.38 |
| United Artists | 33.3 (4) | 50.0 (6) | 16.7 (2) | 22 | 12 | 1.83 |
| Universal/ Columbia | 67.5 (27) | 20.0 (8) | 12.5 (5) | 41 | 40 | 1.05 |
| Paramount | 52.1 (49) | 43.6 (41) | 4.3 (4) | 86 | 94 | 0.92 |
| All US | 33.5 (149) | 40.2 (179) | 26.3 (117) | 969 | 445 | 2.18 |
| British renters | 39.1 (63) | 35.4 (57) | 25.5 (41) | 347 | 161 | 2.16 |
| **Total** | 35.0 (212) | 38.9 (236) | 26.1 (158) | 1316 | 606 | 2.17 |

**Table 7.5** Percentage of renters' British supporting features achieving at least one Leicester booking

| Radio | 85.3 |
|---|---|
| MGM | 78.5 |
| Fox | 75.0 |
| WB | 70.1 |
| United Artists | 66.7 |
| British renters | 61.2 |
| Paramount | 44.9 |
| Universal/Columbia | 32.5 |

The surviving data on exhibition in Leicester clearly questions some of the fundamental assumptions about the appeal and distribution of the quota quickies. In Leicester, American renters were more successful at distributing BSFs than British renters, despite the vertical integration of Gaumont and ABC. Four of the five American majors had a better bookings strike rate than British renters. Moreover, in spite of endless contemporary criticism of the quality of quota films offered by US renters, British firms appear to have distributed a higher proportion of films which exhibitors regarded as unbookable (39 per cent).

American rental companies differed considerably in their ability to attract bookings for their BSFs. Radio (later RKO) was by far the most successful. This is attributable in large part to its association with Julius Hagen's Twickenham production unit, which consistently produced exhibitor-friendly pictures in the mid-1930s. However, the company's success was also helped by the astute marketing and promotional policies put in place by its chairman, Sol G. Newman, and his right-hand man Earl Kramer. As the last American major to establish a rental business in Britain (in August 1930), Radio seem to have courted rather than bullied exhibitors, and established friendly regional branches in the Midlands, the North and in Scotland. This intent was clear from the beginning:

> Extraordinary care has been taken in the selection of Branch Managers, who have been chosen not only for their long-standing association with the trade and their knowledge of territories, but for their tact and courtesy. It is the aim of Radio Pictures, and especially of its Managing Director, to set a standard of business which involves on every hand a full realisation of both sides of the case – that of the exhibitor as well as that of the renter.
>
> Behind this principle is the knowledge that the creation of a cordial relationship between Radio Pictures and exhibitors is one of the finest and most permanent assets that could be built up.[7]

As Mark Glancy has pointed out, MGM were often thought to be the main culprit as far as the quality of BSFs was concerned, but MGM was second only to Radio in the percentage of bookable films it distributed.[8] The real pushers of unwanted films were Paramount (which seemed reasonably genuine in its desire to finance and distribute useable films, but lacked a feel for the market), and the 'minors' Universal and Columbia, which seemed to have little interest in the selection and promotion of their BSFs.

The best way to assess the popularity of different renters' product is to look at the BSFs that secured the most bookings (that is, significantly higher than the average for the year). When we examine the 125 most successful BSFs in Leicester we discover a better performance by British renters, whose strike rate of hits is only bettered by Radio and Warners, and is slightly above the average for the US renters; but Radio's strike rate of hits to releases is almost twice as high. Paramount has only two hits in Leicester to show for more than a hundred releases, while Radio's strike rate is around one in three.[9] Half the hits of British distributors are accounted for by those companies associated with the distribution of films produced by BIP/Associated British, which maintained two circuit cinemas in Leicester, and close links with others.

**Table 7.6** Top 125 British supporting features in Leicester 1930–7: renters

| US renters | Number | Per cent |
|---|---|---|
| Radio | 29 | 23.2 |
| WB/FN | 28 | 22.4 |
| Fox | 15 | 12.0 |
| MGM | 11 | 8.8 |
| Paramount | 2 | 1.6 |
| Columbia | 2 | 1.6 |
| United Artists | 2 | 1.6 |
| Universal | 1 | 0.8 |
| **Total US** | 90 | 72.0 |
| | | |
| **British renters** | | |
| Wardour/ABFD/ABPC/Pathe | 17 | 13.6 |
| British Lion | 3 | 2.4 |
| Gaumont | 2 | 1.6 |
| Ideal | 2 | 1.6 |
| Ace | 2 | 1.6 |
| Other British (9) | 9 | 7.2 |
| **Total British** | 35 | 28.0 |
| **All** | 125 | 100.0 |

6. There were a number of problems in interpreting the data. Although most cinemas advertised their programmes regularly, some occasionally neglected to do so. Most supplied the titles of all features on their programmes, but this may not always have been the case, and the presence of some shorter films may have been concealed under the general rubric of 'full supporting programme'. Occasionally, mistakes were made in the titling of some second features, but when these films could be reliably identified, they have been included in the figures. No distinction has been made between those films booked for a week and those booked for three or four days. The language and organisation of display advertising sometimes made it difficult to determine if a film was being shown as a second or a co-feature. The convention appears to have been that 'also' was used to designate the presence of a supporting feature, while 'and' was used to identify a co-feature. The senior partner was invariably the film that was screened last on the programme, and this was placed either above or to the left of the junior attraction in the advertising display. The supporting feature was usually printed in a smaller point size and, unlike the main attraction, normally did not have the names of starring players above its title. These rules of thumb have been used to determine the statuses of films in double bills.

7. *The Bioscope*, 13 August 1930, p. 55. The article no doubt relied heavily on Radio's press release.

8. H. Mark Glancy, 'Hollywood and Britain MGM: and the British "Quota"', in Jeffrey Richards (ed.), *The Unknown 1930s: An Alternative History of British Cinema 1929–1939* (London: I. B. Tauris, 1998), pp. 57–74.

9. Paramount's Leicester performance must have been particularly disappointing to its director of publicity, R. Gittoes Davies, an ex-editor of the *Leicester Mercury*.

10. *Picturegoer* (9 January 1937, p. 24) described it as a 'pleasant little trifle which has a full complement of human feeling and quiet humour'.

11. *Kinematograph Weekly*, 19 May 1932, p. 27.

12. *Kinematograph Weekly*, 13 October 1932, p. 45.

13. *Picturegoer*, 4 February 1933.

14. *Picturegoer*, 16 June 1934.

15. *Picturegoer* (30 May 1936, p. 30) thought the material in *Cheer Up* 'conventional enough', but 'put over to the best effect', and was particularly impressed with the 'promising' Sally Gray.

16. *Picturegoer*, 23 May 1936, p. 30.

17. *Picturegoer*, 6 February 1937, p. 28.

18. Cmd. 5320: 1047.

19. Ibid., Memorandum by Mr S. Rowson, para. 30.

20. Moreover, although supporting features were usually advertised by their title, this was not always the case. We know from the exhibition records of Leicester's Tudor cinema that it showed the PDC comedy *A Lucky Sweep* as a second feature for four days in September 1932, but it did not bother to advertise the film.

21. *Picturegoer* (15 January 1938, p. 24) described Bernerd Mainwaring's *Jennifer Hale* as the 'moderately entertaining story of a chorus girl who is accused of the murder of a mayor who had made her unwelcome proposals.' It benefited from its authentic details of police procedures and the appeal of its star, Rene Ray.

22. Cmd. 5320: Memorandum of the Board of Trade, para. 71.

23. The assumption is that those in the under 2,000 days category were booked by small cinemas with three-day runs. The films above this category probably achieved some bookings at larger city-centre

cinemas that ran programmes for six days. If the average booking was 3.25 days, films in this category would have had at least 615 bookings.

24. The ten memoirs of the area printed in the booklet edited by Karen Barrow, *West End as I Remember It*, Leicestershire Libraries and Information Service, 1985, contain references to surviving on low incomes, but no references to unemployment.

25. Certainly, its transport links were good, close to a major road and tramline into the city (King Richard's Road) and the Great Central's Westbridge railway station.

26. Quoted in Colin Hyde, *Walnut Street: Past, Present and Future* (Leicester: Leicester City Council Living History Unit, 2000), p. 35.

27. The recollections of one Leicestershire film booker suggest that film rental charges were the subject of considerable negotiation: 'In the silent days, and well into the 1930s, films were invariably bought on a flat rate. The film distributor would come to my father's office, or he'd go to Birmingham, to the renter's offices, and they'd strike a price for that film. It could be anywhere between £1–10s and £8 to £10 for a really big one. Later it was realised by the distributors that sometimes they were not getting their fair share and so the percentage terms came into play. It meant very often that the film would be booked at 25%, which is normally the rock bottom of the net takings at the box office. They didn't take the ice-cream takings or chocolate or cigarettes, just a percentage of the initial ticket revenue at the box office. With a really big picture, such as *Gone with the Wind*, the percentage could be as high as 50%. Never over that, 50% was the top.' Edward Deeming, quoted in Carswell and Roberts, np.

28. 'Loose Budgeting Must Stop', *Kinematograph Weekly*, 13 January 1938, p. 159.

29. Both did better than the much more well-known *Hindle Wakes* (3,400) and *Rich and Strange* (only 1,447, but the summer weather was fine).

30. Sue Harper, 'A Lower Middle-Class Taste Community in the 1930s: Admissions Figures at the Regent Cinema, Portsmouth, UK', *Historical Journal of Film, Radio and Television* vol. 24 no. 4, 2004, p. 566.

31. The main attractions reveal a very definite taste for Janet Gaynor at the Tudor.

32. Varney-Serrao returned to the USA in 1933.

33. It had been premiered at London's Marble Arch Pavilion, where it supported *Strangers May Kiss* to good reviews.

34. British Instructional, originally a producer of actuality films, had been taken over by the BIP empire shortly before, and was now dedicated to featurettes.

35. Their pairings with Fox's first features suggest a degree of flexibility in the general release packages offered to cinemas. *Two Crowded Hours* had supported *Daddy Long Legs* in its West End run at the Tivoli. In Leicester, *Daddy Long Legs* was supported by Powell's *My Friend the King*, while *Two Crowded Hours* was teamed with *The Affairs of Annabel*. *My Friend the King* supported *Bad Girl* at the Tivoli, but was replaced by *The Professional Guest* at the Tudor.

36. The films were Twickenham's *Black Coffee*, and Gainsborough's *Night in Montmartre* and *The Hound of the Baskervilles* (all 1931). By 1936–7, the Regal had cut back its British supporting-feature bookings to seven, while increasing its British first features to twenty.

# 8

# Case Study: Film-making

## C.O.D. – Michael Powell's Quota Quickies

There is a young man called Michael Powell, a director of 'quickies' to whom I should like to draw the attention of the British industry. I should like to point out, too, the conditions under which he works, and modestly to suggest a moral. Powell's *Rynox* shows what a good movie brain can do within the strictest limits of economy. This is the sort of workman we need for the new British cinema; this is the sort of pressure under which a real talent is shot red-hot into the world.

C. A. Lejeune[1]

Michael Powell was one of the few directors of quota quickies to transcend that waterlogged acreage in the field of cultural production to become a film-maker of international repute. Between 1931 and 1936 he directed twenty-three quota pictures before making *The Edge of the World*, the film that finally opened the door to prestigious projects. However, not all of his early films can properly be considered quota quickies. At least six played regularly or occasionally as first or co-features. This was not untypical of quota production, as competent directors might be hired to work on films of varying budgets, and the status of their products would then be determined by the responses of critics and exhibitors. To take two examples, *The Night of the Party* (1933), the first of four films Powell directed at Gaumont-British, was conceived as a first feature by Michael Balcon, but was frequently booked as a supporting picture. In Leicester, its creditable six bookings were equally divided between top and bottom of the bill. *The Man behind the Mask* (1936), the Edgar Wallace-style thriller he made for Joe Rock at the close of his quickie period, had seven bookings in Leicester: four as a supporting feature, one as a co-feature and two as the main attraction. Of the remaining seventeen second features, six were commissioned and distributed by Fox, five by Warner Bros., two by United Artists, one by MGM and by Radio, and two by the British distributor Ideal. The absence of any bookings in Leicester supports the conventional wisdom that the two 1932 films for United Artists (*C.O.D.* and *His Lordship*) and MGM's *Born Lucky* (1932) were commercial failures. With the exception of Warners' *The Girl in the Crowd* (1934), *Someday* (1935) and Fox's *The Price of a Song* (1935), the other films appear to have had some degree of success. Two early films – *Two Crowded Hours* (1931, Fox) and *Rynox* (1931, Ideal) – and two later films – *Something Always Happens* (Warners) and *Lazybones* (Radio) booked particularly well in Leicester. All but the latter also enjoyed considerable critical success.

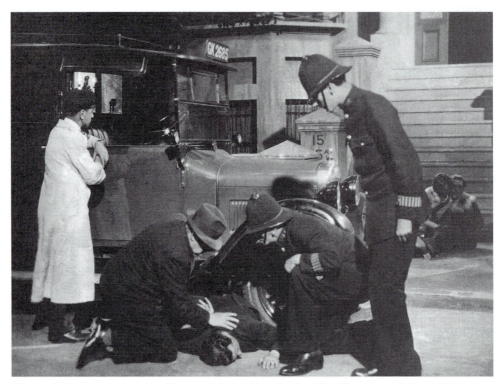

The end of the beginning: the climax to Michael Powell's first film, *Two Crowded Hours* (1931)

## Two Crowded Hours

Most of Powell's early films were made with the young American producer Jerry Jackson, a partnership that was initially called Film Engineering, and then Westminster Films. The first two features were made virtually back-to-back for different distributors. *Two Crowded Hours* was made
for Fox, which at the time was commissioning films at a rate of more than one per month: comedies and thrillers from George King and Starcraft, mainly shot at Twickenham, or occasionally
at the Nettlefold Studios at Walton-on-Thames. Powell's film, a comedy thriller, was scripted by
Jefferson Farjeon, the author of Hitchcock's *No. 17* (1932), and went before the cameras at
Walton on 1 June 1931 under a contract that was standard for American renters: 'The contract
was for a forty minute film', Powell recalled. 'Allowing for trims and editing, that meant shooting four minutes of finished film a day for twelve days, for which we were to be paid a pound
a foot on delivery.'[2] On his first day, Powell took the unit to two locations on the streets of
London, bustled back to Nettlefold and shot additional scenes both on the studio floor and in
an adjacent street:

> By now the crew were getting into their stride, and used to my way of working. They said, 'What's
> next, Mickey?' with tails wagging, and I knew what was next and I told them. They were not used
> to associating high quality with high speed, and they liked it. . . . We finished the first day ahead of
> schedule, and finished the picture on time.[3]

*Two Crowded Hours* was completed at a cost of 17 shillings and sixpence per foot, leaving a profit of 4,000 half crowns, or £500 for the parsimonious production company. Within a week Powell had moved on to his second film, *Rynox*, a mystery by Philip MacDonald, which was financed and distributed by the British company Ideal Films. It had a slightly larger budget – £8,000 in one of Powell's estimates and £4,500 in another – although its running time was five minutes longer at forty-eight minutes. A running time under fifty minutes was perfect for a purpose-made supporting feature in the early 1930s when the double bill was in its infancy and most suburban cinemas restricted their programmes to between 120 and 150 minutes, allowing two full programmes in one evening. The title *Two Crowded Hours* can therefore be seen as an acknowledgment of the demands of the packed two-feature programme, which might also include a trailer, a newsreel or cinemagazine, and even a cartoon or actuality short. Powell's first two films were each released as supporting features, but one indication that Ideal was more concerned about the marketing of its product than Fox (which could write off its film against the profits made by its Hollywood pictures) is the fact that *Rynox* was given a trailer rather than the glass advertising slides that usually sufficed for supporting features. The American renters did not use trailers for their quota films until Radio began to try to extend its sales success by commissioning trailers from the National Screen Service in the mid-1930s. Fox, like Warners, did not follow suit until after the 1938 Quota Act.

In fact, *Two Crowded Hours* was a considerable financial and critical success for Fox, who followed its custom of trade showing it at the Palace Theatre, Cambridge Circus as a curtain raiser to their latest Hollywood feature *The Affairs of Annabel*. Powell recalled a response that was quite out of the ordinary for a supporting feature:

> *Two Crowded Hours* came on first, so a lot of the professional audience arrived half way through. They must have thought they had come to the wrong house. People were roaring with laughter or tensely quiet, and even clapping in the middle. Before we came to the dazzling montage at the end, we knew we had a surprise hit. They put the house lights up. . . . Half the people gathered round us and the other half left, leaving very few people to see Annabel's predictable affairs.[4]

*Two Crowded Hours* ran for six weeks (August–September 1931) in the West End as support to Fox's *Daddy Long Legs* at the Tivoli. The *CEA Film Report* awarded it a staggering nine points, describing it as an 'excellent second feature' and 'very capably directed' in spite of its 'somewhat improbable' narrative. The *Report* praised the film's 'light vein of humour and good characterisation', and the way it maintained 'a tense holding interest'.[5] The *Bioscope* described it as 'a skilful blend of tragedy and comedy' with an effective climax.[6] A vital part of the appeal of *Two Crowded Hours* lay in the way in which an ordinary man – a London cabbie played by Jerry Verno – was made the protagonist of the film. This offered London audiences a strong point of identification. *The Times* hardly ever reviewed quota quickies, but noticed Powell's film and was also impressed with Verno's performance, which was 'so good that his audience have little difficulty in imagining that they are riding in his cab and sharing with him the excitements of a chase through some of the busiest parts of London'. It concluded that the future of its young director 'will certainly be watched with interest'.[7]

A few months later, an American journalist friend of Powell and Jackson wrote an article for *Film Weekly* singling out Powell as 'the most promising of young directors in England today', and 'destined to make British pictures a form of entertainment to be proud of'.[8] The article helped to ensure that, when Ideal showed *Rynox* to the trade that same week, the house was packed.[9] The film-makers were delighted:

> We could hardly believe it, but we had another smash hit. We were riding high. The great ladies of the Sunday newspapers, C. A. Lejeune and Dilys Powell . . . came to see *Rynox* and wrote it up. They had missed *Two Crowded Hours*, but knew all about it. Miss Lejeune said I was a 'red-hot talent shot molten into the world'.[10]

Caroline Lejeune was not the only distinguished member of the cinema community to praise *Rynox*: John Grierson wrote that 'there never was an English film so well made', and asserted that its direction, 'beautiful settings' and 'superb photography' compared well with the products of Hollywood.[11] *Kinematograph Weekly* did not go quite that far, but judged *Rynox* a 'Good Quota supporting offering for the majority of halls', and commented:

> Michael Powell has treated the fantastic story with imagination, and uses his camera to advantage. The settings have the stamp of the modernity, and things are kept well on the move. Although one has a fair idea who the mysterious character is, one can never be sure, and this compels concentration and keeps the interest and entertainment alive.[12]

*The Bioscope* was less enthusiastic, judging Stewart Rome's make-up to be 'so grotesque as to be comical', but conceded that there were passages in which Powell 'succeeds in riveting the attention of his audience'.[13] *Picturegoer* commended the originality of the story, the camerawork and the briskness of the action.[14] Viewed today, it is hard to see what Lejeune and Grierson found quite so exciting in *Rynox*. Geoffrey Faithfull's cinematography is crisp and insightful, and Powell certainly gives his *mise en scène* a modernist American gloss which complements the film's focus on the affairs of a business corporation rather than the usual landed gentry; but the acting is stagey and sometimes cries out for a second take.

Powell's own assessments of the two films are worth quoting because they undermine the conventional wisdom that stylistically and formally, low-budget second features were all alike:

> *Two Crowded Hours* was obviously influenced by Continental films. There were lots of clever angles and quick-cutting, but it was also obvious that the director meant to entertain first and foremost. The shocks and suspense were of the most primitive kind, but they worked. There was plenty of good observation, but no scene to bring a blush to a maiden's cheek. . . . In its detachment about the plot, in its interest in people, it was like the films of H. G. Clouzot after the war. . . . The climax of the film [was] a bang-up finish with a kaleidoscopic montage of images inspired by Soviet cinema. *Rynox*, on the other hand, was much more like a Hollywood film. There were two reasons for the change of style. One was that the screenplay of *Rynox* was adapted from a book. *Two Crowded Hours* had been an action picture, a director's picture. I had to create the scene. But *Rynox* could just as easily have been a stage play as a film, and was more of a talkie. The plot was ingenious; it had a

Molten talent: Powell's modernist *mise en scène* for *Rynox* (1931). Author's collection

clever twist in it, and lots of suspense. There was a certain slickness about the script that nagged me. I got away with it by good casting.

All the same, there is no doubt in my mind that the success of our first two films was due to good scripts. We had plenty of time to write them and rewrite them . . . Never again would Jerry and I give such loving enthusiasm to every word of dialogue and every stage direction.[15]

Here, then, we have two low-budget thrillers, but of very different types and styles. The cheaper of the two is the one closest to the director's heart perhaps because it is the least conventional and the nearer to silent cinema. The extreme paucity of budget, it seems, did not prevent the expression of directorial flair and invention, given a willing and able crew and time to prepare the script. Rather than cramping Powell's style, working for peanuts from an American renter seems to have granted the director a freedom of expression that an increased budget from a British company would still not allow. While the sparse thriller structure of the first film creates space for pictorial invention and character exploration, MacDonald's more densely plotted mystery of a man who stages his own death confines the director and militates against his attempt to bring his characters to life. What works in a novel can be difficult to translate for the screen. Powell feels obliged to work against that 'certain slickness' which challenges the reality of characterisation. With only forty-five minutes' screen time, Powell is faced with too many words and too much plot. The script, relatively polished and professional for a

quickie, is overpowering – clever enough to impress, but something of a millstone for the creative director's neck. He is forced to rely on the ability of his cast to keep his head up. After
only his second film, Powell was showing the first signs of a fatigue that would lead him to
dismiss the career direction that led him to make more than four films per year for the next
five years as being sent 'up the wrong track'.[16] As quickie followed quickie over the next few
years, the time available for creative thinking and the arrival of inspiration would be cut back
further and further and the director's stamina would be put under severe strain.

Powell and Jackson thankfully held on to the formula that had pleased critics and audiences,
but success can be the murderer of innovation. *The Bioscope* had been sufficiently impressed with
Jerry Verno's 'ready wit, droll comments and powers of repartee' in *Two Crowded Hours* to suggest that another appearance might be in order in the future.[17] *My Friend the King* (1931) duly
recast Verno in another taxi-cab thriller, and the film was completed and trade shown well before
*Rynox*. Unfortunately, the subsequent review in *The Bioscope* thought that the picture deterio-
rated into knockabout farce when, in order to outwit the film's villains, Verno adopts the disguise of a woman, and that 'a better vehicle should have been devised for a comedian of such
ability as Verno' (it was seemingly unaware of the pun).[18] Powell dismissed the picture as a 'flop',
but the *CEA Film Report* again awarded it nine marks and recommended it as a 'very useful
second feature anywhere'. There was praise for its acting, its cockney humour, 'fluent direction,
excellent photography, and good pictorial values'.[19] *Picturegoer* was also impressed with the film's
action sequences and rural photography and, while confessing that it was 'not great stuff',
thought it a picture that 'helps pass three-quarters of an hour quite pleasantly'.[20]

Powell's next two films for Fox reverted to the more intricate plotting of Philip MacDonald, and adopted the American formula of an investigative reporter who tracks down criminals.[21]
Ironically, *The Rasp* (1931), a MacDonald adaptation, was praised for its 'refreshing English

Blunt instrument. The police remain baffled in Powell's lost film, *The Rasp* (1931)

atmosphere' and 'picturesque English countryside settings', although it was recognised that the film suffered in comparison to American genre originals, and that the story was 'not told with a great deal of conviction'.[22] As we have seen, the critics tended to be particularly severe on British films that aped American styles and attitudes, and *The Bioscope* complained about the picture's un-British depiction of its detective as a numbskull: 'When will this "guying" of the British police cease? In imported films we expect to find something of this nature, but in our own product it is inexcusable and an unjustified slur to which the censor should put a stop.'[23]

Again, Powell was disappointed with his inability to bring a book alive as a film.[24] He was happier handling MacDonald's original screenplay for *The Star Reporter*, which was trade shown the following week and used to support Columbia's *Platinum Blonde*, a lavish $600,000 production directed by Frank Capra and starring Jean Harlow. Powell's budget of £3,700 would barely have paid for Miss Harlow's gowns. *The Star Reporter* caused little sensation at its trade screening. The *CEA Film Report* complained about an 'indifferent cast', 'artificial story' and 'mediocre direction', but thought that the 'element of suspense and excitement' might make it 'a tolerable second feature for the minor halls'.[25] *Kinematograph Weekly* was a little more enthusiastic, noting what was fast becoming a Powell trademark – good London exteriors – and praising the film's tempo and climax. There was, the reviewer thought, 'a little to appeal to everybody'.[26] *The Bioscope* also picked out the pace of Powell's direction as a saving grace of a 'somewhat unsophisticated' drama in which characters might have been treated with more realism.[27] Certainly the plot, with its inevitable theft of a diamond, was strictly regulation for the period. By the time the film was released, however, the 'buzz' about Powell among fashionable critics had become louder. *Picturegoer* thought Powell might have discovered a new star in Isla Bevan (one of the *CEA Film Report*'s 'indifferent cast').[28] More significantly, the film was selected for praise by the London *Evening News*'s influential reviewer, Jympson Harman:

> At the end of a long and not very inspiring day of seeing new films, I saw a little picture, *Star Reporter*, which jolted my tired brain into renewed enthusiasm. *Star Reporter* packs into three-quarters of an hour as much story as most films that last an hour and a half, cost £30,000 and take six weeks to make. It is absolutely without trimmings and tells an exciting crook story with a smoothness of direction and crispness of acting and cutting which would be a credit to the more ambitious picture.[29]

John Grierson continued his paeon of praise, applauding Powell for his 'slick businesslike job' and his 'solid certainty of himself'. Grierson was particularly impressed with Powell's 'unique power of observation' evidenced in his selection of shots: 'His angles are strong, his continuity, shot by shot, direct and definite. Powell can certainly see things.'[30]

## Taking the mickey: irony and allegory

Powell would look back to 1932 as a missed opportunity. In hindsight, he believed he should have tried to raise some proper finance on the basis of enthusiastic reviews from influential figures and established a serious reputation as an English film-maker. He blamed his business partner:

The films that we were making were just footage. Some of them were downright bad. Jerry was perfectly happy with this sort of hit-and-miss existence, but films were my life, my art, my mistress, my religion. And I was betraying all of them by making potboilers.[31]

But Powell kept faith with Jackson. Their partnership was re-named Westminster Films and established at Nettlefold, which prided itself as 'perfect' for the independent producer, and was where many of Powell's pictures were cut by John Seabourne.[32] The studio used for shooting, however, would vary according to availability and the arrangements of the films' paymasters. Powell and Jackson's last picture as Film Engineering was shot at Nettlefold, and was again a Philip MacDonald tale starring Jerry Verno, but for perhaps the first time, Powell seems to have imbued the story with personal and allegorical significance. The film is notable for a Hitchcockian cameo appearance by Powell playing an eavesdropper – a 'Listening' Tom, if you like. Verno played an ambitious bank clerk who inherits a run-down seaside hotel where some stolen jewels have been hidden. His character seems to have much in common with his director: both experienced a transition from banking to hotel management. The run-down hotel with the grand name has clearly known better days, and is an apt analogy for a British film business struggling to survive on foreign patronage, its 'jewels' yet to be discovered. The sense of wish-fulfilment is palpable when Verno recovers the missing necklace and we see a painting of the dilapidated hotel 'morfing' into a truly splendid property. 'Give me the resources,' Powell seems to be saying, 'and I could make something really special.'

Allegory? Jerry Verno is the proud proprietor of *Hotel Splendide* (1932). Author's collection

Ideal's *Hotel Splendide* supported the George Arliss picture, *The Silent Voice*, at both the Regal Marble Arch and the London Pavilion in April 1932, With the exception of Powell's number one fan, Caroline Lejeune, who thought it a 'professional job', the critics where generally underwhelmed.[33] *Kinematograph Weekly* declared it a serviceable 'light second feature', with a 'high note of comedy' to compensate for its 'far-fetched' plot.[34] *The Bioscope* described it as 'one of those unostentatiously produced British pot-boilers, made with an eye to the cash box, which may be expected to hold its own in the family house, chiefly as a second feature'. It was thought that its combination of comedy and mystery would 'get it past an unsophisticated audience', but that Powell's direction might have been more forceful.[35] *Picturegoer* felt that, as a crime comedy, it fell between two stools.[36]

Supporting features were judged strictly on how effectively they filled an hour while audiences waited for the star attraction. They were not expected to have anything to say, and they were certainly not granted a licence to disguise their meanings or discourses on the biography of the film-maker. However, with an urgent desire to make films of real substance, Powell was tentatively beginning to twist and stretch the formats of the quota film to accommodate his own stylistic innovations and comments on the film industry and society. Like *Two Crowded Hours*, the title of his next picture was self-reflexive. Standing for 'cash on delivery', the title *C.O.D.* was a description of the system of payment by American renters for the quota films made by independent production units like Powell's. United Artists may have had a reputation for releasing superior British product, but the film Powell made for them was one of his more poorly received. Now sadly lost, *C.O.D.* was another adaptation from a story by Philip MacDonald that Powell gave a tongue-in-cheek treatment. *Kinematograph Weekly*'s critic was dismayed by the picture's unevenness: 'A fantastic, far-fetched crime drama, which vacillates between the serious and the unconsciously comic, with such uncertainty that it can never be taken seriously.' The reviewer would have preferred the material – a corpse in the library, a lady in distress and a suspicious trunk in the left-luggage at St Pancras station – to have been treated more seriously and 'turned into an eerie, sensational thriller', but at least felt that the cinematography established 'a good London atmosphere'.[37] *The Bioscope* also blamed the director for the film's lack of any 'semblance of probability', and thought the cast – which included Garry Marsh and Hope Davey – better than the material supplied.[38]

Trade previewed within a week of each other, these two films suddenly showed that Powell was no longer on quite the same wavelength as the gentlemen of the film press. They expected bread-and-butter pictures, and might have been forgiven for thinking that the pretentious Powell wanted to put jam on his. Not only were his films getting longer, but he seemed wilfully to refuse to treat his material with seriousness. He preferred to poke gentle fun at its absurdities and to exaggerate for satiric effect. His approach was arch and camp – well before anyone had coined the term. In fact, his position within the field of cultural production gave him a particular opportunity to develop this approach. The quota quickies are usually thought of in terms of the restrictions placed on creative film-making, but the acclaim given to some of Powell's first films, coupled with the idea that his clients among the American renters were just paying for 'footage', gave him space to experiment and to lampoon the very system of production and distribution that paid his bills.

Critical bewilderment with Powell's irreverent approach peaked with his next film for United Artists, the notorious musical comedy *His Lordship*, in which the reliable Jerry Verno played a reluctant peer who, in a satirical reversal of the prevailing snobbery, prefers to be a plumber. His endeavours to hide his title from his Communist girlfriend (Polly Ward) are threatened by her mercenary comrades, played as comedy Bolsheviks by Michael Hogan and V. C. Clinton-Baddeley. The film alienated critics and audiences by taking Verno's plausible working-class character and placing him in implausible situations. Powell had done much the same thing in *My Friend the King*, but this time he added gloriously absurd song-and-dance sequences that parodied contemporary tastes in musical talkies. In its plot and treatment, *His Lordship* again held up a distorting mirror to the popular British cinema of the day with its class masquerades and phony sophistication. Its topsy-turvy world of social pretence and frustrated romance punctuated by musical interludes is reminiscent of a Gilbert and Sullivan operetta. One of its primary targets was the film publicity machine – here personified by a Hollywood star and her cynical American publicist (Janet McGrew and Ben Welden) – and its manufacture of counterfeit imagery and dubious journalism. The film even has a sequence of dancing charladies, as if to acknowledge that cinema cleaners were likely to be the principal West End audience for a quota quickie like this.

Ironically enough, Powell's satirical picture itself briefly became emblematic of all that was wrong with British film production. As musicals were in vogue, United Artists probably hoped that *His Lordship* might make a serviceable co-feature and allowed it to run to seventy-seven minutes – a decision that would seem to be vindicated by Ralph Smart's witty script and Powell's confident handling of the material. However, it was barracked off screen when it opened for a week at London's Dominion in September 1932 as support to Ben Lyon in *By Whose Hand?*. Trade reviews had been perplexed and not particularly enthusiastic. *Kinematograph Weekly* thought the film lacked 'cohesion and definite purpose', that the song-and-dance sequences seemed out of place and the film contained passages 'which have no definite place in entertainment'. However, the picture was also thought to be redeemed by its satirical wit and 'popular streak of cockney humour', which ought to make it 'a usable quota booking for popular areas'. Technically, the film was perfectly satisfactory.[39] But after the response of the Dominion audiences, the reviews in the fan magazines were more scathing. *Picturegoer* thought *His Lordship* 'a queer mixture of musical comedy, burlesque and satire', while *Film Pictorial* accused the picture of bringing the British film industry into disrepute:

> This is the type of production that does not improve Britain's film prestige. It opens slowly and never at any time does it seem to be on the track of improving. Each minute becomes drearier and drearier; the yawns around us become more and more frequent and the depression ends eventually, about seventy-five minutes after it began. We gather it was supposed to be a comedy. You've probably heard of *The Comedy of Errors* . . .? This was the other one![40]

Provincial exhibitors who had booked the film became so worried that they lobbied the Cinematograph Exhibitors Association to negotiate a release from their contracts with United Artists.[41]

The wags at MGM showed Powell's ninth film *Born Lucky* to the trade on the very day that the luckless *His Lordship* was sheepishly sent onto general release. Based on the popular novel *Mops* by Oliver Sandys (real name: Marguerite Barclay), this musical was even longer than *His*

Bringing the British film industry into disrepute: Janet McGrew, Jerry Verno and Ben Welden in
*His Lordship* (1932)

*Lordship* and would have been a real squeeze to accommodate on most suburban double bills
without unauthorised trimming. The original title of this story of an East End orphan (Rene
Ray) who becomes a star of the stage (as well as again giving a nod to charladies), might have
reminded Powell of his first job in films: as a mop man for Rex Ingram's MGM unit in Nice.[42]
Although Miss Ray was herself a rising star, her film failed to clean up the mess left by *His Lordship*.[43] Powell and Jackson, however, did get a lucky break when they were offered the opportunity to make some films on decent budgets with Michael Balcon at ritzy Gaumont-British.
For the first time, the bright young film-makers were going to work with their own original
scripts, but, as it turned out, they were first obliged to address a project that Balcon had been
keeping on the back burner for some time: a hackneyed whodunit called *Murder Party*. Although
Powell and Jackson were aware that they were being handed a standard quota script, they were
seduced into taking on the project by the offer of a more stellar cast than usual, and the subsequent film – retitled *The Night of the Party* – was packed with Gaumont's contracted artists. But
in spite of prominent advertisements in the trade press, it played second on the bill to Lee Tracy
in *Advice to the Lovelorn* when it opened at the Tivoli in London's West End in March 1934.

Happily, *The Night of the Party* is one of less than a dozen Powell films from the era to have
survived, and proves to be a deliciously camp deconstruction of the society murder mystery,
although one might hardly have realised this from the film's synopsis or reviews. *Kinematograph*

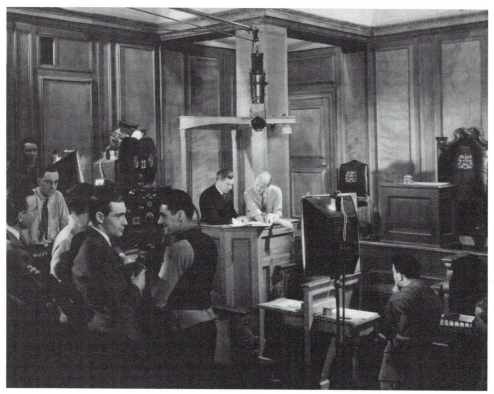

Murder and the creative artist: Powell directs *The Night of the Party* (1934)

*Weekly* seemed unaware that Michael was taking the mickey when it described the film as a 'conventional crime drama', and complained that the direction lacked 'the slickness and kick which is so essential to the complete success of this type of manufactured thriller'. The reviewer could not understand why suspense had been 'weakened to a point where the unexpected becomes commonplace', or why an ending so 'wildly incredible' had been allowed.[44] The aesthetic dispositions and ironic sensibilities now so familiar in the reception of postmodern film were not widespread in the 1930s, and few could recognise blank parody when it screamed in their face like Ernest Thesiger. Powell's picture displays his frustration with the oh-so-polite conventions of the English whodunit. 'It was one of those Agatha Christie stories where everybody's a character and it ends up with an Old Bailey court case', he once recalled, adding 'I was bored to death with it but I did the best I could.'[45] Powell did his best, one might add, to dig the grave of the moribund middle-brow detective mystery, which might pass a post-prandial couple of hours on the West End stage, but hardly stretched the potential of the cinema. His film pays only lip service to the rules, and exposes the genre as a game – a game which, in the words of one of its players, is 'getting on my nerves'.

Powell appears deliberately to over-draw his characters, displaying their shallowness, pretentiousness and moral bankruptcy. High society seems to be populated by lecherous lords, faithless wives, ungentlemanly blackmailers and vain artists. Their capacity for self-deception is nicely satirised in the evidence of the guest of honour at the 'murder party', the Princess: 'They were all *nice* people at the party, people who don't do that kind of thing. After all, you can't eat a man's dinner and then shoot him afterwards – that kind of thing isn't done, especially shooting him twice.' The reason why practically any of the guests might have murdered the host has less to do with a superfluity of motives than the sad fact that they barely muster a moral conviction between the lot of them. In the end, the killer turns out to be a self-styled 'creative artist' who enacts revenge on a corrupt critic. One wonders how fanciful it might be to suggest that, in the figure of the murdered newspaper magnate Lord Studholme, that creative artist Michael Powell might have imagined the head of Gaumont-British Pictures, Michael Balcon. After all, it was Balcon who had insisted on filming the 'stinker' of a script to keep his studio occupied during a production hiatus.[46] Given his pick of contract players, it seems as if Powell took a perverse delight in making sure the picture was suitable only as a supporting feature, a position from which it could gently mock others like itself. The material, he felt, was not worthy of his talents, and he probably wanted to ensure that it was not offered for critical judgment as his debut main feature. He made it under-length, and did not complete additional filming until he had directed *The Fire Raisers* (1933), his own script and one on which he was happier to be judged. In fact, *The Night of the Party* was released after both *The Fire Raisers* and Powell's next film for Balcon, *Red Ensign* (1934). Any danger of *The Night of the Party* being shown in the USA was avoided by having an ending in which the murderer commits suicide – a closure prohibited by the American Production Code.

Many of the modest quota pictures Powell made may be considered disguised films about British cinema: its possibilities and restrictions. They offer a discursive commentary on the hopes and aspirations of the film-maker within an expanding industry reliant on American patronage and hamstrung by conventional ideas. As the early work of a visionary artist, they often imagine the possibility of transformation. *Red Ensign*, which seems to have been booked mainly as a co-feature, is a case in point.[47] More serious than his previous pictures, it is virtually a polemic on the need for a new aesthetic cinema that would wed the visual achievements of the documentary movement with the emotional power tapped by narrative film-making. Although it is ostensibly about shipbuilding, its protagonist's argument that protective quota legislation provides a window of opportunity in which new creative ideas could flourish, has evident application to the work of indigenous film-makers. 'Patriotism is good business,' declares David Barr (Leslie Banks), a partial self-portrait of Powell as a headstrong young leader intent on letting nothing interfere with his creative vision. Like Barr, Powell's job as a director was to 'get things done'.

If the allegorical intent is not immediately obvious, the naming of some characters soon betrays the trope. The cautious chairman of the company is Lord Dean, the same surname as Basil Dean, the powerful impresario and studio head, notorious for his penchant for adapting stage plays to make films.[48] When Dean remarks of a fleet of merchant vessels that 'most of those ships are less than five years old and yet they are rotting at their anchors', he might easily be describing the British films made under the Quota Act, which had been operating for just five years when *Red Ensign* was made. 'The best riveter in the yard' is named Grierson, presumably after John Grierson, the founder of the British documentary movement and a staunch supporter of Powell's attempts to bring originality and style to low-budget pictures.[49] If the name were not enough, the film is full of visual homage to Griersonian cinema in its heroic industrial montages. At the time, Powell was consulting another leading documentarist, Robert Flaherty, who was cutting his *Man of Aran* (1934) in Gaumont's editing rooms.

For Barr, like Powell, the key to success is design. Significantly, his revolutionary new ship is built to the 'artform design', and is not for sale to anyone who plans to sail it under a foreign flag. When Manning, a shady shipping magnate, offers to purchase a fleet of Barr's boats he is rebuffed as an unpatriotic exploiter who evades Board of Trade regulations and crews his vessels with 'sweated, underpaid seamen'. The Board of Trade, of course, was also the body which administered the 1927 Films Act, and Manning may represent some of the less scrupulous quota quickie merchants who were supplying films to American renters. 'Your type of cut-throat competition has already hit British shipping,' Barr tells Manning, 'and unless British shipping prospers, this firm goes out of business.' This was the sort of reasoning that would have delighted Michael Balcon who, at the time, was battling to establish Gaumont-British as a rival to the major Hollywood studios and viewed the American-sponsored quota films as an irritant to his attempts to bolster the prestige of British cinema. Manning is further assured that making craft for him 'might keep us in work for a while, but it will help to ruin our best customer: British ship owners'. On the other hand, Barr's new design will bring 'a revival of British shipping that will mean prosperity for the whole country'. Transposed into the world of film-making, this is a strident critique of the short-termism of quota production and the problems involved in securing adequate investment in the future of an industry vital to British cultural and political influence. When Basil Dean set up his ATP production company at the beginning of 1930, he announced that it would 'make possible the effective presentation of the British point of view in the Dominions and all parts of the British Empire'.[50] In *Red Ensign*, Barr tells Lord Dean that, if nothing is done, 'the ships that were once the means of this country building up the Empire, and on which this country depends for supplies, would cease to exist'. The parallel is clear: if ships helped to build the Empire, it is films that are essential to its maintenance. Powell and Balcon both believed that, like ships, films are a vital means of carrying the culture of Britishness to other parts of the globe. Balcon's dictum was that 'we shall become international by being national', while Powell regarded 'the whole world' as his audience.[51] One member of that audience was sufficiently impressed to congratulate producer, director and cast in a letter to *Film Weekly*: 'The film was really British in outlook and atmosphere; it contained a good story and well-thought-out dialogue; the acting was excellent.'[52]

*Red Ensign* has been remembered largely for its third act in which, with a 'man-to-man' appeal for trust and loyalty, Barr counters worker unrest fostered by agitators in the pay of the unscrupulous Manning. However, Manning eventually succeeds in sabotaging the new ship, and consequently the film was considered dangerously political for a time of industrial crisis. Even *Kinematograph Weekly*, which usually did its best to ignore any hint of ideology in films, commented that 'politically and ethically it leaves itself wide open for criticism'. Apart from the film's 'sidelights on character', 'good melodrama' and 'hint of romance', its saving grace commercially appeared to be its 'popular patriotism'. Thus, it could be deemed 'safe for juveniles'.[53] The *Monthly Film Bulletin* also seemed relieved that this 'melodramatic story showing the hazardous conditions prevailing in the shipbuilding industry . . . avoids controversy'.[54] Michael Powell might not have been so pleased by the calming critical oil poured on the troubled waters of his campaigning picture – the first he regarded as revealing that there was 'something special' about his film-making.

One wonders what acerbic social critique from Powell might be obscured by the *Monthly Film Bulletin's* bland summary of Warners' *Someday* (1935) – the story of an impoverished young couple (Margaret Lockwood and Esmond Knight) 'up against the law' – as 'a pleasant unpretentious story, pleasantly told'.[55] We may never know, as it remains a lost film, but plot synopses suggest that class tensions are ultimately resolved in a consensual manner. Certainly, Powell seems to have tried to represent his working-class characters with verisimilitude, although his efforts were not appreciated by every viewer as one letter to *Picturegoer* revealed:

> Both production and acting were very good and yet the film was spoilt for the simple reason that the stars, just because they were playing parts of employees, were talking as if they had never been educated at all. They were continually saying 'ain't yer' 'av yer' etc. I'm sure most filmgoers will agree that so much of that talk is unnecessary.[56]

The film's trade advertising emphasised that *Someday* was a '*British* Romance', describing it as 'The Sweetest Love Story ever told . . . the laughter and tears, romance and adventure of two against the world!'[57]

Powell wound up his contract at Gaumont-British with *The Phantom Light* (1935), a successful thriller based on a stage play. Like *The Fire Raisers*, it was a first feature and so will not be discussed here, but it marked the end of Powell's thirteen-film partnership with Jerry Jackson. Having tasted film-making on adequate budgets with Balcon, Powell crept back to quota production for one of the American renters. This time it was Warners. *Something Always Happens*, his first film at Teddington, was about a businessman who lives on his wits, and might be considered a tribute to his erstwhile partner. Certainly, Peter Middleton, the protagonist of Brock Williams' script, was a character study of the sort of men that produced quota pictures in spite of all the financial obstacles. Middleton survives by 'selling something I haven't got to someone who doesn't want it' – the type of sleight-of-hand practised daily by the merchants of the quota. Powell was happy with the picture: 'We played it all out for laughs; great speed, excellent dialogue.'[58] The critics agreed, and *Something Always Happens* was among the best-received quota quickies. *Kinematograph Weekly* praised Powell's 'resourceful direction', commenting:

> Here is a neat, entertaining romantic comedy, smartly written and presented. The story, pleasantly extravagant, is compact and smoothly balanced, and the dialogue, which has moments of bright humour, is refreshingly natural. The acting of the principals, too, is above the average. In fact, every department of this unpretentious offering is sound and it represents an attractive two-feature programme proposition for all types of audiences.[59]

Such unqualified enthusiasm was rare, but *Something Always Happens*, the story of a resourceful young man who succeeds by refusing to let setbacks dampen his spirits, struck just the right chord of optimism in the depths of economic depression.

The other films that Powell made for Irving Asher at Warner Bros. were a mixed bag. *The Girl in the Crowd*, a modest comedy of mistaken identity, which introduced a future British star in Googie Withers, was dismissed by its director as 'a complete failure', something Asher had whipped out of a drawer and said, 'For God's sake, shoot this'. Powell believed that 'nobody ever

Prototype noir: Powell on the set of *Crown v. Stevens* (1936) with Patric Knowles and Beatrix
Thompson

saw it'.[60] If its lack of any booking in Leicester is anything to go by, he might have been right,
but *The Girl in the Crowd* received an above average trade review from *Kinematograph Weekly*,
which recommended Powell's 'airy trifle' as 'a very usable quota booking'. Although the plot was
'disjointed' and the whole was only 'mildly amusing', it had 'technical polish', excellent London
exteriors and was 'quite competently directed'.[61]

   *The Brown Wallet* and *Crown v. Stevens* (1936) both utilised the talents of Asher's 'discovery',
Patric Knowles. Powell thought *The Brown Wallet*, a story by Stacy Aumonier of an impecunious
young publisher who finds a wallet full of money and is almost hanged as a murderer, was 'a very
ingenious little thriller – too ingenious', meaning that its plot complexities militated against its
cinematic potential.[62] *Kinematograph Weekly*, on the other hand, approved of its plot complica-
tions and the eventual 'discovery of the least likely person as the murderer'.[63] *Film Weekly*
thought it 'patchy' and unevenly paced. The picture's main deficiency, however, was less the fault
of its director than its star:

   Although director Michael Powell has given the film a wealth of detail and many ingenious situations, one can never quite believe that the hero is behaving naturally. Perhaps this is the fault of
   Patric Knowles who, though he has a pleasant personality and much promise, is too inexperienced
   to give the characterisation the necessary light and shade.[64]

Knowles received slightly better notices in *Crown v. Stevens*, a prototype film noir in which a woman kills a pawnbroker and then tries to poison her husband. But, although *Picturegoer* found Knowles 'likeable enough', it did not care much for the film, which it thought 'conventional in presentation and theme'.[65] However, critical reservations did not prevent Patric Knowles being shipped off to Hollywood.

## Behind the mask

Between making films at Teddington, the peripatetic Powell also completed a very well-received first feature for Geoffrey Rowson's New Ideal company at Beaconsfield (*Her Last Affaire*, 1935) and two more pictures for Fox at Wembley (*The Love Test*, 1935, and *The Price of a Song*).[66] He also made a quota quickie at Twickenham Studios, shortly before Julius Hagen decided to concentrate on more prestigious fare. With conscious irony, *Lazybones* – a story by Ernest Denny about a man who struggled to get out of bed in the morning – was a film that exemplified the feverish production schedule that drove the industry in the mid-1930s. The picture was made during the night shift at Twickenham, after its leading actors – Ian Hunter and Claire Luce – had finished their West End stage work. Like so many of Powell's other quota films, its theme has a wider resonance. Its impecunious titled family looking to revive its fortunes by the marriage of the eldest son (Hunter) to an American heiress (Luce) who has bought the local pub, can be read as a comment on the dependency of a cash-strapped British film industry on Hollywood finance. If one looks a little harder, one can see in the protagonist's contrary reluctance to propose to the heiress until he learns that she has lost her money, Powell's own ambivalent feelings towards Hollywood: admiring its artistry, but resenting its economic domination. Of course no contemporary reviewers pointed this out, and probably none noticed.[67] *Today's Cinema* deemed *Lazybones* 'pleasant popular entertainment', which was all most quota films aspired to, but for Powell must again have seemed a dispiritingly bland assessment. The camerawork was 'competent', the settings (as usual) were 'realistic', and the direction was 'smooth'; but the whole was let down by its 'crook element' which was judged 'nebulous'. The picture's strength was felt to lie elsewhere: 'The entertainment is on safer ground, it seems, on its amusing romantic comedy, and on its piquant characterisation', which included the leads and supporting roles.[68]

Fox's *The Love Test* was an apparently unassuming romantic comedy that was also condescendingly praised as 'a pleasant little film'.[69] There is little doubt, however, that *The Love Test* had allegorical intent, and is worth examining in more detail because it reveals something of the scope of Powell's ambition, even on 'little' films. The story may have been by pulp playwright Jack Celestin, and the script by Selwyn Jepson, another pulpmeister best known for penning the book on which Hitchcock based *Stage Fright* (1950), but Powell's handwriting is all over it (metaphorically, at least).[70] His directorial credit appears over the image of a bubbling chemical flask, as if to acknowledge responsibility for cooking up this concoction. 'To find a formula for fire-proofing celluloid is a very difficult problem,' repeats the vice-president of the film's research and development company, and inflammability was clearly a very real practical difficulty for film distribution, projection and preservation. But, it is also an apt metaphor for the impermanence of so much cinema of the period. Powell worked in an industry in which perhaps 90 per cent of its products had a life span not much longer than a mayfly's. Even main features were lucky

Laboratory lovers: Judy Gunn and Louis Hayward take *The Love Test* (1935)

to outlast an initial circuit release, and quota quickies like *The Love Test* were almost guaranteed to disappear from public view after a few days of exhibition over the course of nine to twelve months. There was no second or third life on television or home video, although a limited survival on 16mm film was sometimes possible. Such a level of ephemerality must have bothered someone like Powell, who believed in the artistic potential of cinema.

*The Love Test*'s recurring image is of a mass-produced celluloid kewpie doll quickly consumed by flames. It is an image that invokes both the manufactured and standardised character of popular genre cinema and the conveyor belt of disposable female 'talent' used to service its needs – fodder for the casting couch, the 'love test'. Young women like Judy Gunn, the film's leading lady, were rapidly consumed by quota production, and replaced by newer faces. Gunn's career in second and co-features began with great enthusiasm but lasted only four brief years and a dozen films. She disappeared soon after starring as Beauty in Twickenham's *Beauty and the Barge* at the age of twenty-three.[71] Her leading man, Louis Hayward, on the other hand, enjoyed a fifty-year career going immediately to Hollywood and starring as *The Man in the Iron Mask* (1939) for United Artists. But only a lucky few actresses, like Googie Withers, achieved the longevity denied to the inflammable kewpie doll. In this film, it is Withers who asks Hayward if he ever takes a girl to the pictures, as if to hint self-reflexively to the subtext of the picture in which she is appearing.

Like the laboratory in Powell's film, lovingly explored by Arthur Crabtree's tracking camera, the quota quickie studios were a testing ground. Actors, technicians and directors could all be given a chance to develop outside of the spotlight of attention given to more prestigious film-making. Crabtree would go on to direct his own films, while Bernard Miles, who made his acting debut in *The Love Test*, would become a distinguished knight of the cinema. The men and women who work at the benches in Powell's laboratory are not unlike those in the studio where it was filmed: they are dedicated, industrious and long-suffering, but they are prone to professional jealousies and egotism. They are also divided by gender, both physically – the men's and women's common rooms are segregated – and psychologically. Professionalism is constantly undercut by a sexual tension encouraged by Googie Withers' Americanised office siren and expressed in the romantic-instrumental love triangle composed by Mary (Gunn), John (Hayward) and Thompson (David Hutcheson), the ambitious misogynist who resents 'taking orders from a woman' and wants to be the lab's top dog. But while the workforce has a vitality enriched by its combustible gender mix, the company management is depicted as a comical collection of old men of limited competence. The chief chemist (Gilbert Davis), for instance, cannot even find a cure for his own hiccups, while the president cannot conceive of a modern office without 'hot-air'. Again, the impatient and frustrated young Powell may have had in mind the management of his own industry and its continuing inability to facilitate the wide-scale development of a cinema of permanent significance. He confessed in his autobiography to being 'impatient with the men who financed the struggling British film industry'.[72]

The one saving grace of Powell's fictional managers (unlike those that managed fictions) is their willingness to promote on merit, even if it means putting a woman in charge; and, in its portrait of a capable young female scientist, the film also registers a significantly progressive approach to gender representation unusual in pre-war British cinema. The proto-feminist Mary may be disturbed and distracted by her submerged sexuality, but the film never questions the fact that she is, in the assertion of her colleague and lover, 'a very good chemist'. So good, in fact, that seduction is proposed as the only way of undermining her professional effectiveness. She may, according to the character played by Bernard Miles, have 'the feel of a Bunsen burner', but she has yet to be ignited by any of her male colleagues. Mary's apparently non-flammable nature is, of course, in contrast to the celluloid dolls that burst into flames at the slightest provocation. Thus, the male chemists are trying to inflame the passions of one 'doll' while struggling to render the others fire-proof. Powell delights in the delicious irony of all this, relishing the taxi-cab conversation in which Mary discourses on the sex life of bees, looking forward to the emergence of a new form of human: 'a neuter, without sex'. Her suitor John flatters her as a 'queen', telling her that her hands are 'far too pretty to hide under rubber gloves', but she thinks of herself as a 'worker'. As John visibly shrinks on the taxi seat like a derided erection, she assures him that 'My mind and my faculties function to the order of my will; I have eliminated sex.' We know, of course that this cannot be the case, not least because this is, after all, a romantic comedy.

One of the most prominent themes of Powell's mature cinema would be the disruption of repressive regimes and circumstances by eruptions of desire – a coterminant of the transformative power of art. It would find its most memorable expression amid the colony of celibate sisters in *Black Narcissus*, but it is already present twelve years earlier among the industrious chemists of *The Love Test*. When Mary returns to her 'worker's room', the camera's concentration on a single rosebud – a symbol of a sexuality waiting to be awakened – sent by an anonymous admirer (it turns out to be the scheming Thompson) anticipates the famous colour transmutation scene in *A Matter of Life and Death* (1946). Her subsequent transformation into a self-conscious object of desire is Powell's rehearsal for the more celebrated lipstick application by Sister Ruth (Kathleen Byron) in *Black Narcissus*, although the emphasis is on sensuality rather than danger. Prefaced by an inspired cut from a collection of chemical containers to an array of perfume bottles, Powell's dreamy feminisation montage includes the same erotic ritual of lip enhancement, as well as the sensuous handling of diaphanous lingerie and stockings, and the final placing of a rose in her hair, the transplanting of romantic expression to her body.[73] To emphasise its erotic significance, the sequence is intercut with another scene showing John being given tips in love-making by Googie Withers' character. The appearance of the newly 'dolled-up' Mary at work precipitates another bout of hiccups from her immediate boss, and his replacement by Mary, now properly the Queen of the Lab. Appropriately for Powell's cinema, the search for fire-proof film is resumed with a new passion and sensuality, until a breakdown in their relationship sets John and Mary the sternest of love tests. The chemical solution, when it is found, is also a romantic resolution, and is delivered in the form of a doll, a lover's gift to Mary.

The reviewer in *Today's Cinema* was certainly impressed with the film's 'charm of characterisation' which compensated for an 'occasional lethargy of tempo'. 'There is a novelty of setting and a general fluency of production which lift it from the rut of British-produced romantic dramas. For one thing, its characters savour more of living people than the generality of its type, and certainly they are entirely new as to profession and behaviour.'[74] The *Monthly Film Bulletin* also noted the freshness of the setting, but dismissed the film as merely 'adequate.[75] *Picturegoer* and *Film Weekly* both thought it 'fairly entertaining', with *Picturegoer* commending the 'competent acting' and a 'sufficiency of technical skill', and *Film Weekly* suggesting that 'fairly skilful direction and good performances from the principals make this rather better than one might think'.[76] In hindsight, of course, *The Love Test*'s conflicted heroine can be seen as the precursor of more celebrated Powell and Pressburger women who are torn between duty and desire, work and romance, in films like *I Know Where I'm Going* (1945), *The Red Shoes* (1949) and *Gone to Earth* (1950).[77] However, none of the surviving reviews of *The Love Test* remark on the picture's striking discourse on the newly emancipated woman's struggle to reconcile feminism and femininity and to establish her place in male-dominated professions. The film's allegorical significance and Powell's intelligent and witty use of montage, mobile and mediated camerawork, striking visual motifs (like the circular imagery that frequently enlivens the frame) and innovative editing techniques are similarly ignored.

The quota quickie phase of Powell's career ended with *The Man behind the Mask*, a less than satisfactory picture in the British 'shocker' tradition made for the Anglo-American independent studio run by Joe Rock. The story and treatment are an uneasy combination of the sort of sharp-witted thriller being produced by Alfred Hitchcock and the super-villain serials churned out by the American 'B' movie studios. The contemporary reviews were remarkably indulgent, even suggesting that Powell had 'done everything possible to give plausibility to the tale', but the picture demonstrates little of Powell's flair.[78] Its bizarrely paced and exaggerated dénouement may indicate a contempt for the material or it might be a coded attempt to identify the

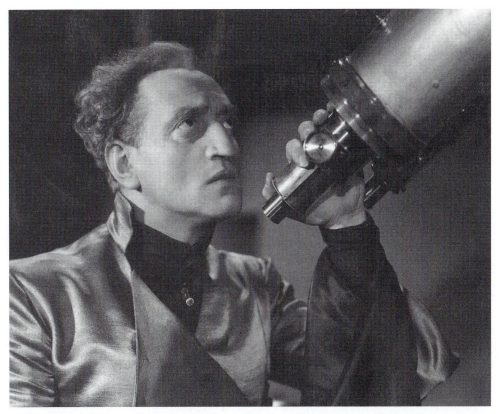

The magus: Maurice Swartz draws his inspiration from the heavens in *The Man Behind the Mask* (1936)

visionary antagonist (Maurice Swartz) with the frustrated director. 'The Master' (aka, Paul Melchior, a reversal of Michael Powell's initials) is a megalomanic magus who speaks 'too many languages', draws his inspiration from the heavens and wants to save the world with the aid of a mystical shield. The Master is pronounced mad, and Powell may well have felt that he was heading towards a similar state of derangement if he continued to suffer the conventionalising pressures of his production environment. His heart is clearly already on Foula, where Joe Rock would give him the opportunity to revitalise his imagination and realise his full potential. When the Chief of the International Police Bureau puts his arm round The Master and leads him away with the promise to help him save the world, we might substitute Joe Rock taking pity on Powell. With *The Edge of the World*, the man behind the mask would be truly revealed.

Two years after quitting the quota quickies, Powell told *Film Weekly* that many second features were really 'mass-produced mediocrities and did the cinema much harm'.[79] His own supporting features demonstrate both continuities with, and divergences from, the prevailing modes of second-feature production in the 1930s. They certainly exemplify the hit-and-miss quality of quota production, and exhibit that threadbare quality that severe budget constraints gave to the textual cloth; but they also show what riches could sometimes be wrung from the poorest of raw material by film-makers of invention. Cameraman Leonard Harris, who assisted Arthur Crabtree on *The Love Test*, believed Powell was too harsh in judging his own early work:

I think that some of them were his best work, because he made some excellent pictures which must have been on a shoestring. You know it was not so difficult, I would say, to make a good picture if you've got a big budget and can go back and retake things. But if you've got to go out there and do it one day, sort of thing, it requires a bit of skill you know.[80]

As Caroline Lejeune so astutely discerned in her review of *Rynox*, quoted at the beginning of this chapter, the quota factories were blast furnaces that could force real talent to reveal itself. Some of Powell's high-pressure products won critical plaudits, some were panned. Some were popular successes, others were box-office disasters. Most juxtaposed successful and unsuccessful sequences within the same picture, but all allowed a talented film-maker to experiment and develop his craft. Within many of these films (most with scripts attributed to other writers) we can find sequences, characterisations and themes that would reappear in more sophisticated form in the subsequent Powell and Pressburger pictures. All those dynamic and enterprising young men who kick against staid conventions to get things done, for instance, would discover their ideal type in Spud (James McKechnie), the go-getting young officer in *The Life and Death of Colonel Blimp* (1943). The magus figure crudely caricatured in *The Man behind the Mask*, would, as Robert Murphy has noted, be more subtly drawn in films like *A Matter of Life and Death* and *The Red Shoes*.[81] But rather than being mere apprentice pieces, with occasional flashes of inspiration, many of Powell's quota quickies can stand as thoughtful and thought-provoking films in their own right. They were, pre-eminently, films with ideas – often ideas about the industry of which they were a part – and, if we care to look, we can find coded within them witty, stylised portraits of the film-maker and the people and institutions that were important to him. Finally, and perhaps most remarkably, even though Powell's quota quickies borrowed freely from European stylistics, frequently adapted American generic forms, and were mostly made for American companies, they remained, like their director 'English to the core, as English as a Cox's Orange Pippin'.[82]

## Notes

1. *Observer*, 13 December 1931.
2. Michael Powell, *A Life in Movies* (London: Methuen, 1987), p. 216.
3. Ibid., p. 218.
4. Ibid., pp. 220–1.
5. *CEA Film Report*, 11 July 1931.
6. *The Bioscope*, 15 July 1931, p. 28.
7. *The Times*, 12 August 1931, p. 8. The film even attracted the attention of *Variety*'s London correspondent who described it as 'Just a quota quickie, but much better than many more ambitious pictures turned out this side'. Quoted in Allen Eyles and David Meeker (eds), *Missing Believed Lost* (London: BFI, 1992), p. 34.
8. Frank Scully, 'Youth and British Films', *Film Weekly*, 7 November 1931.
9. Although Powell remembered it as just a week or two, the trade shows for *Two Crowded Hours* and *Rynox* were four months apart.
10. Powell, *A Life in Movies*, p. 221.
11. John Grierson, 'As Good as Hollywood', *Everyman*, 10 December 1931.

12. *Kinematograph Weekly*, 12 November 1931.

13. *The Bioscope*, 11 November 1931.

14. *Picturegoer*, 5 March 1932. The 'spoiler' revelations carelessly tossed into the review could not have helped readers' subsequent enjoyment of the film.

15. Powell, *A Life in Movies*, pp. 219–20.

16. Ibid., p. 215.

17. *The Bioscope*, 15 July 1931, p. 28.

18. *The Bioscope*, 16 September 1931, p. 34.

19. *CEA Film Report*, 19 September 1931.

20. *Picturegoer*, 13 February 1932.

21. The press sleuth idea would be used again in Paramount's *Scoop*, directed by Maclean Rogers, but this time the reporter would be revealed as the murderer.

22. *Kinematograph Weekly*, 10 December 1931, p. 33.

23. *The Bioscope*, 9 December 1931, p. 20. This did not stop *Film Weekly* (12 December 1931, p. 3) recommending *The Rasp* together with *Rynox*, as an 'ideal' supporting feature.

24. Powell, *A Life in Movies*, p. 223.

25. *CEA Film Report*, 12 December 1931.

26. *Kinematograph Weekly*, 17 December 1931, p. 24.

27. *The Bioscope*, 16 December 1931.

28. *Picturegoer*, 7 May 1932. Young Isla from the Isle of Wight never achieved the escape velocity to take her out of the quota quickies.

29. Quoted in Eyles and Meeker, *Missing Believed Lost*, pp. 39–40. John Gammie in *Film Weekly* (30 January 1932, p. 23) was in no doubt that a conventional programmer had been transformed into something more substantial 'thanks to Michael Powell', who had demonstrated 'what a resourceful director can do with a commonplace, highly incredible story, unambitious settings, and players who are adequate without being anything more'.

30. John Grierson, 'Directors of the Thirties', in Forsyth Hardy (ed.), *Grierson on Documentary* (New York: Harcourt Brace, 1947).

31. Powell, *A Life in Movies*, p. 225.

32. Future film director Muriel Box who worked as a continuity girl on one of the first Powell quickies, was taken on as secretary and script reader. Muriel Box interview, BECTU Oral History Project,

33. *Observer*, 24 April 1932.

34. *Kinematograph Weekly*, 31 March 1932, p. 36.

35. *The Bioscope*, 30 March 1932.

36. *Picturegoer*, 16 July 1932.

37. *Kinematograph Weekly*, 24 March 1932, p. 24.

38. *The Bioscope*, 23 March 1932, p. 22. *Picturegoer* came to a similar conclusion when the film went on general release. 20 August 1932.

39. *Kinematograph Weekly*, 9 June 1932, p. 43.

40. *Picturegoer*, 3 December 1932; *Film Pictorial*, 3 December 1932, p. 19.

41. Eyles and Meeker, *Missing Believed Lost*, p. 43; *Kinematograph Weekly*, 20 October 1932, p. 47.

42. A detailed plot description of *Mops* is available on Steve Crook's invaluable website: <www.powell-press burger.org>.

43. *Picturegoer* (1 April 1933) thought it 'all very naïve' and lacking in cohesion. *Born Lucky* is currently 'lost'.

44. *Kinematograph Weekly*, 8 February 1934.

45. Ian Christie (ed.), *Powell, Pressburger and Others* (London: BFI, 1978), p. 15.

46. Powell, *A Life in Movies*, p. 231. Powell's comment on Balcon was that he 'was not an exciting leader'. Ibid., p. 236.

47. Based on its five Leicester bookings.

48. Dean was keen to use country locations in his films but acknowledged in his autobiography that his cinema had been too much influenced by the theatre: 'I realise now that I tended to regard film-making as an extension of my work in the theatre. This was a fundamental error which . . . did influence my choice of subjects and general approach to what is basically a different art.' Basil Dean, *Mind's Eye* (London: Hutchinson, 1973), p. 257.

49. John Grierson would have been less flattered by the character of his namesake in *The Price of a Song* (1935), the film Powell made for Fox the following year. This Grierson was a murderer. Had the pair fallen out?

50. Dean, *Mind's Eye*, p. 110.

51. Michael Balcon, *Michael Balcon Presents . . . A Lifetime of British Films* (London: Hutchinson, 1969), p. 61; Powell, *A Life in Movies*, p. 189.

52. Letter from C. G. Rice of Bristol, *Film Weekly*, 4 May 1934, p. 69. *Film Weekly*'s reviewer, on the other hand, thought *Red Ensign* was 'lacking in excitement and interest' (1 July 1934, p. 37).

53. *Kinematograph Weekly*, 8 February 1934.

54. *Monthly Film Bulletin*, May 1934. *Film Weekly* (1 July 1934, p. 37) failed to find any controversy in what its reviewer thought an 'uninspired treatment of a topical subject'.

55. *Monthly Film Bulletin*, July 1935. The film was shot under the title *Young Nowheres*, perhaps indicative of a socially critical approach.

56. Letter from Evelyn Selby of Brighton, *Picturegoer*, 16 November 1935, p. 38.

57. *The Cinema*, 17 July 1935.

58. Christie, *Powell, Pressburger and Others*, p. 16.

59. *Kinematograph Weekly*, 28 June 1934, p. 21. See also the positive reviews in *Picturegoer*, 8 December 1934 and *Picture Show*, 15 December 1934.

60. Christie, *Powell, Pressburger and Others*, p. 16.

61. *Kinematograph Weekly*, 6 December 1934. *Picturegoer* (18 May 1935, p. 32) considered 'this mildly amusing comedy' to be 'a trifling affair, weak in continuity but generally competently directed'. Although it detected an occasional 'atmosphere of amateur theatricals' about it.

62. Christie, *Powell, Pressburger and Others*, p. 21.

63. *Kinematograph Weekly*, 27 February 1936.

64. *Film Weekly*, 18 June 1936, p. 36. *Picturegoer*'s Lionel Collier thought one or two situations were 'neatly handled', in spite of the 'surplus of dialogue', but rated Knowles as only 'fair', and awarded the acting honours to the 'minor characters' (18 July 1936, p. 34). *Kinematograph Weekly* had also been more impressed by the supporting cast than the leading player. The *Monthly Film Bulletin* (March 1936), on the other hand, thought the supporting parts stereotypical and overdrawn.

65. *Picturegoer*, 1 August 1936, p. 27. On Knowles' performance and the film's dramatic deficiencies, see also *Kinematograph Weekly*, 2 April 1936.

66. In its review of *The Price of a Song*, *Picturegoer* (5 October 1935, p. 36) was critical of Powell's handling of what was quite an ingenious plot: 'neither the treatment nor the acting get the best out of it . . . the suspense is spoiled by rather clumsy production'.

67. This included the BFI's *Monthly Film Bulletin*, which thought the film would have benefited from a faster pace and a lighter touch. January 1935.

68. *Today's Cinema*, 18 January 1935, p. 8. *Picturegoer* (22 June 1935) pretty much agreed, describing *Lazybones* as 'Simple comedy with a transparent plot, but quite well presented and competently acted.'

69. *Picture Show*, 6 July 1935.

70. Interviewed by Kevin Gough-Yates in 1973, Powell indicated that, in his quota quickie period, he did not simply film the scripts he was given. He had 'a lot to do with' the script for *The Phantom Light*, for instance. <www.powell-pressburger.org/Reviews/Europalia73html>.

71. Judy Gunn (real name: Joan Winfindale) was RADA's youngest entrant, and established a stage reputation before she was twenty, playing opposite Bobby Howes in *She Wanted Adventure*. *Film Pictorial* (19 May 1934, p. 14) remarked on her single-minded dedication to her screen-acting career, and anticipated 'a very loud report' from Gunn: 'Judy is very young, full of ambition, and promises to go far'. She was put under contract at Twickenham Studios after appearing in *Vintage Wine*, and starred in Bernard Vorhaus's *The Last Journey* before taking lead roles in a short string of films for other quota producers. Her retirement from the screen might also have been attributable to her three-year-old marriage to stockbroker Anthony Hue-Williams.

72. Powell, *A Life in Movies*, p. 189.

73. The sequences involving Mary's female neighbour offer rich possibilities for 'queer' readings, noting the connotations of lesbian desire in the way in which Mary is rendered loveable by another woman, and the reaction of that woman to the arrival of John. The fetishistic handling of stockings would reappear in *Contraband* (1940), while the fascination with lipstick reminds one of Powell's account of the seduction techniques of his erstwhile flatmate, Lee Planskoy, who would say to a potential conquest: 'Your lipstick. You have such a beautiful mouth. It could stand a brighter red than Number 12. Let me try it on you. (He had lipsticks lying about everywhere.) Here's a tissue. Wipe that off. Now! Let me show you. That lovely upper lip needs to be fuller.' Ibid., p. 188.

74. *Today's Cinema*, 9 January 1935.

75. *Monthly Film Bulletin*, January 1935.

76. *Picturegoer*, 29 June 1935; *Film Weekly*, 28 June 1935.

77. Natacha Thiery, 'That Obscure Subject of Desire: Powell's Women 1945–1950', in Ian Christie and Andrew Moor (eds), *The Cinema of Michael Powell: International Perspectives on an English Film-Maker* (London: BFI, 2005), pp. 224–38.

78. *Kinematograph Weekly*, 26 March 1936. See also the reviews in *Monthly Film Bulletin*, April 1936 and *Picturegoer*, 22 August 1936, p. 27.

79. *Film Weekly*, 20 August 1938, p.6.

80. BECTU interview.

81. Robert Murphy, 'Strong Men: Three forms of the magus in the films of Powell and Pressburger', *Screen* vol. 46 no. 1, Spring 2005, pp. 63–71.

82. Powell, *A Life in Movies*, p. 232.

# 9

# The Quickie and the Dead:
# Casualties of the Second Quota Act

It is no use beating about the bush – most of us want to give the British Quota Act a nice funeral.
It has served its purpose and it is time it went.

Leeds exhibitor, Harry Hopkins[1]

1935 was a potential tipping point for the Quota Act. In May, when the number of British long films registered under the Act passed 1,000, the proportion of British films reached two in every seven available for distribution.[2] Trade analysts, aware of the efforts being made by most American renters to improve their British-produced pictures, detected signs of a quality up-turn among second features. P. L. Mannock noted that 'those engaged on working on them are getting more and more experienced in turning out presentable results on slender budgets', and was pleased to report 'a marked improvement in the quality of "quota" subjects generally'. Although the worst were as bad as ever, the other films were 'often fit for any hall'.[3] His impression was to receive support from the *CEA Report* for the year, which judged that, of the 173 British films trade shown in 1935, 42 per cent were of a good Hollywood standard, and only 35 per cent were poor. This represented a considerable improvement on previous years, although the long tail remained a concern.[4] This optimistic view was not shared by the indefatigable London branch of the CEA, which continued to insist that the quality of American renters' quota pictures was still falling and the 'menace' was growing.[5] The Leeds branch was equally militant, while the Scots branch also added its voice to the call for the quota to be reduced.[6] Most CEA branch discussions tended to favour a reduction in the quota (usually to 10 per cent) rather than outright abolition, but it was a close call.[7]

In June, the president of the Board of Trade was again pressed in the House of Commons on the issue of quality.[8] Further pressure was applied by the leading cinema economist, Simon Rowson, who called for a £10,000 quality threshold for registration under the Act (still only about half of the average cost of a British picture). 'There are,' he admitted, 'far too many bad British films, and too many of these bad films do not deserve the sympathy we might be prepared to reserve for honourable failures. They are bad because no effort has been exerted to make them otherwise.' Moreover, using *CEA Film Report* review markings, Rowson argued that, compared to foreign films, a disproportionate percentage of British pictures were poor.[9] Consequently, there were proposals from exhibitors to use the *CEA Film Report* scores as a basis for quota qualification, as well as calls for a Board of Examiners to adjudicate on the quality of quota offerings.[10] Just before Christmas, the independent exhibitors received an early present when

the news leaked out from the beleaguered Board of Trade that its advisory committee had recommended a minimum production cost test for quota registration.[11]

By New Year 1936, it seemed that the battle to blunt the Quota Act was almost won, but
dispatches from the production front were again suggesting that quality was already improving
so much that legislative change would hardly be necessary. Reviewing the prospective offerings from renters, *Kinematograph Weekly* announced that 'British producers and Renters have
now signed the death warrant of the "quickie" .'[12] P. L. Mannock was a little more cautious,
foreseeing the eventual demise of the quickies but not 'their early disappearance'. As always,
he was also wary of using the much-maligned pictures as a scapegoat for the ills of British
production:

> But it is all very well for the more responsible studios to grumble at 'quickies'. Some of our largest
> studios continue to turn out pictures which are hopelessly below the standard of Hollywood's
> 'programme' product, and have not the quickie-maker's excuse of limited spending powers.[13]

Mannock's caution towards the corpse of the quickie turned out to be well founded. In March
1936, the latest quota picture from Fox, one of the more progressive producers, was still being
lambasted by the *Kinematograph Weekly* reviewer:

> Comedy melodrama so old-fashioned in story technique, poorly enacted, indifferently directed and
> poverty-stricken in presentation as to finish inevitably amongst the also-rans. The quota angle is no
> excuse for this misguided essay in entertainment, best served by the Americans.[14]

In May 1936, as the advisory Moyne Committee convened to consider changes to the
Quota Act, the film industry was bitterly divided and sliding into financial crisis. In *Kinematograph Weekly*, an anonymous 'prominent member of the industry' summed up the situation thus:
'The producers want as much quota as they can get: the exhibitors as little as can be got, while
the renters would prefer no quota at all, or one based on value rather than footage.'[15] While the
Moyne Committee heard evidence from all interested parties, the findings of a questionnaire
distributed to exhibitors in the London and the Home Counties were published. Significantly,
exhibitors from the three largest circuits (Gaumont-British, ABC and Union cinemas) had
declined to respond. One of the problems in assessing support and opposition for the quota and
concern about low-quality supporting features is that the surviving evidence is skewed towards
one particular interest group: the independent exhibitors. It was the views of these struggling
showmen that were represented week after week in *Kinematograph Weekly* and *The Cinema* via
the CEA branch meetings. The more powerful renters, circuits and large production houses were
less (publicly) vocal, but probably had more direct access to the Board of Trade. Ordinary filmgoers had few opportunities to articulate their views except indirectly via a trade questionnaire
completed by cinema managers. The views of the 275 cinemas that completed the survey were
as follows:

1. Do you think the quota should be abolished entirely; for both exhibitor and renter?
   No: 67%.

2. Do you think the quota on renters should be retained?
   No: 67%. Yes: 29%.
3. If a new quota act should follow the present one, what period of years should it legislate for?
   Less than 5 years: 21%. 5 years: 31%. 10 years: 40%.
4. Do you find any serious difficulty in profitability complying with quota requirements?
   Yes: 49%. No: 50%.
4a. If Yes to question 4; is this due to your audience disliking British productions?
   Yes: 22%.
4b. Is this due to the non-availability of suitable product in your situation?
   Yes: 41%.
5. If a quota on exhibitors is to be continued, what do you regard as a fair percentage?
   Less than 10% quota: 6%. A 10% quota: 47%. A 12.5 or 15% quota: 11%.
   A 20% quota: 12%.
5a. What should be the corresponding percentage on renters?
   Less than 10% quota: 6%. A 10% quota: 47%. A 12.5 or 15% quota: 18%.
   A 20% quota: 17%. More than 20% quota: 12%.[16]

Clearly, the principle of a quota had become widely accepted, even among independent exhibitors, but perhaps the most revealing finding here is the low percentage of exhibitors who say their audiences dislike British productions. Only a little over 10 per cent of those showing the lower-quality British product (assuming the large circuits showed the more expensive films) recorded a problem. Difficulties with quota obligations were much more likely to stem from distribution restrictions imposed by the major circuits, although these might imply that alternative British films from American renters were considered unsuitable. In its evidence to the Moyne Committee, the CEA asserted that in 1935 thirty-three quota films had been definitely unshowable, and thirty-one inferior. 'American houses', it maintained, 'were responsible for most of these.[17]

Meanwhile, British producers, with haughty disdain for small showmen, recommended an exhibitors' quota rising to 50 per cent after ten years.[18] This was a strategy that was presumably designed to force the independents to sell their businesses to the large producer/distributor circuits while deflecting blame onto the American houses for failing to supply sufficient appropriate quota product. The American renters were obliged vigorously to deny allegations that low-grade British films had been made to prejudice the indigenous production industry, and signal their willingness to move towards the production of first features in England. They conceded that quality could only be improved by reducing the number of films they each made by two-thirds to five or six a year. As much as £7 per foot could then be spent on these productions. However, the Moyne Committee preferred to accept the complaints of small exhibitors and published a ringing indictment of the Americans:

the majority of foreign-controlled renters appear to have made arrangements for the production of British films at the minimum of expense, regardless of quality. Such films were not in a position to attract the exhibitors, save in so far as they needed the films to satisfy their quota and indeed they were not, in the main, worthy of exhibition. It was admitted by the renters in evidence before us that the majority of films made for them to enable them to satisfy their quota obligations are worthless and remain in their offices largely unsold and unused.[19]

The Moyne Committee apparently saw its job as finding ways of curbing the abuses practised by the American renters, symbolised by the despised quota quickie.[20] The quickie was the single issue around which the warring factions of the cinema trade could unite. No faction, not even the technicians kept in work by them, could publicly defend bad films; and nobody was prepared to contest the conventional wisdom that the quickies offered little entertainment value. Moyne finally recommended a continuance of the quota system, but with a quality test, based directly on a viewing of the picture by the administering authority, for films counting towards the renter's quota.[21] The committee also recommended a toughening of the regulations covering block booking to prevent renters forcing exhibitors to accept inferior films in package deals with more desirable product – even though it had been repeatedly told that packages were consensual. By and large, the film trade was unhappy with the Moyne recommendations, particularly their call for the establishment of an independent Film Commission, which would be the arbiter of 'quality'. This was seen on all sides as an unwelcome intrusion of bureaucrats and outsiders into the affairs of the industry. The Board of Trade was also unhappy with the idea of a Commission over which it had no direct authority.[22] The recommendation of a quality assessment meant that renters generally felt more hard-done-by than exhibitors and producers. Both renters' and producers' organisations expressed the fear that the uncertainties of quality assessment would act as a disincentive to film finance.[23] Like the film technicians, they preferred a system that would decide quota eligibility on cost per foot.

While the filmgoing public remained oblivious to much of this debate, the endangered status of the double bill was raised in *Picturegoer* in the spring of 1937 under the heading 'Two-feature Programmes Doomed?' Readers were told that 'The biggest bid yet to kill the two-feature film programme is now in progress', and that the double bill 'is now being assailed from all sides'. Front-rank producers were said to be unhappy that 'class B' pictures devalued the film product as a whole, and that part of their solution was to make longer 'A' pictures to 'squeeze out the second feature'. At the same time, exhibitors were keen to exploit a really successful 'A' film by packing in extra screenings via a shortening of the programme. On the other hand, it was conceded that there was a serious scarcity of good shorts to fill out the abbreviated programme and that some 'B' films had proved popular enough to rise to first-feature status.[24]

One of the first reactions to Moyne's recommendations was the call for a separate quota system for first and second features, with the aim of increasing the proportion of first features made by the American renters. The rationale for the scheme, first proposed by the Bristol branch of the CEA, revealed the extent to which supporting features dominated the production schedules of these companies. In 1936, it was claimed, MGM and Fox had handled forty-three British films, but only three had been first features. Warners, First National, Radio, Paramount and Columbia between them had handled fifty-five, of which only eight were first features. Therefore, with the exception of United Artists which dealt almost exclusively with first features, almost 88 per cent of the American renters' British product consisted of supporting features.[25] Very few of these films were shown in the USA. The conclusion:

[T]he only way to put British films on the map is to amend the law so that there is a quota for first features and a quota for second features. Every renter would have to register his film as either a first or second feature, and when selling this would have to be on the contract. . . . No doubt there would be all kinds of objections against this system, especially from the American renters, whose first objection would no doubt be that they could not define which were the first or second features, yet any of their travellers can mark off on his list at once those films which he is allowed to sell as first and second features.[26]

While no direct evidence to support this assertion has come to light, the major circuits seem to have had the status of a film written into their centralised booking contracts, as Jack Rockett, an area manager for the Gaumont circuit remembered:

You had occasions where a manager would say could he show the second features as the feature. He wasn't allowed to do so because of contractual [sic] – but sometimes it could turn out that the second feature was in fact better than the feature as far as the public were concerned. Then you'd got others that were 50/50, where you could show either way.[27]

The examination of actual exhibition practice, however, suggests that, in a minority of cases, making a hard-and-fast classification of a film as a main or supporting feature was not a straight-forward task, and depended as much on critical and audience responses as on registration. More-over, to judge from the contemporary trade reviews, the usual complaints about the poor quality of American-financed British supporting features were beginning to appear out of date. Films like Warners' *The Perfect Crime* and Paramount's *The Cavalier of the Streets* (both 1937) were gar-nering better reviews than most Hollywood second features. *Picturegoer's* influential Lionel Col-lier picked out the latter film for a feature review immediately after its trade show rather than waiting for its general release:

It is not often that I find a place for quota pictures in these pre-views, but in the case of *The Cava-lier of the Streets* I feel the space allocated to it is fully justified. In fact, if all quota pictures were on such a high level of acting and production we shall have little need to grouse about them.[28]

Directed by Harold French and starring Margaret Vyner and Patric Barr, *Cavalier* was a 'well-told' story of blackmail and murder with 'clever characterisations and what is so often lacking in British productions, clever and polished dialogue' (by George Barraud and Ralph Neal).[29]

Warners and Fox were accelerating the trend towards first-feature production. As part of its 'Bigger British' policy, Warners had considerable success with Max Miller vehicles like *Educated Evans* (1937); while 20th Century-Fox produced an adaptation of Shakespeare's *As You Like It*, as well as Britain's first all-Technicolor full-length feature *Wings of the Morning* (both 1937). MGM, now under the guidance of Michael Balcon, began to plan British-made productions on an international scale like *A Yank at Oxford* (1938). It was really only RKO and Paramount, the first of the American houses to make films in England and now operat-ing from the new Pinewood Studios, that stuck with a policy of predominantly second-feature production.[30]

At the annual CEA conference in Harrogate, the new Films Bill, based on the Moyne recommendations, split the Association's general council into independent and circuit exhibitor factions, and all hope of a unified response dissolved. The majority of members continued to favour
a quality test rather than a minimum production budget as the best hope of eliminating inferior
films. They found themselves in opposition to the major British producers and American renters,
as well as the government on the issue, but refused to recognise that they were flogging a dead
horse. However, there was support from the smaller independent producers, led by Widgey
Newman, who regarded the minimum cost test as a serious threat to their survival.[31] Thus,
ironically, the independent exhibitors, the most vocal critics of quota quickies, found themselves
in alliance with some producers of the despised films. The Films Bill crawled through its committee stage, weighed down by countless amendments, and British production was largely sus-
pended until the results were known. The final debates in Commons and Lords provided a
rollercoaster ride for the trade as amendments continued to be adopted or dropped.

In the end, the Films Act softened the Commission to an advisory council, composed of
trade representatives and an independent element, and much like the one that had operated since
1928. This, coupled with the increased flexibility of the Act in comparison to its predecessor,
also pleased exhibitors. But at the eleventh hour, the new Act rejected the quality test in favour
of a minimum cost strategy that would encourage larger investment by the American companies
and put the fly-by-night operations out of business. This was a considerable relief to the American renters who feared investing in films that might be barred from quota registration. The
qualification for registration for the new renters' quota of 15 per cent was a minimum of £1 per
foot spent on labour costs, which were to total at least £7,500. However, more expensive films
could count as double or even treble quota.[32] The treble quota was bitterly opposed by
exhibitors and technicians, who feared that it would reduce the volume of production in British
studios and lead to exhibition shortfalls. The exhibitors' quota was to be 12.5 per cent, and there
was to be a new quota, of the same percentage, for British short films. It was hoped that these
shorts would replace the supporting feature on most programmes.

The 1938 Films Act was a direct assault on the costly two-feature programme, which most
of the film trade had never liked and only the public championed.[33] What was needed was con-
sumer training, the lowering of expectations that had been profligately over-fed in the past. The
public had to be persuaded that one decent film, a newsreel and a couple of shorts should be
enough entertainment. As Odeon chairman Oscar Deutsch put it:

> We must educate the public *out* of this quantity complex, and, as much as we have foisted this spate
> of films on them, educate them *into* what they first had in the early days of our Trade – quality of
> the period and good value for their money. . . . With shorter programmes exhibitors could turn
> round more often and take increased money at the box office.[34]

Thus, in the privacy of an address to fellow exhibitors, Deutch laid bare the economic under-
pinnings of the campaign against the quota quickies. If the quickie could be thoroughly dis-
credited and abolished, the two-feature programme – the biggest barrier to greater exhibitor
profits – would soon follow. The effect of the new Films Act was likely to be the elevation of
the vast majority of British films to the top of the bill, and the erosion of the hegemony of the

double feature. With short films having to be accommodated on already crowded cinema programmes, the prospects for the British second feature looked bleak indeed. *Kinematograph Weekly*
had already confidently assured its readers that 'Quickie production, in the worst sense, will be
killed by the new Act.'[35] Ralph Hanbury, the managing director of RKO-Radio, a company
that had consistently produced the most successful British second features, was quite prepared
to act as their gravedigger:

> One film of outstanding merit is sufficient as a box-office attraction, and more than that, the film
> industry, as it is to-day constituted, cannot afford to provide increased budgets for films that are to
> be shown on a dual programme. It is curious, but the West End has, for many years, provided a
> lesson that has been completely ignored. That is, the public are prepared to pay high prices to see
> only one major feature supported by a choice selection of short subjects. Then why do producers
> continue to produce both 'A' and 'B' films? . . . If we are to abolish the double-feature programme,
> it must be a Trade and not an individual matter, and must be general throughout the country.[36]

Alas, poor quickie. Its grave dug by Deutch and Hanbury, there were, among exhibitors, no shortage of pallbearers eager to speed the passage of its casket. One member of the CEA general council, for instance, chimed in with complaints about the excessive length of programmes and an
assurance that, 'When you play one good picture on its own, you always take more money and
never get any complaints.'[37] Dismissed as 'mere footage', the possible merits of the supporting feature – as a source of variety within a programme, a replacement for the declining music hall and
an outlet for culturally indigenous drama and situation comedy in the days before television – went
unrecognised. The parochial pleasures of domestic audiences cut little ice with cinema magnates
like John Maxwell, whose declared aim was 'rebuilding the British film production business on the
basis of worthwhile pictures that will command respect in the international field and secure world
markets and prosperity for the British film industry'.[38] Any residual demand for second features,
he believed, could be met by those pictures that had failed to win bookings as main attractions.[39]

## A brief new dawn

> 'Quickie' nowadays doesn't necessarily mean the awful rubbish we've been used to enduring under
> that name. More money is being spent on them, more care, more brains.
>
> E. G. Cousins[40]

The 1938 Films Act effectively abolished the informal category of the quota quickie. Hence-
forth, the trade would adopt the term widely used in the USA: the 'B' film. This phrase was
already part of the language of the KRS, whose viewing committee had begun to classify films
as 'A' or 'B'. Films in the former category were to be rented in return for a percentage of box-
office takings, while those in the latter were to be rented for a flat fee.[41] These new 'grading'
arrangements were hotly disputed by the CEA, which sought to prevent circuit houses introducing programmes consisting of two grade 'A' films – a practice already adopted by a few
London cinemas – and thus presenting unanswerable competition for the independent
exhibitor. Under pressure from exhibitors, the KRS agreed to abandon its grading scheme,

Registration rush: Enid Stamp Taylor and Gordon Harker in *Blondes for Danger*, one of 38 British 'B' films trade shown in March 1938

allowing cinemas to continue to decide which films should be programmed as second features.[42] It was a decision that had the backing of *Film Weekly*, which had warned its readers that the grading system was 'vitally important to filmgoers' because it might 'decide the fate of the double-feature programme'. It was particularly worried that 'costly productions may be graded as "A" pictures whether they are good entertainment or not', thus obliging audiences to pay for the 'squandermania' of producers.[43]

The small independent film-makers felt thoroughly abandoned by the government. Their disappointment was summed up by one anonymous producer who complained that, 'The Bill purported to assist the production of British films, but all that it secures is the making of American films in British studios.'[44] A year later, the CEA's assessment of the operation of the Films Act largely supported the independent producers' case:

> Exhibitors are very much concerned at the almost complete absence of British independent production. . . . British quota pictures today are made chiefly by American companies. . . . It is the extra pictures made by independent British producers which are necessary in order to give exhibitors freedom of choice.[45]

While the consequences of over-funding and under-performance had been particularly tough for big-budget pictures, they had also impacted on supporting features. Production had contracted by around 40 per cent and many of the mushroom companies had been culled. In June 1937, the Association of Cine-Technicians calculated that, of the 640 production companies registered over the previous twelve years, only 3 per cent had films in production, and at least 85 per cent would never make another picture.[46] Even before the new Films Act became law, exhibitors were expressing fears that there would be a grave shortage of what had become their 'bread-and-butter' picture as far as programming was concerned. However, there was to be one final fling. In January 1938, Paramount alone had four films in production at four different studios, and in March, the final month of the first Quota Act, there was a veritable stampede to register second features before the rules changed. Films were being registered at a rate of more than one per day, with that single month accounting for almost twice as many supporting features as the whole year that followed. Ace registered six Windmill revue films, all directed by R. A. Hopwood, and Widgey Newman's company registered five pictures, three of which he directed himself. They may have been dashed off before the deadline, but not all of these quickies disappointed film fans: one reader in Richmond wrote to *Film Weekly* to recommend Fox's *Murder in the Family* (1938) as 'well worth seeing' thanks to its excellent story.[47]

But, even as this registration was taking place, most of the supporting feature factories stood idle. At the dawn of the new Quota Act there were no films on the floors of Beaconsfield, Ealing, Hammersmith, Isleworth, Sound City, Teddington or the Rock Studios. At Cricklewood, the ever-industrious Admiral Films were finishing *Bedtime Story* (1938), which some might have considered an appropriate title for the slumbers of quota production. They might also have considered the title of the film being finished at Wembley – *Second Thoughts* (1938) – to be an auspicious one for Fox, which was planning to close its studio.[48] The consequences of this production shut-down would be felt the following year. While March 1938 yielded thirty-eight 'B' films, March 1939 saw only three trade shown. Nor was the shortfall made up by American imports. MGM and Fox had decided to produce no more 'B' grade pictures.[49] A US Department of Commerce Survey would confirm that Hollywood studios were increasingly limiting their exports to 'A' grade films and confining 'B' pictures to their home market. By reducing exports to the films with greatest profit potential, the Hollywood companies could minimise the proportionate number of films required to be produced abroad under quota legislation, and differentiate a 'superior' Hollywood product from that of 'inferior' local film-makers. The Survey offered the following advice to producers:

> It is unwise for us to try to export mediocre films. Foreign audiences in numerous countries get an abundance of that kind of picture from their own studios. American distributors should send only their choice Grade 'A' films to the foreign market. If the choice is between our 'B' type of films and a picture from a native studio, the latter (one need hardly say) is almost invariably preferred. . . . Plainly, before all else, we must emphasise the contrast between our good American pictures and the typical product of local producing industries abroad. We must make that contrast as vivid, as striking, as impressive as it can possibly be made. Persistently and adroitly we must make the foreign movie-goer acutely conscious that the American picture is a product of *decidedly superior* quality. We must make this 'High Quality' factor so universally recognized that the audiences abroad will have no desire to see inferior films that owe their existence simply to some Government legislation or subsidy.[50]

While this policy created opportunities for British second features, it also militated against the continued survival of the two-feature programme.

As British studios became active again after the hiatus created by the uncertainties of the Films Act's provisions, it became clear that 40–50 per cent fewer films were being produced compared to the boom years of the mid-1930s. The reduction in supporting-feature production was far greater. Three months after the Act was passed, six studios remained unused. There was no activity on the floors of Fox's Wembley Studios, while Teddington continued to make modest 'A' grade films using the directorial talents of Arthur Woods. Norman Loudon would later claim that the turnover of Sound City Studios decreased by almost £100,000 in 1938.[51] The long-suffering Paramount would signal their retirement from second-feature production at the end of the year by announcing a new policy of making triple-quota films in Britain for the world market.[52] But, before that, its production unit at Pinewood under Anthony Havelock-Allan, had an overdue success with *This Man Is News* (1938). Made for just £15,000, this film, directed by David Macdonald and starring Barry K. Barnes and Valerie Hobson, demonstrated the potential of a new type of quickie, sweeping into hundreds of cinemas as a first feature, and enjoying distribution in the USA. Briefly, its triumph was hailed as vindication of the new quota regulations, but many producers were more circumspect about the new minimum cost rules. With technicians' wages fixed by union agreements, extra money was going to actors, writers and directors. By and large, this meant that experienced personnel were being employed and opportunities for new entrants to the business were reduced. 'I've got to spend the money,' commented George Smith, 'so I might as well have people who I know are worth it.'[53] Leading actors in previous productions were reduced to supporting roles and new directors could not be risked. Smith's next picture, *You're the Doctor* (1939), made at the reopened Worton Hall, would star the ubiquitous Barry K. Barnes and Googie Withers, with Gus McNaughton in support. However, Smith was in no doubt that there was still a substantial niche for second-feature production, and planned to slightly reduce the length of his films to accommodate the increasing length of first features.[54] When the production of *The Relief of Lucknow*, scheduled for Walton-on-Thames, was scuppered by government intervention via the BBFC, Smith reverted to type. Ever the opportunist, he grabbed the unemployed crew and hired Worton Hall to make *Miracles Do Happen* (1938) – a comedy about a formula for synthetic milk – in less than ten days.[55] George King took longer to consider his position in the light of the new Act, but eventually decided to continue much as before with another Tod Slaughter melodrama, *The Face at the Window*, which went into production at Beaconsfield early in 1939.

While the bigger players in independent production, such as Smith and King, prepared plans for more expensive features, smaller players like Widgey Newman switched their attention to the new subjects of the quota: short films. Newman quickly won contracts from Warners and Paramount to produce six shorts at Bushey, and brought in George Cooper as a scriptwriter. Always prepared to swim against the tide, one of Newman's ex-employees, Roy Boulting, formed Charter Films with his brother John, and demonstrated that featurettes could still be made under the new conditions. One of the great benefits of cheap supporting features was that their low production costs allowed talented individuals entry to the film-making club. The Boultings just squeezed through the door before the price of admission was raised by the 1938 Films Act. The twins began by making shorts, as Roy Boulting recalled:

There were three or four friends of mine who had this idea that I knew something about making films and they were sort of fairly well-off and we weren't seeking millions in those days. For a few thousand pounds you could make a film and so they put up the dough for me and it worked out pretty well. The very first film was at a studio that I'd used when I was working for Ace. I didn't know the big studios at all. The Marylebone studios was a converted non-conformist chapel, and it was run by two men: one called Henry Halstead and the other a fellow called Scott. Very nice men, but a terrible studio.[56]

For some of the old stagers, however, the 1938 Act was the final curtain. George Pearson made his last quota picture – aptly titled *The Fatal Hour* – in 1937. He recalled:

I had no place since quickie-makers had lost caste . . . to become social outcasts working in a contemptible calling. . . . For two years I was 'on the street', no work save a script for Sinclair Hill's *Follow Your Star*, two odd jobs of writing given me by the kindness of Balcon and Pen Tennyson, and an abortive effort with some colour 'shorts' for a small company that suddenly went broke. I had to suffer the agony of unemployment, made more painful by the realisation of being unwanted.[57]

Pearson was rescued only by the outbreak of war and the propaganda needs of the Ministry of Information.

Everyone believed that the new Quota Act would replace the despised quickies with new super productions; but seven months after the act became law, things were not going entirely to plan. Touring around Britain's larger studios, P. L. Mannock found a succession of empty floors, waiting for big-budget films to be given green lights. Only half the films promised for 1938, he thought, would actually be made. Instead, what pulse the industry still had could best be felt in the smaller studios:

I am more and more inclined to pay less and less attention to the costly super-picture and more to the little unit in the small studios, where staffs trained in the cheese-paring economy of the quick-ies are now able to give far better accounts of themselves. I am becoming less and less impressed by the selection of a Hollywood star, a famous director, a best-selling novel, as reliable film ingre-dients. Nearly every Hollywood importation is already 'on the way out' in popularity: the ace director is powerless without the kind of organisation that has made his fame possible: and the costly rights of books is the silliest of all superstitions.[58]

Mannock found that the smaller production units were leaner and fitter, free from the 'megalo-mania and waste' practised among their richer counterparts. He was probably responsible for commissioning a special article by George Smith in the same issue of *Kinematograph Weekly*. Smith painted an unglamorous picture of his film-making as 'a normal business routine', pro-ducing films which were demonstrably well received by the public, despite not being reviewed in the national newspaper press:

I am pleased that it is the bread-and-butter pictures which should form the solid background for the film industry in this country. Including the Empire, we have a great home market which is quite enough to make films pay without a thought to foreign markets: why not, then, make reasonable priced films for this market? . . . Modestly priced films have been, and are, the finest training grounds for artists, directors and technicians. Here these young people are given real opportunities to emerge from obscurity. The artists are given real parts to test them – not two-line bits: technicians are asked to use their brains and not the producer's money for their effects: and of the successful directors now working – how many of them studied in the so-called Quota School? Three names immediately spring to mind – Brian Desmond Hurst, David MacDonald and Michael Powell. And I know there are many more.[59]

When *Kinematograph Weekly* came to review the first nine months of the new Films Act, it discovered that the medicine administered to drive out the quota quickies had damn near done for the patient. As the resulting shortage of films became increasingly acute, sympathy for honest producers of programmers like George Smith began to grow. It was as if the British supporting feature could only really be appreciated when the consequences of its disappearance were obvious from the blank spaces in exhibitors' booking diaries. From being a *bête noir*, the supporting picture suddenly acquired the protected status of an endangered species:

> It is clear that by some means or other we must have such a readjustment that a definite encouragement is given to makers of the ordinary programme film. . . . So long as the ordinary kinema wants to run two features, and this, of course, is while the public demands it, we ought to be having something like two pictures where we are now getting one. . . . But the year opens with no such expectation. The independent producer in this country has watched the tide ebb until he felt it must be near the turn, but what prospect is there of this? None that the businessman could call a practical one. The excellent work done by the British side of American firms has not found its quality supported by its quantity, and the purely native production is far behind our needs.[60]

A phrase like 'the excellent work done by the British side of American firms' really was a sharp about face for a trade press that, a year before, had criticised the American renters for bringing disgrace on the industry. Oscar Deutsch made an impassioned plea to exhibitors to reduce the length of their programmes by abandoning variety acts and the second feature, but the public seemed to be in no mood to accept the reduction in the quantity of entertainment bought by their admission tickets.[61] Harold Birch, a Bolton accountant, wrote to *Picturegoer* to suggest that there were worse aspects of cinema programmes than the supporting feature: 'the paying public would rather see the much-reviled "quota quickie" than sit through a long interval and watch a never-ending line of superfluous advertisements'.[62] As Manchester exhibitor T. H. Hartley confessed: 'Once-nightly houses operated by independents who had to face strong opposition must have two features. It would mean bankruptcy to carry on without.'[63]

Only 103 British films were made during the first year of the 1938 Films Act, a fall of 55 per cent from the previous year. The majority was made by or for the American renters. The proportion of second features fell from 50 to around 20 per cent. The ACT, complained that there was 'hardly a technician in the industry in permanent employment'.[64] The legal consequences of under-production were starkly revealed when, in February, the Board of Trade announced that seventy-one exhibitors and no less than ten renters had failed to meet their quota obligations in 1938.[65] There were no prosecutions.[66] Independent distributors like Liberty, New Realm and Equity British began reissuing films in an attempt to meet the shortage of second features. Some, like *How's Chances?* had their title changed (to *The Bedroom Diplomat*), while others were also severely trimmed in length. John Baxter's *Song of the Plough* was cut to forty-five minutes and re-named *County Fair*. By the end of 1938, the shortage was so acute that a few stalwarts of low-budget production began to make supporting features regardless of their quota eligibility. Ivar Campbell made *Too Many Husbands* for Liberty, and Widgey Newman returned to the fold with *Men Without Honour*, receiving the usual trashing from the CEA's *Film Report*.[67] Thus, once laid in its coffin, the deceased quota quickie had to be revived and put to work anew. But the Board of Trade, under the advice of the new Films Council, held its nerve and declined to amend quota levels or to bow to pressure to abolish the treble-quota.

By the spring of 1939, few of the old quickie studios were still in the quota business. Teddington were mixing in the odd 'B' film with their co-features, Worton Hall was kept in its accustomed employment by Venture Films, which made four undistinguished pictures under the direction of Walter Tennyson (before he joined the Army Film Unit), and there was some activity at Highbury, including a well-liked creepy thriller called *Mrs. Pym of Scotland Yard* (1939), in which Mary Clare played an undercover policewoman who unmasks a fake medium as a killer. But surpisingly, the most notable investigator of the sub-world of the second feature was the Church. Once J. Arthur Rank had demonstrated that film could be a useful tool of religious propaganda, the devout audience began to be targeted by costume films like the Columbia featurette *Governor Bradford* (1938), which described the persecution of the 'hot gospellers' in seventeenth-century England and their treaty with native Americans in Virginia.[68] Christian societies themselves also began to appreciate the potentialities of cinema in spreading their message and, on the principle that the Devil should not have all the best pictures, the Religious Film Society commissioned Gaumont-British Instructional to make a series of forty-minute morality tales. It probably realised that, in the prevailing conditions of product shortage, there was a reasonable chance that the pictures might get regular cinema bookings. Filming began at the empty Shepherd's Bush Studios at the beginning of 1939 with *The Silence* (later re-titled *Two Minutes*) and continued with *What Men Live By*, the first directed by the documentary maker Donald Carter (aka Donald Taylor?), and the second by Vernon Sewell.[69] Another religious drama, *Beyond Our Horizon* (1938), was made at Pinewood by Norman Walker.

There were other instances of the spirit of the quota quickie living on in more expensive pictures. Anglo-American's crime-comedy featurette *Trouble for Two* (1939) met the new quota criteria, but the old treatment it received from *Kinematograph Weekly* would have reassured anyone who might have believed that they didn't make 'em like that any more: 'The playlet aims at getting by with the unexpected, but so confused is the development and laboured the direction that it ends up without registering a single thrill or laugh. Brevity is its sole virtue. Quota fill-up for the uncritical only.'[70] Michael Powell's old partner, Jerry Jackson – now with Warner Bros. – produced Roy William Neill's *A Gentleman's Gentleman* (1938), a comedy derided for its 'poor script, unimaginative direction and feeble dialogue'.[71] The screenplay for George A. Cooper's musical vehicle for child star Hughie Green, *Down Our Alley* (1939), was so 'flimsy' that nobody was prepared to own up to it in public.[72] More positively, the second-feature system

Grand National winner: a trade advertisement for *Happy Event* (1939), the first British second feature in colour. Author's collection

continued to produce stars. The future Gainsborough leading lady, Phyllis Calvert – who had been given her first break as a bit-part player in the Paramount quickie *Anne One Hundred* (1933) – was given a starring role in Venture Film's *Two Days to Live* (1939). Happily, her life on screen lasted considerably longer.

Hardly any field of cultural production is entirely without innovation, and it is perhaps fitting that the very last batch of second features trade shown in the 1930s should contain the first picture in colour. In the midst of the phony war's blackout, the film distributors Grand National unveiled Patrick Brunner's *Happy Event* (1939) in soft and sensuous Dufaycolor, a process which had already been used by the venerable George Pearson (and Humphrey Jennings) to make a few short films.[73] Made by Anglo-French Productions, this thirty-six-minute docu-drama scripted by D. B. Wyndham-Lewis could not have been more appropriate to its distributors as it described the preparation of a racehorse for a Grand National victory.

War sometimes accomplishes what legislation cannot achieve, and although the second Quota Act might have failed to see off the British supporting feature, World War II would at least force it into mothballs for much of the duration. As war approached, the second-feature slot was increasingly used for propaganda films such as Ace's Technicolor documentary *Cavalcade of the Navy* (1939), and GFD's naval drama *Full Speed Ahead* (1938), made with the full co-operation of the Admiralty, but 'amateurish' in its acting and direction.[74] More controversially, Associated British civil defence featurette, *The Warning*, divided opinion more than any previous supporting feature, provoking a deluge of letters to *Picturegoer* from those who thought the film unnecessarily terrifying in a medium intended for entertainment, and those who regarded its message as timely and important.[75]

The Warning was a call to readiness to serve the nation, but, in a way, the British supporting feature was no stranger to patriotic duty. It had supported the development of a fully fledged industry – as opposed to a handful of studios – during the lean years of the 1930s. It had trained a whole generation of technicians, and nurtured directorial and producer talent. It had asked for no plaudits and received few. It remained content with its role as a subaltern cinema, quietly doing its job and leaving the death and glory stuff to the generals: the Kordas, the Balcons and the Wilcoxes. But with war came a new set of needs and priorities. The intensification of the conflict would force the closure or requisition of some of the smaller studios, and the production facilities and place in the cinema programme of the supporting feature would be handed to the makers of public-information and propaganda shorts. Like the legions of POWs, the quota quickie would have to kick its heels and wait for peacetime.

## Notes

1. 'Leeds Condemns Quota Act', *Kinematograph Weekly*, 23 May 1935, p. 13.
2. The proportion of British films would remain at 28 per cent in 1936 and 1937.
3. *Kinematograph Weekly*, 21 February 1935, p. 27.
4. *Daily Telegraph*, 24 April 1936.
5. 'Quota Menace to the Exhibitor', *Kinematograph Weekly*, 16 May 1935, p. 11.
6. 'Scots Attack 20 per cent Quota Demand', *Kinematograph Weekly*, 20 June 1935, p. 5.
7. See, for example, the branch reports in *Kinematograph Weekly*, 12 September 1935, pp. 7–8.
8. 'Commons Questions on Quickies', *Kinematograph Weekly*, 20 June 1935, p. 5.
9. More than 25 per cent of British but less than 8 per cent of foreign films were given marks of less than seven out of ten in the CEA reviews of the previous year. Simon Rowson, 'The Future of the Films Act', paper to the CEA conference in Cardiff, June 1935, published in *Kinematograph Weekly*, 27 June 1935, pp. 7, 53.
10. 'Combating the "Quickie"', *Kinematograph Weekly*, 5 September 1935, p. 3.
11. *Kinematograph Weekly*, 19 December 1935, p. 5.
12. *Kinematograph Weekly*, 9 January 1936, p. 49.
13. '1936 a Landmark for British Pictures', *Kinematograph Weekly*, 9 January 1936, p. 93.
14. Review of *Under Proof* (1936), *Kinematograph Weekly*, 5 March 1936.
15. *Kinematograph Weekly*, 30 April 1936, p. 3.
16. *Kinematograph Weekly*, 21 May 1936, p. 7.
17. *Report of a Committee appointed by the Board of Trade to consider the position of British films*, Cmd 5320, HMSO: 1936, para 11.
18. 'Trade Gives Evidence on Quota', *Kinematograph Weekly*, 25 June 1936, p. 15.
19. Cmd. 5320: Memorandum of the CEA, para 54.

20. John Maxwell certainly believed that the desire to abolish the quota quickie was 'the main grievance that led to the appointment of the Moyne Committee'. 'Maxwell Defends the Treble Quota', *Kinematograph Weekly*, 3 March 1938, p. 3.

21. This was preferred to a minimum-cost test because that 'might be a serious hardship to smaller film producers'. Ibid., p. 21.

22. The extension of government control over the film business suggested by the Committee led many within the industry to see its recommendations as essentially interventionist, and even socialist. *Kinematograph Weekly*, 3 December 1936, pp. 3, 5, 13.

23. *Kinematograph Weekly*, 4 February 1937, pp. 3,19.

24. *Picturegoer*, 3 April 1937, p. 6.

25. I checked these figures against the 1936 registrations listed in Gifford's *British Films Catalogue*. The number of first features corresponds exactly, but they constitute a slightly higher proportion of the long features handled by the American renters (excluding United Artists and Universal): eleven out of eighty, or almost 14 per cent, when shorts are excluded. In all, ninety-nine British long features were handled by American renters, of which seventy-one were second features.

26. *Kinematograph Weekly*, 25 February 1937, p. 8.

27. Jack Rockett interview, BECTU 5, 22 August 1988.

28. *Picturegoer*, 3 April 1937, p. 28.

29. Ibid.

30. RKO did branch out from second features to distribute Herbert Wilcox's hit *Victoria the Great*. Paramount's costs remained rigidly controlled by Pinewood production supervisor Anthony Havelock-Allan, who kept a close eye on the number of takes required for each shot. Rachael Low, *The History of the British Film, 1929–1939* (London: Allen and Unwin, 1985), p. 188. The American renters' move towards bigger British pictures should be understood in the context of the contracting world market for Hollywood films as World War II approached. See Sarah Street, 'The Hays Office and the Defence of the British Market in the 1930s', *Historical Journal of Film, Radio and Television* vol. 5 no. 1, 1985, pp. 38–9.

31. 'Independent Producers Move to Stop Cost Clause', *Kinematograph Weekly*, 24 June 1937, p. 65.

32. Double quota began at £3 per foot and £22,500 labour costs; treble at £5 per foot and £37,500 labour costs.

33. See, for example, the views of Arthur Moss, general manager of Associated British Cinemas, on the uneconomic nature of the long programme in *Kinematograph Weekly*, 12 January 1939, p. 45.

34. 'Overloaded Programmes Are Illogical and Create a Dishonest Policy', *Kinematograph Weekly*, 12 January 1939, p. 47.

35. *Kinematograph Weekly*, 13 January 1938, p. 135.

36. 'Single-Feature Programmes Are Sufficient', *Kinematograph Weekly*, 12 January 1939, p. 57.

37. F. B. B. Blake, 'Public Bored by Mediocre Second-features', *Kinematograph Weekly*, 12 January 1939, p. 73.

38. 'Maxwell Defends the Treble Quota', *Kinematograph Weekly*, 3 March 1938, p. 3.

39. Cmd. 5320: 1024.

40. *Picturegoer*, 21 May 1938, p. 13.

41. Margaret Dickinson and Sarah Street, *Cinema and State: The Film Industry and the British Government 1927–84* (London: BFI, 1985), p. 96.

42. CEA Annual Report, *Kinematograph Weekly*, 9 March 1939, p. 7.

43. Editorial: 'A's and B's', *Film Weekly*, 7 May 1938, p. 3.

44. 'The New Films Act and the Trade', *Kinematograph Weekly*, 31 March 1938, p. 3.

45. 'CEA Opposed to Quota Increases', *Kinematograph Weekly*, 9 March 1939, p. 3.

46. Wood (ed.), *British Films 1927–1939*, p. 51.

47. Letter from Peter Nicholls of Richmond, *Film Weekly*, 16 September 1938, p. 8.

48. In the end, the Wembley Studios remained open, and Fox made the rather more ambitious POW drama *Who Goes Next?* (1939), directed by Maurice Elvey under the terms of the new minimum-cost provision.

49. 'B Grade Films out of Majors' Schedule', *Kinematograph Weekly*, 24 March 1938, p. 3.

50. Annual Survey of Trade Conditions Aboard, US Department of Commerce, quoted in, 'Quota Reason for US Export Limitations', *Kinematograph Weekly*, 27 April 1939, p. 5.

51. 'Films Act's Effect on Sound City', *Kinematograph Weekly*, 1 December 1938, p. 3.

52. *Kinematograph Weekly*, 11 August 1938, p. 19.

53. 'Production Schools Now Closed!', *Kinematograph Weekly*, 23 June 1938, p. 27. While the expanded cast budget accounted for most of Smith's additional expenditure, E. G. Cousins did confirm after a visit to the set of Smith's *His Lordship Goes to Press* (1938) that 'the greater expenditure allows for more time to be spent on each scene'. *Picturegoer*, 2 July 1938, p. 13.

54. *Kinematograph Weekly*, 22 December 1938, p. 18.

55. *Picturegoer*, 7 January 1939, p. 13.

56. Roy Boulting. Unpublished interview by Alan Burton. 1998.

57. George Pearson, *Flashback* (London: Allen and Unwin, 1957), p. 198.

58. *Kinematograph Weekly*, 27 October 1938, p. 38.

59. Ibid.

60. 'The Revival that Failed', *Kinematograph Weekly*, 12 January 1939, p. 4.

61. 'Overloaded Programmes Are Illogical and Create a Dishonest Policy', p. 47.

62. *Picturegoer*, 20 August 1938, p. 26.

63. *Kinematograph Weekly*, 6 April 1939, p. 7.

64. *Kinematograph Weekly*, 20 April 1939, p. 5.

65. *Kinematograph Weekly*, 16 February 1939, p. 3.

66. *Kinematograph Weekly*, 16 March 1939, p. 3.

67. *Film Report*, 11 March 1939.

68. *Kinematograph Weekly* was not impressed: 'The treatment is anaemic, and the story seems about to fade out altogether at times through sheer inertia.' 10 March 1938, p. 26.

69. Freda Bruce Lockhart, 'Celluloid Sermons', *Film Weekly* 29 January 1938, p. 23. Denis Gifford credits Norman Walker as the director of *Two Minutes*.

70. *Kinematograph Weekly*, 25 May 1939, p. 21.

71. *Film Report*, 29 April 1939. Neill's *My Brother's Keeper* received a much better reception.

72. *Film Report*, 22 July 1939.

73. The first full-length feature in Dufaycolor was Maurice Elvey's *Sons of the Sea* (1939), which was trade shown at the same time as *Happy Event*.

74. *Film Report*, 6 May 1939.

75. *Picturegoer*, 5 August 1939, p. 30.

# Conclusion: The Pointing Finger

I have been thinking about the films I saw last year. . . . The film that remained most clear cut in my memory, for the sincerity of the acting and the realism of the story, was a modest effort from a British studio, one which cannot have cost much and was boosted very little. The film was *Reunion*, with Stewart Rome in the leading part.

Letter to *Film Weekly*[1]

## The long Good Fridays

On Good Friday 1931, the manager of a small cinema on England's south coast awaited the delivery of a supporting feature to complete his programme. When it failed to arrive, he wrote 'NO SHOW. FINISH' on one of his walls before shooting himself. This sad little tale, related in passing by Sue Harper in her study of film exhibition in Portsmouth in the 1930s, seems a fitting epitaph to a history of quota quickies completed on Good Friday 2006.[2] 1931 is the year when the double bill became an established part of film exhibition. Some of the conditions that gave birth to the double feature were the same ones that caused the death of the man who ran the Queen's cinema in Portsea: economic recession and dwindling disposable incomes that resulted in an urgent desire to receive value for money. As the dole queues lengthened, those at the Queen's grew shorter, and shorter still as council re-housing schemes moved customers away from the area. Without paying customers, the Queen's could not make the improvements to its ageing premises demanded by that same council.[3] The double feature was the last hope to bring back the crowds.

There has been a largely unstated assumption in the historiography of British film that the second feature was an insignificant and insubstantial part of the story of the national cinema, just one of those 'footnotes to the film'. Well, the man who ran the Queen's did not think so, and nor do I, some seventy-five Easters after his suicide. What was true for the Queen's cinema, Portsea in 1931 was true for the King's and Queen's cinema, UK, in that year and in decades to follow: no supporting feature, 'NO SHOW. FINISH'. Without the employment and training supplied by 'B' pictures the British film industry would have been – financially, technically and artistically – more impoverished, and less able to compete with the superpower of Hollywood. And without the 'B' films' relatively undiluted representations and discourses of Britishness, audiences would have been left with films made with one eye on international sales.

'Sincerity and realism': Stewart Rome (left) leads the way in Baxter and Campbell's *Reunion* (1932)

## The tin can on the tail?

*Picturegoer's* E. G. Cousins once suggested that the absence of a quality clause in the first Quota Act allowed the American renters 'an opportunity to tie a tin can to the tail of the rapidly improving British talkie industry'.[4] Certainly, 'quota quickies' became a crucial phrase in the rhetorical dismissal of British cinematic achievement, but how should we evaluate the contribution to the national cinema of the actual second features themselves? First, as a production sector, the quickies acted as a counter-balance to the excesses of the long party that was British movie-making after the success of *The Private Life of Henry VIII*. In this fools' paradise, film-makers believed that they should spend in excess of £40,000 on a production when the average box-office return from the domestic market was only around £10,000. The much-maligned quota quickie was a beacon of sanity. Without wide-scale foreign distribution, their frugal four-figure budgets were really all that the native industry could afford if it wanted to remain a going concern. Like servants at a drunken feast, the quickies may have suffered derision from the revellers, but they maintained their sobriety and knew their station. Their costumes may have been more simple and their actions more restrained than those of the party guests, but their fiscal prudence stood in sharp contrast to the extravagances of their 'betters'. Life below stairs may have been garrulous, repetitive and impoverished, but without the support it provided, life above stairs would have been much more problematic. The household management of the British film industry of the 1930s depended on the reliable contribution of the modest production units and their largely American clients.

Under the insistence of the Quota Act, the Hollywood companies steadily injected increasing amounts of finance into the indigenous production sector, mitigating the insecurities of the capital extracted from insurance companies and economic adventurers. In return, they received abuse as exploiters, parasites and cultural imperialists. This failure to distinguish between economic exchange and exploitation, and between cultural contribution and imperialism goes right back to the chauvinistic polemics of John Grierson. For Grierson, 'foreign films made in Britain' were likely to be culturally less authentic and valuable than 'British films made in Britain', because 'playing with the Americans' was likely to destroy 'British identity'.[5] While the movies made in Hollywood, which made their profits in Britain, might, with some justification, be regarded as culturally imperialist, the pictures that the same companies filmed in Britain made little attempt to sell the American way of life or promote American tastes. Most were made by British crews and British casts for almost exclusively British audiences. The films of Teddington and Wembley may have had American scriptwriters or directors, and may even have featured the occasional American actor, but most can still be considered part of an indigenous popular culture. Overall, the quickies sponsored by Hollywood companies recruited their casts from music hall, radio and the West End stage. They gave characteristically British treatments to indigenously produced material; and, in spite of their tendency towards London-centricity, they made some attempt to represent cultural life in most regions of the UK.

Ironically, it was those British studios that aspired to international distribution that exhibited the greater degree of cultural compromise and hybridity. They were the more likely to incorporate American idioms and actors in the interests of easing their films' passage across the Atlantic. Thus, a picture like BIP's *The Tenth Man* could distort its representation of parliamentary elections in order to make the political process more recognisable to American audiences. If there was, in Grierson's phrase 'a truly British cinema' in the 1930s, it was not to be found among the émigré film-makers of Denham, or the Ruritanian fantasies of Elstree, but on the floors of Sound City, Worton Hall, Cricklewood, Twickenham and the other 'B' film factories. Although usually artistically impoverished, the films made at these sweat shops often exhibited Grierson's desired qualities of a 'really intimate contact with the national idiom' and 'a British point of view' – be it typically from the perspective of West End or music-hall stage.[6] They were able to retain a cultural integrity because they were not required to please diverse audiences or meet critical standards of international quality. They could safely target the tastes and sensibilities of (primarily) English provincial filmgoers and hope for a very modest profit from the legions of independent exhibitors. Nor were they expected by their American sponsors to communicate a Hollywood vision of the world or promote an American lifestyle. Because, ultimately, it was the footage that was more important than messages, cultural representations or even profitability, the American renters could leave their British producers to their own devices once their budgetary limits had been set. Thus, while financial control might have been in 'alien' hands, creative control was largely a British affair. This was not always the case in some of the larger British studios, where, for Grierson, films 'written, produced, starred, shot, cut and musicked [sic] by foreigners' presented 'a real problem'.[7]

The importance of quota production in developing the skills of British film-makers should not be under-estimated. Ealing sound recordist John Mitchell has confessed that 'Quota quickies did some good in offering a proving ground for many a director or technician whose first chance to gain experience would stand them in good stead for the future.'[8] Even Ronald Neame, who is totally dismissive of the quota pictures, has admitted that 'they did help us with our training – as a young cameraman, I learnt so much from them'.[9] John Baxter was less reserved in his assessment of the benefits of quota production: 'The quota films came in for much abuse and criticism . . . but for me and some others they provided opportunities we were grateful to accept and the results were very successful.'[10]

As a training ground, the quota quickies were invaluable, but they were also crucial in establishing connections that would make possible some of the most celebrated collaborations of the war and post-war years. The magic of Powell and Pressburger's *Black Narcissus* would not have been the same without the fabulous glass mattes of Poppa Day, a contact from Powell's days at Teddington. Ronald Neame was invited to photograph *In Which We Serve* (1942) and then *This Happy Breed* (1944) in large part because he had worked with their producer Anthony Havelock-Allan on the Paramount quickie *The Scarab Murder Case* (1936). With David Lean, who had honed his editing skills on 1930s' programmers, they would form Cineguild to make *Brief Encounter* (1946), and the celebrated Dickens adaptations *Great Expectations* (1947) and *Oliver Twist* (1948). Thus, some of the keynote British films of the 1940s had their roots firmly planted in the quota hot-houses of the previous decade, but so too did more populist pictures. The Gainsborough melodramas equally relied on talent nurtured at £1 a foot: Margaret Lockwood, Phyllis Calvert, James Mason, Jean Kent, Patricia Roc, Arthur Crabtree, Leslie Arliss and Elizabeth Haffenden all benefited from early opportunities given to them by the detested quota quickie.

If one part of the legacy of the quota quickies was inherited, via its creative talents, by the mainstream British cinema of the 1940s and 1950s, the other was bequeathed, via the post-war 'B' films, to television comedy and drama of the 1960s and 1970s. The low-budget, mass-produced sitcoms and adventure series and cop shows that filled the broadcasting schedules after the launch of ITV had their origins in the quickies of the 1930s, and were frequently made in the same studios.

Looking back from the vantage point of the new quota regulations at the end of 1938, John Paddy Carstairs was by no means as dismissive of the sort of films on which he had worked as his colleagues would be a few decades later:

> A lot of unkind things have been said about the old Quota Quickies. People glibly derided them who often did not know which was the feature picture and which the maligned quickie! Yet often these quickies saved a dreary programme, and were extremely entertaining. Further, they were very useful as a satisfactory medium in which to try out and build promising youngsters. . . . True, there were a number of appalling quickies, but there were, recently, also a great number of good ones. So that 'quickie' is a word that can only be used to describe the time the picture took to make, *not* the quality – for some of them had more entertainment packed into them than many Hollywood super-productions.[11]

Carstairs may over-state his case a little, but there is no denying that some British second features were popular with contemporary filmgoers and many enabled genuine directorial and acting talent to develop. A few were influential in ways that have never been fully appreciated. Carstairs, himself, made an unassuming little mystery thriller with George King for Paramount called *Double Exposures* (1937). Its story (by Gerald Elliott) of crooks falling out is unremarkable except for a plot detail in which the killer is accidentally exposed by a photograph taken for another purpose. When it was trade shown in May, Graham Greene was still battling with the construction for his celebrated novel *Brighton Rock* (1938). Greene's thriller would eventually exhibit a very similar plot device.[12] At the time, Greene was moonlighting as a film reviewer, and although he never reviewed *Double Exposures*, he did attend a screening of another Paramount picture, *Make Way for To-morrow*, that was released at the same time. His review reveals that he had seen the Paramount promotional literature of the time.[13] In the introduction to his collected film criticism, Greene wrote:

> I remember opening the envelopes, which contained the gilded cards of invitation, for the morning Press performances (mornings when I should have been struggling with *Brighton Rock* and *The Power And The Glory*) with a sense of curiosity and anticipation. These films were an escape – escape from that hellish problem of construction in Chapter Six . . .[14]

Did one of those gilded cards invite him to view *Double Exposures*, one wonders, and did that help to solve his 'hellish problem'? If so, it is simply another example of creative bricolage: art fabricated from the raw materials provided by commercial culture.

The quota quickies, themselves, might not have aspired to the status of art, but the contemporary distinction between quota and quality now, in many cases, seems questionable. The vulgar and the facile were clearly not the exclusive preserves of Poverty Row. Seventy years on, it is hard to believe that, in a decade which gave rich rewards to the gormless strumming of George Formby, the shrill screeching of Gracie Fields, the Brylcreamed badinage of Jack Hulbert and the jolly hockey stickery of his partner, Cicely Courtneidge, so much ire was directed at cheap pictures made for less than the fee of any of these irritating stars. But then, in the same issue of *Film Pictorial* in which Carstairs re-evaluated the quickies, Alfred Hitchcock's indelible *The Lady Vanishes* (1938) was judged third best film – not of the year, but merely of the week![15] Critical judgment has always been easier with hindsight.

## Cultural eugenics

Finally, then, what has been the point of disinterring the quota quickie from its pauper's grave and performing this 100,000-word autopsy? Yes, we now know more about how it lived and died, the work it did and the contempt and affection in which it was held. We can more accurately assess its contribution to the national cinema. But, ultimately, this is not what has sustained thirty months of study. For me, the quota quickie is a paradigm case of the operation of cultural subordination, the disciplining and punishment of an unruly and uncongenial field of cultural production by more powerful interests. In its time, the quickie propped up a hierarchy of value that was structured by the dominant interests of bigger players in the British film business. Virtually programmed for failure by its penny-pinching budget and therefore posing no economic competition, it was used by the producers of 'quality' British films as a convenient point of comparison, a means to bolster distinction. When its usefulness for the purposes of cultural differentiation began to be outweighed by its potential to stigmatise the entire field of production, the quickie was summarily suppressed. In the years that have followed, its mourners have been few. Pejoratively named and defined by its secondary status, the quickie has been dismissed as unworthy of serious consideration, despite the labour of countless hands and minds that were once dedicated to its creation.

In arguing that supporting features constituted a subordinated culture, it is of course tempting to situate them within the class struggle that was such a prominent feature of 1930s' society. Although superficially attractive, it is difficult to sustain an argument that quota quickies were a proletarian cinema of the dispossessed. They were impoverished films, but not necessarily films only for the poor. In truth, they were made to appeal to most sections of the population by capitalist companies, which sometimes employed the most patrician of figures. Their workers, though subject to conditions that would make a shop steward weep, were well remunerated by contemporary standards. This is, perhaps, more an issue of caste than class. Heuristically, however, it might be more fruitful to think of supporting-feature production as a parallel cinema produced by a process of cloning, guilty about the circumstances of its creation and shy of scrutiny, an inexpensive reproduction of an authentic entity. Its subordination was not so much a battle in a class war as a process of imagined cultural purification. Perhaps appropriately for the 1930s, what we are dealing with here is a matter of cultural eugenics, the struggle to eliminate the supposed inferior via the equivalent of genetic cleansing. In this process, naming and shaming is usually a necessary preliminary to the final elimination. In the 1930s, the name 'quota quickie' was used as a label to designate film products of low cultural value, and associate them with illegitimate foreign powers. The label still sticks to their corpse because the cadaver cannot easily be accommodated in the hallowed ground that is British national cinema.

American programmers have been valued because they seem to represent something essential in national life and culture: a restless spirit that craves action and is prepared to make something out of every opportunity, no matter how slight; and a commercialism that unashamedly peddles the brash, the tawdry and the meretricious. Poverty Row film-making can, therefore, be seen as an authentic cultural expression of an entrepreneurial impulse that refuses to take no for an answer, and pushes on with meagre resources. In the 1930s, the English had a rather different self-conception as a settled nation that took things at a leisurely pace, with good humour and produced products of quality and good taste. Thus, the term 'quickie' could not only connote a lack of quality, but something fundamentally un-English. As J. B. Priestley, perhaps the most astute theorist of national character, argued in 1933:

> It is folly to attempt the high-speed American tempo in British films, for American life is lived at a different pace. It is more melodramatic, and, for that reason, more obvious film material. When a murder is committed in America a police car comes screaming down the street like a fire-engine. In this country, probably, two men in bowler hats would arrive on foot. The American method of catching murderers is no more effectual in reality, but makes better film stuff. Now we can't do that, because it doesn't belong in this country. It isn't real.[16]

Whether it was 'real' or not, Priestley's remarks are evidence of the beliefs that informed film culture at the time. The English were not to be rushed. They were also not to be patronised and told what they must do or see. Thus the term 'quota' was also anathema in a country weaned on free trade and libertarian ideals. A quota was a measure imposed by the strong on the weak, and it smacked of a socialist planned economy. Its acceptance by an imperial nation that thought of itself as a dominant trading force was an implicit recognition of commercial defeat, an insult to virility and a wound to pride. Linguistically, then, 'quota quickie' became an appellation of humiliation, something inappropriate to a British product. It is little wonder that British cinema historiography has chosen to ignore those films that were so designated.

The effective denunciation of these films as injurious to national welfare was accomplished in spite of their thoroughly British ethnocentricity and frequently patriotic content. What they were, and what they contained, was secondary to their usefulness as a cultural marker. The quickies were the victims of dominant discourses in the emergent national cinema that, after *The Private Life of Henry VIII*, emphasised the possibilities of international success and influence. These gelled perfectly with earlier imperialist discourses that identified the role of films as the promotion of British values and lifestyles in the Empire and beyond. Within the rhetoric of expansionism and internationalism there was no room for parochial circumcision or the acceptance of second-class status. Whatever practical use it might have in the business of film exhibition, the supporting feature was damned by its own lack of ambition. According to the strange eugenic reasoning of prevailing film and political culture, once the quota quickie had served its purpose in the system of differentiating the genetically rich from the poor, it had to be culled for the good of the species as a whole. If this logic had been able to run its course, the health of the bloated bodies in the green pastures of 'quality' production might have been tested. As it was, the bodies were forcibly slimmed and the field scorched as a result of the intervention of that arch eugenicist, Adolf Hitler. After the war, the supporting feature would be reprieved and assigned a place in the 'New Jerusalem' of film production and exhibition in which every picture had a role to play in national reconstruction.

Few of these films seem to have left a lasting impression on their viewers. Leslie Halliwell's memoirs of cinemagoing in Bolton are virtually unique in remembering the title and content of a quota quickie:

> It was at the Embassy that a long-forgotten British quickie called *The Pointing Finger* [1933] gave me a night or two of bad dreams. It was set in one of those stately homes full of secret panels, and featured an ancestral portrait with removable eyes so that the villain could peep through.[17]

The finger has been pointed at the vacant eye sockets of quota production these last seven decades, and the villain peeping through has always been imagined to be the American distributor. The memory of ten years of misdemeanours has continued to give bad dreams to film-makers and historians alike, and the quota quickie has been one of those ancestral portraits that British cinema has preferred to turn to the wall: the black sheep of the family. This book has taken on the role of dogged investigator, feeling around the walls of the stately home to find the secret panel and shed light on what has lain hidden behind the dust of myth. Like dust, the myths have grown deeper with time. Their origins in truth have become harder to decipher, but some at least have been blown away: that all British supporting features were quota quickies; that all quota quickies were bad and unpopular pictures; that they were hardly ever shown to the public; that American renters were responsible for all the bad films; and that the quickie was their secret weapon to destroy the British film industry. Time to point the finger at something else.

## Notes

1. Letter from E. C. of Weston-super-Mare, *Film Weekly*, 20 April 1934, p. 29.
2. Sue Harper, 'A Lower Middle-Class Taste Community in the 1930s. Admission Figures at the Regent Cinema, Portsmouth', *Historical Journal of Film, Radio and Television*, vol. 24 no. 4, 2004, p. 566.
3. *Kinematograph Weekly*, 9 April 1931, p. 25 and 14 May 1931, p. 29.
4. *Picturegoer*, 14 April 1934.
5. John Grierson, 'The Film Situation', *London Mercury*, September 1937, pp. 459–63.
6. John Grierson, 'The Fate of British Films', *The Fortnightly*, July 1937.
7. Ibid. This issue of the excessive involvement of European émigrés at the prestige end of native film-making was one that also concerned Graham Greene. The writing of both Grierson and Greene, however, displays a degree of anti-Semitism.
8. John Mitchell, *Flickering Shadows – A Lifetime in Films* (Malvern Wells: Harold Martin & Redman, 1997), pp. 23–4.
9. Interviewed by Matthew Sweet, NFT, 19 October 2003.
10. John Baxter, 'Stepping Stones', unpublished manuscript, BFI Special Collections, p. 15.
11. John Paddy Carstairs, 'Thanks for the Remittance', *Film Pictorial*, 31 December 1938, p. 17.
12. A picture taken by a street photographer allows Rose to identify Spicer as the leaver of the incriminating card at her café.
13. *Night and Day*, 1 July 1937.
14. John Russell Taylor (ed.), *The Pleasure Dome: Graham Greene, The Collected Film Criticism 1935–40* (Oxford: Oxford University Press, 1980), p. 1.
15. It was beaten by *Pygmalion* and *The Adventures of Robin Hood*, and described as 'Disappointing for a film directed by Alfred Hitchcock'. *Film Pictorial*, 31 December 1938, p. 18.
16. J. B. Priestley, 'Writing for the Screen', *Film Weekly*, 26 May 1933, p. 48.
17. Leslie Halliwell, *Seats in All Parts* (London: Granada, 1985), p. 66.

# Filmography: British Supporting/Second Features 1928–39

Below is a list of films of over 3,000 feet made in Britain after the 1927 Quota Act and before the outbreak of World War II, which are believed to have had a significant proportion of their bookings as second features. The criteria of selection have been described in the Introduction and in Note 6 to Chapter 7. Please note that no date was collected for film exhibition in Leicester in 1939.

Key
Q = critical evaluation scores calculated in David Quinlan, *British Sound Films*.
Genre = as classified in Denis Gifford, *The British Film Catalogue*.
L = Leicester
b = second feature
co = co-feature
a = first feature
For example, 2bL = two bookings as a second feature in Leicester

| Title | Minutes | Filming began | Trade show/ Leicester bookings | Production company/ studio | Director | Distributor | Q Genre/synopsis |
|---|---|---|---|---|---|---|---|
| **1928** | | | | | | | |
| Adam's Apple | 79 | 3/28 | 9/28 10/29 bL | BIP / Elstree | Tim Whelan | Wardour | Silent Comedy. American on Paris honeymoon arranges mother-in-law's kidnap. |
| Adventurous Youth | 54 | 1928 | 1928 | Pall Mall | Edward Godal | WB | Silent Adventure set during Mexican revolution. |
| The Bells of St. Mary's | 60 | 1928 | 11/28 4/30 bL | GP Productions / Worton Hall | Redd Davis | JMG | Silent Comedy. Vicar confronts Sussex bullies. |
| Cocktails | 67 | 8/28 | 10/28 | BIP / Elstree | Monty Banks | Wardour | Silent Comedy. Cocaine planted on heiress. |
| First Born | 86 | 5/28 | 10/28 11/29 bL | BIP / Elstree | Miles Mander | W&F | Silent Drama. Deception concerning the offspring of a knight. |
| Houp-la! | 75 | 4/28 | 7/28 5/29 bL | British Screen Production / Worton Hall | Frank Miller | British Screen | Silent Drama. In Cornwall, zoologist framed for theft, becomes lion tamer. |
| The Lady of the Lake | 57 | 9/28 | 12/28 | Gainsborough/Islington | James Fitzpatrick | Select | Silent Adventure. Adaptation of Scott's epic poem of Scottish romance. Sound added 1931. |
| Little Miss London | 76 | 7/28 | 3/29 10/29 bL | BIF / Bushey | Harry Hughes | Fox | Silent Comedy. Fake bankrupt poses as workman while daughter loves fake peer. |
| Love's Option (A Girl of Today) | 66 | 5/28 | 9/28 | Welsh-Pearson-Elder / Cricklewood | George Pearson | Paramount | Silent Adventure. Competition over claims to Spanish copper mine. |
| Man in the Saddle (retitle: A Reckless Gamble) | 48 | 9/28 | 10/28 | Cinema Exclusives | Widgey Newman | PDC | Silent Sport. Horse-racing drama. |
| Night Patrol (retitle: City of Shadows) | 48 | ?/28 | 1929 | H. B. Parkinson / Worton Hall | Norman Lee | JMG | Silent Drama. Unemployed miner helps London's Flying Squad. OR documentary on the homeless. |
| Not Quite a Lady (The Cassilis Engagement) | 80 | 2/28 | 7/28 6/29 bL | BIP / Elstree | Thomas Bentley | Wardour | Silent Comedy. Rich woman gets rid of son's unsuitable fiancée. |
| Paradise | 80 | 5/28 | 10/28 11/29 bL | BIP / Elstree | Denison Clift | Wardour | Silent Romance. On Riviera, doctor saves woman from gigolo. |
| The Second Mate | 44 | 10/28 | 1/29 10/29 bL | H. B. Parkinson / Worton Hall | J. Steven Edwards | Pioneer | Silent Adventure. Ship saved by captain's daughter. |
| Smashing Through (Face) | 78 | 6/28 | 10/28 8/29 a,2bL | Gaumont / Shepherd's Bush | W. P. Kellino | Gaumont | Silent Sport. Motor-racing. Vamp persuades inventor to race friend. |
| The Tallyman | 35 | 1928 | 1928 | Homestead Films | Maurice Sandground | Film Distributors | Silent Comedy. Tallyman's Blackpool holiday. |
| The Thoroughbred | 62 | 6/28 | 1928 10/29 bL | London Screen Plays / Twickenham | Sidney Morgan | Gaumont | Silent Sport. Horse-racing drama. |

| Title | Mins | Date | Date | Production | Director | Distributor | Description |
|---|---|---|---|---|---|---|---|
| Three Men in a Cart | 57 | 7/28 | 1929 / 7/30 bL | British Screen Productions / Worton Hall | Arthur Phillips | Universal | Silent Comedy. Three friends discover treasure. |
| Two Little Drummer Boys | 83 | 5/28 | 6/28 / 4/29 bL | G.B. Samuelson / Southall | G. B. Samuelson | GBS | Silent Drama. Boy soldier demonstrates heroism and self-sacrifice. |
| The Valley of the Ghosts | 57 | 7/28 | 11/28 | British Lion | G. B. Samuelson | JMG | Silent Crime. Edgar Wallace thriller. Murder of a blackmailer. |
| Warned Off | 72 | 10/28 | 11/28 / 7/30 bL | B&D / Cricklewood | Walter West | JMG | Silent Sport. Troubled owner's horse wins Grand National. |
| The Warning (Introspection) | 75 | 10/28 | 11/28 / 5/30 bL | British Projects / Welwyn | Reginald Fogwell | Pro Patria | Silent Drama. Mother tells story to persuade daughter not to elope. |
| What Money Can Buy | 71 | 4/28 | 7/28 / 8/29 a,2bL | Gaumont / Shepherd's Bush | Edwin Greenwood | Gaumont | Silent Drama. Cleric provides alibi for woman accused of killing husband. |
| When Knights Were Bold | 79 | 8/28 | 2/29 / 2/30 3bL | B&D / Cricklewood | Tim Whelan | W&F | Silent Comedy. Unpopular heir dreams he lives in Middle Ages. |
| Widecombe Fair | 71 | 8/28 | 12/28 / 10/29 bL | BIP / Elstree | Tim Whelan | Wardour | Silent Romance. Rich widow aids poor squire. |
| Would You Believe It? | 57 | 12/28 | 5/29 / 3/30 a,2bL | Archibald Nettlefold / Walton | Walter Forde | Butcher's | Silent Spy Comedy. Tank runs amok. [3] |

### 1929

| Title | Mins | Date | Date | Production | Director | Distributor | Description |
|---|---|---|---|---|---|---|---|
| After Many Years | 70 | 1929 | 2/30 | Savana Films | Lawrence Huntington | JMG | Silent Crime. Murdered policeman's son catches killer in Peru. |
| Alf's Carpet | 65 | 7/29 | 11/29 / 6/30 bL | BIP / Elstree | W. P. Kellino | Wardour | Comedy. Busman's adventures with magic carpet. |
| Auntie's Antics | 57 | 1929 | 5/29 | G&S / Preston (Brighton) | Wilfred Gannon | G&S | Silent Comedy. |
| The Bondman | 95 | 6/28 | 1/29 / 12/29 3bL | B&D / Cricklewood | Herbert Wilcox | W&F | Silent Adventure. In Sicily, blinded revolutionary saved from gallows by half-brother. |
| A Broken Romance | 75 | 7/29 | 10/29 / 5/30 bL | H. B. Parkinson / Worton Hall | J. Steven Edwards | Fox | Silent Romance. Disabled actress meets author at film trade show. |
| The Chamber of Horrors | 55 | 2/29 | 1929 | BIF / Welwyn | Walter Summers | PDC | Silent Horror. Man goes mad in Madame Tussaud's. |
| The Dizzy Limit (retitled: Kidnapped) | 63 | 11/29 | 2/30 | Edward Whiting / Worton Hall | Edward Dryhurst | PDC | Silent Comedy. Jewel thief kidnaps conjuror's assistant. Music added later. |
| The Flying Scotsman | 61 | 2/29 | 5/29 / 6/30 3bL | BIP / Elstree | Castleton Knight | WB | Silent Drama. Railway driver vs stoker. Sound added 1930. [4] |
| Frozen Fate | 56 | 1929 | 5/29 | British Screen Productions | Ben R. Hart, St John L. Clowes | JMG | Silent Adventure. Death and despair in Lapland. |
| Human Cargo | 48 | 1928 | 1/29 | H. B. Parkinson / Worton Hall | J. Steven Edwards | Pioneer | Silent Crime. Girl poses as crook to expose bent policeman. |

| Title | Minutes | Filming began | Trade show/ Leicester bookings | Production company/ studio | Director | Distributor | Genre/synopsis | Q |
|---|---|---|---|---|---|---|---|---|
| The Lady from the Sea (The Goodwin Sands) | 62 | 4/29 | 1929 | BIP / Elstree | Castleton Knight | Paramount | Silent Adventure. Sea rescue leads to romance. Sound added 1930. | 4 |
| Life's a Stage (Encore) | 65 | 1/29 | 3/30, 5/30 bL | Encore / Worton Hall | Arthur Phillips | Argosy | Silent Crime. Busker confesses to murder to save amnesiac film star daughter. | |
| London Melody | 59 | 11/29 | 8/30 | British Screen Productions / Worton Hall | Geoffrey Malins, Donald Stuart | British Screen Productions | Musical Romance. | 2 |
| Lure of the Atlantic | 50 | 1929 | 10/29, 5/30 bL | H. B. Parkinson / Worton Hall | Norman Lee | Fox | Silent Drama-doc. First transatlantic flight. | |
| Naughty Husbands | 62 | 1929 | 1/30 | Geoffrey Benstead | Geoffrey Benstead | Geoffrey Benstead | Silent Comedy. Convict's dream of running a marriage agency. | |
| Nick's Knickers | 55 | 8/29 | 10/29 | G&S / Preston | Wilfred Gannon | G&S | Silent Comedy. | |
| Over the Sticks | 37 | 1929 | 1/30 | Cinema Exclusives | G. B. Samuelson, A. E. Coleby | Fox | Silent Sport. Racecourse drama. | |
| Riverside Melodies | 49 | 1929 | 10/29 | Electrochord | | Butcher's | Musical. | |
| The Streets of London | 39 | 9/28 | 1/29, 10/29 bL | H. B. Parkinson / Worton Hall | Norman Lee | Pioneer | Silent Crime. Embezzlement drama. | |
| The Third Gun | 36 | 1929 | 1929 | BSFP | Geoffrey Barkas | Universal | Crime. Poacher accidentally kills man. | |
| Wolves | 57 | 8/29 | 5/30 | B&D / Elstree | Albert de Courville | W&F | Adventure in the Arctic. | 3 |
| You'd Be Surprised | 65 | 7/29 | 4/30, 9/30 b,aL | Archibald Nettlefold / Walton | Walter Forde | Butcher's | Musical Comedy. Songwriter mistaken for convict. | 3 |
| **1930** | | | | | | | | |
| Amateur Night in London | 34 | 1930 | 2/30, 6/30 bL | PDC / Elstree | Monty Banks | PDC | Comedy. Amateur talent competition. | |
| Bedrock | 40 | 1930 | 6/30 | Piccadilly / Twickenham | Carlyle Blackwell | Paramount | Drama set in Canada. | |
| Beyond the Cities (Reparation) | 70 | 5/30 | 11/30, 7/31 bL | Piccadilly / Twickenham (?) | Carlyle Blackwell | Paramount | Drama. In Canada, sportsman saves girl from marrying rich cad. | 3 |
| The Black Hand Gang | 63 | 9/30 | 10/30, 7/31 bL | BIP / Elstree | Monty Banks | Wardour | Comedy. Variety star Wee Georgie Wood's boy gang catch a criminal. | 2 |
| Brown Sugar | 70 | 9/30 | 4/31, 11/31 bL | Julius Hagen / Twickenham | Leslie Hiscott | WB | Drama. Actress struggles for acceptance as lord's wife. | 1 |
| Comets | 61 | 1/30 | 1/30, 6/31 bL | Alfa / Twickenham | Sasha Geneen | JMG | Revue. | |

| Title | No. | Date | Date | Company / Studio | Director | Distributor | Description | |
|---|---|---|---|---|---|---|---|---|
| Contraband Love | 67 | 8/30 | 3/31 12/31 2bL | British Screenplays / B&D Elstree (Cornwall) | Sidney Morgan | Paramount | Crime. Smugglers and undercover policeman. | 3 |
| Cross Roads (The Warning) | 58 | 2/30 | 1930 | British Projects / Welwyn | Reginald Fogwell | Paramount | Drama. Domestic melodrama of killing of unfaithful husband. | 2 |
| Dangerous Seas | 53 | 5/30 | 3/31 | Edward G. Whiting | Edward Dryhurst | Filmophone | Crime Romance. Cornish customs investigator and smugglers. | 2 |
| Down River | 73 | 10/30 | 5/31 2/32 bL | Gaumont / Shepherd's Bush | Peter Godfrey | Gaumont | Crime. Head of smuggling ring unmasked by customs' agent. | 4 |
| Enter the Queen | 42 | 1930 | 11/30 7/31 bL | Starcraft / Beaconsfield | Arthur Varney-Serrao | Fox | Comedy. Masquerade ends in romance. | 4 |
| Eve's Fall | 34 | 1/30 | 2/30 6/30 bL | Gordon Bostock / BIP Elstree | Monty Banks | PDC | Musical. Adventures of an amnesiac girl. | |
| Flames of Fear | 62 | 1930 | 9/30 | Argyle Art / Tamworth | Charles Barnett | EB | Silent Drama. Miner saves woman from fire. | |
| Guilt | 65 | 7/30 | 1/31 8/31 2bL | Reginald Fogwell / Worton Hall | Reginald Fogwell | Paramount | Drama. Melodrama of unfaithful wife. | 2 |
| His First Car | 35 | 1930 | 5/30 | PDC | Monty Banks | PDC | Comedy. Husband wins money and buys car. | |
| House of the Arrow | 76 | 1/30 | 3/30 | Twickenham / Twickenham | Leslie Hiscott | WB | Crime. In France, detective solves the murder of a rich woman. | 4 |
| Infatuation | 35 | 1/30 | 1/30 7/30 bL | Alpha / Twickenham | Sasha Geneen | PDC | Romance. Youth discovers he is in love with his mother. | |
| Kiss Me, Sergeant | 56 | 5/30 | 8/30 3/31 bL | BIP / Elstree | Monty Banks | Wardour | Comedy. Leslie Fuller gets into scrapes in India. | 2 |
| The Last Tide | 57 | 1930 | 2/31 | Argyle Art / Tamworth | John Argyle | EB | Silent Romance. Devon fisherman. | |
| Leave It to Me | 40 | 9/30 | 10/30 2/31 bL | George King / Twickenham | George King | Fox | Comedy. Man thwarts blackmailer. | 3 |
| Morita | 38 | 1930 | 1/31 | Patrick K. Heale / Worton Hall | Fred Paul | Britivox | Musical. Hawaiian beachcomber and pearl diver. | |
| The Musical Beauty Shop | 34 | 1/30 | 3/30 | PDC | Monty Banks | PDC | Musical. Beautician puts on cabaret. | |
| The New Waiter | 35 | 1/30 | 2/30 | PDC | Monty Banks | PDC | Musical. Drunken waiter unmasks thief. | |
| The Night Porter | 45 | 9/29 | 3/30 | Gaumont / Shepherd's Bush | Sewell Collins | Ideal | Comedy. Hotel porter and honeymooners. | 3 |
| No Exit | 69 | 2/30 | 7/30 | WB / Welwyn | Charles Saunders | WB | Comedy. Romantic story of mistaken identity. | 3 |
| No Lady | 72 | 8/30 | 5/31 10/31 bL | Gaumont / Shepherd's Bush | Lupino Lane | Gaumont | Comedy. Man mistaken for crook wins glider race at Blackpool. | 4 |
| Not so Quiet on the Western Front | 50 | 4/30 | 5/30 5/30 aL | BIP / Elstree | Monty Banks | Wardour | Comedy. Leslie Fuller in WWI French café. | 3 |

| Title | Minutes | Filming began | Trade show/ Leicester bookings | Production company/ studio | Director | Distributor | Genre/synopsis | Q |
|---|---|---|---|---|---|---|---|---|
| An Obvious Situation (retitle: Hours of Loneliness) | 65 | 1930 | 2/31 | Carlton / Teddington | Guarino C. Glavany | WB | Crime. Blackmail on the Riviera. | 2 |
| Old Soldiers Never Die (Show a Leg) | 58 | 12/30 | 3/31 7/31 2a,2bL | BIP / Elstree | Monty Banks | Wardour | Comedy. Leslie Fuller joins Army in WWI. | 3 |
| Painted Pictures | 56 | 4/30 | | Bernard Smith | Charles Barnett | Fox | Silent Drama about reforming artist. | |
| The Road to Fortune (Moorland Terror) | 60 | 5/30 | 8/30 | Starcraft / Twickenham (Cornwall) | Arthur Varney–Serrao | Paramount | Crime. Girl saves boyfriend from a life of crime. | 1 |
| School for Scandal | 76 | 5/30 | 8/30 3/31 bL | Albion / BIP Elstree | Maurice Elvey | Paramount | Comedy adaptation of Sheridan's play set in 1771. | 3 |
| Scrags | 63 | 1930 | 3/30 10/30 bL | H. B. Parkinson | Norman Lee | JMG | Silent. Adventure of a stray dog. | |
| Should a Doctor Tell? | 59 | 7/30 | 9/30 5/31 b,coL | British Lion / Beaconsfield | Manning Haynes | British Lion | Drama of illicit affairs. | 3 |
| Terrors | 47 | 1930 | Erle O. Smith | Erle O. Smith | Universal | Fantasy. | Scots boys imagine tunnelling to Australia. | |
| Thread O'Scarlet | 35 | 1930 | 11/30 4/31 bL | Gaumont / Shepherd's Bush | Peter Godfrey | Gaumont | Crime. Innocent blacksmith hanged. | |
| Too Many Crooks | 38 | 1930 | 8/30 10/30 2bL | George King / Twickenham | George King | Fox | Comedy. Playboy catches spy. | |
| What a Night (Wanted) | 58 | 11/30 | 3/31 10/31 2bL | BIP / Elstree | Monty Banks | FN-Pathe | Comedy. Leslie Fuller at haunted inn. | 2 |
| Who Killed Doc Robin? | 36 | 1930 | 2/31 | Gainsborough / Islington | W. P. Kellino | Ideal | Comedy. Nightclub hostess is mother of gangster rivals. | |
| The Woman from China aka The Girl from China | 81 | 2/30 | 3/30 7/30 3bL | Edward C. Whiting / Worton Hall | Edward Dryhurst | JMG | Silent Crime. Wife helps Chinaman kidnap girl. | |
| The Woodpigeon Patrol | 44 | 1930 | 1930 | Pro Patria | Ralph Smart, P. R. Lucas | Pro Patria | Silent Adventure with boy scouts. | |
| **1931** | | | | | | | | |
| Alibi | 75 | 1/31 | 4/31 | Twickenham / Twickenham | Leslie Hiscott | W&F | Crime. Detective solves suicide mystery in country house. | 3 |
| Almost a Divorce | 58 | 4/31 | 8/31 2/32 bL | B&D / Elstree | Arthur Varney–Serrao | W&F | Comedy of marital disagreement. | 1 |
| Aroma of the South Seas | 36 | 1931 | 4/31 | Gainsborough / Islington | W. P. Kellino | Ideal | Comedy. Shipwrecked valet and master. | |
| Bachelor's Baby | 57 | 9/31 | 5/32 10/32 bL | BIP / Elstree | Harry Hughes | Pathe | Comedy. Young man finds abandoned baby. | 3 |

| Title | | | | | | | Description |
|---|---|---|---|---|---|---|---|
| The Bad Companions | 45 | 11/31 | 4/32 8/32 bL | BIP-BIF / Welwyn | John Orton | Pathe | Comedy. Sacked worker wins back his girl. |
| The Beggar Student | 65 | 11/31 | 12/31 2/32 bL | Amalgamated / Beaconsfield | John Harvel Victor Hanbury | British Lion | Musical romance in Heidelberg. Bilingual versions. 3 |
| Betrayal | 66 | 12/31 | 1932 8/32 bL | Fogwell Films / Elstree | Reginald (Fogwel) | Universal | Drama. Crime of passion leads to perjury. 3 |
| Bill and Coo | 42 | 6/31 | 7/31 1/32 bL | BIP / Elstree | John Orton | Wardour | Revue. Romance among variety artists. 3 |
| Bill's Legacy | 57 | 4/31 | 11/31 5/32 a,5bL | Julius Hagen / Twickenham | Harry J. Revier | Ideal | Comedy. Leslie Fuller rises from rags to riches. 2 |
| Birds of a Feather | 52 | 1931 | 6/31 | Macnamara / Worton Hall | Ben R. Hart | G&L | Romance. Love among artists. 2 |
| Black Diamonds | 53 | 6/31 | 1932 | Hammer / Goldthorpe (Yorks) | Charles Hammer | Wardour | Drama. Exposé of the hazards of mining. |
| Bracelets | 50 | 7/30 | 1/31 9/31 2bL | Gaumont / Shepherd's Bush | Sewell Collins | Gaumont | Comedy Thriller. Jeweller and con men. 3 |
| Bull Rushes | 37 | 1930 | 2/31 | Gainsborough / Islington | W. P. Kellino | Ideal | Comedy. Englishman fights bull in Spain. |
| Captivation | 76 | 1/31 | 5/31 | John Harvel / Beaconsfield | John Harvel | W&F | Romance. On Riviera, girl woos famous novelist. 3 |
| Chin Chin Chinaman (USA: Boat from Shanghai) | 52 | 7/31 | 8/31 3/32 bL | Real Art / Twickenham | Guy Newall | MGM | Crime. Detectives in disguise trap jewel thief. 3 |
| Dance Pretty Lady (Carnival) | 63 | 7/31 | 12/31 5/32 b,2coL | BIP / Welwyn | Anthony Asquith | Wardour | Drama. Dancer marries the wrong man. 2 |
| Deadlock | 84 | 4/31 | 9/31 2/32 bL | George King / Walton | George King | Butcher's | Crime. Actor murdered on film set. 4 |
| Fascination | 70 | 4/31 | 4/31 10/31 b,2aL | Regina / BIP Elstree | Miles Mander | Wardour | Romance. A young husband falls for an actress but returns to his wife. 2 |
| The Final Reckoning | 64 | 1931 | 3/32 | John F. Argyle / Tamworth | John F. Argyle | Equity British | Silent Crime. Attempted murder among miners. Sound added. 1 |
| A Gentleman of Paris | 77 | 5/31 | 12/31 4/32 2bL | Gaumont / Cricklewood & Shepherd's Bush | Sinclair Hill | Gaumont | Crime. Parisian judge tries ex-mistress for murder he knows she did not commit. 4 |
| The Girl in the Night (The Knight Errant) | 65 | 4/31 | 7/31 3/32 2b,3coL | Henry Edwards / BIP Elstree | Henry Edwards | Wardour | Crime. Couple sheltering from storm discover diamond smugglers. 3 |
| The Great Gay Road | 84 | 7/31 | 10/31 2/32 2bL | Stoll / Cricklewood | Sinclair Hill | Butcher's | Romance. Tramp returns home and falls in love. 4 |
| Her Reputation (Passing Brompton Road) | 67 | 4/31 | 7/31 | London Screenplays / B&D Elstree | Sidney Morgan | Paramount | Comedy. Wife tries unsuccessfully to divorce husband. 1 |

| Title | Minutes | Filming began | Trade show/ Leicester bookings | Production company/ studio | Director | Distributor | Genre/synopsis | Q |
|---|---|---|---|---|---|---|---|---|
| Hot Heir | 39 | 1930 | 2/31 9/31 bL | Gainsborough / Islington | W. P. Kellino | Ideal | Comedy. King replaced by dancer. | |
| The House of Unrest | 58 | 2/31 | 3/31 | Associated Picture Productions/ Cricklewood | Leslie Howard Gordon | PDC | Crime. Diamond thieves. | 3 |
| How He Lied to Her Husband | 33 | 1930 | 1/31 8/31 bL | BIP / Elstree | Cecil Lewis | Wardour | Comedy. G. B. Shaw's play about a rich man who suspects his wife loves poet. | |
| Immediate Possession | 42 | 12/30 | 2/31 11/31 bL | Starcraft / Twickenham | Arthur Varney-Serrao | Fox | Comedy. Estate agent sells 'haunted' house. | 3 |
| In a Lotus Garden | 47 | 8/30 | 2/31 | Patrick K. Heale / Worton Hall | Fred Paul | Paramount / W&F | Musical. In China, fiancée saves naval officer. | 1 |
| Jealousy | 56 (78) | 4/31 | 8/31 | Majestic–New Era / Worton Hall | G. B. Samuelson | WB | Drama. Guardian tries to spoil ward's romance. | 2 |
| A Lucky Sweep | 56 | 12/31 | 3/32 | National Talkies / Blattner, Elstree | A.V. Bramble | PDC | Comedy. Girl buys sweepstake ticket for anti-gambling fiancé. | 3 |
| The Lyons Mail | 76 | 1/31 | 4/31 | Twickenham / Twickenham | Arthur Maude | W&F | Crime. In France, man is mistaken for murderer. | 3 |
| The Man at Six (USA: The Gables Mystery) | 71 | 5/31 | 7/31 3/32 co,2bL | BIP / Elstree | Harry Hughes | Wardour | Crime. Woman detective unmasks crooks at country house. | 2 |
| Many Waters | 76 | 8/31 | 11/31 3/32 coL | Associated Metropolitan / BIP Elstree | Milton Rosmer | Pathe | Drama. Couple look back over their lives. | 3 |
| Midnight | 45 | 11/30 | 1/31 5/31 2bL | George King / Walton | George King | Fox | Crime Comedy. Secret agent vs spies. | 4 |
| Murder on the Second Floor | 69 | 9/31 | 1/32 6/32 3bL | WB–FN / Teddington | William McGann | FN | Crime. Novelist imagines murder of fellow tenants. | 2 |
| My Friend the King | 46 | 8/31 | 9/31 2/32 2bL | Film Engineering / Walton | Michael Powell | Fox | Comedy. Cabby saves Ruritanian king from revolutionaries. | 3 |
| My Old China | 35 | 1931 | 8/31 | Gainsborough / | W. P. Kellino | Ideal | Comedy. Newsreel cameramen vs Chinese bandit. | |
| Nine Till Six | 75 | 12/31 | 3/32 8/32 3bL | ATP / Ealing | Basil Dean | Radio | Romance. Dressmaker accused of theft of ball-gown. | 4 |
| Number Please | 41 | 4/31 | 7/31 10/31 2bL | George King / Walton | George King | Radio | Crime. Telephonist flirts with crooks. | 2 |
| The Officers' Mess | 66 | 3/31 | 5/31 12/31 2bL | Harry Rowson / Walton | Manning Hayes | Paramount | Comedy. Lieutenant gets involved with stolen jewels. | 2 |

| Title | No. | Year | Dates | Production / Studio | Director | Distributor | Description |
|---|---|---|---|---|---|---|---|
| The Other Mrs. Phipps | 39 | 1931 | 12/31 | Real Art / Twickenham | Guy Newall | FN | Comedy. Cross-dressing lord foils kidnappers. |
| Other People's Sins | 63 | 1/31 | 2/31 8/31 b,coL | Associated Picture Productions / Cricklewood | Sinclair Hill | PDC | Crime. Father takes blame for daughter's crime. 4 |
| The Other Woman | 45 (64) | 1931 | 6/31 | Majestic Films / ? | G. B. Samuelson | UA | Romance. Woman wins back neglected husband. 1 |
| Paradise Alley (Black Diamonds) | 56 | 1931 | 3/31 | Argyle Art / (Tamworth) | John Argyle | Argyle Art | Silent Crime. Miner takes blame for barrister's crime. |
| Peace and Quiet | 42 | 2/31 | 6/31 11/31 2bL | GS Enterprises / Twickenham | Frank Richardson | Fox | Comedy. Nervous lord thwarts crook. 3 |
| Poor Old Bill (Bill's War Debt) | 52 | 1/31 | 6/31 8/31 3bL | BIP / Elstree | Monty Banks | Wardour | Comedy. Leslie Fuller tries to evict guest. 2 |
| The Professional Guest | 44 | 5/31 | 10/31 4/32 3bL | George King / Walton | George King | Fox | Comedy. The *nouveau riche* in polite society. |
| Pyjamas Preferred (Pyjama Knights in Paris / Red Dog) | 51 (46) | 8/31 | 12/32 5/33 2bL | BIP-BIF / Welwyn | Val Valentine | Pathe | Comedy. In France, president of Purity League runs nightclub. 2 |
| The Rasp | 44 | 9/31 | 12/31 5/32 bL | Film Engineering / Walton | Michael Powell | Fox | Crime. Journalist solves minister's murder. 3 |
| Rodney Steps In | 42 | 5/31 | 6/31 12/31 bL | Real Art / Twickenham | Guy Newall | Fox | Comedy. Young man helps girl who is posing as jewel thief. 3 |
| Romany Love | 58 | 10/30 | 2/31 | Patrick K. Heale / Worton Hall | Fred Paul | MGM | Musical romance among gypsies. 2 |
| Rynox | 47 | 6/31 | 11/31 2/32 4bL | Film Engineering / Walton | Michael Powell | Ideal | Crime. Bankrupt fakes his own murder. 4 |
| A Safe Affair | 52 | 7/31 | 10/31 5/32 2bL | Langham / Walton | Bert Wynne | MGM | Drama involving the papers of a Ruritanian countess. 2 |
| Self-Made Lady (Sookey) | 68 (77) | 12/31 | 3/32 7/32 bL | George King / Walton | George King | UA | Romance. Loves of an upwardly mobile slum girl. 2 |
| Shadows (Press Gang) | 57 | 1/31 | 3/31 | BIP / Elstree | Alexandre Esway | Wardour | Crime. Press lord's son tracks down kidnapper. 2 |
| The Star Reporter (Special Assignment) | 43 | 10/31 | 12/31 5/32 2bL | Film Engineering / Walton | Michael Powell | Fox | Crime. Journalist recovers stolen jewels. 2 |
| Stepping Stones (England through the Ages) | 50 | 1/31 | 1932 | Geoffrey Benstead / Worton Hall | Geoffrey Benstead | Geoffrey Benstead | Musical. Nostalgia for the music hall. 2 |
| Stranglehold | 66 | 8/31 | 10/31 3/32 bL | Henry Edwards / Teddington | Henry Edwards | WB | Drama. Schoolmaster's marriage is ruined. 2 |
| The Third String | 65 | 9/31 | 2/32 8/32 coL | Welsh-Pearson / Cricklewood | George Pearson | Gaumont | Comedy. Sailor Sandy Powell boxes champion. 2 |

| Title | Minutes | Filming began | Trade show/ Leicester bookings | Production company/ studio | Director | Distributor | Genre/synopsis | Q |
|---|---|---|---|---|---|---|---|---|
| Thoroughbred | 64 | 5/31 | 3/32 | Argyle / Tamworth | Charles Barnett | Equity British | Silent Sport. Amnesiac racehorse trainer saves heiress from unwise marriage. Sound added. | 2 |
| Tin Gods | 51 | 10/31 | 4/32 | BIP / Elstree | F. W. Kraemer | Pathe | Adventure. Marines rescue ship attacked by pirates in China Seas. | 3 |
| To Oblige a Lady | 75 | 11/30 | 3/31 | British Lion / Beaconsfield | Manning Haynes | British Lion | Comedy. Wife lets flat to couple wanting to impress rich uncle. | 3 |
| Two Crowded Hours | 44 | 6/31 | 7/31 2/32 3bL | Film Engineering / Walton | Michael Powell | Fox | Crime. Escaped convict tries to kill witness. | 3 |
| Two Way Street | 44 | 10/31 | 12/31 | Nettlefold / Walton | George King | UA | Romance. Cross-class love triangle. | 3 |
| Verdict of the Sea | 63 | 8/31 | 6/32 1/33 bL | Regina Films / BIP Elstree | Frank Miller, Sydney Northcote | Pathe | Drama. Crewman foils mutiny on tramp steamer. | 1 |
| We Dine at Seven | 44 | 1/31 | 4/31 10/31 bL | GS Enterprises / Twickenham | Frank Richardson | Fox | Comedy. Newlywed gets involved with another man's wife. | 3 |
| The Wrong Mr. Perkins | 38 | 1930 | 1/31 4/31 2bL | Starcraft / Twickenham | Arthur Varney-Serrao | Fox | Comedy. Banker mistakes the identity of a poor man. | |
| **1932** | | | | | | | | |
| Above Rubies | 44 | 11/31 | 1/32 | Ralph J. Pugh / Walton | Frank Richardson | UA | Comedy set in Monte Carlo. | 1 |
| Account Rendered | 35 | 1/32 | 3/32 8/32 bL | PDC / Cricklewood | Leslie Howard Gordon | PDC | Crime. Bankrupt financier is prosecuted. | |
| After Dark | 45 | 9/32 | 10/32 5/33 2bL | Fox / Walton | Albert Parker | Fox | Crime Comedy. Jewel theft and search for hidden gems. | 4 |
| The Barton Mystery | 77 | 9/32 | 11/32 4/33 2bL | B&D-Paramount / Elstree | Henry Edwards | Paramount | Crime. Fake medium proves girl innocent of blackmailer's murder. | 2 |
| The Blind Spot | 75 | 3/32 | 9/32 4/33 bL | WB-FN / Teddington | John Daumery | WB | Crime. Amnesiac girl weds barrister who prosecutes her father. | 2 |
| Born Lucky (Mops) | 78 | 10/32 | 12/32 | Westminster/ Wembley | Michael Powell | MGM | Musical. Cockney cleaner becomes singing star. | 3 |
| The Call-Box Mystery | 73 | 1/32 | 3/32 12/32 b,2aL | Samuelson / Cricklewood | G. B. Samuelson | UA | Crime. Detective and girlfriend prove suicides are murders. | 2 |
| Called Back | 50 | 12/32 | 2/33 9/33 3bL | Real Art / Twickenham | Reginald Denham, Jack Harris | Radio | Crime. Spain. Revolutionary doctor foiled by man who has recovered his sight. | 2 |
| Castle Sinister | 49 | 1932 | 4/32 | Delta / Bushey | Widgey R. Newman | Filmophone | Horror. Devon. Mad doctor tries to transplant girl's brain into apeman. | 3 |
| C.O.D. | 65 | 1/32 | 3/32 | Westminster / | Michael Powell | UA | Crime. Girl hires thief to help her hide stepfather's body. | 3 |

| Title | No. | Date 1 | Date 2 | Production / Location | Director | Distributor | Description |
|---|---|---|---|---|---|---|---|
| Come into My Parlour | 46 | 1/32 | 3/32 | GEM / Blattner, Elstree | John Longden | MGM | Crime. Manicurist shelters barber who thinks he has killed burglar. 3 |
| The Crooked Lady | 75 | 2/32 | 3/32 8/32 b,3aL | Real Art / Twickenham | Leslie Hiscott | MGM | Crime. Jewel thief falls for female detective. 3 |
| Daughters of Today | 74 | 11/32 | 3/33 | FWK Production / Cricklewood | F.W. Kraemer | UA | Drama. Country sisters seek adventure in London. 1 |
| Don't Be a Dummy | 50 | 11/32 | 12/32 | WB-FN / Teddington | Frank Richardson | FN | Comedy. Gambling peer becomes a ventriloquist. 2 |
| Double Dealing | 48 | 3/32 | 5/32 8/32 4bL | Real Art / Twickenham | Leslie Hiscott | Fox | Comedy. Puritan politician's private life exposed. 3 |
| Down Our Street | 75 | 3/32 | 5/32 | B&D-Paramount / Elstree | Harry Lachman | Paramount | Drama. Cockney girl elopes with youth of dubious character. 4 |
| Ebb Tide | 74 | 11/31 | 2/32 | B&D-Paramount / Elstree | Arthur Rossen | Paramount | Drama. Sailor weds orphan while fiancée is in jail. 2 |
| The Face at the Window | 52 | 1932 | 10/32 1/33 2bL | Real Art / Twickenham | Leslie Hiscott | Radio | Crime. In Paris, detective exposes count as robber. 2 |
| Flat No. 9 (Stormy Weather) | 49 | 3/32 | 1932 8/32 5bL | V.E. Deucher / Twickenham | Frank Richardson | Fox | Comedy. Young man and married woman rent the same flat. 3 |
| Forging Ahead (Easy Money) | 48 | 12/32 | 3/33 | Harry Cohen / Wembley | Norman Walker | Fox | Comedy Thriller. 'Haunted' house is base for crooks. 2 |
| The Game of Chance (His Promise) | 65 | 5/31 | 2/32 | Equity British / Tamworth | John F. Argyle | Equity British | Silent Sport. Horse-racing drama involving crooked bookie. Sound added. |
| Her Night Out (Alone at Last) | 45 | 7/32 | 10/32 | WB-FN / Teddington | William McGann | WB | Comedy. Quarrel leads couple into contact with bank robber. 2 |
| Heroes of the Mine | 48 | 4/32 | 8/32 | Delta / Bushey | Widgey R. Newman | Butcher's | Drama of Welsh miners trapped underground. 3 |
| High Society | 50 | 5/32 | 7/32 7/33 2bL | WB-FN / Teddington | John Rawlings | FN | Comedy. Cockney maid poses as rich woman. 2 |
| His Lordship | 76 | 1932 | 6/32 | Westminster Films / Walton | Michael Powell | UA | Musical. Plumber who is really a peer gets engaged to film star. 2 |
| His Wife's Mother (Double Trouble) | 70 | 7/32 | 10/32 5/33 2bL | BIP / Elstree | Harry Hughes | Wardour | Comedy. Husband poses as double to fool mother-in-law. 2 |
| Holiday Lovers | 48 | 10/32 | 11/32 | Harry Cohen / Wembley | Jack Harrison | Fox | Romantic Comedy. Brighton. Couple tries to fool each other that they are rich. 2 |
| Hotel Splendide | 53 | 1/32 | 3/32 7/32 2bL | Film Engineering / Walton | Michael Powell | Ideal | Comedy. Seaside hotel built over buried loot. 2 |
| A Hundred to One | 45 | 12/32 | 1/33 8/33 bL | Julius Hagen / Wembley | Walter West | Fox | Sport. Nag produces Derby-winning foal. 2 |
| The Impassive Footman (USA: Woman in Bondage) | 69 | 1/32 | 6/32 10/32 2bL | ATP / Ealing | Basil Dean | Radio | Drama. Doctor loves wife of cruel patient killed by servant. 3 |

| Title | Minutes | Filming began | Trade show/ Leicester bookings | Production company/ studio | Director | Distributor | Genre/synopsis | Q |
|---|---|---|---|---|---|---|---|---|
| The Iron Stair | 51 | 11/32 | 1/33 6/33 3bL | Real Art / Twickenham | Leslie Hiscott | Radio | Crime. Twin jailed for his brother's crime. | 3 |
| A Letter of Warning | 33 | 1/32 | 2/32 9/32 bL | WB-FN / Teddington | John Daumery | WB | Drama. Actors receive poison pen letters. | |
| Life Goes On (Sorry You've Been Troubled) | 77 | 1932 | 3/32 2/33 bL | B&D-Paramount / Elstree | Jack Raymond | Paramount | Crime. Crook hides dead financier and frames his fiancée. | 3 |
| Little Fella | 45 | 1932 | 10/32 4/33 6bL | WB-FN / Teddington | William William McGann | FN | Comedy. Baby helps girl to win major. | 3 |
| Little Waitress | 49 | 7/32 | 11/32 | Delta / Bushey | Widgey Newman | Ace | Musical. Romance of poor tourist and rich German waitress. | 3 |
| Love on the Spot | 65 | 5/32 | 6/32 12/32 bL | ATP / Ealing | Graham Cutts | Radio | Romance. Love among thieves. | 4 |
| Lucky Ladies | 74 | 6/32 | 9/32 | WB-FN / Teddington | John Rawlings | FN | Comedy. Sisters win Irish sweep and lose winnings to con man. | 2 |
| The Marriage Bond | 82 | 2/32 | 3/32 9/32 co,2bL | Twickenham / Twickenham | Maurice Elvey | Radio | Romance. Alcohol leads to marriage break-up and problems for children before reconciliation. | 3 |
| The Melody Maker | 56 | 8/32 | 3/33 8/33 4bL | WB-FN / Teddington | Leslie Hiscott | FN | Comedy. Composer rewrites fiancée's sonata. | 2 |
| Men of Steel | 71 | 5/32 | 9/32 2/33 a,bL | Langham / Walton | George King | UA | Drama. Sheffield steelworks manager is softened by accident to secretary. | 3 |
| The Merry Men of Sherwood | 37 | 1932 | 9/32 | Delta / Bushey | Widgey R. Newman | Filmophone | Adventure. Outlaw restores King to throne. | |
| Money Means Nothing | 70 | 1932 | 8/32 1/33 3bL | B&D-Paramount / Elstree | Harcourt Templeman | Paramount | Comedy. Butler inherits fortune and daughter marries his master. | 2 |
| Mr. Quincy of Monte Carlo | 53 | 12/32 | 1/33 7/33 4bL | WB-FN / Teddington | John Daumery | FN | Comedy. Bank clerk becomes millionaire. | 3 |
| Naughty Cinderella | 56 | 10/32 | 1/33 3/33 bL | WB-FN / Teddington | John Daumery | FN | Comedy. Danish girl outwits and marries guardian. | 2 |
| The New Hotel | 49 | 1932 | 3/32 8/32 2bL | PDC / Cricklewood | Bernerd Mainwaring | PDC | Musical. Opening of new hotel. | 3 |
| Old Spanish Customers (Toreadors Don't Care) | 69 | 3/32 | 9/32 3/33 2bL | BIP / Elstree | Lupino Lane | Wardour | Comedy. Leslie Fuller takes a trip to Spain. | 3 |
| On Thin Ice | 62 | 1932 | 2/33 | Hall Mark / | Bernard Vorhaus | Equity British | Crime. Blackmailer uses girl to bleed her father. | 2 |
| Once Bitten | 48 | 1/32 | 3/32 8/32 3bL | Real Art / Twickenham | Leslie Hiscott | Fox | Comedy. Amnesiac believed to have killed blackmailer. | 3 |

| Title | Length | | | Studio / Location | Director | Distributor | Description |
|---|---|---|---|---|---|---|---|
| One Precious Year (Driven) | 76 | 11/32 | 2/33 | B&D-Paramount / Elstree | Henry Edwards | Paramount | Romance. Neglected wife with one year to live is vulnerable to cad's advances. 2 |
| Partners Please | 34 | 1932 | 1932 | PDC / Cricklewood | Lloyd Richards | PDC | Comedy. Fiancé becomes nightclub gigolo. |
| Puppets of Fate (USA: Wolves of the Underworld) | 72 | 11/32 | 1/33 | Real Art / Twickenham | George A. Cooper | UA | Crime. Escaped con blackmails murderous doctor into helping him. 4 |
| Reunion | 60 | 10/32 | 11/32 5/33 3bL | Sound City / Shepperton | Ivar Campbell, John Baxter | MGM | Drama. Ex-major helps out corporal. 4 |
| The River House Ghost | 52 | 10/32 | 12/32 4/33 4bL | WB-FN / Teddington | Frank Richardson | FN | Comedy Thriller. Girl unmasks crooks pretending to be ghosts. 2 |
| A Safe Proposition | 46 | 1932 | 6/32 2/33 bL | Real Art / Twickenham | Leslie Hiscott | Fox | Comedy. Man saves girl's jewellery from bogus count. |
| Send 'em Back Half Dead | 44 | 12/32 | 5/33 | Cecil Landeau / Blattner, Elstree | Redd Davis | Fox | Parody. Spoof anthropology film. |
| The Shadow | 74 | 12/32 | 3/33 9/33 2bL | Real Art / Twickenham | George A. Cooper | UA | Crime. Writer helps police unmask murderous blackmailer. 4 |
| She Was Only a Village Maiden | 60 | 9/32 | 2/33 | Sound City / Shepperton | Arthur Maude | MGM | Comedy. Sister tries to win inheritance. 3 |
| Side Streets | 47 | 11/32 | 3/33 | Sound City / Shepperton | Ivar Campbell | MGM | Drama. Ex-boxer saves future mother-in-law from blackmailing husband. 3 |
| The Silver Greyhound | 47 | 6/32 | 9/32 3/33 bL | WB-FN / Teddington | William McGann | WB | Comedy thriller. Man retrieves stolen papers from spy. 1 |
| Smilin' Along | 38 | 1932 | 12/32 | Argyle Talking Pictures | John Argyle | EB | Comedy. Girl poses as maid at boyfriend's engagement party. |
| The Spare Room | 34 | 1932 | 3/32 8/32 bL | PDC / Cricklewood | Redd Davis | PDC | Comedy involving hen-pecked husband. |
| The Stolen Necklace | 48 (40) | 11/32 | 2/33 11/33 3bL | WB-FN / Teddington | Leslie Hiscott | WB | Crime. Competition for stolen jewels. 2 |
| Strange Evidence (Dance of the Witches) | 72 | 11/32 | 1/33 10/33 bL | London / B&D Elstree | Robert Milton | Paramount | Crime. Wife suspected of poisoning husband. 1 |
| The Strangler (Four Winds) | 45 | 8/31 | 3/32 6/32 bL | BIP-BIF / Welwyn | Norman Lee | Pathe | Crime. Murder of actor. 3 |
| Strictly Business | 46 | 10/31 | 1/32 7/32 3bL | BIF / Welwyn | Jacqueline Logan, Mary Field | Pathe | Comedy. Heiress saved from blackmailer. 2 |
| Strip! Strip! Hooray! | 36 | 1932 | 1932 | BIP / Elstree | Norman Lee | Pathe | Comedy. Puritan exposed at sunbathing resort. |
| Taking Ways | 40 | 12/32 | 12/33 | Sound City / Shepperton | John Baxter | Universal | Comedy about a jewel theft. |
| The Television Follies | 45 | 12/32 | 6/33 2/34 bL | English Films / Worton Hall | Geoffrey Benstead | English Films | Revue. Music-hall acts seen through television. |

| Title | Minutes | Filming began | Trade show/ Leicester bookings | Production company/ studio | Director | Distributor | Genre/synopsis | Q |
|---|---|---|---|---|---|---|---|---|
| The Temperance Fete | 45 | 8/31 | 1/32 8/32 2bL | Fogwell Films / Worton Hall | Graham Cutts | MGM | Comedy. . George Robey subverts temperance social. | 3 |
| That Night in London (USA: Overnight) | 78 | 8/32 | 11/32 6/33 bL | London / B&D Elstree | Rowland V. Lee | Paramount | Crime. Dancer falls for embezzler she has been sent to con. | 4 |
| A Tight Corner | 49 | 5/32 | 8/32 3/33 bL | Real Art / Twickenham | Leslie Hiscott | MGM | Comedy. Detectives foil blackmailers. | 3 |
| To Brighton with Gladys (To Brighton with a Bird) | 45 | 12/32 | 2/33 8/33 2bL | George King / Ealing | George King | Fox | Comedy. Nephew takes penguin to uncle in Brighton. | 3 |
| A Voice Said Goodnight | 35 | 1932 | 3/32 7/32 3bL | WB-FN / Teddington | William McGann | WB | Crime. Usurer killed in revenge for woman's suicide. |  |
| The Water Gipsies | 79 | 8/31 | 3/32 8/32 2bL | ATP / Beaconsfield | Maurice Elvey | Radio | Romance. Beautiful bargee accidentally drowns fiancé. | 4 |
| When London Sleeps | 78 | 3/32 | 7/32 10/32 bL | Twickenham / Twickenham | Leslie Hiscott | APD | Crime. Gambling den owner kidnaps cousin to usurp title. | 3 |
| The Wonderful Story | 72 | 8/32 | 11/32 | Reginald Fogwell (Devon) | Reginald Fogwell | Sterling | Romance. Young farmer and disabled brother love same girl. |  |
| The World, the Flesh and the Devil | 53 | 10/32 | 11/32 5/33 bL | Real Art / Twickenham & Beaconsfield | George A. Cooper | Radio | Crime. Lawyer based in docklands pub tries to dispossess heir. | 3 |
| A Yell of a Night | 42 | 1932 | 7/32 | C. a Becket Williams | Gustave Minzenty | Universal | Comedy. Crooks look for loot in waxworks. |  |
| Yes, Madam | 46 | 12/32 | 2/33 7/33 5bL | British Lion / Beaconsfield | Leslie Hiscott | Fox | Comedy. Man must keep job to secure legacy. | 3 |
| **1933** | | | | | | | | |
| Anne One Hundred | 66 | 3/33 | 6/33 2/34 3bL | B&D-Paramount / Elstree | Henry Edwards | Paramount | Drama of woman's struggle to retain her soap factory. | 2 |
| As Good as New | 49 | 2/33 | 3/33 | WB-FN / Teddington | Graham Cutts | WB | Romance. Girl becomes a gold-digger after romantic misunderstanding. | 2 |
| Ask Beccles | 67 | 10/33 | 12/33 6/34 bL | B&D-Paramount / Elstree | Redd Davis | Paramount | Comedy thriller of complications surrounding a diamond theft. | 3 |
| The Bermondsey Kid | 75 | 8/33 | 11/33 4/34 a,2bL | WB-FN / Teddington | Ralph Dawson | FN | Sport. Boxer is forced to fight sick friend. | 3 |
| Beware of Women (With the Best Intentions) | 51 | 4/33 | 5/33 | WB-FN / Teddington | George King | FN | Comedy. Lord's son takes jewels by mistake. | 3 |

|  | | | | | | | |
|---|---|---|---|---|---|---|---|
| The Black Abbot | 56 | 11/33 | 1/34 9/34 2bL | Real Art / Twickenham | George A. Cooper | Radio | Crime. Lord held to ransom in his home. 2 |
| Borrowed Clothes | 68 | 1933? | 2/34 | Maude Productions | Arthur Maude | Columbia | Comedy. Woman accidentally acquires couturiers. 2 |
| Call Me Mame | 59 | 1933 | 6/33 | WB-FN / Teddington | John Daumery | WB | Comedy. Heir to peerage embarrassed by mother. 1 |
| Chelsea Life | 69 | 8/33 | 11/33 | D&B-Paramount / Elstree | Sidney Morgan | Paramount | Drama of life among bohemian artists. 2 |
| Cleaning Up | 70 | 1933 | 5/33 7/33 3a,3bL | British Lion / Beaconsfield | Leslie Hiscott | EB | Comedy. Lord's son engages in various masquerades. 3 |
| Commissionaire | 72 | 5/33 | 10/33 9/34 bL | Granville / Cricklewood | Edward Dryhurst | MGM | Crime. Commissionaire blamed for son's robbery. 3 |
| Counsel's Opinion | 76 | 12/32 | 3/33 9/33 2bL | London / B&D, Elstree | Allan Dwan | Paramount | Comedy. Widow poses as lord's wife to win barrister. 4 |
| The Crime at Blossoms | 76 | 1/33 | 3/33 12/33 bL | B&D-Paramount / Elstree | Maclean Rogers | Paramount | Crime. Wife is obsessed with death of previous tenant of cottage. 3 |
| Crime on the Hill | 68 | 9/33 | 12/33 6/34 co,2a,2bL | BIP / Welwyn | Bernard Vorhaus | Wardour | Crime. Vicar proves man innocent of murder. 3 |
| The Crimson Candle | 67 | 1933 | 2/34 5/35 bL | Bernerd Mainwaring / Wembley | Bernerd Mainwaring | MGM | Crime. Doctor proves maid is murderer. 2 |
| Dora | 40 | 1933 | 5/33 | H&S Film Service | St John L. Clowes | H&S | Comedy. The frustrations of an American tourist. |
| Doss House | 52 | 6/33 | 6/33 12/33 2bL | Sound City / Shepperton | John Baxter | MGM | Drama. Reporter and detective pose as tramps to catch escapee. 4 |
| Double Bluff | 35 | 1933 | 1933 | British Pictorial | R. E. Jeffrey | Universal | Crime. Cardsharper fakes his own death. |
| Double Wedding (Double Trouble) | 50 | 1/33 | 3/33 | WB-FN / Teddington | Frank Richardson | WB | Comedy. Two couples on honeymoon. 2 |
| Enemy of the Police | 51 | 1933 | 10/33 | WB-FN / Teddington | George King | FN | Comedy. Moral reformer is mistaken for criminal. 1 |
| Excess Baggage | 59 | 2/33 | 5/33 9/33 2bL | Real Art / Twickenham | Redd Davis | Radio | Comedy. A colonel goes ghost hunting. 3 |
| Eyes of Fate (All the Winners) | 67 | 5/33 | 12/33 | Sound City / Shepperton | Ivar Campbell | Universal | Fantasy. Bookmaker acquires tomorrow's newspaper and reads of his death. 2 |
| Faces | 68 | 1933 | 1/34 | B&D-Paramount / Elstree | Sidney Morgan | Paramount | Romance. Beautician falls for client's husband. 2 |
| Facing the Music (The Jewel Song) | 69 | 2/33 | 6/33 4/34 bL | BIP / Elstree | Harry Hughes | Wardour | Stanley Lupino comedy with music. Publicity stunt backfires. 4 |
| The Fear Ship | 66 | 1933 | 10/33 | ASFI-J Steven Edwards / Wembley | J. Steven Edwards | Paramount | Adventure. Mate saves sailing ship. |
| Flat no. 3 | 45 | 9/33 | 2/34 9/34 2bL | British Lion / Beaconsfield | Leslie Hiscott | MGM | Crime. Lawyer helps woman who believes she has killed blackmailer. 2 |

| Title | Minutes | Filming began | Trade show/ Leicester bookings | Production company/ studio | Director | Distributor | Genre/synopsis | Q |
|---|---|---|---|---|---|---|---|---|
| The Flaw | 67 | 8/33 | 9/33 | Patrick K. Heale / Wembley | Norman Walker | Paramount | Crime. Victim turns tables on poisoner. | 3 |
| Follow the Lady | 49 | 5/33 | 6/33, 9/33 3bL | George Smith / | Adrian Brunel | Fox | Comedy. Frenchwoman blackmails bachelor. | 2 |
| The Fortunate Fool | 74 | 9/33 | 11/33, 3/34 bL | ATP / Ealing | Norman Walker | ABFD | Comedy. Author poses as poor man to adopt girl and ex-boxer. | 3 |
| General John Regan | 74 | 8/33 | 10/33 | B&D-Paramount / Elstree | Henry Edwards | Paramount | Comedy. Irish villagers invent mythical hero to fool American. | 4 |
| The Ghost Camera | 68 | 6/33 | 7/33, 1/34 b,3aL | Real Art / Twickenham | Bernard Vorhaus | Radio | Thriller. Camera contains evidence of theft and murder. |  |
| The Girl in Possession | 71 | 1/33 | 2/34, 8/34 6bL | WB-FN / Teddington | Monty Banks | WB | Comedy. American girl is duped into believing she has inherited stately home. | 4 |
| Going Straight | 51 | 8/32 | 3/33 | WB-FN / Teddington | John Rawlins | WB | Comedy. Ex-crooks save man from romantic mistake. | 1 |
| The Golden Cage | 62 | 2/33 | 4/33, 2/34 2bL | Sound City / Shepperton | Ivar Campbell | MGM | Romance. Girl marries rich man but still loves poor boy. | 4 |
| Great Stuff | 50 | 3/33 | 6/33, 9/33 4bL | British Lion / Beaconsfield | Leslie Hiscott | Fox | Comedy. Parents try to stop daughter's wedding. | 2 |
| Guest of Honour (Gay Lord Strathpeffer) | 53 | 10/33 | 3/34, 1/35 4bL | WB-FN / Teddington | George King | FN | Comedy. Lord unmasks blackmailer. | 2 |
| Head of the Family | 66 | 6/33 | 8/33, 2/34 2bL | WB-FN / Teddington | John Daumery | FN | Melodrama of bankrupt who catches son attempting robbery. | 1 |
| Hearts of Oak | 49 | 1933 | 7/33, 1/34 bL | International Productions | M. A. Wetherell | International Productions | War. The battle of Zeebrugge 1918. |  |
| Her Imaginary Lover | 66 | 8/33 | 10/33, 3/34 bL | WB-FN / Teddington | George King | FN | Comedy. Heiress invents lover to keep suitors at bay. | 3 |
| High Finance | 67 | 1933 | 6/33, 12/33 2bL | WB-FN / Teddington | George King | FN | Drama. Selfish magnate redeemed by jail. | 2 |
| Hiking with Mademoiselle | 40 | 1933 | 3/33 | International Productions | Edward Nakhimoff | International Productions | Comedy. French tourist foils London robbery. |  |
| His Grace Gives Notice | 57 | 4/33 | 7/33, 1/34 a,2bL | Real Art / Twickenham | George A. Cooper | Radio | Comedy. Butler keeps quiet about inheriting title. | 2 |
| The House of Trent (Shepherd's Warning / Trent's Folly) | 75 | 10/33 | 11/33, 2/34 a,bL | Ensign / Ealing | Norman Walker | Butcher's | Romance. Doctor's patient dies while he is with press baron's daughter. | 3 |
| I Adore You | 74 | 8/33 | 11/33 | WB-FN / Teddington | George King | WB | Musical. Actor is mistaken for owner of film studio. | 3 |

| Title | Length | Trade show | Released | Production | Director | Distributor | Notes | No. |
|---|---|---|---|---|---|---|---|---|
| I'll Stick to You | 67 | 5/33 | 7/33 1/34 3a,2bL | British Lion / Beaconsfield | Leslie Hiscott | British Lion | Comedy. Girl thwarts attempt to cheat glue inventor. | 2 |
| I'm an Explosive (High Explosive) | 49 | 2/33 | 3/33 9/33 3bL | George Smith / Walton | Adrian Brunel | Fox | Comedy. Professor's son drinks liquid explosive. | 3 |
| Important People | 48 | 11/33 | 2/34 6/34 bL | George Smith / Wembley | Adrian Brunel | MGM | Comedy. Quarrelling couple stand as rivals at election. | 3 |
| The Jewel | 67 | 1933 | 10/33 4/34 2bL | Venture Films | Reginald Denham | Paramount | Thriller. Man saves his aunt's diamond. Edgar Wallace. | 2 |
| Keep It Quiet | 64 | 11/33 | 3/34 9/34 2bL | British Lion / Beaconsfield | Leslie Hiscott | British Lion | Comedy. Man gets mixed up with a gang of thieves. | 2 |
| The Lady Is Willing | 74 | 8/33 | 1/34 10/34 bL | Columbia / B&D Elstree | Gilbert Miller | Columbia | Comedy. In Paris, man kidnaps wife of financier who ruined him. Leslie Howard. | 2 |
| The Laughter of Fools | 47 | 9/33 | 10/33 5/34 2bL | George Smith / Walton | Adrian Brunel | Fox | Drama. Mother wants to wed daughter to rich captain. | 1 |
| Little Miss Nobody | 52 | 1/33 | 2/33 | WB-FN / Teddington | John Daumery | WB | Comedy. Danish girl on the British stage wins film contract. | 2 |
| Little Napoleon (Her Man of Destiny) | 44 | 6/33 | 7/33 3/34 bL | George Smith / Walton | Adrian Brunel | Fox | Drama. Playwright exposes fiancée's father as counterfeiter. | |
| Long Live the King | 44 | 9/32 | 4/33 2/34 bL | WB-FN / Teddington | William McGann | FN | Comedy. Cockney woman rescues baby prince from Ruritanian revolutionaries. | 2 |
| The Lord of the Manor | 71 | 1/33 | 5/33 12/33 5bL | B&D-Paramount / Elstree | Henry Edwards | Paramount | Comedy. Lord and general's hopes for the marriages of their offspring are dashed. | 4 |
| Love at Second Sight (USA: The Girl Thief) | 71 | 11/33 | 4/34 10/34 bL | Radius-BIP / Elstree | Paul Merzbach | Wardour | Comedy. Match magnate's daughter feigns love for inventor of everlasting match. | 2 |
| The Love Wager | 64 | 6/33 | 1933 | Anglo European / | A. Cyran | Paramount | Romance. Couple succeed in meeting father's conditions for marriage. | 2 |
| The Luck of a Sailor (Contraband) | 66 | 11/33 | 5/34 12/34 2bL | BIP / Elstree | Robert Milton | Wardour | Romance. Ruritanian queen abdicates to wed English sea captain. | 2 |
| Lucky Blaze | 48 | 1933 | 8/33 1/34 bL | Ace | Widgey R. Newman | Ace | Sport. Squire's daughter helps jockey win race. | 3 |
| The Lure | 66 | 5/33 | 8/33 4/34 bL | Arthur Maude / Wembley | Arthur Maude | Paramount | Crime. Murder mystery. | 1 |
| Maid Happy (Maid to Order) | 74 | 2/33 | 6/33 12/33 bL | Bendar / BIP Elstree (Switzerland) | Mansfield Markham | WP | Musical. In Switzerland, schoolgirl poses as older woman to win diplomat. | 2 |
| The Man I Want (Digging Deep) | 68 | 11/33 | 3/34 | British Lion / Beaconsfield | Leslie Hiscott | MGM | Comedy. Man discovers stolen jewels. | 2 |
| The Man Outside | 52 | 3/33 | 5/34 1/34 4bL | Real Art / Twickenham | George A. Cooper | Radio | Thriller. Hidden diamonds in country house. | 2 |
| Mannequin | 54 | 10/33 | 12/33 8/34 3bL | Real Art / Twickenham | George A. Cooper | Radio | Romance. Boxer in love triangle. | 1 |

| Title | Minutes | Filming began | Trade show/ Leicester bookings | Production company/ studio | Director | Distributor | Genre/synopsis | Q |
|---|---|---|---|---|---|---|---|---|
| Marooned | 67 | 8/33 | 11/33 | British Lion / Beaconsfield | Leslie Hiscott | Fox | Thriller. Lighthouse-keeper shelters escaped convict. | 3 |
| Master and Man | 44 (54) | 6/33 | 3/34 | BIP / Welwyn | John Harlow | Pathe | Comedy. Tramps save house from arsonists. | 2 |
| Matinee Idol | 75 | 2/33 | 3/33 10/33 2bL | Wyndham Films / Wembley | George King | UA | Crime. Actress proves sister did not murder lover. | 3 |
| Mayfair Girl | 67 | 6/33 | 8/33 5/34 4bL | WB-FN / Teddington | George King | WB | Thriller. American girl framed for murder. Sally Blane. | 1 |
| The Medicine Man | 52 | 1/33 | 2/33 8/33 3bL | Real Art / Twickenham | Redd Davis | Radio | Comedy. Youth impersonates doctor. | 3 |
| Meet My Sister | 70 | 5/33 | 8/33 | Pathe / Welwyn | John Daumery | Pathe | Comedy. Poor lord's sister is fiancée of his future father-in-law. | 3 |
| Mixed Doubles | 69 | 8/33 | 9/33 5/34 bL | B&D-Paramount / Elstree | Sidney Morgan | Paramount | Comedy. Romantic complications in two marriages. | 2 |
| A Moorland Tragedy | 39 | 1933 | 3/33 | GEM Productions | M. A. Wetherell | EB | Crime. Rich man kills his love rival, a poacher. | 3 |
| Mrs Dane's Defence | 67 | 9/33 | 11/33 6/34 2bL | National Talkies / Wembley | A. V. Bramble | Paramount | Drama. Problems with securing parental approval for marriage. | 1 |
| Murder at the Inn (Other Men's Women) | 55 | 10/33 | 2/34 | WB-FN / Teddington | George King | WB | Crime. Elopers involved in the killing of blackmailing landlord. | 2 |
| My Lucky Star | 63 | 1933 | 6/33 | Louis Blattner / Elstree | Louis Blattner, John Harlow | W&F | Comedy. Shopgirl posing as film star loves porter posing as artist. Florence Desmond. | 2 |
| The Night of the Party (Murder Party) | 61 | 5/33 | 2/34 7/34 3a,3bL | Gaumont / Shepherd's Bush | Michael Powell | Gaumont | Crime. Secretary framed for murder of boss. | 3 |
| Nine Forty-Five | 58 | 11/33 | 4/34 10/34 4bL | WB-FN / Teddington | George King | WB | Crime. Doctor proves 'murder' was suicide. | 2 |
| No Funny Business | 76 | 1/33 | 3/33 10/33 bL | John Stafford / B&D Elstree | Victory Hanbury, John Stafford | UA | Comedy. On Riviera, professional co-respondents mistake each other for clients. | 3 |
| Oh No, Doctor! | 62 | 1933 | 2/34 11/34 bL | George King | George King | MGM | Comedy. Doctor tries to frighten ward's fiancé to death. | 2 |
| Oh, What a Night! (The Irresistible Marmaduke) | 59 | 12/33 | 3/35 | Edward G. Whiting / Wembley | Frank Richardson | Universal | Comedy about an amnesiac. | 1 |
| Out of the Past | 51 | 1932 | 2/33 8/33 4bL | WB-FN / Teddington | Leslie Hiscott | WB | Crime. Manageress blackmailed for posing as co-respondent. | 3 |
| Paris Plane | 52 (56 orig) | 6/33 | 9/33 7/34 bL | Sound City / Shepperton | John Paddy Carstairs | MGM | Crime. Detective catches killer aboard plane. | 3 |

| Title | | | | | | | Description |
|---|---|---|---|---|---|---|---|
| The Pointing Finger | 68 | 10/33 | 12/33 5/34 4bL | Real Art / Twickenham | George Pearson | Radio | Crime. Man tries to kill half brother to inherit. 2 |
| A Political Party (Bill MP) | 73 | 5/33 | 1/34 9/34 a,2bL | BIP / Elstree | Norman Lee | Pathe | Comedy. Chimney sweep's son helps opponent in by-election. Leslie Fuller. 4 |
| Purse Strings | 69 | 4/33 | 7/33 5/34 bL | B&D-Paramount / Elstree | Henry Edwards | Paramount | Drama. Miser's wife becomes shoplifter. 2 |
| The Right to Live (The 'K' Formula) | 72 | 8/33 | 10/33 | Fox / Ealing | Albert Parker | Fox | Crime. Intrigue over the formula to neutralise poison gas. 2 |
| The River Wolves (Lion and Lamb) | 56 | 11/33 | 1/34 6/34 5bL | Real Art / Twickenham | George Pearson | Radio | Crime. Skipper saves girl from blackmailer. John Mills stars. 2 |
| The Roof | 58 | 9/33 | 11/33 6/34 3bL | Real Art / Twickenham | George A. Cooper | Radio | Crime. Jewel theft from lawyer. 1 |
| A Royal Demand | 62 | 6/33 | 8/33 | Moorland Films | Gustave Minzenty | Paramount | Drama. Royalist escapes by posing as Roundhead. 1 |
| Seeing Is Believing | 70 | 12/33 | 2/34 11/34 bL | B&D-Paramount / Elstree | Redd Davis | Paramount | Comedy. Policeman mistakes girl for thief and follows her aboard ship. William Hartnell. 1 |
| A Shot in the Dark | 53 | 9/33 | 10/33 7/34 a,5bL | Real Art / Twickenham | George Pearson | Radio | Mystery. Who killed the hated recluse? 2 |
| The Silver Spoon | 64 | 11/33 | 12/33 | WB-FN / Teddington | George King | WB | Comedy. Man confesses to murder to protect woman he loves. Cecil Parker. 1 |
| Smithy (The Man with a Million) | 53 | 7/33 | 10/33 3/34 3bL | WB-FN / Teddington | George King | WB | Comedy. Clerk comes into fortune. 3 |
| Song Birds | 36 | 1933 | 10/33 1/34 2bL | BIP / Welwyn | John Harlow | Pathe | Comedy. Tramps at Christmas party. |
| Song of the Plough | 68 | 6/33 | 12/33 6/34 aL | Sound City / Shepperton | John Baxter | MGM | Drama. Farmer saved from ruin by winning sheepdog trials. 2 |
| The Stickpin | 44 | 4/33 | 6/33 11/33 2bL | British Lion / Beaconsfield | Leslie Hiscott | Fox | Crime. Man framed for blackmailer's murder. 3 |
| Strictly in Confidence | 42 | 5/33 | 7/33 | WB-FN / Teddington | Clyde Cook | FN | Comedy. Journalists catch con man. |
| Strike It Rich | 76 | 7/33 | 10/33 3/34 bL | British Lion / Beaconsfield | Leslie Hiscott | British Lion | Comedy. Diffident clerk takes over firm. 2 |
| A Taxi to Paradise (Third Man Lucky) | 44 | 12/32 | 2/33 5/33 3bL | George Smith / Wembley | Adrian Brunel | Fox | Comedy of marital infidelity. 3 |
| That's My Wife | 67 | 1/33 | 3/33 8/33 bL | British Lion / Beaconsfield | Leslie Hiscott | British Lion | Comedy. Beautician poses as solicitor to save uncle from scandal. 3 |
| The Thirteenth Candle | 68 | 3/33 | 3/33 12/33 3bL | WB-FN / Teddington | John Daumery | WB | Mystery. Who killed the squire? 2 |
| This Acting Business | 54 | 9/33 | 12/33 | WB-FN / Teddington | John Daumery | WB | Comedy. Newlyweds separate because of parents' interference. 2 |

| Title | Minutes | Filming began | Trade show/ Leicester bookings | Production company/ studio | Director | Distributor | Genre/synopsis | Q |
|---|---|---|---|---|---|---|---|---|
| Three Men in a Boat | 60 | 1933? | 5/33 3/34 2bL | ATP / Ealing | Graham Cutts | ABFD | Comedy. Three men on boating holiday. | 3 |
| Tiger Bay | 66 | 6/33 | 9/33 3/34 2a,2bL | Wyndham / Elstree | J. Elder Wills | ABFD | Drama. Chinese woman saves orphan from brutal sea captain. Anna May Wong. | 2 |
| Till the Bells Ring | 54 | 1933 | 4/33 | BSFP / | Graham Moffatt | Bayley | Comedy. Scotsman woos widow he thinks is rich. | |
| Too Many Wives (This Is the Wife) | 58 | 1/33 | 3/33 8/33 2bL | WB-FN / Teddington | George King | WB | Comedy. Maid poses as wife for important clients. | 2 |
| Trouble in Store | 39 | 1933 | 1/34 | WB-FN / Teddington | Clyde Cook | FN | Comedy. Shop assistants catch burglars. | |
| Two Wives for Henry | 45 | 1933 | 1/34 9/34 3bL | GS Enterprises | Adrian Brunel | Fox | Comedy. Bootmaker takes a substitute 'wife' to Brighton. | 3 |
| The Umbrella | 56 | 5/33 | 7/33 2/34 2bL | Real Art / Twickenham | Redd Davis | Radio | Comedy. Man acquires pickpocket's umbrella by mistake. | 2 |
| Up to His Neck | 73 | 6/33 | 8/33 5/34 a,2bL | B&D / Elstree | Jack Raymond | UA | Comedy. Bank clerk uses legacy to stage drama. | 4 |
| Veteran of Waterloo | 48 | 1933 | 7/33 | National Talkies | A. V. Bramble | Paramount | Drama. Old corporal recalls battle. | 1 |
| The Warren Case (Crime Reporter / Fleet Street Murder) | 75 | 12/33 | 3/34 7/34 bL | BIP / Welwyn | Walter Summers | Pathe | Crime. Deranged reporter strangles mistress and frames fiancé of employer's daughter. | 2 |
| White Ensign | 84 | 11/33 | 3/34 8/34 2a,5bL | Sound City / Shepperton | John Hunt | MGM | Adventure. In Santa Barbara, British Navy quells revolution. | 3 |
| Without You | 66 | 12/33 | 3/34 | British Lion / Beaconsfield | John Daumery | Fox | Comedy. Trial separation of composer and wife. | 2 |
| **1934** | | | | | | | | |
| Ace of Spades | 66 | 10/34 | 2/35 9/35 3bL | Real Art / Twickenham | George Pearson | Radio | Drama. Election candidate suspected of murder. | 3 |
| The Admiral's Secret | 63 | 1/34 | 2/34 9/34 2bL | Real Art / Merton Park, Twickenham | Guy Newall | Radio | Comedy. Spanish crooks search for jewels stolen by admiral. | 3 |
| Adventure Limited (Trust Barclay) | 69 | 7/34 | 10/34 | B&D–Paramount / Elstree | George King | Paramount | Adventure. Rescue of South American president. | 1 |
| Annie, Leave the Room! (The Cat's Whiskers, One Crazy Week) | 76 | 12/34 | 2/35 | Twickenham / Twickenham | Leslie Hiscott | Universal | Comedy. Cash-strapped lord hires home to American film company. | 3 |
| Anything Might Happen | 66 | 3/34 | 9/34 | Real Art / Twickenham | George A. Cooper | Radio | Crime. Reformed gangster mistaken for criminal. | 1 |

| Title | | | | | Director | Distributor | Description |
|---|---|---|---|---|---|---|---|
| Badger's Green | 67 | 5/34 | 9/34, 4/35 aL | B&D-Paramount | Adrian Brunel | Paramount | Comedy. Cricket match played to decide development issue. 4 |
| Bagged | 40 | 1934 | 6/34 | BIP / | John Harlow | Pathe | Comedy. Anarchist dupes tramps into delivering bomb. |
| Big Business | 53 | 7/34 | 10/34 | WB–FN / Teddington | Cyril Gardner | WB | Comedy. Businessman's double revives firm. 2 |
| The Big Splash | 66 | 9/34 | 5/35, 11/35 2bL | British Lion / Beaconsfield | Leslie Hiscott | MGM | Comedy. Millionaire hires double. 2 |
| Blind Justice (Recipe for Murder) | 73 | 8/34 | 10/34, 7/35 4bL | Twickenham / Twickenham | Bernard Vorhaus | Universal | Crime. Woman is blackmailed over cowardice of her brother. 2 |
| Borrow a Million | 49 | 10/34 | 11/34, 12/35 bL | Fox / Wembley | Reginald Denham | Fox | Comedy. Teashop owner starts restaurant chain. 2 |
| Brides to Be (Sign Please) | 67 | 3/34 | 5/34 | B&D-Paramount / Elstree | Reginald Denham | Paramount | Crime. Crooks intervene in romance between shopgirl and millionaire. 1 |
| The Case for the Crown | 70 | 7/34 | 11/34, 7/35 2bL | B&D-Paramount / Elstree | George A. Cooper | Paramount | Crime. Suicide made to look like murder to save woman's reputation. 2 |
| Crazy People (Safety First) | 67 | 1/34 | 9/34, 12/34 3bL | British Lion / Beaconsfield | Leslie Hiscott | MGM | Comedy. Man tries to fool rich aunt. 2 |
| The Crucifix | 48 | 1934 | 3/34 | New Era | G. B. Samuelson | Universal | Drama. Companion steals dead woman's crucifix without knowing it has been left to her. 4 |
| Dangerous Companions | 44 | 1934 | 3/34 | A. N. C. Macklin | A. N. C. Macklin | Beacon | Crime. Jewel thief saves girl from kidnappers. Stars A. N. C. Macklin. |
| Dangerous Ground | 67 | 2/34 | 4/34 | B&D-Paramount / Elstree | Norman Walker | Paramount | Crime. Dead detective's girl exposes murderer. David Lean editor. 3 |
| Death Drives Through | 62 | 9/34 | 2/35, 11/35 bL | Clifford Taylor / Ealing | Edward L. Cahn | ABFD | Sport. Drama of motor-racing rivals. 2 |
| The Double Event | 68 | 1/34 | 3/34, 10/34 a,2bL | Triumph / Hammersmith | Leslie Howard Gordon | PDC | Comedy. Cleric's daughter becomes bookmaker. 4 |
| Easy Money | 69 | 2/34 | 8/34, 3/35 2bL | B&D-Paramount / Elstree | Redd Davis | Paramount | Drama of a cheating bookmaker. 1 |
| Eight Cylinder Love | 42 | 7/34 | 12/34 | Tribune / Marylebone | Peter Saunders | Columbia | Sport. Racing driver eludes kidnappers and wins race. |
| Father and Son | 48 | 2/34 | 9/34, 3/35 3bL | WB–FN / Teddington | Monty Banks | WB | Crime. Bank clerk takes the blame for theft he thinks his father committed. 1 |
| The Feathered Serpent | 72 | 10/34 | 12/34, 6/35 bL | George Smith / Walton | Maclean Rogers | Columbia | Crime. Journalist proves actress did not murder fiancé. 1 |
| Flood Tide | 63 | 6/34 | 11/34, 7/35 4bL | Real Art / Twickenham | John Baxter | Radio | Romance. Lock-keeper's son marries bargee's daughter. 2 |
| Full Circle | 55 | 9/34 | 4/35, 5/35 3bL | WB–FN / Teddington | George King | WB | Crime. Burglar steals and returns will. 1 |
| Get Your Man | 67 | 1934 | 8/34, 5/35 bL | B&D-Paramount / Elstree | George King | Paramount | Comedy. Son resists father's attempt to wed him to rival manufacturer's daughter 2 |

| Title | Minutes | Filming began | Trade show/ Leicester bookings | Production company/ studio | Director | Distributor | Genre/synopsis | Q |
|---|---|---|---|---|---|---|---|---|
| The Girl in the Crowd | 52 | 8/34 | 12/34 | WB–FN / Teddington | Michael Powell | FN | Comedy. Man decides to marry girl picked at random. | 4 |
| The Girl in the Flat | 65 | 4/34 | 6/34 12/35 bL | B&D–Paramount / Elstree | Redd Davis | Paramount | Crime. Lawyer's fiancée is blackmail victim. | 2 |
| Girls Will Be Boys (The Last Lord) | 71 | 5/34 | 9/34 3/35 co,bL | BIP / Elstree | Marcel Varnel | Wardour | Comedy. Girl poses as grandson of lord. | 4 |
| A Glimpse of Paradise | 56 | 8/34 | 10/34 | WB–FN / Teddington | Ralph Ince | FN | Crime. Ex-con saves daughter from blackmailer. | 2 |
| His Majesty and Company | 66 | 11/34 | 1/35 9/35 bL | Fox / Wembley | Anthony Kimmins | Fox | Musical. Man opens London restaurant with Ruritanian royal family in exile. | 3 |
| How's Chances? | 73 | 2/34 | 5/34 10/34 bL | Sound City / Shepperton | Ivar Campbell | Fox | Musical. Ballerina poses as diplomat's fiancée. | 4 |
| Hyde Park | 48 | 8/34 | 11/34 6/35 2bL | WB–FN / Teddington | Randall Faye | WB | Comedy. Socialist refuses to let daughter marry peer's son. | 1 |
| The Immortal Gentleman (Will Shakespeare) | 61 | 9/34 | 3/35 | Bernard Smith | Widgey R. Newman | Equity British | Drama. Shakespeare discusses clientele of inn with friends. | 2 |
| The Invader (The Intruder) (USA: An Old Spanish Custom) | 61 | 10/34 | 1/36 4/36 bL | British & Continental / Worton Hall | Adrian Brunel | MGM | Comedy set in Spain. Starring Buster Keaton. | 3 |
| Irish Hearts (USA: Norah O'Neal) | 70 | 7/34 | 10/34 | Clifton Hurst / Cricklewood | Brian Desmond Hurst | MGM | Drama. Doctor in love with two nurses fights epidemic. | 2 |
| It Happened in Paris | 68 | 12/34 | 6/35 2a,co,2bL | Wyndham / Ealing | Robert Wyler, Carol Reed | ABFD | Romance. Art student finds love in Paris. | 2 |
| It's a Bet (Hide and I'll Find You) | 69 | 8/34 | 2/35 | BIP / Elstree | Alexandre Esway | Wardour | Comedy. Reporter hides in Devon to win bet. Gene Gerrard. | 3 |
| Josser on the Farm | 63 | 8/34 | 11/34 5/35 3bL | Fox / Cricklewood | T. Hayes Hunter | Fox | Comedy. Farmhand elected as magistrate. Last of Ernie Lotinga series. | 2 |
| Key to Harmony | 69 | 11/34 | 3/35 12/35 3bL | B&D–Paramount / Elstree | Norman Walker | Paramount | Romance. Girl's love life is threatened by success. | 1 |
| King of Whales | 44 | 1934 | 6/34 3/35 bL | Argonaut | Challis Sanderson | MGM | Adventure. Whale ship in African waters. | |
| The Lash | 63 | 3/34 | 5/34 11/34 2bL | Real Art / Twickenham | Henry Edwards | Radio | Drama. Millionaire father horsewhips wife-neglecting son. | 2 |
| Lazybones | 65 | 9/34 | 1/35 7/35 6bL | Real Art / Twickenham | Michael Powell | Radio | Comedy. Marriage of heir and heiress. | 3 |
| Leave It to Blanche (February 29th) | 51 | 4/34 | 8/34 | WB–FN / Teddington | Harold Young | FN | Comedy. Confusion over whether husband has killed wife's lover. | 2 |

| Title | No. | Date | Date | Location | Director | Dist. | Description |
|---|---|---|---|---|---|---|---|
| Lend Me Your Wife | 62 | 6/34 | 10/35 3/36 co,2bL | Grafton / BIP Elstree | W. P. Kellino | MGM | Comedy. Man borrows friend's wife to fool rich uncle. 2 |
| Lest We Forget | 60 | 1/34 | 8/34 11/34 2bL | Sound City / Shepperton | John Baxter | MGM | Drama. Poignant pretence at service reunion. Re-working of 1932's *Reunion*. 3 |
| The Life of the Party | 53 | 1934 | 4/34 3/35 3bL | WB-FN / Teddington | Ralph Dawson | WB | Comedy. Wife tries to conceal drunken neighbour from husband. 1 |
| Little Stranger | 51 | 1934 | 3/34 9/34 3bL | George King | George King | MGM | Drama. Old man adopts child. 2 |
| Lord Edgware Dies | 82 | 5/34 | 8/34 2/35 3bL | Real Art / Twickenham | Henry Edwards | Radio | Crime. French detective solves mystery of lord's death. 3 |
| Lost over London | 38 | 1934 | 1934 | Rex Green | Rex Green | Columbia | Drama. The travels of a stolen pound note. |
| Love, Mirth and Melody (Smile, Vicar, Smile) | 64 | 5/34 | 9/34 | Mancunian / Albany | Bert Tracy | Universal | Revue. Variety acts. |
| The Love Test | 63 | 10/34 | 1/35 9/35 3bL | Fox / Wembley | Michael Powell | Fox | Romantic Comedy. Love and laughter among research chemists. 3 |
| Lucky Loser | 68 | 2/34 | 4/34 10/34 bL | B&C-Paramount / Elstree | Reginald Denham | Paramount | Comedy. Man sells desk containing winning sweepstake ticket. 2 |
| The Man Who Changed His Name | 80 | 1/34 | 3/34 9/34 a,bL | Real Art / Twickenham | Henry Edwards | Universal | Crime. Husband poses as murderer to prevent wife leaving. 3 |
| The Medium | 37 | 1934 | 9/34 1/36 bL | Film Tests | Vernon Sewell | MGM | Horror. Psychic reveals that mad sculptor hid body in statue. |
| Money Mad (Monday at Ten) | 68 | 2/34 | 9/34 6/35 bL | Champion / Worton Hall | Frank Richardson | MGM | Drama. Struggle to save the pound. 1 |
| Mr. What's-His-Name | 66 | 11/34 | 4/35 10/35 4bL | WB-PN / Teddington | Ralph Ince | FN | Comedy. Amnesiac businessman meets his wife again. 4 |
| Music Hall (Say It with Song) | 75 | 3/34 | 6/34 2/35 3a,2bL | Real Art / Twickenham | John Baxter | Radio | Musical. Modern showmanship saves old music hall. 4 |
| Night Club Queen | 88 | 2/34 | 3/34 7/34 bL | Real Art / Twickenham | Bernard Vorhaus | Universal | Crime. Barrister's wife runs nightclub and is framed for murder. 4 |
| Night Mail | 54 | 4/34 | 5/35 12/35 2bL | British Lion / Beaconsfield | Herbert Smith | MGM | Thriller. Reporter attempts to prevent murder of a judge aboard express train. 3 |
| No Escape | 70 | 1934 | 6/34 12/34 2bL | WB-FN / Teddington | Ralph Ince | WB | Drama. Malayan planter is suspected plague carrier. 4 |
| The Office Wife | 43 | 4/34 | 8/34 | WB-FN / Teddington | George King | WB | Romance. Love triangle between publisher, wife and secretary. 4 |
| Once in a New Moon (Lucky Star) | 63 | 7/34 | 12/34 | Fox / Shepperton | Anthony Kimmins | Fox | Fantasy. Village postmaster is thrown into space. 3 |
| Open All Night | 61 | 7/34 | 10/34 5/35 4bL | Real Art / Twickenham | George Pearson | Radio | Drama. Girl saved from murder charge by suicide of exiled Russian duke. 4 |
| Ovanga (USA: Love) | 68 | 1934 | 9/34 | Ouanga / West Indies | George Terwilliger | Paramount | Horror. Black woman turns to voodoo when her white lover becomes engaged. |

| Title | Minutes | Filming began | Trade show/ Leicester bookings | Production company/ studio | Director | Distributor | Genre/synopsis | Q |
|---|---|---|---|---|---|---|---|---|
| The Outcast | 74 | 1/34 | 3/34 9/34 2bL | BIP / Welwyn, Elstree | Norman Lee | Wardour | Comedy. Pet greyhound of bankrupt bookie wins race. | 3 |
| Passing Shadows | 67 | 2/34 | 5/34 1/35 bL | British Lion / Beaconsfield | Leslie Hiscott | Fox | Crime. Burglar convinces chemist that he has killed man. | 2 |
| The Path of Glory | 68 | 1/34 | 3/34 | Triumph / Hammersmith | Dallas Bower | PDC | Comedy. Two Ruritanian countries try to lose a war. | 3 |
| The Perfect Flaw | 51 | 5/34 | 6/34 10/34 bL | Fox / Ealing | Manning Hayes | Fox | Crime. Clerk tries to kill stockbroker. | 2 |
| The Poisoned Diamond | 73 | 1934 | 12/34 | Grafton | W. P. Kellino | Columbia | Drama. Bankrupt gets revenge on those who ruined him. | 3 |
| The Price of Wisdom | 67 | 12/34 | 2/35 2/36 bL | B&D-Paramount / Elstree | Reginald Denham | Paramount | Drama. Country girl's adventures in the city. | 1 |
| The Primrose Path (The Flowery Walk) | 71 | 5/34 | 7/34 | B&D-Paramount | Reginald Denham | Paramount | Romance. Wife and daughter in love triangle. | 1 |
| The Public Life of Henry the Ninth | 60 | 11/34 | 1/35 7/35 2bL | Hammer / Ealing | Bernerd Mainwaring | MGM | Comedy. Potman at London pub becomes celebrity. | 3 |
| Romance in Rhythm | 73 | 1/34 | 9/34 11/35 bL | Allied / Cricklewood | Lawrence Huntington | MGM | Musical (Crime). Songwriter suspected of nightclub manager's murder. | 1 |
| The Rugged Island | 44 | 1934 | 1934 | Zenifilms | Jenny Brown | | Drama. A crofter and his girl. | |
| Sabotage (Menace) (USA: When London Sleeps) | 65 | 1934 | 2/36 | Sound City / Shepperton | Adrian Brunel | Reunion | Crime. Railway owner wrecks trains during brainstorms. | 2 |
| Say It with Diamonds | 64 | 11/34 | 3/35 7/35 2bL | Redd Davis / Walton | Redd Davis | MGM | Comedy. Mancunian retrieves necklace from thieves. | 2 |
| The Scoop | 68 | 6/34 | 10/34 12/35 bL | B&D-Paramount / Elstree | Maclean Rogers | Paramount | Crime. Reporter kills traveller in self-defence. | 1 |
| The Secret of the Loch | 79 | 3/34 | 6/34 12/34 co.2bL | Wyndham / Ealing | Milton Rosmer | ABFD | Fantasy. Diver discovers Loch Ness monster. | 2 |
| Smith's Wives | 61 | 12/34 | 2/35 9/35 3bL | Fox / Wembley | Manning Hayes | Fox | Comedy. Bookie and parson called Smith live in neighbouring flats. | 2 |
| Something Always Happens | 69 | 4/34 | 6/34 1/35 6bL | WB-FN / Teddington | Michael Powell | WB | Comedy. Car salesman in love. | 4 |
| Sometimes Good | 68 | 2/34 | 5/34 | Grafton / BIP Elstree | W. P. Kellino | Paramount | Comedy. Girl posing as colonel's daughter loves ex-employer's son. | 1 |
| Spring in the Air | 74 | 9/34 | 12/34 6/35 bL | John Stafford / BIP Elstree | Victor Hanbury, Norman Lee | Pathe | Musical. In Budapest, girl poses as a maid to win scientist. | 2 |
| Street Song | 64 | 12/34 | 3/35 11/35 5bL | Real Art / Twickenham | Bernard Vorhaus | Radio | Musical. Street singer is helped by pet shop owner. | 2 |

| Title | Length | Date 1 | Date 2 | Studio / Location | Director | Distributor | Notes | Rating |
|---|---|---|---|---|---|---|---|---|
| Strictly Illegal | 69 | 12/34 | 2/35 | Leslie Fuller / Cricklewood | Ralph Cedar | Gaumont | Comedy. Bookie believes he has killed someone. | 3 |
| Swinging the Lead | 63 | 1934 | 1/35 | Weiner, MacKane and Rogers | David MacKane | Universal | Comedy. Smuggling of drug that changes personality. Stars William Hartnell. | 3 |
| Tangled Evidence | 57 | 1/34 | 3/34 10/34 bL | Real Art / Merton Park, Twickenham | George A. Cooper | Radio | Crime. Inspector proves that girl did not kill her uncle. | 2 |
| The Tell Tale Heart (USA: Bucket of Blood) | 49 | 1934 | 3/34 | Clifton–Hurst Blattner | Brian Desmond Hurst | Fox | Horror. Killer tormented by the heartbeats of his victim. | 5 |
| The Third Clue (The Shakespeare Murders) | 72 | 8/34 | 12/34 | Fox / Ealing | Albert Parker | Fox | Crime. Rival crooks go after jewels hidden in old house. | 1 |
| To Be a Lady | 68 | 6/34 | 7/34 | B&D-Paramount / Elstree | George King | Paramount | Drama. Hairdresser is wrongly convicted of theft. | 2 |
| Too Many Millions | 57 | 6/34 | 9/34 5/35 bL | WB-FN / Teddington | Harold Young | WB | Romance between millionairess and poor artist. | 1 |
| The Unholy Quest | 56 | 1934 | 3/34 | Widgey R. Newman | R. W. Lotinga (Newman) | Equity British | Horror. Mad doctor tries to revive embalmed crusader. | 2 |
| Virginia's Husband | 71 | 8/34 | 9/34 1/35 co, 3bL | George Smith / Walton | Maclean Rogers | Fox | Comedy. Woman hires man to pose as her husband to fool rich aunt. | 3 |
| Warn London | 68 | 3/34 | 5/34 | British Lion / Beaconsfield | T. Hayes Hunter | British Lion | Crime. Detective poses as tramp to outwit German master criminal. | |
| The Way of Youth | 65 | 9/34 | 11/34 8/35 bL | B&D-Paramount / Elstree | Norman Walker | Paramount | Crime. Casino owner saves grand-daughter from blackmail. | 1 |
| What Happened Then? | 61 | 6/34 | 9/34 3/35 2bL | BIP / Welwyn | Walter Summers | Wardour | Thriller of a man wrongfully convicted of murder. | 3 |
| What Happened to Harkness? | 53 | 5/34 | 8/34 3/35 2bL | WB-FN / Teddington | Milton Rosmer | FN | Comedy. Village Bobby investigates miser's 'murder'. | 3 |
| What's in a Name? | 47 | 7/34 | 10/34 6/35 3bL | WB-FN / Teddington | Ralph Ince | FN | Comedy. Clerk posing as composer loves fake film star. | 1 |
| Whispering Tongues | 55 | 2/34 | 3/34 9/34 bL | Real Art / Twickenham | George Pearson | Radio | Crime. Son steals gems from those who caused father's suicide. | 2 |
| Who's Your Father? | 63 | 12/34 | 3/35 8/35 2bL | Lupino Lane – St George / Walton | Lupino Lane | Columbia | Comedy about marriage, mixed-marriage and widowhood. | 2 |
| Wishes | 35 | 1934 | 9/34 | BIP | W. P. Kellino | Pathe | Comedy. Tramps find wish-granting talisman. | |
| Womanhood | 61 | 1934 | 11/34 | Louis London | Harry Hughes | Butcher's | Crime. Ex-con seeks revenge on reporter who jailed him. | 3 |
| Youthful Folly (Intermezzo) | 72 | 8/34 | 11/34 | Sound City / Shepperton | Miles Mander | Columbia | Romance. The love life of the son and daughter of a lady. | 3 |

**1935**

| Title | Length | Date 1 | Date 2 | Studio / Location | Director | Distributor | Notes | Rating |
|---|---|---|---|---|---|---|---|---|
| Alibi Inn | 53 | 1935 | 7/35 12/35 3bL | Central | Walter Tennyson | MGM | Crime. Inventor breaks out of jail to prove his innocence. | 3 |

| Title | Minutes | Filming began | Trade show/Leicester bookings | Production company/studio | Director | Distributor | Genre/synopsis | Q |
|---|---|---|---|---|---|---|---|---|
| All at Sea (Mr. Faintheart) | 60 | 1/35 | 10/35 | Fox / Wembley | Anthony Kimmins | Fox | Comedy. Clerk poses as author on cruise. | 1 |
| The Awakening | 65 | 10/35 | 3/38 | Victory / Bushey | Anthony Frenguelli | Cosmopolitan | Melodrama. Two doctors in love with the same woman. | 1 |
| Bargain Basement aka Department Store (Johnson's Stores) | 66 | 2/35 | 5/35, 10/35 2co,5bL | Real Art / Twickenham | Leslie Hiscott | Radio | Crime. Crooked store manager mistakes ex-con for employer's heir. | 3 |
| Big Ben Calling | 44 | 1935 | 1935 | Norman Loudon | Ivar Campbell | | Musical. Pirate radio station in London. | |
| Birds of a Feather (The Rift in the Loot) | 69 | 8/35 | 10/35 | Baxter & Barter | John Baxter | Universal | Comedy. Poor peer poses as servant to locate hidden treasure. | 4 |
| Black Mask (Gentleman in Black) | 67 | 6/35 | 12/35, 2/36 4bL | WB-FN / Teddington | Ralph Ince | WB | Crime. Robin Hood charity worker is falsely accused of murder. | 2 |
| Breakers Ahead (The Lady of Pendower) | 58 | 6/34 | 1/35 | Anglo Cosmopolitan / Shepperton | Tony Gilkison | Reunion | Drama. Rivalry among Cornish fishermen. | 2 |
| Calling the Tune | 71 | 11/35 | 7/36, 2/37 bL | Phoenix-IFP / Ealing | Reginald Denham | ABFD | Musical. Record manufacturer's daughter loves son of man he cheated. | 2 |
| Captain Bill (Waterways) | 81 | 5/35 | 11/35, 6/36 2bL | Leslie Fuller / Rock, Elstree | Ralph Cedar | ABFD | Comedy. Bargee saves schoolteacher from gunrunners. | 2 |
| Checkmate | 68 | 1935 | 10/35, 4/36 co,bL | B&D-Paramount / Elstree | George Pearson | Paramount | Crime. Detective discovers fiancée's father is a gang boss. | 2 |
| Cheer Up | 72 | 4/35 | 2/36, 8/36 4a,3bL | Stanley Lupino / Ealing | Leo Mittler | ABFD | Musical. Mistaken for millionaire, author finances show. | 4 |
| Children of the Fog | 61 | 11/35 | 2/37 | Jesba / Southall | Leopold Jessner, John Quin | NPFD | Melodrama. Man marries step-sister and they take his sick brother to Australia. | 2 |
| Crime Unlimited | 72 | 4/35 | 8/35, 2/36 7bL | WB-FN / Teddington | Ralph Ince | FN | Crime. Undercover detective catches jewel thieves. | 3 |
| Cross Currents (Nine Day Blunder) | 66 | 5/35 | 7/35 | B&D-Paramount / Elstree (Budleigh Salterton) | Adrian Brunel | Paramount | Comedy. Devon vicar suspected of killing love rival. | 2 |
| Crown v. Stevens (Third Time Unlucky) | 65 | 12/35 | 3/36, 10/36 2bL | WB-FN / Teddington | Michael Powell | WB | Crime. Ex-dancer murders usurer and then tries to kill her husband. | 2 |
| Dark World | 73 | 1935 | 12/35, 11/36 2bL | Fox / Wembley | Bernard Vorhaus | Fox | Crime. Jealous man kills the wrong victim. | 4 |
| Death on the Set (USA: Murder on the Set) | 72 | 1/35 | 3/35, 6/36 bL | Twickenham / Twickenham | Leslie Hiscott | Universal | Crime. Film director kills gangster double and frames actress. | 2 |

| Title | | | | | | | Description |
|---|---|---|---|---|---|---|---|
| The Deputy Drummer | 71 | 6/35 | 9/35 | St George's Pictures | Henry George | Columbia | Musical. Jewel thieves caught at house party by composer posing as peer. 2 |
| Don't Rush Me (When We Are Married) | 72 | 9/35 | 1/36 | Fred Karno / Hammersmith | Norman Lee | PDC | Comedy. Moral reformer is forced to become bookie. Robb Wilton. 3 |
| Eliza Comes to Stay | 72 | 11/35 | 4/36 12/36 a,2bL | Twickenham / Hammersmith | Henry Edwards | Twickenham | Comedy. Unruly teenager visits family. Stars Betty Balfour. 2 |
| Expert's Opinion | 71 | 1935 | 10/35 6/36 b,2coL | B&D-Paramount / Elstree | Ivar Campbell | Paramount | Espionage. Spies seek plans for aircraft guns. 2 |
| Faithful | 78 | 10/35 | 3/36 7/36 a,8bL | WB-FN / Teddington | Paul Stein | WB | Musical. Married Viennese singer is tempted by rich woman. 3 |
| Flame in the Heather | 66 | 1935 | 9/35 | Crusade / B&D Elstree | Donovan Pedelty | Paramount | Adventure. 1745. English spy saves Jacobite's daughter. 1 |
| Gaol Break (Bill and Son) | 64 | 11/35 | 3/36 10/36 4bL | WB-FN / Teddington | Ralph Ince | WB | Crime. Man escapes from jail to rescue his son. 4 |
| Gay Old Dog | 62 | 9/35 | 11/35 7/36 7bL | Embassy / Walton | George King | Radio | Comedy. Doctor rescues vet from unwise marriage. 2 |
| Gentleman's Agreement | 70 | 1935 | 4/35 | B&D-Paramount / Elstree | George Pearson | Paramount | Comedy. Gentleman changes places with down-and-out. Stars Vivien Leigh. 1 |
| Handle with Care | 59 | 2/35 | 3/35 11/35 3bL | Embassy / Walton | Redd Davis | Radio | Comedy. Ex-crook beats spies by taking strength pill. 1 |
| The Happy Family (French Salad) | 67 | 10/35 | 8/36 2/37 a,2bL | British Lion / Beaconsfield | Maclean Rogers | British Lion | Comedy. Parents pretend they are broke to shake up family. 2 |
| Hello Sweetheart (The Butter and Egg Man) | 71 | 2/35 | 5/35 | WB-FN / Teddington | Monty Banks | WB | Musical. Americans persuade farmer to finance film. 3 |
| Honours Easy | 62 | 5/35 | 7/35 4/36 coL | BIP / Welwyn | Herbert Brenon | Wardour | Drama. Art dealer frames client's son for theft. 2 |
| Hot News (The Guest Reporter) | 78 | 11/35 | 3/36 9/36 6bL | St George's Pictures / Cricklewood | W. P. Kellino | Columbia | Comedy. Dumb reporter causes Chicago gangsters to kidnap cabaret star by mistake. 1 |
| Inside the Room | 66 | 1935 | 3/35 | Twickenham / Twickenham | Leslie Hiscott | Universal | Crime. French detective unmasks revenge killer. 2 |
| Jimmy Boy | 71 | 4/35 | 8/35 | Baxter & Barter / Cricklewood | John Baxter | Universal | Comedy. Irish bootboy unmasks film star as spy. 2 |
| Jubilee Window | 61 | 4/35 | 6/35 | B&D-Paramount / Elstree | George Pearson | Paramount | Comedy. Crooks try to steal jewels on Jubilee day. 1 |
| King of the Castle | 69 | 7/35 | 2/36 6/36 4bL | City Film / Shepperton | Redd Davis | Gaumont | Comedy. Peer's butler is missing heir. 3 |
| The Last Journey | 66 | 5/35 | 10/35 3/36 b,4aL | Twickenham / Twickenham | Bernard Vorhaus | Twickenham | Drama. Train driver driven mad by imagining his wife's adultery. 4 |

| Title | Minutes | Filming began | Trade show/ Leicester bookings | Production company/ studio | Director | Distributor | Genre/synopsis | Q |
|---|---|---|---|---|---|---|---|---|
| Late Extra | 69 | 8/35 | 11/35 5/36 co,3bL | Fox / Wembley | Albert Parker | Fox | Crime. Reporter catches gunman. | 3 |
| Lend Me Your Husband | 60 | 1935 | 6/35 1/36 3bL | Embassy | Frederick Hayward | Radio | Comedy. Married man spends weekend with friend's wife. | 2 |
| Line Engaged | 68 | 7/35 | 11/35 5/36 bL | British Lion / Beaconsfield | Bernèrd Mainwaring | British Lion | Crime. Detective proves his son innocent of blackmailer's murder. | 3 |
| A Little Bit of Bluff | 61 | 11/34 | 3/35 7/35 bL | GS Enterprises / Walton | Maclean Rogers | MGM | Comedy. Girl poses as detective to retrieve stolen jewels. | 2 |
| Lucky Days | 67 | 6/35 | 8/35 4/36 co,bL | B&D-Paramount / Elstree | Reginald Denham | Paramount | Comedy. Wife passes on astrology tips to husband. Chili Bouchier, Sally Gray. | 2 |
| McGlusky the Sea Rover (USA: Hell's Cargo) | 59 | 9/34 | 7/35 2co,2bL | BIP / Welwyn | Walter Summers | Wardour | Adventure. Stowaway falls in love with Arab woman. | 3 |
| The Mad Hatters | 68 | 6/35 | 7/35 4/36 co,bL | B&D-Paramount / Elstree | Ivar Campbell | Paramount | Comedy. Two hat shop owners fall for French woman. | 2 |
| The Man without a Face | 62 | 7/35 | 9/35 3/36 3coL | Embassy / Walton | George King | Radio | Crime. Framed man escapes from jail and exposes the real culprit. | 2 |
| Maria Marten or the Murder in the Red Barn | 67 | 1/35 | 4/35 7/35 a,b,coL | George King / Shepperton | Milton Rosmer | MGM | Crime Melodrama. Squire kills pregnant mistress to marry heiress. First Tod Slaughter. | 2 |
| Mr Cohen Takes a Walk | 82 | 8/35 | 12/35 10/36 2bL | WB-FN / Teddington | William Beaudine | WB | Drama. Rich retailer poses as pedlar but returns in time to save business. | 3 |
| Murder at Monte Carlo | 70 | 10/34 | 1/35 8/35 bL | WB-FN / Teddington | Ralph Ince | FN | Crime. Professor killed for his winning roulette system. | 3 |
| The Mystery of the Marie Celeste (USA: The Phantom Ship) | 80 | 7/35 | 11/35 6/36 2a,bL | Hammer / Walton | Denison Clift | GFD | Drama. In 1872 mad sailor kills everyone on board ship and jumps into sea. | 3 |
| Old Faithful | 67 | 7/35 | 8/35 3/36 4bL | GS Enterprises / Walton | Maclean Rogers | Radio | Romance among cabbies. | 2 |
| Old Roses | 60 | 3/35 | 7/35 | Fox / Wembley | Bernerd Mainwaring | Fox | Crime. Villager confesses to murder to save rich man's son. | 2 |
| Once a Thief | 67 | 5/35 | 6/35 3/36 b,coL | B&D-Paramount / Elstree | George Pearson | Paramount | Crime. Jewel thief's paint formula stolen while he is in jail. | 3 |
| One Good Turn | 72 | 10/35 | 6/36 12/36 co,2bL | Joe Rock / Elstree | Alfred Goulding | ABFD | Comedy. Coffee stallholders save girl from fake film producer. | 2 |
| Play Up the Band (Sharps and Flats) | 71 | 6/35 | /36 coL | City / Ealing | Harry Hughes | ABFD | Comedy. Yorkshire band travels to London for competition. | 3 |
| The Price of a Song | 67 | 2/35 | 5/35 | Fox / Wembley | Michael Powell | Fox | Crime. Bookie kills step-daughter's husband and frames her lover. | 3 |

| Title | No. | | | Production | Director | Distributor | Notes |
|---|---|---|---|---|---|---|---|
| The Private Secretary | 70 | 7/35 | 9/35 aL / 4/36 aL | Twickenham / Twickenham | Henry Edwards | Twickenham | Comedy. Rich man's nephew avoids creditors. Alistair Sim. 3 |
| Public Nuisance No.1 | 78 | 10/35 | 2/36 / 10/36 bL | Cecil / Beaconsfield | Marcel Varnel | GFD | Musical. On Riviera, shopgirl helps waiter to save uncle's hotel. 2 |
| Railroad Rhythm | 43 | 5/35 | 3/36 | Carnival / Bushey | A. E. C. Hopkins | Exclusive | Musical. Derelict station revitalised by music. |
| A Real Bloke | 70 | 1935 | 8/35 2bL | Baxter & Barter | John Baxter | MGM | Drama. Navvy keeps his redundancy from daughter. 3 |
| Riders to the Sea | 40 | 1935 | 2/37 | Flanagan – Hurst | Brian Desmond Hurst | MGM | Drama. Disaster at sea. |
| The Right Age to Marry | 69 | 3/35 | 6/35 / 3/35 bL | GS Enterprises / Walton | Maclean Rogers | Radio | Comedy. Gold-digger tries to seduce mill owner. 3 |
| The River House Mystery | 56 | 1935 | 10/35 | Imeson – Foulsham | Fraser Foulsham | Universal | Crime. Detective saves girl's jewels but finds he is hoax victim. 1 |
| The Riverside Murder | 64 | 1/35 | 3/35 / 7/35 a,2bL | Fox / Wembley | Albert Parker | Fox | Crime. Detective and girl reporter solve murders of three businessmen. |
| The Rocks of Valpre (USA: High Treason) | 74 | 8/34 | 1/35 / 8/35 3a,2bL | Real Art / Twickenham | Henry Edwards | Radio | Crime. 1880. Disgraced officer freed from Devil's Island saves beloved from blackmailing spy. |
| Royal Eagle | 69 | 10/35 | 6/36 | Quality Films / BIP Elstree | Arnold Ridley, George A. Cooper | Columbia | Crime. Clerk accused of warehouse robbery tracks down real thieves. 3 |
| Runaway Ladies (The Unexpected Journey) | 49 | 9/35 | 6/38 | International Players / Independent Elstree (France) | Jean de Limur | Exclusive | Comedy of mistaken identity set in France. 2 |
| School for Stars | 71 | 3/35 | 5/35 | B&D-Paramount / Elstree | Donovan Pedelty | Paramount | Romance. Waitress finds love and fame at stage school. 2 |
| The Secret Voice | 68 | 12/35 | 2/36 / 10/36 bL | B&D-Paramount | George Pearson | Paramount | Crime. Industrial espionage involving formula for non-inflammable petrol. 2 |
| Sexton Blake and the Bearded Doctor (The River Mystery) | 64 | 5/35 | 5/35 / 1/36 3bL | Fox / Wembley | George A. Cooper | MGM | Crime. Doctor murders during insurance fraud. 1 |
| Sexton Blake and the Mademoiselle | 63 | 1935 | 10/35 / 3/36 co,2bL | Fox / Wembley | Alex Bryce | MGM | Crime. Girl takes revenge on financier who ruined her father. 3 |
| The Shadow of Mike Emerald | 61 | 8/35 | 10/35 / 4/36 3bL | GS Enterprises / Walton | Maclean Rogers | Radio | Crime. Partners seek revenge on crooked financier. 2 |
| The Small Man | 70 | 2/35 | 3/35 / 3/36 3bL | Baxter & Barter | John Baxter | Universal | Drama. Small shopkeepers unite to fight chainstore. 4 |
| Someday (Young Nowheres) | 69 | 3/35 | 7/35 | WB-FN / Teddington | Michael Powell | WB | Romance between cleaner and lift boy in an apartment block. Stars Margaret Lockwood. 3 |
| Stars on Parade | 82 (51) | 12/35 | 1/36 / 9/36 a,3bL | Butcher's / Cricklewood | Oswald Mitchell, Challis Sanderson | Butcher's | Revue. Played in different-length versions. 2 |

| Title | Minutes | Filming began | Trade show/ Leicester bookings | Production company/ studio | Director | Distributor | Genre/synopsis | Q |
|---|---|---|---|---|---|---|---|---|
| The Stoker | 71 | 1/35 | 7/35 1/36 2a,2bL | Leslie Fuller / Rock, Elstree | Leslie Fuller | Gaumont | Comedy. Gold-digger's activities foiled by stoker. | 2 |
| Sunshine Ahead | 64 | 10/35 | 12/35 2/37 bL | Baxter & Barter / Cricklewood | Wallace Orton | Universal | Musical. Outside broadcast goes ahead despite opposition. | 3 |
| Sweeney Todd, The Demon Barber of Fleet Street (USA: The Demon Barber of Fleet Street) | 68 | 3/36 | 8/36 a,3co,2bL | George King | George King | MGM | Horror (Crime DG) Eighteenth-century London barber kills and robs clients before using their flesh for pies. | 3 |
| That's My Uncle (The Iron Woman) | 58 | 2/35 | 3/35 | Twickenham / Twickenham | George Pearson | Universal | Comedy. Crooks plant stolen wallet on man posing as butler. | 1 |
| Three Witnesses | 68 | 1/35 | 3/35 | Twickenham / Twickenham | Leslie Hiscott | Universal | Crime. Solicitor solves murder of fiancée's brother. | 1 |
| Ticket of Leave | 69 | 11/35 | 1/36 7/36 b,coL | B&D-Paramount / Elstree | Michael Hankinson | Paramount | Crime. Girl joins up with thief after he robs her flat. | 2 |
| Tomorrow We Live | 72 | 10/35 | 10/36 6/37 a,co,2bL | Conquest | Manning Hayes | ABFD | Drama. Suicidal financier helps down-and-outs. | 2 |
| Tropical Trouble | 70 | 10/35 | 10/36 | City Film / Walton | Harry Hughes | GFD | Comedy. Island governor's aide poses as bachelor and his wife as his secretary. | 2 |
| Twice Branded | 69 | 1935 | 1/36 7/36 5bL | GS Enterprises / Walton | Maclean Rogers | Radio | Crime. Innocent ex-con is forced to pose as his family's uncle, James Mason. | 3 |
| The Vandergilt Diamond Mystery (Copperhead) | 59 | 11/35 | 1/36 8/36 5bL | Winwood / Shepperton | Randall Faye | Radio | Comedy. Girl and crooks seek jewellery hidden in golf bag. | 1 |
| The Village Squire | 66 | 1935 | 4/35 | B&D-Paramount / Elstree | Reginald Denham | Paramount | Comedy. Film star saves squire's play and weds daughter. Vivien Leigh. | 2 |
| Wedding Eve | 39 | | 2/35 8/35 6bL | National Progress – Astor | Charles Barnett | Radio | Musical. Sing-song before marriage of Devon publican's daughter. | |
| Wedding Group (USA: Wrath of Jealousy) | 68 | 11/35 | 3/36 1/37 4bL | Fox / Wembley | Alex Bryce | Fox | Romance. Lovers parted by wicked sister. | 3 |
| What the Parrot Saw | 40 | 7/35 | 8/35 | Widgey R. Newman / Bushey | Widgey R. Newman | Butcher's | Romance blossoms during zoo visit. | |
| When the Cat's Away | 34 | 1935 | 8/35 | Central | Walter Tennyson | Zenifilms | Comedy. Husbands go boating and try to photograph girls. | |
| White Lilac | 67 | 2/35 | 6/35 10/35 co,2bL | Fox / Wembley | Albert Parker | Fox | Crime. Who killed unpopular villager? | 3 |
| A Wife or Two | 63 | 1935 | 1/36 7/36 2bL | British Lion / Beaconsfield | Maclean Rogers | British Lion | Comedy. Man tries to convince rich uncle that he is still married to first wife. | 2 |

|  | | | |  |  |  |  |
|---|---|---|---|---|---|---|---|
| Windfall | 65 | 1935 | 7/35 2/36 2b,4coL | Embassy | George King | Radio | Drama. Inheritance turns son into wastrel. 2 |

### 1936

| Title | mins | | dates | studio | director | dist. | description |
|---|---|---|---|---|---|---|---|
| All That Glitters | 72 | 1936 | 12/36 9/37 7bL | GS Enterprises / Walton | Maclean Rogers | Radio | Comedy. Goldmine owner foils swindlers. 3 |
| Apron Fools | 34 | 1936 | 7/36 | Marks Pictures | Widgey R. Newman | Radio | Comedy. Squire's daughter mistaken for servant. |
| Auld Lang Syne | 72 | 11/36 | 2/37 9/37 2bL | Fitzpatrick / Shepperton | James A. Fitzpatrick | MGM | Historical. Adventures of a poet in eighteenth-century Scotland. 2 |
| The Avenging Hand | 65 | 1936 | 4/36 2/37 3bL | John Stafford / Welwyn | Frank Richardson | Radio | Crime. Crooks pose as hotel guests to look for hidden loot. 2 |
| The Bank Messenger Mystery | 56 | 1936 | 12/36 | Hammer | Lawrence Huntington | Renown | Crime. Sacked cashier robs his old bank. 2 |
| Beauty and the Barge | 72 | 6/36 | 2/37 10/37 4b2aL | Twickenham / Hammersmith | Henry Edwards | Wardour | Comedy. Bargee adopts Mayor's runaway daughter who falls for mate. 2 |
| Bed and Breakfast (No. 7 Blank Square) | 58 (47) | 5/36 | 12/37 | Walter West / Southall | Walter West | Coronel | Drama. Old actor solves people's problems. 1 |
| The Belles of St. Clement's | 68 | 11/35 | 1/36 | B&D-Paramount / Elstree | Ivar Campbell | Paramount | Drama. Friendship between two girls at training college. 2 |
| Beloved Imposter (Dancing Boy) | 86 | 1/36 | 3/36 9/36 bL | John Stafford / Welwyn | Victor Hanbury | Radio | Musical. Waiter believes he killed singer. 2 |
| The Big Noise | 65 | 1/36 | 3/36 | Fox / Wembley | Alex Bryce | Fox | Musical. Clerk is fall guy for oil company executives. 2 |
| The Black Tulip | 57 | 6/36 | 2/37 1/38 bL | Fox / Wembley | Alex Bryce | Fox | Adventure. In old Holland, merchant seeks the secret of black tulips. 1 |
| Blind Man's Bluff | 71 | 1/36 | 3/36 12/36 5bL | Fox / Wembley | Albert Parker | Fox | Drama. Blind scientist undergoes secret cure. James Mason. 1 |
| Born That Way | 64 | 6/36 | 7/36 3/37 6bL | Randall Faye, Ace / Walton | Randall Faye | Radio | Comedy. Scots woman looks after brother-in-law's children. 3 |
| Bottle Party | 46 | 1936 | 11/36 4/37 5bL | Ace | R.A. Hopwood | Ace | Revue. Windmill Theatre. Includes Kenneth More. 2 |
| The Brown Wallet | 68 | 9/35 | 2/36 8/36 4bL | WB-FN / Teddington | Michael Powell | FN | Crime. Bankrupt is accused of murdering his rich aunt. 2 |
| Busman's Holiday (Bow Bells) | 68 | 8/36 | 11/36 7/37 6bL | GS Enterprises-Bow Bells / Walton | Maclean Rogers | Radio | Comedy. Busman catches burglars. 3 |
| Café Colette (USA: Danger in Paris) | 71 | 7/36 | 1/37 6/37 a,5bL | Garrick / Wembley | Paul Stein | ABFD | Musical. Russian spy in Paris poses as singer to steal secrets. 2 |
| Café Mascot | 76 | 5/36 | 7/36 | Pascal / Wembley | Lawrence Huntington | Paramount | Romance. Young man helps Irish girl with money found in taxi. 2 |
| Calling All Ma's aka The Biter Bit | 49 | 12/36 | 3/37 | Fox / Wembley | Redd Davis | Fox | Comedy. Husband attempts to escape wife's nagging. 2 |

| Title | Minutes | Filming began | Trade show/Leicester bookings | Production company/studio | Director | Distributor | Genre/synopsis | Q |
|---|---|---|---|---|---|---|---|---|
| Calling All Stars | 79 | 10/36 | 3/37, 10/37 4bL | British Lion / Beaconsfield | Herbert Smith | British Lion | Musical. Line up includes Ambrose, Carroll Gibbons and Arthur Askey. | 3 |
| The Captain's Table | 55 | 11/36 | 11/36 | Fitzpatrick / Shepperton | Percy Marmont | MGM | Crime. Detective poses as steward to catch killer on cruise. | 4 |
| Chinese Cabaret | 44 | 1/36 | 1936 | Bijou Film Co. | Buddy Harris | Columbia | Musical. Detective's daughter unmasks smugglers. | |
| The Crimes of Stephen Hawk (USA: Strangler's Morgue) | 69 | 2/36 | 5/36, 10/36 a,6bL | George King / Shepperton | George King | MGM | Crime. Regency money lender is macabre murderer. | 3 |
| Cross My Heart | 65 | 11/36 | 1/37 | B&D-Paramount / Pinewood | Bernerd Mainwaring | Paramount | Romance. Girl loved by gambler and musician turns lodging house into nightclub. | 1 |
| Darby and Joan | 76 | 12/36 | 2/37, 7/37 5bL | Rock / Elstree | Syd Courtenay | MGM | Romance. Girl marries rich man for the sake of her blind sister, but fiancé returns. | 1 |
| Digging for Gold | 45 | 1936 | 9/36, 12/36 3bL | Ace | R. A. Hopwood | Ace | Revue. Windmill Theatre. | |
| Double Alibi | 40 | 12/36 | 2/37, 9/37 4bL | Fox / Wembley | David Macdonald | Fox | Crime. Robber's alibi broken by rival's girlfriend. | |
| Dream Doctor | 41 | 5/36 | 9/36 | Bernard Smith-Widgey Newman | Widgey R. Newman | MGM | Drama. Gypsy interprets dreams of doctor's patients. | |
| The Early Bird | 69 | 5/36 | 8/36 | Crusade / Highbury (Ulster) | Donovan Pedelty | Paramount | Comedy. Irish villagers rebel against puritanical woman. | 2 |
| The Elder Brother | 67 | 11/36 | 2/37 | Triangle / Shepperton | Frederick Hayward | Paramount | Drama. Man takes blame for his brother's misdeeds. | 1 |
| Everything in Life (Because of Love) | 70 | 7/36 | 11/36 | Tudor / Highbury | J. Elder Wills | Columbia | Musical. On Riviera, playboy poses as forger. | 2 |
| Fair Exchange | 63 | 2/36 | 7/36, 1/37 4bL | WB-FN / Teddington | Ralph Ince | WB | Comedy. Criminologist tries to stop son becoming a detective by staging a theft. | 3 |
| Farewell to Cinderella | 65 | 11/36 | 4/37 | GS Enterprises / Walton | Maclean Rogers | Radio | Romance. Uncle helps family drudge's love life. | 1 |
| Find the Lady | 71 | 2/36 | 3/36, 2/37 2bL | Fox / Wembley | Roland Gillett | Fox | Comedy. Love triangle between a fake faith healer, a poor man and an heiress. George Saunders. | 2 |
| First Offence (Bad Blood) | 66 | 10/35 | 2/36, 10/36 b,coL | Gainsborough / Islington (France) | Herbert Mason | Gaumont | Crime. John Mills stars in a story of car thieves. | 3 |
| Full Speed Ahead | 71 | 1936 | 11/36 | Lawrence Huntington / Wembley | Lawrence Huntington | Paramount | Adventure. Couple elopes on ship that the captain plans to scuttle. | 2 |
| Full Steam | 47 | 1936 | 10/36, 2/37 8bL | Ace | R. A. Hopwood | Ace | Revue. Windmill Theatre. Includes Kenneth More. | |

| Title | | | | Production | Director | Distributor | Description |
|---|---|---|---|---|---|---|---|
| Grand Finale | 71 | 7/36 | 9/36 | B&D-Paramount / Elstree Shepperton | Ivar Campbell | Paramount | Comedy. Actress is courted by her ex-husbands. 1 |
| Gypsy | 80 | 8/36 | 12/36 7/37 5bL | WB-FN / Teddington | Roy William Neill | WB | Romance. Gypsy girl, believing her beloved lion-tamer dead, marries rich man. 2 |
| Hail and Farewell | 74 | 7/36 | 9/36 | WB-FN / Teddington | Ralph Ince | FN | Comedy. The adventures of men on leave from a troopship docked at Southampton. 4 |
| Head Office | 67 | 6/35 | 11/36 4/37 5bL | WB-FN / Teddington | Melville Brown | WB | Drama. Clerk blackmails employer over son's cowardice. 2 |
| Hearts of Humanity | 75 | 6/36 | 11/36 | UK Films / Shepperton | John Baxter | APD | Drama. Outcast vicar helps tramps and catches crooks. 3 |
| The Heirloom Mystery | 69 | 1936 | 11/36 7/37 5bL | GS Enterprises / Walton | Maclean Rogers | Radio | Drama. Cabinet maker's fake antique causes trouble for son. 3 |
| Highland Fling | 67 | 3/36 | 6/36 2/37 4bL | Fox / Wembley | Manning Hayes | Fox | Comedy. Detectives look for lost will at Highland Games. 2 |
| Honeymoon Merry-go-round (Olympic Honeymoon) | 63 | 3/36 | 1/40 | London Screenplays-Fanfare / Ealing | Alfred Goulding | RKO | Comedy. Honeymooner helps English ice hockey team in Switzerland. 3 |
| House Broken | 73 | 4/36 | 6/36 | B&D-Paramount / Rock Elstree | Michael Hankinson | Paramount | Comedy. Wife tries to make husband jealous of Frenchman. 3 |
| The House of the Spaniard | 70 | 4/36 | 10/36 11/37 bL | Phoenix / Ealing | Reginald Denham | ABFD | Crime. Liverpool clerk unmasks employer as Spanish revolutionary counterfeiter. 3 |
| The Howard Case | 64 | 1936 | 3/36 | Sovereign | Frank Richardson | Universal | Crime. Lawyer kills twin cousin and frames partner. 2 |
| If I Were Rich (Humpty Dumpty) | 59 | 4/36 | 5/36 11/36 5bL | Randall Faye / Walton | Randall Faye | Radio | Comedy. Socialist barber inherits earldom. 1 |
| International Revue | 40 | 7/36 | 9/36 2/37 2bL | Medway | Buddy Harris | Medway | Revue. |
| Irish and Proud of It (Never Go Home) | 72 | 9/36 | 11/36 4/37 2bL | Crusade / Wembley | Donovan Pedelty | Paramount | Comedy. In Ireland, manufacturer tackles moonshiners in pay of gangsters. 3 |
| Irish for Luck (Meet the Duchess) | 68 | 8/36 | 12/36 4/37 a,5bL | WB-FN / Teddington | Arthur Woods | FN | Comedy. Three people down on their luck win fame on radio. 4 |
| Knights for a Day (Full Tilt) | 69 | 3/36 | 3/37 | Pearl / Welwyn | Norman Lee | Pathe | Comedy. Ruritanian barber saves prince from revolutionaries. 2 |
| Landslide | 66 | 11/36 | 1/37 | Crusade / Wembley | Donovan Pedelty | Paramount | Crime. Policeman investigates cashier's death when landslide traps actors in Welsh theatre. 2 |
| The Lilac Domino | 79 | 12/36 | 7/37 6/38 a,bL | Grafton-Capitol-Cecil / Welwyn | Fred Zelnik | UA | Musical. In Budapest, count falls in love with mysterious girl. 2 |
| Love at Sea | 70 | 2/36 | 4/36 | B&D-Paramount / Elstree | Adrian Brunel | Paramount | Comedy. Girl falls for suspected thief on cruise. 2 |
| Luck of the Turf (Gay Reality) | 64 | 7/36 | 9/36 4/37 2a,3bL | Randall Faye / Walton | Randall Faye | Radio | Comedy. Tipster gambles to pay for his wedding. 3 |

| Title | Minutes | Filming began | Trade show/ Leicester bookings | Production company/ studio | Director | Distributor | Genre/synopsis | Q |
|---|---|---|---|---|---|---|---|---|
| Make Up | 70 | 11/36 | 7/37 | Standard International / Shepperton | Alfred Zeisler | ABFD | Drama. Italian surgeon becomes clown and proves his ward did not kill lion-tamer. | 3 |
| The Man behind the Mask | 79 | 1/36 | 3/36 9/36 co,2a,4bL | Joe Rock, Elstree | Michael Powell | MGM | Crime. Mad astronomer kidnaps lord's daughter. | 3 |
| Mayfair Melody | 83 | 11/36 | 3/37 8/37 2bL | WB-FN / Teddington | Arthur Woods | WB | Musical. Rich girl helps mechanic become opera star. Chili Bouchier. | 3 |
| Midnight at Madame Tussaud's | 66 | 10/36 | 12/36 | Premier / Highbury | George Pearson | Paramount | Crime (Horror?). Embezzler tries to murder explorer at waxworks. | 1 |
| Murder at the Cabaret | 67 | 1936 | 12/36 | MB Productions | Reginald Fogwell | Paramount | Musical. Singer killed during cabaret act. | 1 |
| Murder by Rope | 65 | 6/36 | 8/36 2/37 2bL | B&D-Paramount / Shepperton | George Pearson | Paramount | Crime. Judge and executioner menaced by (apparently) hanged man. | 1 |
| The Music Maker | 52 | 1936 | 3/36 | Inspiration / ? | Horace Shepherd | MGM | Drama. Musician finishes symphony before his death. | |
| My Partner, Mr. Davis | 58 | 1936? | 1936 | Oxford | Claude Autant-Lara | RKO | Comedy. Unemployed man outwits crooked financier. | |
| No Escape (No Exit) | 83 | 10/36 | 11/36 7/37 2bL | Welwyn /Welwyn | Norman Lee | Pathe | Crime. Writer bets he can hide friend from the police for one month. | 4 |
| Not So Dusty | 70 | 3/36 | 5/36 12/36 3bL | GS Enterprises–Bow Bells / Walton | Maclean Rogers | Radio | Comedy. Crooks go after rare books in the possession of dustmen. | 4 |
| Nothing Like Publicity | 64 | 7/36 | 9/36 4/37 4bL | GS Enterprises / Walton | Maclean Rogers | Radio | Comedy. Actress poses as American heiress. | 2 |
| Pal O'Mine | 42 | 2/36 | 3/36 | Film Sales / Bushey | Widgey R. Newman | Radio | Musical. Thinking his son has robbed the theatre's safe, stage doorman takes blame. | |
| Patricia Gets Her Man | 67 | 12/36 | 3/37 9/37 5bL | WB-FN / Teddington | Reginald Purdell | FN | Comedy. Girl hires gigolo who is really a count. | 2 |
| Pay-Box Adventure (Open House) | 68 | 3/36 | 6/36 | B&D-Paramount / JH, Elstree | W. P. Kellino | Paramount | Crime. Lawyer tries to destroy cinema where cashier is an heiress. Kellino's last film. | 1 |
| Piccadilly Playtime | 49 | 1936 | 12/36 6/36 2bL | Ace | Frank Green | Ace | Revue. Windmill Theatre. | 1 |
| The Prison Breaker | 69 | 1/36 | 2/36 | George Smith / Walton | Adrian Brunel | Columbia | Crime. Secret service agent escapes from jail and catches crook. | 2 |
| Radio Lover | 64 | 2/36 | 10/36 3/37 5bL | City Film / BIP, Elstree | Austin Melford | ABFD | Comedy. Plain singer gets friend to mime on TV. | 3 |
| Reasonable Doubt | 73 | 8/36 | 12/36 7/37 2bL | Pascal / Shepperton | George King | MGM | Crime. Barrister's client turns out to be his son. | |
| Rhythm in the Air | 72 | 4/36 | 9/36 1/36 7bL | Fox / Wembley | Arthur Woods | Fox | Musical. Disabled riveter becomes star tap dancer. | 3 |

| Title | No. | Date | Date | Production | Director | Distributor | Description |
|---|---|---|---|---|---|---|---|
| The Scarab Murder Case | 68 | 10/36 | 11/36 7/37 4bL | B&D-Paramount / Pinewood | Michael Hankinson | Paramount | Crime. Detective proves archaeologist is killer. 2 |
| The Scat Burglars | 46 | 1/36 | 2/37 | New Ideal / Hammersmith | Leslie Rowson | MGM | Comedy. Star's jewels stolen for publicity stunt. 1 |
| Second Bureau | 77 | 10/36 | 12/36 9/37 2b2aL | Premier-Stafford / Shepperton | Victor Hanbury | Radio | War romance. WWI German spy falls in love with French spy. 3 |
| Servants All | 34 | 1/36? | 3/36 1/37 3bL | Fox / Wembley | Alex Bryce | Fox | Comedy. Aristocrats change places with servants. |
| She Knew What She Wanted (Kiss and Make Up) | 74 | 3/36 | 6/36 12/36 co,2bL | Rialto / BIP Elstree | Thomas Bentley | Wardour | Musical. Band leader steals girl's diary and catches jewel thieves. 2 |
| Show Flat | 70 | 7/36 | 10/36 | B&D-Paramount / Shepperton | Bernard Mainwaring | Paramount | Comedy. Couple use vacant flat to impress impresario. 1 |
| Side Street Angel | 65 | 11/36 | 3/37 6/37 4bL | WB-FN / Teddington | Ralph Ince | WB | Comedy. Rich man poses as thief to woo woman who runs reformatory. 3 |
| Silver Blaze (USA: Murder at the Baskervilles) | 70 | 10/36 | 7/37 1/38 2a,2bL | Twickenham / Twickenham | Thomas Bentley | ABPC | Crime. Sherlock Holmes solves death of racehorse owner and groom. 2 |
| Sing as You Swing (Calling All Stars) | 81 | 10/36 | 7/37 | Rock / Elstree | Redd Davis | BIED | Revue. Radio and variety turns with minimal narrative. 3 |
| Someone at the Door | 74 | 2/36 | 5/36 9/36 co,2a,3b | BIP / Elstree | Herbert Brenon | Wardour | Comedy. Reporter fakes murder that then comes true. 2 |
| Song in Soho | 48 | 1936 | 12/36 6/37 bL | Ace | R. A. Hopwood | Ace | Revue. Windmill Theatre. 2 |
| Song of the Road (Horse) | 71 | 9/36 | 2/37 7/37 a,3bL | UK Films / Shepperton | John Baxter | Sound City | Drama. Mechanisation causes old labourer and horse to search for work in Sussex. 3 |
| Strange Cargo (Breakers Ahead) | 68 | 1/36 | 3/36 10/36 bL | Lawrence Huntington / B&D, Elstree | Lawrence Huntington | Paramount | Crime. Stowaway helps captain catch gunrunners. 2 |
| Strangers on Honeymoon | 69 | 5/36 | 11/36 7/36 bL | Gaumont / Shepherd's Bush | Albert de Courville | Gaumont | Comedy. In Canada, peer posing as tramp weds girl to save her from crooks. 3 |
| Such Is Life | 80 | 8/36 | 11/36 5/36 bL | Inc. Talking Films / Shepperton | Randall Faye | NPFD | Comedy. Millionaire poses as clerk to help typist become singer. 3 |
| Take a Chance | 72 | 8/36 | 1/37 7/37 4bL | Grosvenor / Ealing | Sinclair Hill | ABFD | Comedy. Tipster discovers racehorse owner's wife is leaking information. 3 |
| The Tenth Man | 68 | 1936 | 8/36 5/37 a,2bL | BIP / Elstree | Brian Desmond Hurst | Wardour | Drama. Wife supports career of crooked financier. 3 |
| Terror on Tiptoe | 58 | 1936 | 1936 | MB Productions | Louis Renoir | New Realm | Crime. Attempted murder of film star's double. 2 |
| They Didn't Know | 67 | 1936 | 4/36 3/37 bL | British Lion / Beaconsfield | Herbert Smith | MGM | Comedy (no category DG). Engaged couple are the targets of blackmailers. 1 |

| Title | Minutes | Filming began | Trade show/ Leicester bookings | Production company/ studio | Director | Distributor | Genre/synopsis | Q |
|---|---|---|---|---|---|---|---|---|
| This Green Hell | 72 | 1936 | 3/36 | Randall Faye / Walton | Randall Faye | Radio | Comedy. Victim of train crash imagines he is a famous explorer. | 4 |
| To Catch a Thief | 64 | 5/36 | 6/36 3/37 4bL | GS Enterprises / Walton | Maclean Rogers | Radio | Comedy. Inventor catches crooks. | 2 |
| A Touch of the Moon | 67 | 1936 | 2/36 | GS Enterprises | Maclean Rogers | Radio | Comedy. Girl chooses alcoholic over rich fiancé. | 2 |
| Troubled Waters | 71 | 1935 | 2/36 10/36 co,2bL | Fox / Wembley | Albert Parker | Fox | Crime. Crooks try to steal liquid explosive from villagers. | 2 |
| Twelve Good Men | 64 | 2/36 | 3/36 12/36 5bL | WB–FN / Teddington | Ralph Ince | WB | Crime. Vengeful escaped convict is foiled by actor. | 3 |
| 21 Today | 34 | 1936 | 3/36 | Albany Studios | John H. Taylor | MGM | Musical. Performances at a birthday party. | |
| Two on a Doorstep | 71 | 2/36 | 5/36 | B&D–Paramount / Rock Elstree | Lawrence Huntington | Paramount | Comedy. Baliff becomes bookie to help girl's brother. | 1 |
| Under Proof | 50 | 12/35 | 2/36 2/37 2bL | Fox / Wembley | Roland Gillett | Fox | Comedy. Coward takes brandy and foils smugglers. | 1 |
| Unlucky Jim | 34 | 1936 | 5/36 | Master | Harry Marks | Radio | Comedy. Adventures of two boys on a break from school. | |
| The Vicar of Bray | 67 | 11/36 | 3/37 2/38 bL | J. H. Productions / Hammersmith, Twickenham | Henry Edwards | ABPC | Historical. King's ex-tutor intercedes on behalf of imprisoned man. Stanley Holloway. | 2 |
| The Voice of Ireland | 49 | 1936? | 3/36 | Victor Haddick | Victor Haddick | ICC | Musical. Traveller reunited with old friends in Ireland. | |
| Wednesday's Luck | 68 | 3/36 | 5/36 12/36 2bL | B&D–Paramount / Elstree | George Pearson | Paramount | Crime. Detective poses as ex-con to unmask crook. | 1 |
| What the Puppy Said | 39 | 2/36 | 11/36 bL | Widgey Newman / Bushey | Widgey Newman | Butcher's | Animal Drama. Collie dog aids romance on farm. | |
| Windmill Revels | 47 | 1936 | 12/36 6/373bL | Ace | R. A. Hopwood | Ace | Revue. | 2 |
| Wings Over Africa | 63 | 7/36 | 9/36 | Premier Stafford / Shepperton | Ladislaus Vajda | Radio | Adventure. Rival expeditions search for hidden treasure. | 2 |
| **1937** | | | | | | | | |
| The Academy Decides | 49 | 3/37 | 3/37 | UK Films / Shepperton | John Baxter | MGM | Drama. Orphan adopted by buskers tries to kill her seducer. | 2 |
| Against the Tide | 67 | 1/37 | 3/37 10/37 5bL | Fox / Cricklewood | Alex Bryce | Fox | Drama. Conflict between Cornish fisherman's mother and fiancée. | 2 |
| The Angelus (retitled: Who Killed Fen Markham?) | 76 | 4/37 | 6/37 | St Margaret's / Twickenham | Thomas Bentley | Ambassador | Crime. Nun proves actress and fiancé did not murder producer. | 2 |
| Around the Town (Song Writers on Parade) | 68 | 5/37 | 5/38 11/38 bL | British Lion / Beaconsfield | Herbert Smith | British Lion | Musical. Agent escorts US producer and daughter to London shows. | 2 |

|  | | | | | | | |
|---|---|---|---|---|---|---|---|
| Behind Your Back | 70 | 3/37 | 4/37 12/37 co,3bL | Crusade / Wembley | Donovan Pedelty | Paramount | Drama. Author solves actor's problems on play's first night. |
| The Bells of St Mary's | 45 | 6/37 | 12/37 6/38 6bL | Fitzpatrick / Shepperton | James A. Fitzpatrick | MGM | Musical. Chorister marries sexton's daughter in nineteenth-century Devon. |
| Blondes for Danger | 69 | 10/37 | 3/38 8/38 4,6bL | Wilcox / Beaconsfield | Jack Raymond | British Lion | Crime. Cabbie saves prince from assassins. 5 |
| Boys Will Be Girls (Big-hearted Bill) | 66 (70) | 4/36 | 7/37 4/38 2a,4bL | Leslie Fuller / Rock, Elstree | Gilbert Pratt | BIED | Comedy. Man forced to give up smoking and drinking to inherit fortune. 3 |
| Brief Ecstasy (Dangerous Secrets) | 71 | 4/37 | 8/37 6/38 a,bL | IFP-Phoenix / Ealing | Edmond T. Greville | ABFD | Romance. Scientist's wife falls for his ward, a pilot. 2 |
| Captain's Orders | 75 | 8/37 | 12/37 8/38 2co,5bL | Liberty / Worton Hall | Ivar Campbell | Liberty | Drama. Ship's captain racing to US rescues shipwrecked star. 3 |
| Carry On London | 46 | 1937? | 2/37 6/37 4bL | Ace | D. R. Frazer | Ace | Revue. Windmill Theatre. 1 |
| Catch as Catch Can (Reissued as Atlantic Episode) | 71 | 3/37 | 6/37 3/38 2bL | Fox / Wembley | Roy Kellino | Fox | Crime. Crooks try to steal diamonds that girl has smuggled aboard liner. James Mason. 2 |
| The Cavalier of the Streets | 70 | 2/37 | 3/37 12/37 2bL | B&D-Paramount / Pinewood | Harold French | Paramount | Crime. Wife rescued from murder charge by blackmailer's confession 4 |
| The Claydon Treasure Mystery (The Shakespeare Murders) | 63 | 12/37 | 3/38 9/38 5bL | Fox / Wembley | Manning Hayes | Fox | Crime. Author solves murder and finds treasure. 3 |
| The Compulsory Wife | 57 | 2/37 | 3/37 8/37 5bL | WB-FN / Teddington | Arthur Woods | WB | Comedy. Burglar steals clothes of couple who have been obliged to spend the night together. 1 |
| Concerning Mr. Martin (The Crooked Gentleman) | 57 | 1/37 | 3/37 11/37 2bL | Fox / Wembley | Roy Kellino | Fox | Crime. Gentleman thief frames crooked club owner. 3 |
| Concert Party | 45 | 1937 | 5/37 | Ace | R. A. Hopwood | Ace | Revue. Windmill Theatre. |
| The Dance of Death (The Vengeance of Kali) | 64 | 10/37 | 3/38 | Glenrose / Cricklewood | Gerald Blake | Fidelity | Crime. Crook steals lord's cursed jewel and kills dancer. 1 |
| Darts Are Trumps (Match Point) | 72 | 12/37 | 3/38 10/38 3bL | George Smith / Walton | Maclean Rogers | RKO | Comedy. Darts player catches jewel thief. 4 |
| Death Croons the Blues | 74 | 9/37 | 10/37 7/38 4bL | St Margaret's / Twickenham | David Macdonald | MGM | Crime. Drunken reporter proves man innocent of singer's murder. 2 |
| The Derelict | 57 | 1937 | 11/37 | M.V. Gover | Harold Simpson | Independent | Drama. Tramp pays for boy's operation by selling drawings. 1 |
| Devil's Rock | 55 | 8/37 | 3/38 | C. G. Burger / (Ireland) | Germain Burger | Columbia | Musical. Irish concert party's takings are stolen. 1 |
| Dial 999 | 45 | 9/37 | 1/38 7/38 5bL | Fox / Wembley | Lawrence Huntington | Fox | Crime. Detective unmasks head of counterfeiting gang. 2 |

| Title | Minutes | Filming began | Trade show/Leicester bookings | Production company/studio | Director | Distributor | Genre/synopsis | Q |
|---|---|---|---|---|---|---|---|---|
| Dr. Sin Fang | 61 | 3/37 | 9/37 2/38 6bL | Victory/Hammersmith (Elstree?) | Anthony Frenguelli | MGM | Chinese master crook tries to steal cancer cure. | 1 |
| Double Exposures (reissued as Alibi Breaker) | 67 | 2/37 | 5/37 | Triangle/Shepperton | John Paddy Carstairs | Paramount | Crime. Sacked reporter supplies evidence for murder conviction. | 1 |
| Double or Quits | 72 | 12/37 | 3/38 10/38 5bL | WB-FN/Teddington | Roy William Neill | WB | Crime. Thief steals stamps on Atlantic liner. | 2 |
| East of Ludgate Hill | 47 | 9/37 | 12/37 5/38 7bL | Fox/Wembley | Manning Hayes | Fox | Drama. Office workers faced with the loss of their promised bonus. | 4 |
| Easy Riches (In the Money) | 67 | 9/37 | 1/38 6/38 3bL | GS Enterprises/Walton | Maclean Rogers | RKO | Comedy. Rival manufacturers combine forces against con men. | 1 |
| False Evidence | 71 | 1937 | 9/37 | Crusade/Wembley | Donovan Pedelty | Paramount | Crime. Secretary proves her ex-fiancé is innocent of murder. | 2 |
| The Fatal Hour (The Clock) | 65 | 3/37 | 5/37 | B&D-Paramount/Pinewood | George Pearson | Paramount | Crime (Espionage). Agent poses as wastrel to trap spies. | 3 |
| Father Steps Out | 64 | 1937 | 6/37 12/37 3bL | George Smith/Walton | Maclean Rogers | Radio | Comedy. Chauffeur saves his boss from swindlers. | 3 |
| Fifty Shilling Boxer | 73 | 1937 | 5/37 1/38 2bL | George Smith/Walton | Maclean Rogers | Radio | Sport. Boxer returns to the ring after failing as actor. | 1 |
| First Night | 69 | 4/37 | 6/37 | Crusade/Wembley | Donovan Pedelty | Paramount | Romance. Producer helps family drudge to become playwright. | 2 |
| The £5 Man | 76 | 2/37 | 3/37 12/37 1bL | Fox/Wembley | Albert Parker | Fox | Comedy. Framed ex-con poses as butler and unmasks counterfeiters. | 2 |
| Footlights | 44 | 1937 | 6/37 | Ace | R. A. Hopwood | Ace | Revue. Windmill Theatre. | |
| The Gap | 38 | 1937 | 4/37 8/37 5bL | GB Instructional | Donald Carter | GFD | War. Dramatising the consequences of an air raid on London. | |
| The Girl in the Taxi | 72 | 2/37 | 8/37 2/38 co,bL | British Unity/Ealing | Andre Berthomieu | ABFD | Musical. In Paris, captain's wife flirts with moral reformer and son. | 2 |
| Glamour Girl (Love Insurance) | 67 | 11/37 | 2/38 5/38 4bL | WB-FN/Teddington | Arthur Woods | WB | Comedy. Vain photographer reformed by secretary. | 2 |
| The Green Cockatoo (Four Dark Hours) | 65 | 1/37 | 1940 | New World/Denham | William Cameron Menzies | Fox | Crime. Country girl helps man whose brother has been killed by racetrack gang. | 3 |
| Heavily Married | 35 | 1937 | 5/37 | Krackerjack Comedies/Highbury | Clayton Hutton | MGM | Comedy. Man weds circus strong woman and finds she has triplets. | 3 |
| Holiday's End | 70 | 1/37 | 3/37 1/38 bL | B&D-Paramount/Pinewood | John Paddy Carstairs | Paramount | Drama. Teacher unmasks revolutionary bent on assassination. | 3 |

| Title | | | | Production / Studio | Director | Dist. | Plot | |
|---|---|---|---|---|---|---|---|---|
| The House of Silence | 44 | 1/37 | 3/37 8/37 5bL | George King / Shepperton | R. K. Neilson Baxter | MGM | Crime. Journalist unmasks Cornish innkeeper as smuggler. | 3 |
| The Inspector | 35 | | 1/37 | Ace | Widgey R. Newman | WB | Comedy. Moral reformer visits holiday camp. | |
| Intimate Relations | 66 | 1/37 | 11/37 | Tudor / Highbury | Clayton Hutton | ABFD | Musical. Married man flirts with film star who poses as friend's fiancée. | 2 |
| It's in the Blood | 56 | 6/37 | 3/38 10/38 4bL | WB-FN / Teddington | Gene Gerrard | FN | Comedy. On Channel crossing, film fan catches thieves. | 2 |
| It's Never Too Late to Mend | 67 | 1/37 | 3/37 7/37 co,5bL | George King / Shepperton | David Macdonald | MGM | Crime. Nineteenth-century JP schemes to wed farmer's daughter by jailing her fiancé. | 3 |
| It's Not Cricket | 63 | 1/37 | 3/37 7/37 co,5bL | WB-FN / Teddington | Ralph Ince | FN | Comedy. Man tries to elope with his best friend's wife. | 3 |
| Jennifer Hale | 66 | 6/37 | 10/37 6/38 8bL | Fox / Wembley | Bernerd Mainwaring | Fox | Crime. Architect proves girl's innocence of murder. | 3 |
| John Halifax, Gentleman | 69 | 12/37 | 3/38 8/38 bL | George King / Shepperton | George King | MGM | Drama. In 1790 apprentice inherits mill and weds lord's ward. | 2 |
| Lancashire Luck | 74 | 9/37 | 11/37 8/38 2bL | B&D-Paramount / Pinewood | Henry Cass | Paramount | Comedy. Girl is lucky in love while father is lucky on the pools. | 2 |
| The Last Chance | 74 | 8/37 | 11/37 | Welwyn / Welwyn | Thomas Bentley | Pathe | Crime. Gunrunner breaks jail to prove he was framed for murder. | 2 |
| The Last Curtain | 67 | 6/37 | 7/37 | B&D-Paramount / Pinewood | David Macdonald | Paramount | Crime. Insurance investigator poses as crook to expose theatre manager as fence. | 2 |
| The Last Rose of Summer | 60 | 5/37 | 9/37 5/38 2bL | Fitzpatrick / Shepperton | James A. Fitzpatrick | MGM | Musical. Love life of a poet. | 2 |
| The Live Wire (Three Men on a Horse / Plunder in the Air) | 69 | 4/37 | 10/37 5/38 a,co,4bL | Tudor / Beaconsfield | Herbert Brenon | British Lion | Comedy. Reformed con man turns worthless land into spa. | 3 |
| The Londonderry Air | 47 | 6/37 | 12/37 7/38 4bL | Fox / Wembley | Alex Bryce | Fox | Romance. Irish pedlar persuades servant girl to run away with him. | 3 |
| Lucky Jade | 69 | 1/37 | 3/37 | Welwyn | Walter Summers | Paramount | Crime. Maid posing as actress is accused of stealing jade. | 2 |
| Macushla | 59 | 7/37 | 12/37 | Fox / Wembley | Alex Bryce | Fox | Crime. Irish farmer's daughter loves policeman who is hunting her brother. | 2 |
| Member of the Jury | 61 | 2/37 | 3/37 11/37 2bL | Fox / Wembley | Bernerd Mainwaring | Fox | Crime. Juror's employer goes on trial. | 1 |
| Merely Mr. Hawkins | 71 | 11/37 | 1/38 | George Smith / Walton | Maclean Rogers | RKO | Comedy. Hen-pecked husband outwits con men. | 2 |
| Missing, Believed Married (Missing from Home) | 66 | 7/37 | 9/37 | B&D-Paramount / Pinewood | John Paddy Carstairs | Paramount | Comedy. Market traders protect amnesiac heiress from fortune hunters. | 1 |

| Title | Minutes | Filming began | Trade show/ Leicester bookings | Production company/ studio | Director | Distributor | Genre/synopsis | Q |
|---|---|---|---|---|---|---|---|---|
| Mr. Smith Carries On (Death Adds Up) | 68 | 6/37 | 9/37 4/38 bL | B&D-Paramount / Pinewood | Lister Laurance | Paramount | Drama. Secretary accidentally shoots tycoon but clinches deal. | 3 |
| Murder in the Family | 75 | 10/37 | 2/38 10/38 2bL | Fox / Wembley | Albert Parker | Fox | Crime. Which member of the family killed rich aunt? | 2 |
| Murder Tomorrow | 69 | 12/37 | 2/38 | Crusade / Cricklewood | Donovan Pedelty | Paramount | Crime. Woman who accidentally killed her husband is helped by lawyer. | 3 |
| Museum Mystery (Museum Peace) | 69 | 2/37 | 4/37 | B&D-Paramount / Pinewood | Clifford Gulliver | Paramount | Crime. Museum theft foiled by student and curator's daughter. | 1 |
| Night Ride | 71 | 4/37 | 6/37 2/38 bL | B&D-Paramount / Pinewood | John Paddy Carstairs | Paramount | Drama. Sacked lorry driver starts own business and helps to save trapped miners. | 2 |
| Oh Boy! (Old Boy) | 73 | 1937 | 3/38 10/384 bL | ABPC / Elstree | Albert de Courville | ABPC | Comedy. Scientist turns himself into a baby and saves the Crown Jewels. | 1 |
| Overcoat Sam | 44 | 1937 | 3/37 10/37 bL | UK Films / Shepperton | Wallace Orton | MGM | Crime. Thief steals coat containing ticket for trunk believed to contain corpse. | 1 |
| Passenger to London (The Black Trunk) | 57 | 3/37 | 6/37 3/38 2bL | Fox / Wembley | Lawrence Huntington | Fox | Crime (Espionage). British agent saves secret documents from spies. | 1 |
| Pearls Bring Tears | 63 | 2/37 | 3/37 11/37 4bL | GS Enterprises / Walton | Manning Hayes | Columbia | Comedy. Two men try to regain lost pearls. | 4 |
| The Perfect Crime (Copper-proof) | 69 | 2/37 | 4/37 10/37 6bL | WB-FN / Teddington | Ralph Ince | WB | Crime. Clerk fakes suicide and robs employer. | 3 |
| The Price of Folly (Double Error) | 53 | 6/36 | 2/37 | Welwyn | Walter Summers | Pathe | Crime. Lawyer kills blackmailer who faked girl's death. | 1 |
| Quiet Please | 69 | 8/37 | 1/38 9/38 5bL | WB-FN / Teddington | Roy William Neill | FN | Comedy. Buskers save jewels from thieves. | 2 |
| Racing Romance | 63 | 1937 | 9/37 6/38 6bL | GS Enterprises | Maclean Rogers | Radio | Sport (Romance). Garage owner buy's girl trainer's racehorse, which wins. | 3 |
| Remember When aka Riding High | 68 | 7/37 | 7/39 | Embassy / Shepperton | David Macdonald | British Lion | Comedy. In 1879. Solicitor helps village blacksmith win race on his newly invented bicycle. | 3 |
| Return of a Stranger | 70 | 3/37 | 5/37 12/37 co,3a,4bL | Premier-Stafford / Shepperton | Victor Hanbury | Radio | Crime. Disfigured returning exile finds fiancée has married. | 2 |
| Strange Experiment | 75 | 10/36 | 1/37 6/37 4bL | Fox / Wembley | Albert Parker | Fox | Crime. Pharmacist catches gang who forced him to help with robbery. | 2 |
| The Reverse Be My Lot | 66 | 2/37 | 1/38 | Rock / Elstree | Raymond Stross | Columbia | Romance. Scientist and son both love girl who is their guinea pig. | 2 |
| Rhythm Racketeer | 84 (73) | 1/37 | 10/37 5/38 3bL | Rock / Elstree | James Seymour | BIED | Musical. Band leader is double framed for jewel theft on liner. Harry Roy. | 3 |
| Sam Small Leaves Town | 79 | 7/37 | 11/37 7/38 co,5bL | British Screen Service / Highbury | Alfred Goulding | BSS | Comedy. Actor poses as holiday-camp handyman for bet. | 3 |

| Title | Length | | | Production / Studio | Director | Distributor | Description | |
|---|---|---|---|---|---|---|---|---|
| Saturday Night Revue | 77 | 7/37 | 10/37 10/38 6/38 bL | Welwyn / Welwyn | Norman Lee | Pathe | Musical. Reformed club owner reunites blind busker with partner. | 3 |
| The Schooner Gang | 71 | 8/37 | 9/37 | New Garrick / Cricklewood | W. D. Hackney | Butcher's | Crime. Robbers force innkeeper to help them steal jewels. | 1 |
| Screen Struck | 38 | 1937? | 3/37 | UK Films / Shepperton | Lawrence Huntington | MGM | Comedy. American producer oversees British film company. | |
| Scruffy | 61 | 9/37 | 4/38 | Vulcan / Cricklewood | Randall Faye | BIEF | Drama. Burglars adopt runaway and his dog. | 2 |
| Sexton Blake and the Hooded Terror (Sexton Blake and the Master Criminal) | 69 | 11/37 | 2/38 7/38 5bL | George King / Shepperton | George King | MGM | Crime. Detective unmasks criminal mastermind. | 4 |
| Ship's Concert | 44 | 2/37 | 4/37 8/37 4bL | WB-FN / Teddington | Leslie Hiscott | WB | Revue. Compered by Jack Hulbert with a slight story to link the acts. | |
| Shooting Stars | 69 also 40 | 4/37 | 10/37 | Viking / Cricklewood | Eric Humphries | Viking | Revue. | 2 |
| Silver Top | 66 | 12/37 | 1/38 | Triangle / Shepperton | George King | Paramount | Crime. Old lady reforms crook posing as lost son. | 1 |
| Spring Handicap | 69 | 3/37 | 5/37 8/37 b,co,aL | ABPC / Elstree | Herbert Brenon | ABPC | Comedy. Wife stops miner from gambling away his legacy. | 2 |
| Starlight Parade | 38 | 1937? | 2/37 | Viking | Eric Humphries | | Revue. | |
| The Strange Adventures of Mr. Smith | 71 | 1937 | 5/37 1/38 5bL | George Smith / Walton | Maclean Rogers | Radio | Comedy. Artist posing as businessman is accused of murdering himself. | 2 |
| Tea Leaves in the Wind aka Hate in Paradise | 63 | 8/37 | 11/38 | Chesterfield / (Ceylon) | Ward Wing | BSS | Crime. Planter's assistant plans to take over plantation. | 2 |
| Television Talent (Television Trouble) | 56 | 6/37 | 11/37 | Alexander Films | Robert Edmunds | Ambassador | Comedy. Music teacher is framed for forgery but still wins talent competition. | 2 |
| There Was a Young Man | 63 | 5/37 | 9/37 | Fox / Wembley | Albert Parker | Fox | Comedy. Man mistaken for heir foils Orientals seeking sacred relic. | 1 |
| The Ticket of Leave Man | 71 | 8/37 | 10/37 5/38 4bL | George King / Shepperton | George King | MGM | Crime. Nineteenth-century philanthropist frames his rival. | 1 |
| Twin Faces (Press Button B) | 67 | 6/37 | 8/37 | Premier / Highbury | Lawrence Huntington | Paramount | Crime. Art dealer's nephew is double of jewel thief. | 1 |
| Under a Cloud | 67 | 6/37 | 8/37 | Triangle / Shepperton | George King | Paramount | Crime (Social Melodrama – Pg). Returning father proves son did not kill blackmailer. | 2 |
| Uptown Revue | 45 | 1937 | 4/37 4/38 4bL | Ace | R. A. Hopwood | Ace | Revue. Windmill Theatre. | |
| Variety Hour (Variety Stars of 1937) | 66 | 1/37 | 3/37 10/37 4bL | Fox / Wembley | Redd Davis | Fox | Revue. | 2 |

| Title | Minutes | Filming began | Trade show/Leicester bookings | Production company/studio | Director | Distributor | Genre/synopsis | Q |
|---|---|---|---|---|---|---|---|---|
| The Vulture | 66 | 10/36 | 2/37 9/37 5bL | WB-FN / Teddington | Ralph Ince | FN | Comedy. Detective poses as Chinaman to catch jewel thieves. | 3 |
| Wanted | 71 | 11/36 | 2/37 | Embassy / Shepperton | George King | Sound City | Comedy. Crooks mistake clerk for jewel thief. | 3 |
| West End Frolics | 46 | 1937 | 3/37 | Ace | R. A. Hopwood | Ace | Revue. Windmill Theatre. | |
| West of Kerry (Island Man / USA: Men of Ireland) | 47 | 5/37 | 3/38 | Irish National Film Corp / Bushey (Ireland) | Patrick K. Heale | Butcher's | Romance. Island girl falls for visiting medical student. | 2 |
| When the Devil Was Well | 67 | 1937 | 3/37 12/37 4bL | George Smith / Walton | Maclean Rogers | Radio | Comedy. Mother's attempts to make her son marry heiress. | 3 |
| When the Poppies Bloom Again | 45 | 2/37 | 5/37 4/38 bL | George King / Shepperton | David Macdonald | MGM | War. WWI nurse loves blinded soldier suspected of being a spy. | 3 |
| Who Killed John Savage? (The Lie Detector) | 69 | 7/37 | 11/37 5/38 6bL | WB-FN / Teddington | Maurice Elvey | WB | Crime. Manufacturer fakes his death to collect insurance. | 3 |
| Why Pick on Me? | 64 | 6/37 | 7/37 3/38 4bL | GS Enterprises / Walton | Maclean Rogers | Radio | Comedy. Hen-pecked clerk gets into trouble when drunk. | 3 |
| The Wife of General Ling | 72 | 1/37 | 4/37 12/37 a,2bL | Premier-Stafford / Shepperton | Ladislao Vajda | Radio | Adventure. Wife of Chinese bandit aids British agent. | 3 |
| The Windmill | 62 | 1/37 | 3/37 11/37 7bL | WB-FN / Teddington | Arthur Woods | FN | War. WWI spy blackmails innkeeper's adopted German daughter. | 2 |
| Wise Guys | 67 | 4/37 | 8/37 a,3bL | Fox / Wembley | Harry Langdon | Fox | Comedy. Couple must raise money before they can inherit loan company. Naughton and Gold. | 3 |
| You Live and Learn | 80 | 3/37 | 9/37 6/38 bL | WB-FN / Teddington | Arthur Woods | WB | Comedy. US showgirl finds the rich landowner she is to marry is fake. | 2 |
| **1938** | | | | | | | | |
| The Awakening | 64 | 1/38 | 3/38 | Cosmopolitan | Alfonse Frenguelli | Cosmopolitan | Romance. Love triangle among doctors. | 1 |
| Bad Boy (Branded) | 69 | 2/38 | 3/38 | Radius / Cricklewood | Lawrence Huntington | RKO | Crime. Ex-con goes on rampage. | 3 |
| Bedtime Story | 71 | 2/38 | 3/38 | Admiral / Cricklewood | Donovan Pedelty | Grand National | Comedy. Orphan tries to run away to America and ends up on a farm. | 1 |
| Behind the Tabs | 48 | 1938 | 3/38 | Ace | R. A. Hopwood | Ace | Revue. Windmill Theatre. | |
| Beyond Our Horizon | 42 | 1938 | 3/39 | GHW / Pinewood | Norman Walker | Unity | Drama. Norwegian pastor tries to cure wife's paralysis. | |
| Blarney | 67 | 1938 | 5/38 | O.D. / Ireland | Harry O'Donovan | ABFD | Comedy. In Ireland, man accidentally takes stolen gems. | 2 |

|  | | | | | | | |
|---|---|---|---|---|---|---|---|
| Breakers Ahead | 37 | 1938 | 7/38 | GB Instructional | Vernon Sewell | GFD | Drama. Cornish fisherman saves estranged brother from wreck. |
| Chinatown Nights (The Return of Sin Fang) | 70 | 1938? | 3/38, 12/38 bL | Victory | Anthony Frenguelli | Columbia | Crime. Girl kidnapped by Chinese crooks. 2 |
| Coming of Age | 68 | 1938 | 3/38 | George Smith | Manning Hayes | Columbia | Comedy. Couple flirt with singer and her husband. 2 |
| Consider Your Verdict | 37 | | 12/38 | Charter / Highbury | Roy Boulting | Anglo | Crime. Juror falsely confesses to murder to save accused. |
| Crown Trial | 35 | 1/38 | 3/38 | AIP | John Ruffin | Exclusive | Comedy. Youth-restoring drug leads to treason trial in ancient Greece. |
| Father O'Nine | 47 | 2/38 | 3/38 | Fox / Wembley | Roy Kellino | Fox | Comedy. Sacked man searches for nine children. 2 |
| Full Speed Ahead | 60 | 1/38 | 5/39 | Educational & General Services / Cricklewood | John Hunt | GFD | Drama. Destroyer's commander saves girl from burning cargo ship. 3 |
| The Gables Mystery | 66 | 1/38 | 3/38 | Welwyn / Welwyn | Harry Hughes | MGM | Crime. Female detective unmasks woman's killer. 1 |
| A Gentleman's Gentleman | 70 | 9/38 | 5/39 | WB-FN / Teddington | Roy William Neill | WB | Comedy. In Switzerland, valet blackmails master. 2 |
| Governor Bradford (USA: Governor William Bradford) | 33 | 1/38 | 3/38 | AIP | Widgey Newman | Columbia | Drama. Pilgrim fathers sail in *Mayflower*. |
| His Lordship Goes to Press | 80 | 8/38 | 10/38 | George Smith (Canterbury) / Walton | Maclean Rogers | RKO | Comedy. Lord poses as farmer to fool female reporter. 2 |
| His Lordship Regrets (Bees and Honey) | 78 | 5/38 | 7/38 | George Smith (Canterbury) / Walton | Maclean Rogers | RKO | Comedy. Poor peer woos fake heiress but loves secretary. 2 |
| Horse Sense | 39 | 1/38 | 3/38 | AIP | Widgey Newman | Columbia | Drama. Old farm horse saved from slaughter. |
| If I Were Boss | 72 | 1/38 | 3/38 | George Smith / Walton | Maclean Rogers | Columbia | Drama. Clerk inherits firm and is used by crooks. 1 |
| Incident in Shanghai | 67 | 9/37 | 1/38, 8/38 a,3bL | B&D-Paramount / Pinewood | John Paddy Carstairs | Paramount | War. Red Cross chief's wife loves British pilot flying for the Chinese. |
| Interrupted Rehearsal | 39 | | 3/38 | Ace | R. A. Hopwood | Ace | Revue. Windmill Theatre. |
| The Landlady | 35 | 9/38 | 9/38 | Charter | Roy Boulting | Fidelity | Drama. Landlady ejects girl who becomes actress. |
| The Last Barricade | 58 | 1/38 | 3/38 | Fox / Wembley | Alex Bryce | Fox | Drama. Spanish Civil War journalist rescues spy's daughter. 2 |
| Many Tanks, Mr. Atkins | 68 | 7/38 | 12/38 | WB-FN / Teddington | Roy William Neill | FN | Comedy. Trooper saves his tank supercharger invention from spies. 3 |
| Me and My Pal | 74 | 10/38 | 2/39 | Welwyn / Welwyn | Thomas Bentley | Pathe | Comedy. Police try to expose insurance fraudsters. 2 |

| Title | Minutes | Filming began | Trade show/ Leicester bookings | Production company/ studio | Director | Distributor | Genre/synopsis | Q |
|---|---|---|---|---|---|---|---|---|
| Men without Honour | 59 | 11/38 | 3/39 | Smith & Newman / Bushey | Widgey Newman | Equity British | Crime. Lawyer poses as crook to trap sharepushers. | 1 |
| Miracles Do Happen | 59 | 12/38 | 1939? | George Smith / Worton Hall | Maclean Rogers | New Realm | Comedy. Professor's nephew tries to get financial backing for artificial milk. | 2 |
| Murder in Soho (USA: Murder in the Night) | 70 | 9/38 | 2/39 | ABPC / Elstree | Norman Lee | Associated British | Crime. | 2 |
| My Irish Molly | 69 | 9/38 | 12/38 | Argyle British / Welwyn | Alex Bryce | ABPC | Musical. Orphaned Irish girl becomes radio star. | 2 |
| Night Journey | 76 | 11/38 | 12/38 | British National-Butcher's / Walton | Oswald Mitchell | Butcher's | Crime. Lorry driver saves woman from crooks. | 2 |
| On Velvet | 70 | 1/38 | 3/38 | AIP | Widgey Newman | Columbia | Comedy. Bookie and punter set up TV station. | 1 |
| Paid in Error | 68 | 1938? | 2/38 8/38 7bL | George Smith / Walton | Maclean Rogers | Columbia | Comedy. Boarder tries to retain money paid to him by mistake. | 3 |
| Queer Cargo (USA: Pirates of the Seven Seas) | 61 | 4/38 | 8/38 | ABPC / Elstree | Harold Schuster | ABPC | Adventure. China Seas pirate captures smuggled cargo. | 1 |
| Revue Parade | 35 | 1938 | 3/38 | Ace | R. A. Hopwood | Ace | Revue. Windmill Theatre. | |
| Romance a la Carte | 72 | 2/38 | 3/38 | George Smith / Walton | Maclean Rogers | RKO | Comedy. Restaurant manager vs chef. | 2 |
| Second Thoughts | 61 | 2/38 | 3/38 | Fox / Wembley | Albert Parker | Fox | Drama. Chemist suspects that his wife loves playwright. | 2 |
| Simply Terrific | 73 | 11/37 | 2/38 | WB-FN / Teddington | Roy William Neill | WB | Comedy. Playboys promote hangover cure. | 2 |
| A Sister to Assist 'er | 72 | 2/38 | 3/38 | AIP / Elstree | Widgey Newman, George Dewhurst | Columbia | Comedy. Poor woman poses as rich twin to fool landlady. | 2 |
| The Sky Raiders | 57 | 1/38 | 3/38 | Sovereign / Pinewood | Fraser Foulsham | FN | Crime. Bullion thieves kidnap girl. | 1 |
| Smugglers' Harvest | 43 | 1/38 | 3/38 | Cantaphone / Cornwall | John R. Phipps | Exclusive | Adventure. Cornish smugglers vs coastguards. | |
| Special Edition | 68 | 1/38 | 3/38 | Redd Davis / Worton Hall | Redd Davis | Paramount | Crime. Reporter proves photographer is killer. | 3 |
| Spotlight | 39 | 1938 | 3/38 | Ace | R. A. Hopwood | Ace | Revue. Windmill Theatre. | |
| Star of the Circus | 68 | 1/38 | 5/38 | ABPC / Elstree | Albert de Courville | Associated British | Romance. In Germany, tightrope walker loves dancer. | 3 |
| Swing | 37 | 1938 | 3/38 | Ace | R. A. Hopwood | Ace | Revue. Windmill Theatre. | |

| Title | mins | | | Studio / Location | Director | Distributor | Synopsis |
|---|---|---|---|---|---|---|---|
| 13 Men and a Gun | 64 | 2/38 | 6/38 | Two Cities–Pisorno / Italy | Mario Zampi | BIED | Drama. Search for WWI German gunners who revealed their position. 4 |
| Too Many Husbands | 59 | 3/38 | 12/38 | Liberty / Worton Hall | Ivar Campbell | Liberty | Comedy. Adventures of con man and fake countess on Riviera. 2 |
| Two Men in a Box | 49 | 1938 | 3/38 | Ace | R. A. Hopwood | Ace | Revue. Windmill Theatre. 2 |
| Uncle Nick | 60 | 1/38 | 3/38 | Hibernia | Tom Cooper | Hibernia | Comedy. Set in Ireland. |
| The Villiers Diamond | 50 | 11/37 | 2/38 9/38 5bL | Fox / Wembley | Bernérd Mainwaring | Fox | Crime. Retired crook blackmailed by ex-partner, fakes robbery. 2 |
| The Viper | 74 | 10/37 | 1/38 10/38 4bL | WB–FN / Teddington | Roy William Neill | FN | Comedy. Detective in disguise saves woman's diamond. 1 |

## 1939

| Title | mins | | | Studio / Location | Director | Distributor | Synopsis |
|---|---|---|---|---|---|---|---|
| Blind Folly (Money for Nothing) | 78 | 8/39 | 11/39 | George Smith / Walton | Reginald Denham | RKO | Comedy. Man inherits nightclub from crooked brother. 2 |
| The Body Vanishes (The Murder Action) | 45 | 5/39 | 12/39 | Venture / Worton Hall | Walter Tennyson | New Realm | Crime. Thief fakes death to escape partner. 2 |
| The Briggs Family | 70 | 12/39 | 3/40 | WB–FN / Teddington | Herbert Mason | WB | Drama. An everyday story of an English family. |
| Crimes at the Dark House | 69 | 11/39 | 2/40 | Pennant / Elstree | George King | British Lion | Crime. Melodrama of Victorian wife-killer. 4 |
| Dead Men Are Dangerous | 69 | 9/38 | 2/39 | Welwyn / Welwyn | Harold French | Pathe | Crime. Author changes clothes with dead man and is accused of murder. 3 |
| Dr. O'Dowd | 76 | 8/39 | 1/40 | WB / Teddington | Herbert Mason | WB | Drama. Son accuses doctor father of drunkenness, causing him to be struck off. |
| Down Our Alley | 56 | 5/39 | 7/39 | British Screen Services / Highbury | George A. Cooper | British Screen | Musical. Boy gang substitute for nightclub singer. 2 |
| The Face at the Window | 65 | 2/39 | 4/39 | Pennant / Beaconsfield | George King | British Lion | Crime. French count and mad brother murder and rob banks in 1880s' Paris. 1 |
| The Flying Squad | 64 | 5/39 | 4/40 | ABPC / Elstree | Herbert Brenon | Associated British | Crime. Drug smuggler kills brother of girl investigator. 2 |
| Happy Event | 36 col | 1939 | 12/39 | Anglo-French | Patrick Brunner | Grand National | Sport. Trainer's daughter raises horse to win Grand National. |
| His Brother's Keeper (Dressed to Kill) | 70 | 6/39 | 9/39 | WB–FN / Teddington | Roy William Neill | FN | Drama. Brothers fall out over gold-digging singer. 3 |
| Inquest | 60 | 7/39 | 12/39 | Charter / Highbury | Roy Boulting | Grand National | Crime. Coroner suspects widow of murder. 3 |
| Jail Birds | 73 | 10/39 | 12/39 | Butcher's / Walton | Oswald Mitchell | Butcher's | Comedy. Tough thief bullies meek con into joint jailbreak. 3 |
| Law and Disorder | 71 | 10/39 | 3/40 | British Consolidated / Highbury | David Macdonald | RKO | Comedy. Young solicitor infiltrates gang of saboteurs. 3 |

| Title | Minutes | Filming began | Trade show/ Leicester bookings | Production company/ studio | Director | Distributor | Genre/synopsis | Q |
|---|---|---|---|---|---|---|---|---|
| Meet Maxwell Archer (Archer Plus Twenty) | 74 | 6/39 | 9/39 | RKO / Rock, Elstree | John Paddy Carstairs | RKO | Crime. Amateur detective solves murder and unmasks spies. | 3 |
| Mistaken Identity (I'm Not Rich) | 48 | 1939 | 12/39 (released 1942) | Venture / Worton Hall | Walter Tennyson | New Realm | Comedy. Producer mistakes shy conjuror for millionaire. | 1 |
| Mrs. Pym of Scotland Yard | 65 | 7/39 | 10/39 | Hurley / Highbury | Fred Elles | Grand National | Crime. Woman detective unmasks fake medium and saves heiress. | 4 |
| Murder Will Out | 65 | 4/39 | 9/39 | WB-FN / Teddington | Roy William Neill | WB | Crime. Doctor's wife is blackmailed by crooks. | 2 |
| Secret Journey (The Man from MI5 USA: Among Human Wolves) | 72 | 3/39 | 6/39 | British National / Elstree | John Baxter | Anglo-American | Crime. Rival spies pursue German chemist's secret formula. | 2 |
| Shadowed Eyes | 68 | 6/39 | 9/39 | Savoy (George Smith) / Worton Hall | MacLean Rogers | RKO | Drama. Mad surgeon operates on barrister who convicted him of murder. | 2 |
| They Came by Night | 72 | 7/39 | 2/40 | 20th Century / Islington | Harry Lachman | 20th Century-Fox | Crime. Jeweller poses as thief after brother's suicide. | 1 |
| Trouble For Two | 46 | 2/39 | 46/39 | Venture / Worton Hall | Walter Tennyson | Anglo-American | Crime. Detective in disguise catches jewel thieves. | 2 |
| Trunk Crime (USA: Design For Murder) | 51 | 2/39 | 4/39 | Charter / Elstree | Roy Boulting | Anglo-American | Crime. Student tries to bury his tormentor alive. | 3 |
| Two Days to Live | 44 | 3/39 | 6/39 | Venture / Worton Hall | Walter Tennyson | Anglo-American | Comedy. Hypochondriac takes to burglary. | 2 |
| Two Minutes (The Silence) | 42 | 1/39 | 1/39 | G-B Instructional | Donald Carter | Exclusive | Drama. Armistice Day silence convinces man to stay with invalid wife. | 2 |
| What Men Live By | 41 | 1939 | 11/39 | G-B Instructional | Vernon Sewell | Exclusive | Drama. Destitute man is taught carpentry and turns out to be an angel. | |

# Index

## List of Illustrations

Whilst considerable effort has been made to correctly identify the copyright holders, this has not been possible in all cases. We apologise for any apparent negligence and any omissions or corrections brought to our attention will be remedied in any future editions.

*The Bondman*, British and Dominions Film Corporation; *Midnight*, Fox Film Company; *Tangled Evidence*, Twickenham Film Studios Productions; *Strictly Business*, British Instructional Films; *Badger's Green*, Paramount British Productions/British and Dominions Film Corporation; *How He Lied to Her Husband*, British International Pictures; *Too Many Crooks*, George King Productions; *I'm an Explosive*, George Smith Enterprises; *The Water Gipsies*, Associated Radio Pictures/Associated Talking Pictures; *Murder at Monte Carlo*, Warner Bros. First National Productions; *All at Sea*, Fox-British Pictures; *The Shadow*, Real Art Productions; *After Dark*, Fox-British Pictures; *Dangerous Seas*, Edward G. Whiting Productions; *First Offence*, Gainsborough Pictures; *Night Ride*, British and Dominions Film Productions; *Warn London*, British Lion Film Corporation; *The Night Porter*, Gaumont-British Picture Corporation; *Prison Breaker*, George Smith Enterprises; *Murder on the Second Floor*, Warner Bros. First National Productions; *Doss House*, Sound City; *Going Straight*, Warner Bros. First National Productions; *Chelsea Life*, British and Dominions Film Corporation/Paramount British Productions; *Something Always Happens*, Warner Bros. First National Productions; *The Third Clue*, Fox-British Pictures; *The Wrong Mr Perkins*, Starcraft; *The Brown Wallet*, Warner Bros. First National Productions; *The Tell Tale Heart*, Clifton-Hurst Productions; *The Secret of the Loch*, Wyndham Productions; *The Impassive Footman*, Associated Talking Pictures; *Strip! Strip! Hooray!*, © British International Pictures; *Mayfair Girl*, Warner Bros. First National Productions; *The Lash*, Twickenham Film Studios Productions; *Leave It to Blanche*, Warner Brothers First National Productions; *Old Faithful*, George Smith Enterprises; *A Real Bloke*, Baxter and Barter Productions; *Lancashire Luck*, British and Dominions Film Corporation/Paramount British Productions; *The Village Squire*, British and Dominions Film Corporation/Paramount British Productions; *A Taxi to Paradise*, George Smith Enterprises; *Matinee Idol*, Wyndham Productions; *Tiger Bay*, Wyndham Productions; *The Ghost Camera*, Real Art Productions; *The House of Unrest*, Associated Picture Productions; *Down River*, Gaumont-British Picture Corporation; *To Brighton with Gladys*, George King Productions; *Sweeney Todd*, ATS Productions; *Crime Unlimited*, Warner Bros. First National Productions; *Immediate Possession*, Starcraft; *Two Crowded Hours*, Film Engineering Company; *Rynox*, Film Engineering Company; *The Rasp*, Film Engineering Company; *Hotel Splendide*, Film Engineering Company; *His Lordship*, Westminster Films; *The Night of the Party*, Gaumont-British Picture Corporation; *Crown v. Stevens*, Warner Bros. First National Productions; *The Love Test*, Fox-British Pictures; *The Man Behind the Mask*, Joe Rock Productions; *Blondes for Danger*, Herbert Wilcox Productions; *Happy Event*, Anglo-French; *Reunion*, Sound City.